Handbook on Grandparenthood

Handbook on Grandparenthood

Edited by
Maximiliane E. Szinovacz

GREENWOOD PRESS
Westport, Connecticut • London

Library of Congress Cataloging-in-Publication Data

Handbook on grandparenthood / edited by Maximiliane E. Szinovacz.
   p. cm.
   Includes bibliographical references and indexes.
   ISBN 0–313–29886–6 (alk. paper)
   1. Grandparents—Social conditions. 2. Grandparenting.
  3. Grandparent and child. I. Szinovacz, Maximiliane.
  HQ759.9.H36   1998
  306.874'5—DC21   97–32009

British Library Cataloguing in Publication Data is available.

Library of Congress Catalog Card Number: 97–32009
ISBN: 1–313–29886–6

First published in 1998

Greenwood Press, 88 Post Road West, Westport, CT 06881
An imprint of Greenwood Publishing Group, Inc.

Printed in the United States of America

The paper used in this book complies with the
Permanent Paper Standard issued by the National
Information Standards Organization (Z39.48–1984).

10 9 8 7 6 5 4 3 2 1

Our grandparents inspired us—
we dedicate this book to them.

Contents

Contents

Acknowledgments

This handbook truly reflects a team effort—the contributors to this volume encouraged me to design and pursue the project, devoted their creativity and insight to writing their chapters, and inspired my own chapters. They also accepted revision suggestions with much good humor and patience. My heartfelt thanks to all of them.

Thanks are also due to the AARP–Andrus Foundation, which sponsored my research on grandparenting during 1994–1996. Chapter 18 and the development of the bibliography were supported in part by the Foundation.

I am grateful to the editors at Greenwood Press in charge of this handbook—first Mildred Vasan and then Nita Romer—who supported this project with enthusiasm, advice, and much patience with missed deadlines.

David Ekerdt, Lynne Gershenson Hodgson, and Vira R. Kivett offered suggestions for my own chapters, and Stanley DeViney helped me with methodological questions.

Rosa McElroy checked and integrated the reference lists from individual chapters.

Handbook on Grandparenthood

Chapter 1

Grandparent Research: Past, Present, and Future

Maximiliane E. Szinovacz

Grandparents born during the first decades of this century knew economic hardship during the Great Depression and benefitted from the New Deal, some fought in World War II or worked in the war-time weapon industries, and many of those raised in rural communities worked on farms. They faced racial segregation in schools and public transportation, saw youth (some of them their grandchildren) revolt against yet another war, and experienced a technical revolution spanning from the beginnings of flight to the exploration of outer space. Some of them did not survive their grandchildren's childhood while others are still alive.

Today's new grandparents were born during or in the aftermath of World War II and at the beginning of the baby boom. They fought in very different wars, are well accustomed to crossing the country and even continents in hours rather than days or weeks, and have started to converse with their growing grandchildren via the Internet. They saw cycles of recession and inflation followed by economic booms, and some of those raised on farms left amid bankruptcies and foreclosures. Many of them have profited from affirmative action and some from relatively generous welfare and Social Security programs but now face an erosion of these programs as they enter this new stage in life. Most of them will survive beyond their grandchildren's childhood, and many will experience their grandchildren's adulthood and their own great-grandparenthood.

Beginning this chapter with a doubtless somewhat overgeneralized depiction of grandparenthood then and now serves not only as an illustration of social changes impacting on grandparenthood itself, but also as a reminder that grandparenthood research reflects and is influenced by changes in historical and social structures and climates. Expanding on this thought, the first section of this chapter explores the legacies underlying grandparent research since the 1940's. An overview of this volume is presented next, followed by an outlook on and recommendations for future research.

THE PAST: LEGACIES AND TURNING POINTS

Grandparent research is at the crossroads of several disciplines and research traditions. Pioneers came from anthropology, psychology, psychiatry, and sociology, as well as the multidisciplinary perspectives of family studies and gerontology (Barranti, 1985; Hader, 1965; Kivnick, 1984). Early studies on grandparents have hovered at the margins of research on families, the elderly, and intergenerational relations (Barranti, 1985; P. K. Smith, 1991). To understand these legacies of grandparent research, it is necessary to look back at both the social and scientific currents of this time.

The Beginnings (1940–1959)

Grandparenthood as a distinct research topic emerged during the late 1940's and 1950's. This era is marked by family upheaval during and following World War II and the beginnings of the baby boom. Couples were rejoined after war-time separations, war-time marriages split up or were dissolved by death, war-time households were restructured, and following the war children were born in close intervals. It is also marked by demographic and social trends that started well before the mid century. They include increases in longevity, migration from farms to urban areas, greater independence of elders after the institutionalization of Social Security, and nuclear household formation (Gratton & Haber, 1996; Haber & Gratton, 1994; Hareven, 1994; Uhlenberg, 1980). Family values changed as well. The authority of older family members, based on farm ownership, declined as younger families moved to urban centers (Gratton & Haber, 1996), "permissive" child rearing was advocated (Bretherton, 1993), and emancipatory movements (civil rights for blacks, a new wave of feminism) were on the horizon.

These trends set the stage for grandparents' roles in the middle of this century as well as for early research on grandparenthood. One of the earliest sociological articles on grandparenthood, (von Hentig, 1946) emphasizes grandmothers' function as "rescuers" of families and grandchildren during times of war and postwar family crises:

the grandmother in countless cases stands ready to shelter the divorcee and her children, to receive children and grandchildren in her home when apartments cannot be found, or the man is out of work. The lower mobility of the older generation renders her more shockproof to the contingencies and fortunes of industrial life. The rural habitat of grandmothers is another asset in war and postwar crisis. (von Hentig, 1946: 391)

He also comments on the special role of black grandmothers as well as the educational function of Native American grandmothers. Von Hentig's work reflects concern with the disruptive effects of World War II and its aftermath on families as well as the functional orientation in sociological thinking of this time, hence the primary focus on the grandmother's contributions to the nuclear family or subfamily. Notably, the grandmother's function was seen primarily in a positive light.

As war-time pressures declined, prevailing norms of generational independence once again dominate popular thinking as well as expert advice (Gratton & Haber, 1996). Parsons' (1954/1943) depiction of the "isolated nuclear family" reflects this trend and, perhaps, gives rise to a dualism in family studies—an emphasis on the nuclear family unit, especially in its early stages (Barranti, 1985; P. K. Smith, 1991) and an interest in kinship though not grandparenthood per se (Sussman, 1953).

Albrecht's (1954) research, well in line with the concept of the *structurally*[1] isolated family, confirms the renewed emphasis on independence between the generations. Grandparents are "stimulated" and "enriched" by contacts with their grandchildren but follow a "hands off" policy as far as their adult children's child-rearing practices are concerned and prefer active social participation without responsibility for their grandchildren. However, they do assume responsibility if "the intervening generation fails" (p. 203). In a similar vein, Koller (1954) addresses problems encountered in multigenerational households. His research suggests "a striking ambivalence towards the creation of a three-generational household" (p. 206). While adult children feel obliged to assist their elderly parents, they nonetheless view three-generational households as "a hazardous type of family living in which the combined virtues of a diplomat, statesman, and saint are needed" (p. 206).

Early anthropological research on grandparenthood, grounded in functionalism and no doubt influenced by social norms and popular thought, focused on authority relations among the generations. In view of the prevailing image of "strict" and "formal" grandparents in Western societies, anthropologists were intrigued by "joking" and relatively egalitarian relationships between grandparents and grandchildren in pre-industrial societies. Apple's (1956) classic study constitutes the culmination of this line of inquiry. She found that "formality between grandparents and grandchildren is related to association of grandparents with family authority, while the indulgent, close, and warm relationship is fostered by dissociation of grandparents from family authority" (p. 662).

Kinship studies of that time also convey an image of "indulgent" grandparents (Young & Willmott, 1957). However, in contrast to the "hands off" rules described by Albrecht (1954), the London working-class families studied by Young and Willmott accept grandparents' involvement: "some wives, and more husbands, do not agree with Mum (the maternal grandmother) all the time. But even if they resent her interference, she is a presence in their lives," (Young & Willmott, 1957: 60).

Later research on blue-collar families in the United States confirms this pattern (Rubin, 1976). Young and Willmott (1957) further note favoritism for the first-born grandchild, "paramountcy" of the wife's mother, as well as competition between maternal and paternal grandparents "for the affections of their grand-children" (p. 59).

For developmental psychologists, interest in grandparenthood derives from concerns about "appropriate" child-rearing techniques and grandparents' role as socialization agents (Tinsley & Parke, 1984). Even though developmental psychologists largely discounted socialization influences by family members out-side the nuclear family until the 1980's, a focus Tinsley and Parke (1984) at-tribute to the acceptance of the isolated nuclear family metaphor, one early study did consider such influences. Comparing child-rearing attitudes of grandmothers and mothers, Staples and Smith (1954) found that grandmothers are more strict than mothers, and that grandmothers residing in households with their grand-children are particularly strict. Staples and Smith do not comment on the im-plications of their findings, but within the context of an increasing emphasis on permissive child-rearing techniques (Bretherton, 1993), the research question itself suggests concerns about grandparents' participation in parenting, once again in line with prevailing norms of independence and noninterference.

Clinical case studies by psychiatrists constitute the most frequent outlet for publications on grandparents before the 1960's. Given the emphasis on the mother-child bond in psychoanalytic thinking (Bretherton, 1993), it is not sur-prising that these contributions view grandparents primarily (though not exclusively) in a negative light (Hader, 1965; Kivnick, 1984). A typical example is Rappaport's (1957) description of the "Grandparent Syndrome":

the presence of the grandparent infantilizes the parents and creates feelings of omnipo-tence in the grandchild if the grandparent is also weak. In addition, grotesque and bizarre character traits are apt to develop because of grandparental identification. (Hader, 1965: 232)

Very much in contrast to these prevailing views is research on black grand-parents (especially grandmothers). The black grandmother's strength and au-thority is accepted, if not idealized. She offers advice on child rearing to her own offspring, other kin, and her white mistress, and she is a stabilizing force for black families. Frazier (1939) characterizes black grandmothers as "guardian of the generations":

During slavery the Negro grandmother occupied in many instances an important place in the plantation economy and was highly esteemed by both the slaves and the masters. ... She was the repository of the accumulated lore and superstition of the slaves and was on hand at the birth of black children as well as of white. She took under her care the orphaned and abandoned children . . . When emancipation came, it was often the old grandmother who kept the generations together. (p. 114f.)

The legacies, then, of early endeavors are a marginalization of grandparent research (due to the emphasis on the nuclear family and the simultaneous emphasis on kinship in general rather than the grandparent-grandchild relationship) and the establishment of three research themes: (1) grandparents as "rescuers" in family crises; (2) grandparents' role in parenting, including the norm of non-interference, and potential tensions between parents and "interfering" grandparents; and (3) the consequences of extended-household structures, and the special status of black grandmothers.

The 1960's

Developments in grandparent research during the 1960's reflect, on the one hand, the focus on parenting and children in the baby-boom era, and, on the other hand, increasing interest in aging issues among sociologists and psychologists. The earlier emphasis on grandparents' functions is now replaced by a focus on the meaning and content of the grandparent role, either from the perspective of the grandparent or from that of the grandchild.

Neugarten and Weinstein's (1964) classical study, influenced by the Chicago school's symbolic interactionist orientation (Turner, 1982) as well as the emerging focus on life-span development among researchers of the University of Chicago's Committee on Human Development (Cole, 1992), doubtless constitutes the major contribution to grandparent research during this era. Observing that earlier research refers "only obliquely, if at all, to the symbolic meaning of the grandchild to the grandparent" (p. 199), Neugarten and Weinstein (1964) assessed three dimensions of grandparents' role: comfort, significance, and style (p. 200). Their classification of grandparent meaning and styles guide grandparent research to this date.

The other new perspective evolves from the home economics tradition. Oriented more toward younger than older families, these researchers focus on grandchildren and their perceptions of grandparents (see Barranti, 1985).

Thus, the 1960's studies establish grandparenthood as an agenda in the field of aging and, thematically, turn attention toward grandparents' and grandchildren's perceptions of the grandparent role and grandparent activities.

The 1970's

Amid radical family changes (divorce and single parenthood, women's labor force participation, teenage pregnancy) and political unrest, as well as concern about elders' "disengagement" in a youth-oriented society (Hochschild, 1976; Holman & Burr, 1980), grandparent research continues to focus on grandparents' role as one of the few significant roles of aging individuals (Kahana and

Kahana, 1971). It also reflects, though only marginally as yet, changes in family structure during this time: parents' authority in child rearing is emphasized as is grandparents' role as rescuers in family crises.

The significance attached to the grandparent role shows in more widespread recognition that grandparenthood constitutes a component of family and kin relationships and of the role repertoire of aging individuals. Thus, grandparenthood is increasingly mentioned in studies on parenting, later-life families, widowhood, or black families (Hess & Waring, 1978; Jackson, 1971; Lopata, 1973; Troll, Miller, & Atchley, 1979). In addition, more efforts are vested into the conceptualization and measurement of the grandparent role. Wood and Robertson (1976) propose a two-dimensional typology of the grandparent role, while Kahana and Kahana (1971) differentiate among several levels of analyses in grandparent studies and stress the impact of kinship structure and residence (community versus institution) on grandparent meaning and activities.

There also is continued interest in grandchildren's perceptions of and relationships with grandparents. Using a developmental framework, Kahana and Kahana (1970) explore age-related changes in grandchildren's views of grandparents, and Robertson (1976) notes grandparents' influence on grandchildren as well as grandchildren's feelings of responsibility toward grandparents. Mead (1974), focusing on grandparents' role as educators in times of social change, proposes that grandparents may help bridge the generation gap by providing a link to the past.

Two old themes—grandparents' authority and grandparents' function as family "rescuers"—reemerge in a new coat. While earlier studies focused on authority relations among grandparents, parents, and children and raised concerns about grandparents' interference in child rearing, research during the 1970's shifts to a view of the middle generation as "lineage bridge" (Hill et al., 1970) and "mediator" (Robertson, 1975) of the grandparent-grandchild relationship. Implicit in this new emphasis is, of course, the assumption that the middle generation is in control not only over their children but also over grandparents and grandchildren as they relate to each other.

Crises associated with family structural change—divorce, single parenthood, teenage childbearing—once again promote interest in grandparents' supportive function and the consequences of extended households. Both Furstenberg (1976) and Kellam, Ensminger, and Turner (1977) document that the presence of the grandmother or a grandmother figure can have ameliorative influences on children of teenage or single mothers.

To summarize, grandparent research in the 1970's is, for the most part, a continuation and refinement of earlier efforts on grandparents' role. However, the fledgling interest in grandparents' supports to teenage and single parents already offers a glimpse of the major shifts in grandparent research that were to occur in the following decades.

The 1980's

The political and social climate of the 1980's distinguishes itself by a turn toward more conservative views, especially on economic and family issues. Having undergone considerable structural change during the preceding decade (changes that stabilized but for the most part did not decline), families were further burdened by economic hardship, drug addiction, and AIDS among their members, as well as cutbacks in social and welfare programs. These burdens were further compounded by the increasing care needs of longer surviving but frail relatives as well as the unmet needs for child care among the continuously growing number of employed mothers.

In family studies these societal trends resulted in a plentitude of studies on divorce and reconstituted families, the impact of women's employment, or the consequences of teenage pregnancy, most of them with a focus on young parents and their children (Berardo, 1990), as well as a turn toward feminist and critical theorizing and complex family systems and ecological models. Gerontology experienced an explosion of research on family caregiving. In addition, gerontologists became increasingly interested in intergenerational relationships and social supports, using theories derived from life-course and ecological perspectives, network analysis, and classical works on small groups and social integration (Antonucci, 1990; Bengtson and Roberts, 1991; Roberts and Bengtson, 1990).

Paralleling the activation of grandparent supports during times of family troubles (Aldous, 1985; Cherlin & Furstenberg, 1986b; Hagestad, 1985; Troll, 1983), grandparent research expanded rapidly during these times of family hardship. Studies on grandparents multiplied and diversified, addressing both old and new themes. For the first time, book-length publications on grandparenthood appear (Bengtson & Robertson, 1985; Cherlin & Furstenberg, 1986a; Cohler and Grunebaum, 1981; Johnson, 1988d), and grandparent research emerges as a research topic in its own right rather than as an appendix to research on intergenerational kin and family relations.

By now grandparent research had caught up with changing social and political realities. Issues surrounding family structural change and family problems become center points. Numerous studies address the impact of divorce on grandparent-grandchild relationships, stepgrandparenthood, grandparents' supports to single mothers and grandchildren, as well as the impact of grandparent coresidence and support on grandchildren in single-parent families (Ahrons & Bowman, 1982; Aldous, 1985; Bogolub, 1989; Dornbusch et al., 1985; Duffy, 1981; Gladstone, 1988, 1989; Johnson, 1983a, 1983b, 1985, 1988a, 1988b; Johnson & Barer, 1987; Johnson, 1981; E. Johnson & Vinick, 1982; Kalish & Visher, 1982; Kaslow & Hyatt, 1981; Matthews & Sprey, 1984; McLanahan & Bumpass, 1988; Sanders & Trygstad, 1989; Spanier & Hanson, 1982; Trygstad & Sanders, 1989). Concern over grandparents' separation from grandchildren of non-custodial parents and new legislation on grandparents' visitation rights also become topics of research and debate (Bean, 1985–1986; Fernandez, 1988; Foster & Freed, 1984; Thompson et al., 1989; Wilson & LeShane, 1982).

Other family troubles are investigated as well. The continued high rate of teenage parenthood gives rise to research on the experience of early ("off-time") grandparenthood (Burton, 1987; Burton & Bengtson, 1985) and on grandparents' role as co- and surrogate parents (Flaherty, 1988; Flaherty, Facteau, & Garver, 1987). Increasing child-care needs of employed mothers are reflected in enhanced research interest in grandparents' childrearing practices in general (Blackwelder & Passman, 1986; Tinsley & Parke, 1984, 1987; Tomlin & Passman, 1989; Wilson, 1984, 1989) and on grandparents' role as child-care providers (Presser, 1989) and surrogate parents (Kennedy & Keeney, 1988) in particular. A few studies also assess grandchildren's experiences with disabled grandparents and grandparents' death (Creasey & Jarvis, 1989; McKeever, 1980) as well as grandparent's reactions to ill grandchildren (Romis, 1981).

As gender-role issues come to the forefront in both family studies and gerontology, the near-exclusive investigation of grandmothers in past research is questioned as well. More studies now include both grandparents (e.g., Cherlin & Furstenberg, 1986a), and several articles are devoted entirely to grandfathers (Baranowski, 1985; Kivett, 1985b; Russell, 1986). These studies are complemented by research reporting gender differences in grandchildren's relations with grandparents (Eisenberg, 1988; Hartshorne & Manaster, 1982; Ponzetti & Folkrod, 1989).

Whereas increases in longevity led to a shift towards research on caregiving in the general field of gerontology, within the grandparent literature they draw attention to the changing demographics of grandparenthood, especially the longer survival of several grandparents (Cherlin & Furstenberg, 1986a; Hagestad, 1988; Hagestad & Burton, 1986; Uhlenberg, 1980) and, consequently, on relations between grandparents and adolescent grandchildren (Baranowski, 1982; Dellman-Jenkins, Papalia, & Lopez, 1987; Matthews & Sprey, 1985) as well as on great-grandparents (Doka & Mertz, 1988).

Perhaps inspired by the conservative movement's call to "revive family values," some researchers of this era claim that grandparents have "abandoned" their grandchildren in pursuit of hedonistic rather than familistic values (Gutmann, 1985; Kornhaber, 1985, 1996; Kornhaber & Woodward, 1981). Kornhaber bases his thesis on findings from mostly clinical case studies. Other research conducted during the 1980's does not support this trend. For example, Cherlin and Furstenberg's (1986a) research, based on a broad sample of over 500 grandparents, indicates that close to three-quarters of grandparents maintained "companionate" or "involved" relationships with their grandchildren. Furthermore, as Cherlin and Furstenberg (1986a: 192) note, "what seems to Kornhaber as detachment is perceived by many grandparents as self-reliance, a quality much valued in American culture."

Indeed, Cherlin and Furstenberg's (1985, 1986a, 1986b) work represents one of the benchmark studies on grandparenthood. They differentiate among three major styles of grandparenting (involved, companionate, remote) and assess variations in the prevalence of each style by gender, race and ethnicity, and grandchildren's ages, as well as geographical distance. Addressing grandparents' relations to different grandchildren, they also note that grandparents "selectively" invest in grandchildren. Their findings further indicate that divorce enhances contacts with custodial but decreases contacts with noncustodial grandparents. This finding adds additional evidence that grandparenting is enhanced during times of family crises (Hagestad, 1985).

Influenced less by societal trends than by theoretical emphases on the life course and life-span development, research on grandparenthood during this decade also turns to issues of change in grandparenthood and grandparent-grandchild relationships over time. Kivnick (1982, 1985, 1986, 1988) and Schultz (1980) tie variations in grandparent-grandchild relationships to children's cognitive development and to grandparents' developmental needs. Numerous others explore the transition to grandparenthood and/or changes especially in mother-daughter relationships following the birth of the first grandchild (Belsky & Rovine, 1984; Cunningham-Burley 1984a, 1985, 1986a, 1986b; Fischer, 1981, 1983, 1988; Hagestad & Lange, 1986; Wilson, 1987). Troll (1985) stresses that grandparent-grandchild relationships are affected by contingencies in both grandparents' and grandchildren's lives, while Hagestad (1985) emphasizes changes in generational structures and the dynamic character of intergenerational transmission. Knipscheer (1988) proposes a theoretical framework based on the temporal embeddedness of grandparenting.

More traditional lines of grandparenthood research also continue throughout the 1980's. There is still interest in the conceptualization of the grandparent role and satisfaction with that role (Crawford, 1981; Kivnick, 1981, 1982, 1983; McGreal, 1986; Thomas, 1986a, 1986b; Timberlake, 1980), in the role of parents as mediators (Thompson & Walker, 1987), in the norms (or lack thereof) guiding grandparent-grandchild relations (Wood, 1982), and in racial and ethnic variations (Jackson, 1986; McCready, 1985; Raphael, 1989; Schmidt & Padilla, 1983; Sotomayor, 1989).

The increased importance and diversification of grandparent research is, perhaps, best documented in Bengtson and Robertson's (1985) edited volume on grandparenthood as well as in the numerous literature reviews appearing during the 1980's (Barranti, 1985; Denham & Smith, 1989; Kivnick, 1984; Peterson, 1989; Sprey & Matthews, 1982; Troll, 1980, 1983; Wilcoxon, 1987; Wood, 1982). Nevertheless, grandparent research still remains—in volume as well as in quality—on the fringes of mainstream research on aging families and intergenerational relations. Thus, Bengtson's (1985) characterization of grandparenthood as heterogeneous and symbolic also fits research on grandparenthood during this era.

Recent Developments

Amid economic recovery in the 1990's, the structurally changed and troubled family of the 1980's was here to stay (Poponoe, 1993). Partially based on the presumption that families can and should take care of their own, welfare reform and cuts in other social programs continued and unleashed a policy debate that cast the generations against each other (Kingson, Hirshorn, & Cornman, 1986; Mullen, 1996). Within this political climate, research on intergenerational relationships and transfers and on aging families takes on new significance.

These developments also leave their mark on grandparent research. The prevalence of extended and especially skip-generation households and their consequences for both grandparents and grandchildren become dominant themes of grandparent research in the 1990's (Barnhill, 1996; Burton, 1992a; Burton & DeVries, 1992; Burton, Dilworth-Anderson & Merriwether-deVries, 1995; Carlson, 1993; Dilworth-Anderson, 1994; Dowdell, 1995; Dressel & Barnhill, 1994; Jendrek, 1993, 1994; Joslin & Brouard, 1995; Karp, 1996; Minkler & Roe, 1993, 1996; Minkler, Roe, & Price, 1992; Minkler et al., 1993; Minkler, Roe & Robertson-Beckley, 1994; Poe, 1992; Roe, Minkler, & Barnwell 1994; Roe, Minkler, & Saunders, 1995; Shore & Hayslip, 1994; Solomon & Marx, 1995; Trupin, 1993) and result in the formation of a special interest group on "grandparents raising grandchildren" in the Gerontological Society of America. New large-scale surveys address the extent of intergenerational transfers (Bass & Caro, 1996; Kronebusch & Schlesinger, 1994), the social, personal, and family conditions that enhance close ties and exchanges of supports between generations, including grandparents and grandchildren (Bengtson & Harootyan, 1994; Eggebeen, 1992a, 1992b; Hogan, Eggebeen, & Clogg, 1993 King & Elder, 1995a), and long-term effects of childhood experiences with grandparents on attitudes toward the elderly in general (Silverstein & Parrott, 1997) and on support of aging parents in particular (Szinovacz, 1997b).

Prompted both by the heightened vulnerability of minority families as well as their ability to secure extended-family support in times of crisis (Stack, 1974), there also is renewed interest in grandparents and extended-household structures especially among blacks (Burton & Dilworth-Anderson, 1991; Hill-Lubin, 1991; Hunter, 1993, 1997; Kivett, 1993; Pearson, et al. 1990; Ruggles, 1994; Scott & Black, 1994; Taylor, 1993; Taylor & Chatters, 1991), Asians (Detzner, 1996; Kamo & Zhou, 1994; Yee, 1992), and Native Americans (Bahr, 1994; Bahr & Bahr, 1993; Weibel-Orlando, 1990). Enhanced attention to grandparents in rural and especially farm families (King & Elder, 1995a) constitutes a new variation on this theme. In addition, divorce and grandparenthood remains a focal research area, now with an emphasis on grandparents' supports to divorced adult children and to grandchildren in divorced or reconstituted families (Bray & Berger, 1990; Clingempeel, et al., 1992; Coleman, Ganong, & Cable, 1997; Cooney & Smith, 1996; Henry, Ceglian, & Matthews, 1992; Henry, Ceglian, & Ostrander, 1993;

Kennedy & Kennedy, 1993; Myers & Perrin, 1993; Pearson, 1993; Serovich, 1991; Spitze et al., 1994).

While problem-oriented grandparent research dominates during this era, there also are numerous studies on diverse other topics. Many of these investigations address themes pursued earlier (e.g., grandparents' roles, their child-rearing techniques, their relationship with grandchildren, or the transition to grandparenthood). However, a few new themes emerge as well. Interest in grandparents' relations with adult grandchildren follows from earlier demographic studies that documented the longer duration of grandparenthood and is facilitated by the convenience of college student samples (Franks et al., 1993; Hodgson, 1992; Kennedy, 1990, 1992a, 1992b; Langer, 1990; Lawton, Silverstein, & Bengtson, 1994b; Montepare, Steinberg, & Rosenberg, 1992; Roberto & Stroes, 1992). Prevailing myths about families of the past inspire historical studies on grandparenthood (Gratton & Haber, 1996; Hepworth, 1995), while the growing aging population and recognition that grandparents provide numerous material supports and gifts to their grandchildren prompt market researchers to create demographic profiles of grandparents (Schlosberg, 1990; Schwartz & Waldrop, 1992).

Several other research themes are theoretically grounded. Life-course theory leads to an emphasis on past family experiences as determinants of current grandparent-grandchild relationships (Silverstein, Lawton, & Bengtson, 1994a or b; Whitbeck, Hoyt, & Huck, 1993). Modernization theory is applied to grandparenthood in Third World countries (Sangree, 1992), and evolutionary thinking transpires in interpretations of gender and lineage effects on grandparenthood (Hogan, Eggebeen, & Clogg., 1993; Leek & Smith, 1991; Rossi & Rossi, 1990; M. Smith, 1991).

Despite these accomplishments, grandparent research remains marginal—not so much in terms of the quantity but rather the quality of existing investigations. As several recent reviewers note, many studies on grandparenthood are methodologically flawed, atheoretical, and lack integration as well as attention to diversity and contextual influences (Aldous, 1995; Kivett, 1991b; Pruchno & Johnson, 1996; Roberto, 1990; Robertson, 1995; M. Smith, 1991; Wilk, 1993). We present this volume in the hope that it will guide grandparent research into the mainstream of research on families and the elderly.

THE PRESENT: AN INTRODUCTION TO THE VOLUME

Over the past 50 years we have learned much about grandparenthood. Yet, there is still much to be learned. This volume is organized around four themes that are crucial to a deeper understanding of grandparenthood: the heterogeneity of grandparenting experiences; the dynamics and contingencies of grandparent-grandchild and extended-family relationships; interventions in grandparenting; and conceptual, theoretical, and methodological issues in grandparent research.

Heterogeneity

Recognition of variations in the grandparent experience can be traced to the earliest scientific studies on grandparenthood (Von Hentig, 1946). By the 1980's, Bengtson (1985) saw heterogeneity as one of the "principal themes" in grandparent research: "The growing body of empirical research points to the heterogeneity among grandparents, to the dangers in stereotyping and overgeneralizing, and to the likelihood of increasing differentiation in grandparents' roles in the future" (p. 11).

Despite such acknowledgments, systematic exploration of differences in grandparenting experiences over time and among diverse population groups remains quite limited. Predominance of cross-sectional designs and lack of historical data led to a static and sometimes even biased view of grandparenthood. Indeed, references to historical changes in grandparenting are often grounded in myths rather than realities. For example, having finally discarded the Walton's image of large coresident extended families (Hareven, 1994), researchers came to question the very existence of grandparenthood in the past (Robertson, 1995). Others maintain that grandparents have become more detached from their grandchildren (Gutmann, 1985; Kornhaber, 1985, 1996). In Chapter 2, Peter Uhlenberg and James B. Kirby explore the realities of historical change in grandparenthood by tracing demographic trends in the prevalence of grandparenthood and in the characteristics of grandparents throughout this century. These analyses debunk several prevailing myths about grandparenthood in the past and about changes in grandparenthood over time. They show, for example, that even at the beginning of this century *most* grandchildren had at least one surviving grandparent at the time they reached adulthood, and that barriers to grandparent-grandchild interactions for the most part *declined* during this century. In addition, Uhlenberg and Kirby caution against oversimplified interpretations of demographic trends. For example, to understand changes in children's coresidence with grandparents, it is essential to consider *simultaneous* influences of cohort trends in fertility, in specific nuclear family structures, as well as in types of extended living arrangements.

Cultural comparisons enhance not only our comprehension of diverse societies and human experiences within such societies but also provide a framework for understanding and evaluating our own social institutions. in Chapter 3, Charlotte Ikels argues that grandparenthood as a social status must be investigated within the context of societal norms and structures. Kinship structures and societal norms define the parameters within which individual grandparent-grandchild relationships are enacted. Kinship rules impact on access to grandchildren, on the formation and acceptance of grandparent-grandchild coresidence, or on the reliance on fictive kin to supplement biological kindred. For example, patrilocality coupled with village exogamy greatly reduces access to maternal grandparents, a pattern quite distinct from the matrifocal kinship structures in the United States and many European countries. Similarly, grandparent-grandchild relationships should be explored within the larger context of the societal status of the elderly. Countering yet another common image, Ikels stresses that modernization does not always undermine the social position of aged individuals. In some societies or societal subgroups, modernization may enhance elders' status as their adult children and grandchildren come to rely more on their grandparents' cultural heritage as well as their economic supports.

Once we recognize the contextual nature of grandparenting, the relatively simple explanatory models used in many grandparent studies can no longer be justified. Instead, research must be guided by theoretical frameworks that treat complexity and heterogeneity of human experiences as core assumptions. The ecological perspective in Chapter 4 presented by Valarie King, Stephen T. Russell and Glen H. Elder, Jr. fulfills this requirement. According to this perspective, relations between grandparents and grandchildren are embedded in societal, enviornmental, cultural, familial, and individual contexts that are interdependent and change over time. Focusing on environmental factors (urban, rural, and farm families) as an illustration, the authors demonstrate how historical change (urbanization), family change (outmigration of grandchildren from rural areas), or community-specific norms (patrifocal structures among farm families) impinge upon grandparents and grandchildren as they relate to each other.

Because research has relied on relatively homogeneous samples as well as on conceptual frameworks derived from studies of whites, subcultural variations in grandparenthood are still not well understood. As Andrea G. Hunter and Robert J. Taylor note in Chapter 5, particularly troublesome is the tendency to study grandparenthood in white families within a noncrisis context and grandparenthood among African Americans and other minorities within the context of family and social problems. For example, a considerable proportion of research on black grandparents is devoted to grandparents raising grandchildren. Even though this living arrangement is more prevalent among minority groups (Fuller-Thomson, Minkler, & Driver, 1997; Szinovacz, 1998), the majority of black grandparents do not raise their grandchildren. Nevertheless, there are some distinct features of grandparenthood in this group. Hunter and Taylor suggest African American grandparenthood is characterized by an emphasis on grandparents' role as socialization agents, high integration of grandparents in family life, or the inclusion of fictive grandparents in personal kindred. They also stress considerable within-group heterogeneity, which deserves further inquiry.

This theme—heterogeneity of grandparenting experiences within minority groups—is further pursued by Norma Williams and Diana J. Torrez in Chapter 6. These authors warn against generalizations of insights derived primarily from research on Mexican Americans to the entire Hispanic population as well as against presumptions that familism and other traditional cultural patterns characterize all Hispanic families. Informed by symbolic interactionism, Williams and Torrez view grandparent roles as emergent and emphasize that families in general and grandparents in particular adapt traditional cultural patterns to present societal and familial conditions. They also point out that differences in acculturation within families and across Hispanic subgroups may lead to considerable diversity between and among Hispanic grandparents and grandchildren.

Relying on available studies as well as his own research, Yoshinori Kamo observes in Chapter 7 both communalities and differences among Asian American grandparents. Norms grounded in Confucian ethics and patrilineal/patrilocal family structures constitute a common link among Asian American families and manifest themselves in upward extended households as well as somewhat formal relationships between grandparents and grandchildren. On the other hand, there also is great variety among Asian American grandparents. They come from societies that differ in economic development, demographic characteristics, and political background, and their families vary in regard to their immigration histories and acculturation patterns. Applying modernization theory to intergenerational dynamics, Kamo further argues that acculturation and assimilation of Asian American grandchildren may undermine grandparents' traditional authority and lead to a pronounced generation gap. However, Asian American grandparents continue to function as transmitters of cultural heritage and of knowledge about their countries of origin.

Gender and lineage differences constitute yet another source of variation in grandparent and grandchild experiences. Although grandfathers were neglected in early research (Baranowski, 1985), gender differences have become a dominant theme in recent grandparent studies. However, as Glenna Spitze and Russell A. Ward emphasize in Chapter 8, our understanding of gender differences in grandparenting remains quite limited. The authors attribute this deficit to a static perspective and insufficient attention to historical, societal, and familial contexts that cause or modify gender influences on grandparenting experiences. Spitze and Ward suggest that a generational framework (differences between grandmothers and grandfathers, between maternal and paternal grandparents, and between granddaughters and grandsons) combined with a life-course and historical perspective may be particularly useful for future research. For example, differences between grandsons and granddaughters may be traced to cohort-specific gender-role socialization not only by their parents but also by their grandparents, and differences between grandmothers and grandfathers may reflect their own gender-role socialization as well as their earlier parental and grandchild roles. Such dynamics are further explored in Part II of this volume.

Dynamics and Contingencies

Grandparenting and grandparent-grandchild relations are best understood as emerging phenomena that reflect changes in individuals' lives as well as past and present interaction processes among family members. Past research addressed some dynamics and contingencies of grandparenting, but many others await inquiry. A few studies have explored the anticipation of and transition to grandparenthood, including the timing of the transition; others investigated intergenerational processes in general and grandparents' influence on grandchildren in particular; and some were devoted to grandparenting under special circumstances such as adult children's divorce or their inability to raise their own children. The chapters contained in the second part of this volume reflect these emphases in past research and point to needed expansions in future studies.

Grandparenthood is initiated by a a dual transition process—the adult child's parenthood and the parent's grandparenthood—and subject to various other transitions in the lives of grandparents, grandchildren, and adult children. Thus, to understand grandparenthood requires an understanding of life-course transitions. In Chapter 9, Vira R. Kivett offers a theoretical and conceptual framework for assessing the impact of transitions on grandparents and on grandparent-grandchild relationships. She distinguishes among different types of transitions, delineates the contexts in which transitions occur, and describes factors that modify the impact of transitions on grandparenting. Kivett argues that past research focused on specific "events" that impact grandparent-grandchild relationships but failed to view them as transitions. Conceptualizing such "events" as transitions acknowledges their processual nature, provides a framework that allows comparisons among various transitions, and promotes deeper understanding of the conditions that facilitate or hinder adaptation processes by grandparents and grandchildren.

An alternative dynamic approach, the intergenerational solidarity model, is presented in Chapter 10 by Merril Silverstein, Roseann Giarrusso, and Vern L. Bengtson. The authors demonstrate the usefulness of their conceptual model for understanding selected features of grandparent-grandchild relationships. Because norms guiding grandparent behaviors are ambiguous, comparisons of intergenerational solidarity structures across generations and over time can shed some light on how the dynamics of grandparent-grandchild relationships differ from relationships in other generational units such as parents and children. Silverstein, Giarrusso and Bengtson further point out that the emphasis on single dimensions of grandparenting (e.g., frequency of contacts) in past research promotes a static and simplified perspective of grandparenthood. In contrast, the multidimensional intergenerational solidarity model enables researchers to track the development of complex relationships over time, in response to past relationship characteristics as well as family-external events.

Another dynamic, though underresearched, feature of grandparent-grandchild relationships is how grandparents and grandchildren exert influence on each other. In Chapter 11, Angela M. Tomlin notes that grandparents influence grandchildren in direct and indirect ways, and that influence processes within the grandparent-parent-grandchild triad should be seen as reciprocal rather than as always directed at the grandchild. Both the influence processes and their outcomes are contingent on a variety of factors ranging from grandchildren's age or grandparents' gender to contextual and family structural conditions. Because earlier studies focused on grandparents' influences on grandchildren (and their parents) and on influence processes and outcomes under selected conditions (e.g., parents' divorce) and over relatively short time periods, multilayered influence processes among grandparents, parents, and grandchildren and their long-term outcomes require further investigation.

Following grandparents and grandchildren over long time spans also will be necessary to fully understand relationships between grandparents and adult grandchildren. In Chapter 12, Lynne Gershenson Hodgson stresses that with the increased duration of grandparenthood, research needs to follow grandparents' "careers" well into their grandchildren's adulthood. Choices made early in the grandparent career (e.g., care for the grandchildren during their mother's work hours or emotional involvement with grandchildren when they were young) as well as the timing of transitions in both grandparents' and grandchildren's lives will account for differential dynamics in the development of relationships between adult grandchildren and their grandparents and may vary considerably among divergent population subgroups. In addition, Hodgson notes, we need to expand our knowledge about the conditions that lead to enhanced or more distant relationships between grandparents and gandchildren once the grandchildren reach adulthood. More research also should be devoted to changes in grandparent-grandchild relationships brought about by increased frailty among older grandparents, for example, when the earlier flow of supports from grandparent to grandchild shifts to supports from the grandchild to the grandparent.

Among the contingencies that have a profound impact on grandparent-grandchild relationships and received some attention in earlier research is adult children's divorce. Colleen L. Johnson in Chapter 13 critiques divorce research that centered on the nuclear family and demonstrates that the middle generation's divorce impacts the entire kin network, including the grandparents. Among maternal grandparents whose daughters typically have custody, divorce tends to trigger the grandparent's role as "family stabilizer," while paternal grandparents sometimes devise complex strategies to ensure continued contact with noncustodial grandchildren. Johnson further notes that the role of grandparents in their adult children's divorce may be heightened by the normative ambiguity that continues to surround the divorce process and its consequences. Furthermore, new kinship ties brought about by adult children's remarriages require further investigation. Although preliminary research evidence points to preferential treatment of biological over stepgrandchildren, further studies need to explore the processes accounting for the development of close or distant ties between stepgrandparents and stepgrandchildren.

The contingent character of the grandparent role is perhaps most evident in situations that trigger grandparents' involvement in their grandchildren's care. In Chapter 14, Barbara A. Hirshorn emphasizes that grandparent-care scenarios vary in regard to time frame and level of responsibility, ranging from occasional baby-sitting to long-term surrogate parenting. In addition, grandparents' involvement in their grandchildren's care evolves from a variety of circumstances, usually in their adult children's lives. However, care for grandchildren is sometimes motivated by the grandparents' needs or wishes, for example, when "cultural conservator" grandparents "actively solicit" live-in grandchildren (Weibel-Orlando, 1990: 121). While several studies point to both benefits and problems surrounding grandparents' involvement in their grandchildren's care—both for the grandparents and the grandchildren, additional research on the outcomes of grandparents' caregiver roles is needed.

Interventions

The potential negative consequences of adult children's divorce on grandparents' access to grandchildren as well as of grandparents' role as surrogate parents have raised concerns among practitioners and policy makers and prompted the development of special programs for grandparents. Such interventions in intergenerational relations are addressed in the third part of this volume.

In Chapter 15, Richard B. Miller and Jonathan G. Sandberg suggest that clinical interventions grounded in family systems theory may be the most appropriate for family therapy involving three generations. For example, problems caused by boundary ambiguity or ambiguous hierarchies, two central concepts in family system theory, often characterize families of grandparents who have major responsibility for the care of the grandchildren, and principles of family systems–oriented divorce therapy may be applicable to disputes about grandparents' access to grandchildren. The authors suggest that family therapists have too often focused on nuclear family units. Thus, greater involvement of family therapists in grandparenting issues is needed as is research documenting the outcomes of clinical interventions in grandparent access disputes or in family problems associated with surrogate parenting.

Such interventions may indeed be needed because, as Joan Aldous claims in Chapter 16, current policies are not conducive to easing family discord over grandparents' access to grandchildren or problems encountered by grandparents who raise their grandchildren. After reviewing current statutes and pertinent research on grandparents' visitation rights, the author concludes that court-enforced visitations may often not be in the best interest of the grandchildren and that mediation may be a better alternative to resolve visitation disputes. Similarly, policies that force grandparents' involvement in the care for their grandchildren (for example, the requirement in new welfare programs that teenage mothers reside with their families) may not always be beneficial for the grandchildren, the teenage parent, or the grandparents. On the other hand, current policies and laws that ensure parents' autonomy in child-rearing often leave grandparents raising grandchildren in a "legal limbo."

Left in this "legal limbo" are now about 10% of black and Hispanic and a smaller proportion of white grandmothers who have sole responsibility for grandchildren in their households (Szinovacz, 1998). It is thus not surprising that programs aimed at surrogate grandparents have taken center stage among other intergenerational programmatic efforts. In Chapter 17, Maximiliane E. Szinovacz and Angela Roberts note that programmatic efforts for surrogate as well as other grandparents are on the rise and increasingly supported by national organizations. They caution, however, that many programs address only some of grandparents' concerns (for example, support groups for surrogate grandparents often do not alleviate legal problems) and that more systematic program evaluations are needed.

In Chapter 18, Maximiliane E. Szinovacz returns to the one theme that inspired and pervades all contributions to this volume: the call for more theoretically grounded and methodologically sophisticated research on grandparenting. She emphasizes that past theorizing and research have failed to capture the heterogeneity, dynamics, and complexity of grandparenting. Relying on insights from all other chapters, Szinovacz proposes specific conceptual, theoretical, and methodological refinements. Her suggestions, as well as those noted by authors throughout this volume and summarized below, represent a challenging agenda for future investigations on grandparenthood.

THE FUTURE: NEEDED RESEARCH ON GRANDPARENTING

The contributers to this handbook summarize, critique, and advance knowledge on grandparenting that accumulated throughout the past half century. Chapters contained in the first part of the volume demonstrate *heterogeneity* in grandparent experiences across time; across cultures, among as well as within subcultural groups; and by gender. They also inspire avenues for future research. First, as King, Russell, and Elder emphasize, recognition of diversity is but an initial step toward understanding *how* historical, cultural, and societal contexts condition and mediate intergenerational processes. We need to develop theories that link the intrafamilial dynamics of grandparent-grandchild relationships to structural conditions that change over time and reflect both cultural influences as well adpative processes by families.

Second, studies of minority grandparents have to be integrated into mainstream research on grandparenthood. As long as investigations of minority grandparents are tied to specific social and familial problems or proceed from a majority perspective, our understanding of subcultural variations in grandparenting will remain limited. We need studies that go beyond quantitative comparisons of grandparent activities and explore qualitative differences in the meaning of grandparenthood, the dynamics of grandparent-grandchild relationships, or in the outcomes of specific grandparent and grandchild experiences. We also have to explore conditions that account for differences in grandparenting experiences among different minority subpopulations as well as within minority groups.

Lastly, research on gender differences in grandparenting has to be theoretically grounded and linked to macro phenomena such as changing gender-role ideologies, trends in women's labor force participation, and changes in child-care policies. From a feminist perspective, it may also be time to question the continued predominance of grandmothers in the care of grandchildren (both inside and outside the household) when an increasing proportion of grandmothers is employed and a growing proportion of retired or semiretired grandfathers are available for support with child care.

Further research efforts also are necessary to fully capture the *dynamics and contingencies* of grandparenting. To achieve this goal, it will first be necessary to move from cross-sectional studies that treat such dynamics and contingencies as "events" (e.g., as variables in regression models) to panel studies that follow grandparents and grandchildren over various transitions and explore the effects of simultaneous and sequential transition processes on grandparent-grandchild relationships.

Second, in designing conceptual, measurement, and exploratory models we have to acknowledge that relationships change over time and differ among generations. Thus, we cannot assume that relationship typologies and factor structures derived from studies of grandparents and adult grandchildren can be generalized to interactions between grandparents and preschool-age grandchildren, or that explanatory models of parent-adult child relationships are equally applicable to relationships between grandparents and grandchildren. Or, to paraphrase Lynne Gershenson Hodgson, we have to move from assessments of *whether* a grandmother and her granddaughter are holding hands to investigations of *how* they are holding hands.

Third, we have to go beyond paying lip service to reciprocal influence processes among family members. This means, at the very least, inclusion of pertinent characteristics and behaviors of all involved family members in explanatory models and reliance on recursive models.

Fourth, research on the effects of divorce or surrogate parenting has to address the circumstances under which these transitions occur and short-term as well as long-term adaptation processes in their aftermath. For example, adult children's divorce may have different consequences for grandparent-grandchild relationships contingent on grandchildren's age, pre-divorce relationships among extended kin, or grandparents' involvement in the divorce process. Moreover, relationships between ex-spouses (and their relations to ex-parents-in-law) may change over time as some disputes are settled and new ones emerge or as the divorcees engage in new relationships.

Similarly, we need large-scale and longitudinal investigations of grandparents' involvement in child care. Only such studies can demonstrate outcomes of grandparents' involvement for the grandchildren, the grandparents, and the parents. In addition, we need to consider the contingencies of such outcomes on various circumstances, ranging from the events that triggered grandparents' involvement to grandchildren's age at the time the care arrangement started or changes in household boundaries during grandparents' care.

Such research on the consequences of divorce, surrogate parenting, or other stressful transitions is especially important to guide clinical interventions, policies, and programs. As Aldous emphasizes, policies that enforce intergenerational relationships should proceed from scientific knowledge rather than from sentimental notions about "family values." Which policies, therapies, or programs "work"—and for whom they work—requires investigations that compare short-term and long-term consequences of alternative choices and interventions (e.g., court-ordered visitation versus mediation-based visitation or surrogate parenting versus foster care) on *all* involved family members.

We have, indeed, much to learn about grandparenting. Perhaps recent funding initiatives for research on grandparenting by the National Institute of Aging (1995) and other agencies will encourage investigators to pursue some of the suggestions for future research offered throughout this handbook.

NOTE

1. The concept of the isolated nuclear family refers to structural isolation (e.g., household structure, authority relations) not to interactions among kin (Parsons, 1971).

Part I

Variations in
Grandparenting Experiences

Chapter 2

Grandparenthood Over Time: Historical and Demographic Trends

Peter Uhlenberg and James B. Kirby

Recent empirical studies have expanded our knowledge of grandparenthood in contemporary society. It is important to recognize, however, that grandparenthood today may be quite different than it was in the past (or what it may be in the future). The number of grandparents, the sociodemographic characteristics of grandparents, and the roles of grandparents are all likely to change in response to changing historical conditions. In this chapter we examine some of the changes in grandparenthood that have occurred in twentieth-century America.

Each of the basic demographic variables (mortality, fertility, migration) has important implications for the experience of grandparent-grandchild relationships in a society. A nice summary of effects of changing mortality and fertility is provided by Cherlin and Furstenberg when they write: "In past times, when birth and death rates were high, grandparents were in relatively short supply. Today . . . grandchildren are in short supply" (1986a: 28).

Other factors being equal, the higher the death rates are among adults, the less likely that children and young adults will have any particular grandparent still living. And, other factors being equal, the lower the fertility rates, the fewer the average number of grandchildren for persons at each stage of later adulthood. Migration patterns affect the geographic proximity of grandparents and grandchildren, and proximity almost certainly has consequences for the nature of the relationship. In addition to supply and geographic distribution of grandparents, changes over time in the characteristics of the grandparent population (such as health status, economic status, educational status, and marital status), affect intergenerational relationships. The following discussion considers how sociodemographic changes over the twentieth century have altered grandparenthood.

MORTALITY

The assertion that children today are more likely than those in the past to have living grandparents is correct, but not precise. Great precision is not possible because direct data on the supply of grandparents for individuals at various stages of life are not available for past times. Nevertheless, a sense of the magnitude of historical change is gained from examining life tables. As data presented in this section will reveal, there is no basis for asserting that, "[v]ery few grandparents were alive at the turn of the century" (Robertson, 1995: 245), or that "[I]t is only within the last half century that people have lived long enough to become grandparents" (Pruchno, 1995: 12). On the other hand, mortality decline occurring over the twentieth century has significantly increased the number of grandparents in the kin networks of children and young adults.

Using life tables for the U.S. population in various years between 1900 and 2000, Uhlenberg (1980, 1996) provides estimates of the proportion of persons at various stages of life who have particular grandparents alive. These calculations are made with an assumption that in each generation, mothers are age 27 and fathers are age 30 when children are born. Thus the probability of a maternal grandmother being alive for a newborn is the probability that a woman survives from age 27 (when her daughter is born) to age 54 (when her daughter's child is born). Similarly, the probability of a paternal grandfather of a 30-year-old being alive is the probability of a male surviving from age 30 (when his son is born) to age ninety (when his son's child is age 30). Given the necessity of making simplifying assumptions in this analysis, the results described below should be interpreted as approximations of historical conditions rather than precise estimates.

The steadily improving prospects of having grandparents alive when individuals arrive at various life-course stages is shown by data in Table 2.1. Mortality conditions existing in 1900 imply that fewer than one-fourth of all newborns would have a complete set of living grandparents, and by age 30, only one-fifth would have any living grandparent. Mortality conditions in 2000 produce a situation where two-thirds of all children begin life with all grandparents alive, and more than three-fourths have at least one grandparent alive when they reach age 30. Without question the mortality revolution of the twentieth century has greatly increased the number of grandparent-grandchild relationships in American society.

Most young children and adolescents at the beginning of the century, as at the end, had a least one living grandparent. In 1900 about 94% of the 10-year-olds and 70% of the 20-year-olds still had a grandparent. Thus it is likely that most persons throughout this century have retained some memory of a grandparent. But typical ages at which persons no longer have surviving grandparents have advanced substantially. Under mortality conditions of 2000, only 3% or 4% of all persons would lose their last grandparent before reaching adulthood (age 20), and three-fourths would still have a grandparent when they reach age

Table 2.1
Percent of Persons at Various Ages Who Have Grandparents Still Living, Under Mortality Conditions Existing in Selected Years: 1900–2000[a]

	All Grandparents Alive at Age:					1 + Grandparent Alive at Age:				
Year	0	10	20	30		0	10	20	30	40
1900	23.8	6.4	0.4	0.0		99.2	94.2	69.6	20.6	1.0
1920	31.0	9.8	0.7	0.0		99.6	96.4	75.5	24.6	1.6
1940	41.3	14.0	1.2	0.0		99.9	98.1	82.5	32.5	2.3
1960	54.8	22.6	3.2	0.0		100.0	99.4	92.0	51.3	6.5
1980	62.7	31.0	6.1	0.1		100.0	99.7	95.8	68.3	15.4
2000	67.8	38.9	9.7	0.3		100.0	99.9	97.4	75.8	21.0

	1 + Grandmother Alive at Age:					1 + Grandfather Alive at Age:				
Year	0	10	20	30	40	0	10	20	30	40
1900	92.5	80.1	52.1	15.4	0.8	89.4	71.1	36.5	6.2	0.2
1920	94.5	84.3	57.4	17.9	1.3	92.6	77.3	42.4	8.1	0.2
1940	97.8	91.2	68.9	25.8	2.0	94.2	78.6	44.0	9.0	0.3
1960	99.3	96.2	83.2	43.2	5.7	96.4	83.5	52.3	14.1	0.8
1980	99.6	97.7	89.3	60.2	14.1	97.7	88.5	60.8	20.4	1.6
2000	99.7	98.3	91.3	66.9	19.1	98.3	92.2	69.7	26.8	2.4

[a]Assuming children are born in each generation to mothers age 27 and fathers age 30.

Source: Uhlenberg, 1996.

30. The growing probability of cosurviving with grandparents over a substantial period of young adult life has potential implication for kin networks, although little is known about actual consequences (Aldous, 1995). For example, are meaningful exchanges of services or social support common between grandparents and their grandchildren who are in their 20's and 30's? (see Hodgson, 1992; Chapter 12). And what is the importance of the increasing frequency of four-generation families? Because most persons now are over 30 before their last grandparent dies, more children must have one or more great-grandparent living when they are born. Do great-grandparents typically play any important

role in the lives of their great-grandchildren? (see Doka & Mertz, 1988; Chapter 12).

Lower death rates for females compared to males over the twentieth century, combined with age differences between spouses, have made it more common for young persons to have grandmothers alive than grandfathers. The older age of fathers compared to mothers implies that paternal grandparents will tend to be older than maternal ones, and hence die sooner. As the gender gap in mortality increased between 1900 and 1980, the differential survival prospects of grandmothers compared to grandfathers grew increasingly large. The ratio of 20-year-olds with only grandmothers living to those with only grandfathers living increased from 1.9 in 1900 to 4.5 in 2000. While the proportion of 30-year-olds with a grandmother still alive increased from 15% to 67% over this century, the proportion with a grandfather still alive increased only from 6% to 27%. Clearly the supply of grandmothers has grown more rapidly than the supply of grandfathers, especially among young adults. This means that a large majority of the great-grandparents in this country are females, and grandmothers comprise about 75% of the living grandparents of persons aged 30.

FERTILITY

While mortality levels affect the supply of grandparents for children in a population, fertility levels affect the supply of grandchildren for older persons. In this section we ask three questions about the relationship between childbearing patterns and the experience of grandparenthood in later life: (1) How have changes in rates of childlessness affected the proportion of persons who never become grandparents? (2) How have changes in fertility rates affected the number of grandchildren that older persons have? and (3) How have changes in timing of childbearing affected the ages at which persons become grandparents? Almost no historical data are available that directly measure any of these aspects of grandparenthood, and literature on these subjects is nearly nonexistent. Nevertheless, we can use fertility information collected in past censuses to gain a sense of how important changes in childbearing patterns over the past century have been.

The first question we want to answer is this: What proportion of women reaching old age in different time periods never became grandmothers? We focus on successive cohorts at the time they occupy the age category 60–64 to trace historical trends in the experience of grandparenthood in later life. Clearly all women in a cohort who are childless in later life will be grandchildless. In addition, those who have children will be grandchildless if none of their children have children. To estimate grandchildlessness among mothers in one cohort, we use data on childlessness among women in the cohort born 30 years later. This is only a rough approximation because the children born to mothers in a cohort span a number of birth years. Nevertheless, this estimate provides a reasonable approximation of historical trends.

An example of how rates of grandchildlessness are calculated will clarify the procedure. Women aged 60–64 in 1900 were members of the birth cohort of 1835–39. Using census reports, we find the following parity distribution for women in this cohort who survived through mid-life: 14.4% had no children, 7.4% had one child, 9.0% had two children, 9.3% had three children, and the remainder had four or more. Childlessness among the children born to the 1835–39 cohort is determined by looking at percent childless among women born in 1865–69, which was 20.2%. Thus our estimate of percent permanently grand-childless for women aged 60–64 in 1900 is 14.4% (those who had no child) +7.4% × .202 (those who had one child, but that child had no children) +9.0 × .202 (those who had two children, neither of whom had a child), and so on. About 16.4% of the women aged 60–64 are estimated to have been grandchild-less. The same procedure applied to successive cohorts of women produces the results displayed in Figure 2.1.

Rates of grandchildlessness increased for women reaching old age up to World War II, when nearly 30% were in this category. Because rates of child-lessness remained high for women born in the first decade of this century, rates of grandchildlessness remained high for women reaching old age up to about 1970. Then grandchildlessness declined rapidly for successive cohorts approach-ing old age for the remainder of this century. Only slightly more than 10% of women in their 60's in the 1990's were permanently grandchildless. This reflects the very low level of childlessness for women born in the 1930's who entered their childbearing stage of life during the baby-boom years. Increasing child-lessness among more recent cohorts is reflected in the growing level of grand-childlessness among women reaching old age after 2000. Because about 20% of the women born around 1960 are expected to remain childless (Chen & Morgan, 1991), rates of grandchildlessness will again reach 25% or higher among those entering old age after 2020.

The second question we ask is how the average number of grandchildren changes over time for women who have at least one child. The technique used to estimate this is similar to the one described above to calculate grandchild-lessness. The average number of grandchildren for mothers in the birth cohort of 1835–39 is obtained by multiplying their average number of children by the average number of children their children had. The fertility of the middle gen-eration is approximated by the average number of children born to women 30 years younger than the grandparent cohort. The estimated number of grandchil-dren for women aged 60–64 in 1900 is 4.59 (average number of children for those in the 1835–39 cohort) times 2.64 (average number of children for the 1865–69 cohort), or 12.1. Results of these calculations for various cohorts are shown in Figure 2.2.

As expected, Figure 2.2 shows a marked decline over the twentieth century in the average number of grandchildren for women entering later life. Reflecting the large decline in family size in the late nineteenth and early twentieth cen-turies, the average number of grandchildren for women aged 60–64 declined

Figure 2.1
Estimated Percent of Women Aged 60–64 Who Are Childless and Grandchildless, 1900–2010

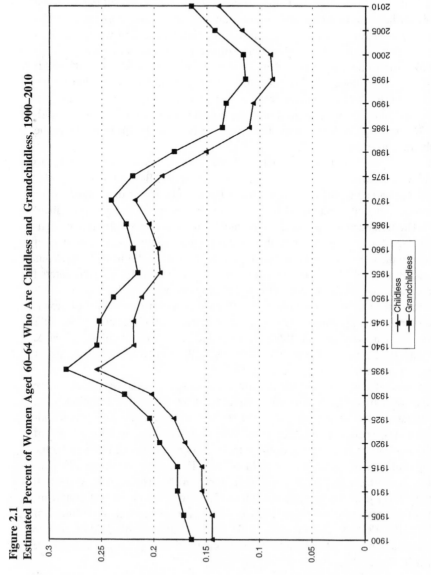

Source: Calculated from the U.S. Bureau of the Census (1945), tables 7–12, and the National Center for Health Statistics (1994), section 1.

Figure 2.2
Estimated Mean Number of Grandchildren for Women Aged 60–64, 1900–1980

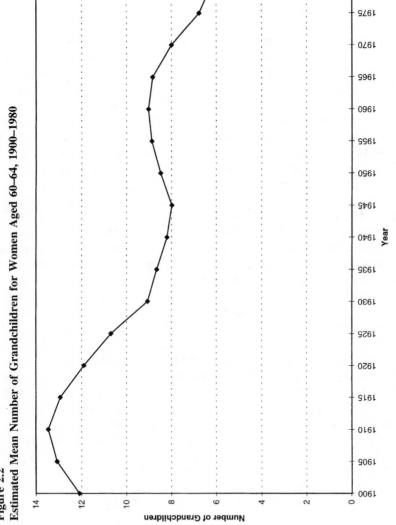

Source: Calculated from the U.S. Bureau of the Census (1945), tables 1–6, and the National Center for Health Statistics (1994), section 1.

from over 13 in 1910 to about 8 in the 1940's. After a slight increase, resulting from the baby boom after World War II, the average number of grandchildren has again declined in recent years. Women reaching old age in the 1990's typically have fewer than six grandchildren, and the downward trend is expected to continue into the next century until it reaches about four (when completed family size in both relevant generations averages about two). There is, of course, a great deal of variation in number of grandchildren that older persons have, but few in the future will have as many as was typical for grandparents in the early twentieth century.

The final question concerns the timing of entrance into grandparenthood. There is no evidence that the age at which persons experience the transition to grandparenthood has changed significantly over the twentieth century (Cherlin & Furstenberg, 1986a). The median age at which women have their first birth has tended to fall within the range of 22 to 24 over this time period (National Center for Health Statistics, 1994; Suchindran & Koo, 1992), suggesting that it has been common to become a grandparent for the first time between ages 45 and 50. Greater change has occurred, however, in the typical age for completing childbearing. As family size declined in the early decades of this century, women were increasingly ceasing their childbearing at younger ages. For example, the proportion of women aged 40–44 who had at least one child under age 5 dropped from 23.6% in 1910 to 11.3% in 1940 and to 10.4% in 1970 (U.S. Bureau of the Census, 1945; U.S. Bureau of the Census, 1975b). When women were bearing children later in their fecund period, it was common for them to be rearing their younger children when they became grandparents. In other words, many new grandparents in the early twentieth century were still actively parenting their own children. Over time it has become less likely for the roles of active parent and grandparent to overlap. On the other hand, early teenage childbearing can produce grandmothers who are still parenting the mother of their grandchild. When very early childbearing occurs in several generations, grandmotherhood can arrive before women reach age 30 (Burton & Bengtson, 1985).

In summary, changing fertility patterns have altered the nature of grandparenthood in several interesting ways: (1) a higher percentage of persons entering old age at the end of the century are grandparents than was true earlier in the century, (2) grandparents now have fewer grandchildren than grandparents in the past, and (3) it has become increasingly uncommon for grandparenting to overlap with active parenting. These changes have consequences for both grandchildren and grandparents. Some writers suggest that grandparents tend to make "selective investments" in grandchildren, that is, to concentrate their attention and support on particular grandchildren (Cherlin & Furstenberg, 1986a). As number of grandchildren per grandparent declines, such a strategy becomes less necessary. With fewer siblings and cousins to compete with, an increasing proportion of children is likely to receive substantial support from grandparents. This change has not escaped the attention of marketing researchers. Finding ways to tap into the growing, affluent grandparent population has become akin

Table 2.2
**Percent of Children Under 18 with Grandparent in Home by Number of Parents
in Home and Race: 1940–1991**

	TOTAL		2 PARENTS		1 PARENT		0 PARENT	
Year	White	Black	White	Black	White	Black	White	Black
1940	10.3	16.0	7.2	5.3	1.8	3.1	1.3	7.6
1950	10.6	18.5	7.7	6.9	1.8	4.0	1.1	7.6
1960	6.8	15.8	4.7	5.2	1.4	4.4	0.7	6.2
1970	5.4	13.0	3.0	3.5	1.2	4.6	0.9	4.9
1980	4.8	12.2	2.3	1.7	1.5	5.7	1.0	4.8
1991	5.3	14.9	2.1	1.1	2.3	8.4	0.9	5.4

Source: Hernandez and Myer (1993), table 3.10, and U.S. Bureau of the Census (1994b), table 12.

to finding the "holy grail" in the marketing industry (Schlosberg, 1990; Crispell, 1993).

CORESIDENCE AND GEOGRAPHIC PROXIMITY

Several studies have demonstrated the important consequences of geographic proximity for frequency of grandparent-grandchild interaction and for the type of role grandparents play (Cherlin & Furstenberg, 1986a; Doka & Mertz, 1988; Kivett, 1985b; Rossi & Rossi, 1990). The most intensive involvement of grandparents, including grandparents acting as surrogate parents, is possible when the generations coreside. Among those living apart, greater distance increases the likelihood that the grandparent role is remote in contrast to active. Census data on coresidence of grandparents and grandchildren are available for years since 1940. Using those data it is possible to look both at the proportion of children living in a grandparent's home and at the proportion of children who coreside with a grandparent (whether or not the grandparent is the household head). Because of racial differences in family structure, patterns for black and white children are examined separately. Few historical data exist related to geographic distance between those who live in separate households, but some inference of change in proximity can be made by looking at historical data on migration patterns.

Information on the proportion of children under age 18 who have a grandparent living in their household for years since 1940 is presented in Table 2.2. In some cases these children are living in the grandparent's house, while in others the grandparent is living with the child's parents. Although no information is available on the role these grandparents play in the child's life, one can assume that this arrangement provides an opportunity for close interaction. The proportion of white children living with a grandparent in the house declined from over 10% in 1940 and 1950 to about 5% in 1970, 1980, and 1991. By looking at the number of parents present in the home it is clear why coresidence with grandparents declined—the arrangement of a grandparent being present along with two parents dropped significantly (from 8% in 1950 to 2% in 1991). The proportion of all children living with a grandparent but no parent present, a clear indicator that the grandparent is a surrogate parent, has remained quite stable (at about 1%). The proportion of children living with one parent and a grandparent in the home increased slightly from a low of 1.2% in 1960 to a high of 2.3% in 1991. Thus despite a rapid increase in one-parent families for children (from 7% in 1960 to over 21% in 1991) living with grandparents has not become a more common experience.

In years since 1940, a larger proportion of black than white children have lived with grandparents in the home, and the racial gap has grown larger over time. In 1991, black children were about three times more likely than white children to coreside with a grandparent. This racial difference occurs because of large differences in living with a grandparent only (black children in 1991 were six times more likely than whites to be in this category) and because the proportion of black children living with one parent and a grandparent increased over time. It should be noted, however, that growth in proportion of all children who live with one parent and a grandparent is due entirely to the growth in the number who live in single-parent families (the proportion of black children who have only one parent increased from 22% in 1960 to 57% in 1991). Among both black and white children living in one-parent families, the proportion who coreside with a grandparent has declined in recent decades. No doubt many grandparents are assisting their grandchildren who lack two parents, but most do not provide them with housing.

If coresidence provides greatest opportunity for intergenerational closeness, then living in different countries is likely to present the greatest obstacle to grandparents and grandchildren developing a relationship. The massive immigration to the United States in the late nineteenth and early twentieth century produced a situation where a significant number of children were first- or second-generation immigrants. Using census data on nativity status of parents, it is possible to track the changing percent of children who were likely to have grandparents living abroad. In 1900, about one-third of the children under age 15 had foreign-born parents. After 1920 the likelihood of having a grandparent living outside the United States began to decline. Since 1950, fewer than 10% of American children have been separated from grandparents by national boundaries. This change over time reflects the curtailment of immigration after restrictive immigration laws were enacted in the 1920s. Recent upturns in immigration will increase the proportion without grandparents in this country, but the level will remain far below that existing in the early twentieth century. Thus changes over this century suggest a decline of 20% to 25% in the proportion of children likely to have limited contact with grandparents because they live in different countries.

Among children with grandparents living in the United States, geographic distance may be an obstacle to forming close relationships. Lacking direct information on geographic proximity of grandparents and grandchildren, it is difficult to determine whether or not change has occurred in the proportion who live far from each other. Several bits of information, however, suggest that it is unlikely that large changes in proximity of kin have occurred. Greater geographic distance between generations would develop over time if an increasing proportion of persons were moving away from their place of origin. Data from various current population surveys, which have measured movement of the population annually since 1948, do not indicate any increase in internal migration rates (Long, 1988). Indeed, the proportion of Americans who move each year has been lower since 1970 than it was in the years between 1948 and 1970 (U.S. Bureau of the Census, 1995a). Consistent with this finding, social surveys since 1962 have repeatedly found that about 75% of all older persons with children have a child living nearby (Uhlenberg, 1993). Finally, census data indicate little change over this century in percent of the native-born adult population living outside of their state of birth. In 1910, about 62% of adults aged 40–60 were living in their state of birth, compared to about 61% in 1980 (Uhlenberg, 1993). Given improvements in transportation and communication technology and the lack of evidence that geographic distance between generations has increased, there is no reason to believe that grandparents and grandchildren have less access to each other now than in the past. Indeed, it is likely that obstacles to interaction have declined over time.

SELECTED CHARACTERISTICS OF GRANDPARENTS

Several changes over the twentieth century, in addition to those discussed above, have implications for grandparent-grandchild relationships. Four of these are considered briefly in this section: health status, poverty status, educational gap between generations, and marital status. In none of these areas are historical data specific to grandparents available. However, because a majority of older persons are grandparents, changes in the characteristics of the older population as a whole provide an indication of changes in the grandparent population.

Health Status

Serious disabilities and chronic illnesses prevent some grandparents from enjoying an active relationship with their grandchildren. Has this become a larger or a smaller problem over time? Some hypothesize that modern medecine has kept alive an increasing proportion of older persons suffering from disabilities and disease (Crimmins, Hayward, & Saito, 1994; Verbrugge, 1984). If this occurred, then a larger proportion of the grandparent population would be ill or disabled now than in the past. Because the duration of most illnesses in the early twentieth century was quite short, being resolved by recovery or death within eight weeks (Riley, 1990), it is likely that the prevalence of chronic illness among the older population has increased.

Nevertheless, the overall effect of changing health status on potential for active grandparent-grandchild relationships has been positive. Although the amount of time that people spend in an unhealthy state toward the end of life increased, the amount of later life spent in a healthy state has increased still more (Manton, Corder, & Stallard, 1993; Rogers, Rogers, & Belanger, 1990). Thus, over time a growing proportion of each successive cohort, measured at any particular age, has been alive and in good health. Therefore, many more young children and adolescents now, compared to the past, have grandparents who are active and healthy. The trade off for young adults is that many who now have disabled old grandparents in the past would not have had those grandparents alive at all.

Poverty Status

Compared to their affluent counterparts, grandparents who live in poverty cannot contribute much to the economic well-being of their grandchildren and may be less able to maintain frequent contact. In the early decades of the twentieth century, before the old-age security programs were established, there is little doubt that a majority of older grandparents had scarce economic resources. The spread of social security and sustained economic growth that followed World War II led to declining poverty among older Americans. Nevertheless, as recently as 1959, 35% of the population over age 65 still lived in poverty. Changes since 1959 have been analyzed extensively (Duncan & Smith, 1989; Holz-Eakin & Smeeding, 1994; Hurd, 1990), and these studies show continued improvement in economic well-being of the older population up to the present. The purchasing power of households headed by older persons grew by 40% between 1971 and 1991 (Holz-Eakin & Smeeding, 1994), and rates of poverty among the old have been reduced to about 12%. When measured in a comprehensive way, "[T]he elderly *as a group* are now as well off as the non-elderly, *as a group*" (Holz-Eakin & Smeeding, 1994: 105). The long trend of improving economic status of older grandparents suggests that financial problems have become less and less of an obstacle to grandparent-grandchild relationships. Decreasing poverty rates have occurred among black as well as white grandparents, although blacks continue to be disadvantaged relative to whites.

Educational Gap

It often is observed that large differences in levels of educational attainment interfere with closeness in social relationships. Because most children are in school, it is not meaningful to compare their educational level with that of their

Table 2.3
Percentage Distribution of Women Aged 25–34 and 55–64 by Years of School Completed: 1930–2000

	% Less Than 8			% 12 or more			Index of
Year	25-34	55-64	Diff.	25-34	55-64	Diff.	Dissimilarity
1930	48.3	73.1	-24.8	32.1	17.9	14.2	24.8
1940	35.1	64.3	-29.2	42.0	22.2	19.8	29.2
1950	27.2	62.9	-35.7	50.0	23.1	26.9	35.8
1960	17.2	54.1	-36.9	59.7	28.7	31.0	37.0
1970	9.6	36.6	-27.0	71.2	42.1	29.1	29.2
1980	5.2	22.1	-16.9	83.8	57.6	26.2	26.2
1990	4.0	13.6	-9.6	87.4	70.4	17.0	17.0
2000	4.0	8.0	-4.0	87.4	80.3	7.1	7.0

Source: U.S. Bureau of the Census, 1995b.

grandparents. The educational milieu of children, however, is shaped by the educational experience of their parents. Therefore, the educational gap between the parents and the grandparents of children might indicate the extent to which differences in educational attainment limit the role that grandparents play. It is assumed that grandparents who have significantly less education than their children will have greater difficulty relating to grandchildren than those with more equal education. Historical change in this generational gap is approximated by comparing the years of school completed by women aged 25–34 (representing the parent generation) with women aged 55–64 (representing the grandparent generation) in various years. Results of this comparison are shown in Table 2.3.

The generational gap in education underwent a major transition over the past 100 years. Although data on educational attainment are not available before 1930, it is likely that the gap was small around 1900 because most children, like their parents, received relatively little formal education. At the end of the century the gap is again small because members of both generations typically completed a high-school education. In the middle of this transition, however, the gap was large because children tended to receive far more education than their parents. It was during the time period when public education was expanding rapidly that cohorts entering childhood experienced greatly expanded opportunities for schooling compared to their parents. As shown in Table 2.3, by 1930 the educational gap between the parents and grandparents of young children was quite large. This gap continued to expand until about 1960, when the parent generation had been in school after World War II and the grandparent generation had completed its education in the early decades of this century. By the end of the twentieth century, grandparents of young children are members of cohorts that completed nearly as much education as the parents of these children. It appears, therefore, that generational gaps in educational attainment now play a smaller role in creating distance between grandparents and grandchildren than they did in the recent past.

Marital Status

The significance of parents' and grandparents' marital status for the relationship that children have with their grandparents is discussed in several chapters of this handbook (see especially Chapters 13 and 16). Divorce in the parental generation is found to intensify contact and affective closeness between young children and their maternal grandparents, while it tends to reduce closeness to paternal grandparents (Cherlin & Furstenberg, 1986a; Matthews & Sprey, 1984). Effects of the grandparents' marital status on the role they play has received less attention, but it is likely that being married facilitates greater involvement, especially for grandfathers.

The proportion of children born in decades since the 1920's who have lived with fewer than two parents before reaching age 17 has been calculated by Hernandez and Myer (1993). Changes in the experiences of children born between 1920 and 1950 were not very large. During this time period, about one-third of all children lived with only one parent during at least part of their childhood. The declining proportion experiencing family disruption due to death of a parent was roughly balanced by an increasing proportion experiencing the divorce of their parents. After 1960, however, increasing divorce in the parental generation, as well as increasing out-of-wedlock childbearing, led to a growing likelihood that children would live with only one parent. By the time the cohort born in 1980 reaches age 17, it is projected that fewer than half will have lived continuously with two parents (Hernandez & Myer, 1993). There are several implications of the increasing number of children in single-parent families and in blended families for grandparents in the United States. The proportion of grandparents (mostly maternal) providing extensive help in caring for grandchildren is likely to increase, and the proportion of grandparents (mostly paternal) blocked from having close relationships with grandchildren also is likely to increase. In addition, a growing number of older persons are entering into the vaguely defined role of stepgrandparent (Glick, 1989; Szinovacz, in press).

Changes in the marital status of persons with young grandchildren is approximated by tracking the marital status of persons aged 55–64 who have ever married (Table 2.4). For men in this age range, the proportion divorced increased as the proportion widowed decreased over the past 100 years, resulting in little change in the percent who are married. Throughout the twentieth century more than 85% of men in the prime ages to be grandfathers of young children have

Table 2.4
Marital Status Distribution of the Ever-Married Population Aged 55–64, by Sex: 1900–1994

Year	Males			Females		
	Married	Widowed	Divorced	Married	Widowed	Divorced
1900	86.5	12.9	0.6	64.8	34.6	0.5
1910	86.3	12.8	0.9	67.0	32.3	0.7
1920	86.5	12.4	1.1	66.9	32.3	0.8
1930	86.9	11.4	1.7	68.2	30.6	1.3
1940	87.8	10.1	2.0	69.2	29.0	1.7
1950	88.8	8.3	2.9	70.6	26.8	2.6
1960	91.2	5.5	3.3	71.8	24.3	4.0
1970	91.6	4.4	4.0	72.9	21.7	5.4
1980	90.5	3.8	5.7	72.4	19.8	7.8
1994	85.5	3.5	11.0	72.4	14.5	13.2

Source: U.S. Bureau of the Census, 1975a, 1995b.

been married. Because of gender differences in mortality, a much larger proportion of grandmothers than grandfathers were widowed at any particular date, and a smaller proportion were married. But widowhood among women aged 55–64 declined more rapidly than being divorced increased, so over time an increasing proportion were married. Assuming that being married increases the ability of persons to play an active grandparent role, conditions now are somewhat better than they were in the past. However, rapidly increasing divorce rates after 1970 suggest that this pattern will not continue.

CONCLUSIONS

A number of writers have commented either on the dearth of research attention to grandparenthood in the first half of the twentieth century or on the proliferation of research in recent decades (Aldous, 1995; Smith, 1991). It is not obvious, however, whether earlier inattention to this topic reflected the small role that grandparents played in the lives of children in the past, or whether researchers in the past were blind to the significant role they played. To resolve this question, it is necessary to have more knowledge about the history of grandparenthood. Did demographic conditions produce a situation where few grandparents were available to relate to children? Did family structure and social conditions exclude grandparents from playing active roles? Or, did misperceptions and prejudices of social researchers lead them to ignore an important family relationship?

A review of changing demographic behavior suggests several reasons why grandparenthood might become increasingly salient over the past century. With the aging of the population, the prevalence of grandparents in the total population has increased substantially. (The ratio of the population over age 50 to the population under age 15 nearly quadrupled between 1900 and 2000—increasing from .38 to 1.26). Children now, compared to the past, on average have more living grandparents and have fewer siblings and cousins who compete for the attention of these grandparents. Further, a larger proportion of children in the early 1900's had grandparents living abroad. As important as these demographic shifts have been, they should not be exaggerated. Throughout this century most children have had one or more living grandparents who resided in the United States, and most older persons have been grandparents.

Several other twentieth-century changes in American society have reduced obstacles that keep some older persons from developing significant relationships with their grandchildren. Grandparents with young grandchildren are increasingly likely to possess the critical resources of good health and economic security. Potential time available for interacting with grandchildren may have increased as the spread of retirement and early cessation of childbearing have reduced the amount of time that grandparents invest in work and child rearing. It should be noted, however, that increasing labor force participation by middle-aged women may mean that fewer grandmothers of young grandchildren are now available to help their daughters with child care. The declining educational gap between the grandparent and parent generations since 1960 may have contributed to less social distance between grandparents and their younger grandchildren. Finally, as more children experience parental divorce, public interest in both the supportive role that grandparents can play and the rights of grandparents to maintain contact with grandchildren has grown (see Chapter 16).

In addition to changing objective conditions, it is important also to consider how changing stereotypes and images of older persons might influence the role of grandparents (and popular perceptions of this role). After a careful review of the literature, Achenbaum concludes, "Virtually every history of aging and the elderly affirms that old age came to be perceived as a 'problem' in western civilization early in the twentieth century, if not before" (1996: 145).

Medical professionals, psychologists, educators, and social workers generally focused on the infirmities and limits of older persons, and the old were widely viewed as "obsolete" (Achenbaum, 1978; Haber, 1983). When old age was viewed as a disease and old people as obsolete, it is not surprising to find negative references to grandparents in the early twentieth century. Using anecdotal evidence, writers in this period warned that grandparents tended to interfere with parental control and to hold views that conflicted with those of parents (see

Chapter 1). Grandparents were seen as creating psychopathology in children and sometimes producing delinquency (Butler & Lewis, 1982; P. K. Smith, 1991). Butler and Lewis note that, "Early psychoanalytic interpretations of grandparenthood were rather grim and villainous" (1982: 156). Although the negative images of grandparents in the past may not have been valid, stereotypes do have consequences. For example, the accepted view of old age as a problem and the related negative view of grandparenthood no doubt contributed to the absence of scholarly work on the grandparent role of older persons before mid-century.

There is a tendency for contemporary research on grandparent-grandchild relationships to be ahistorical—to give little attention to how intergenerational relationships are conditioned by particular social structures. This review suggests that grandparenthood in the past was different in significant ways from what it is now. And one should expect grandparenthood in the future to differ from what it is today. Demographic change, social change, and ideological change all influence the nature of grandparent-grandchild relationships in a society. In each area, changes over the twentieth century have tended to increase opportunities for grandparent-grandchild relationships to flourish.

Chapter 3

Grandparenthood in Cross-Cultural Perspective

Charlotte Ikels

This chapter focuses on grandparenthood in societies other than the contemporary United States. As Fry (1995) points out, there are several important reasons for investigating social phenomena such as grandparenthood outside of our own society. First, from the point of view of theory construction, as social scientists, we need to base our theories on empirical data gathered from a diverse range of societies. We cannot simply assume that characteristics of developed societies or of the West represent cultural universals. Second, we need to have a realistic understanding of the range of human experience. Too often our view of family ties in other times or other places is hampered by a romantic image of a past Golden Age or contemporary Golden Isles inhabited by idyllic loving families (Nydegger, 1983). Encounters with the sometimes ugly ethnographic facts can help us gain perspective. Third, by comparing our experience and cultural models with those of others, we acquire greater insight into our own social institutions. Furthermore, grandparenthood cannot be viewed as an abstract status with a universal set of roles. Rather grandparenthood derives its meaning from the specific social and cultural characteristics of a particular locality. These characteristics include, but are not limited to, kinship organization, (e.g., bilateral versus unilineal descent systems, the presence or absence of adoption, fosterage, or fictive kin relationships), residence patterns, subsistence patterns, and values and attitudes.

EARLY RESEARCH

Cross-cultural researchers, comparativists whose goals include discovering patterns among variables across a wide range of societies and generating theories to explain these patterns, have been struck by the diversity that exists in the grandparent-grandchild relationship. Why is it, they have speculated, that in some societies the relationship is characterized by respect and deference, in others by warmth and affection, and in still others by ribald and insulting behavior on the part of both generations?

One of the earliest cross-cultural studies of grandparenthood is that of Radcliffe-Brown (1940), who had noted the easy familiarity that seems to occur so naturally between grandparents and grandchildren in contrast to the more strained relationship that occurs between parents and children. He attributed this difference to the fact that the responsibilities of child rearing require parents to be both nurturers and disciplinarians and thus introduces special tensions into their interaction with their children. He also pointed out that in some ways, particularly when compared with the parental generation, grandparents and grandchildren are both marginal to the society as a whole, the former gradually withdrawing while the latter are gradually entering. This alleged marginality led not only Radcliffe-Brown but also many comparativists interested in the relationships between age groups to assert that the members of alternate (as opposed to adjacent) generations have, therefore, a special affinity for one another, that is, that they are natural allies against the middle generation, which both view as excluding them from positions of power and prestige.

Looked at another way, grandchildren are the replacements of grandparents or, in societies that see souls cycling between the world of the living and the world of the dead, they are the grandparents returned, that is, grandchildren and grandparents are members of the same generation and should treat each other as equals—with familiarity rather than respect. This interpretation, Radcliffe-Brown argued, helps us to understand the significance of "joking relationships," privileged patterns of teasing—perhaps the ultimate form of familiarity—between particular categories of kin. Radcliffe-Brown argued that joking relationships are a means of erasing real inequalities in a relationship. With reference to stylized joking between grandparents and grandchildren, then, teasing, insults, and suggestive behavior would serve to erase their very real age differences and to assert that these two classes of kin are equal.

Drucker-Brown's (1982) work among the Mamprusi of northeastern Ghana demonstrates that the joking relationship between grandparents and grandchildren can be multifunctional in nature, that is, not only serving as a leveler but also reducing intergenerational tensions. Among the Mamprusi children are required to treat their parents with respect and deference. In seeking goods from parents, they are expected to kneel or crouch, avert their eyes, and speak softly. In seeking goods from grandparents, however, they may make demands in a very discourteous fashion. Similarly, children should not discuss sexual matters with parents (who play an important role in arranging their marriages) but may joke with a grandparent about eloping. Following Radcliffe-Brown, Drucker-Brown observes, that the etiquette of joking releases tensions which may be accumulated between persons with divergent or contradictory interests. A tendency to "open conflict" is thus replaced by "sham conflict" [between grandparents and grandchildren] or avoidance [between parents and children] . . . The joking of grandparent and grandchild does not replace a tendency towards open conflict between them with a sham conflict. Rather it allows the expression of strong emotions suppressed in the avoidance etiquette of the parent-child bond. (1982: 721)

Nadel (1951) took issue with the universality of Radcliffe-Brown's interpretations and argued that since joking relationships are not always present, there has to be another variable that intervenes between generational status and familiarity. Based on his own study of ten Nuba (African) "tribes," he determined that the critical variable in grandfather-grandson interaction is the degree of familial authority possessed by the grandfather: the greater the authority the less the familiarity. Drawing on Nadel's argument and findings but using the Human Relations Area Files (HRAF)[1], Apple set out to test two hypotheses:

Hypothesis I: when the grandparental generation continues to exercise considerable authority over the parental generation after the grandchildren are born, the relation of the grandchildren to the grandparents will not be one of friendly equality. . . .

Hypothesis II: if the grandchildren's relation with one set of grandparents has less friendly equality than with the other, the former grandparents will be those related to the grandchildren through the parent who possesses. . . . more household authority in the nuclear family. (1956: 657)

Apple chose to test two hypotheses because it was well known that while in some societies, such as the United States, there tend to be few patterned differences in the relationships grandchildren have with their paternal and maternal grandparents, in other societies, especially those featuring unilineal descent, there are considerable differences in how grandchildren relate to the two sets of grandparents (see below). Both of Apple's hypotheses were overwhelmingly supported, and her work highlighted the importance of examining the larger kinship context in which grandparenthood is embedded.

Although suggestive of the factors influencing grandparent-grandchild relationships, the studies of Radcliffe-Brown, Nadel, and Apple are based on norms, that is, prescriptive behavior, and not on the observation of actual behavior. Moreover the norms under investigation operate at the highest level of abstraction and fail to differentiate among the behaviors appropriate to the various dyads, for example, grandfather-grandson, grandmother-granddaughter, that constitute the broader category of grandparents-grandchildren. The limitations of these early studies led researchers to conclude that a deeper understanding of the context of grandparenthood was essential before they could safely undertake theory building. They further knew that the most important societal contexts they needed to understand were the kinship system and the overall status of the aged: the kinship system because, after all, grandparenthood is fundamentally a kinship status, and the overall status of the aged because grandparents are, in most societies, members of the oldest segment of the population.

KINSHIP

Although grandparenthood is first and foremost a kinship relationship, this simple biological fact masks considerable diversity in how grandparenthood is experienced and played out in any particular society. Three variables are especially important: (1) the nature of the descent system, (2) the flexibility of the concept of kinship, and (3) household organization and residence patterns.

Descent Systems

Descent systems are mechanisms through which a newborn is assigned membership in a kin group. Anthropologists generally distinguish between two major forms of descent, bilateral descent and unilineal descent. (There are, of course many other distinctions, but I do not wish to burden the reader!) In bilateral descent systems, an individual traces descent through both the paternal and the maternal line, that is, regards consanguineal relatives traced through the father as equivalent for all practical purposes to consanguineal relatives traced through the mother. Most Americans whose origins lie in Europe, for example, trace their descent in this manner, and the principle of kin equivalence is reflected in our kinship terminology. We refer to a male sibling of our parents as "uncle" and nothing more, that is, we do not automatically make clear to the listener that we are referring to our father's brother or our mother's brother. Similarly grandparents are grandparents and nothing more regardless of whether we are talking about our father's parents or our mother's. While it is certainly true that middle-class Euro-American grandchildren in the United States often have different relationships with their two sets of grandparents (and with their parents' sibling sets), these differences are usually the result of situational factors, such as proximity, age, parental marital status, and the like, rather than of norms prescribing different relationships (Johnson, 1983a).

Unilineal descent systems are quite different. As the initial term suggests, one line, the paternal in patrilineal descent and the maternal in matrilineal descent, is emphasized substantially more than the other. In this type of system an individual is affiliated to one set of kin without fully relinquishing his or her ties to the other. Allegiance (in disputes and conflicts), rights and privileges (access to land or to inheritances), and obligations (providing assistance to elderly relatives), however, are obtained from or owed primarily, and sometimes exclusively, to the unilineal descent group. Kinship terminology usually reflects at least some elements of these distinctions. Traditional Chinese society, for example, is typical of those practicing patrilineal descent, and the Chinese language reflects this. There are four distinct terms for grandparents (FaFa, FaMo, MoFa, and MoMo) and a minimum of five distinct terms for parental siblings

(FaOlBro, FaYoBro, FaSi, MoBro, and MoSi)—because birth order is important in the patrilineage, it also is marked in the terms used to designate paternal male relatives. Grandchildren are divided into two basic categories that are further differentiated by sex. The two categories are "grandchildren" (the children of one's son) and "outside grandchildren" (the children of one's daughter)—outside because they belong to their own father's patrilineage and not their maternal grandparent's patrilineage (Feng, 1967).

For our purposes, one of the most important aspects of unilineal descent systems is that one set of grandparents is privileged over the other. Chinese paternal grandparents, for example, customarily are owed support by their sons and their sons' sons but not by their sons' daughters nor by their daughters and their daughters' children. By contrast among the Navajo who practice matrilineal descent, when parents are unable to provide for their children, every effort is made by tribal authorities to place the children with their maternal grandmother or other matrikin before placing them with their paternal grandmother (Shomaker, 1989).

Kinship Flexibility

Becoming a grandparent normally is the result of being a parent, but in all societies there is usually a minority of individuals who for one reason or another are childless and would, thereby, seem to be precluded from grandparenthood. In societies lacking a flexible concept of kinship, that is, providing no alternatives to a direct biological linkage for the creation of parental or grandparental ties, such individuals are severely disadvantaged in old age. Most societies, however, allow adoption, fosterage, or fictive kinship ties to compensate for reproductive shortcomings. In some societies even purchase of a child has been possible. Sangree (1992) contrasts the fates of the biologically childless in two patrilineal societies, the Tiriki of Kenya and the Irigwe of Nigeria. The Tiriki are unusual among East African populations in not facilitating adoption. Sangree points out that "people feared punishment from the vengefully jealous spirits or ghosts of the children's true begetters or bearers" (p. 339). In addition, all adult male Tiriki learned a form of sorcery that would make other people sterile; this sorcery had the inhibiting side effect of rendering its user sterile. A sterile older male, however, would not only not be inhibited by this side effect but might also be especially jealous of people who had numerous progeny and use the sorcery against them. Similar beliefs were held about childless old women who were not infrequently accused of being witches and bringing death to other people's children. Life was made so unpleasant for the childless elderly that they were either "driven from the community or died one way or another before they reached an advanced age" (Sangree, 1992: 340).

The situation among the Irigwe was totally different. Sangree estimates that some 20% of Irigwe women never had any live-born children, but they told him this fact quite openly and did not seem unduly distressed by it. The reason was that sterility could easily be overcome by both adoption and fosterage. In fact, "begging" children from a clan brother or sister with numerous progeny was done not only by the childless but also by middle-aged parents whose biological children had all grown up. Not to yield to the pleas of the childless or the lonely was to risk being stigmatized as stingy.

The reasons older people around the world are motivated to acquire a young child through adoption or fosterage are diverse. Among the Herero, a pastoral population living in Botswana, fosterage is viewed primarily as a means of providing an elder with a young helper (Keith et al, 1994). A similar pattern is described by Shomaker (1989) for early twentieth-century Navajo. Citing earlier studies, she describes how

grandchildren served as eyes, ears, hands, and feet for their frail grandparents. The grandchildren were usually about eight years of age; their duties were, among other things, to haul water, chop wood, work in the fields, and herd sheep, from which they became known as "little sheepherders" ... giving a grandchild to its grandparents was understood as a demonstration of respect to the grandparents, as well as a means of minimizing friction with elders and thus, in some instances, reducing the possibilities of the elders exercising witchcraft. (Shomaker, 1989: 2–3)

At the time of her own fieldwork in the early 1980's, however, Shomaker found that the main reason (86% of 107 cases) for the transfer of a child to a grandmother was difficulties or deaths in the child's natal family that made effective parenting impossible. Weibel-Orlando (1988) cites the same reason for informal adoption of orphans or children from impoverished or disrupted homes among the Sioux. Contemporary Navajo grandmothers have not become entirely altruistic in providing care to grandchildren; they make deliberate efforts to inculcate the value of reciprocity in their biological and fostered grandchildren. Though, as Shomaker (1990) reports, by the time the elders actually need care, the grown-up youngsters are often no longer coresident. In their stead the grandchildrens' own biological mother may provide the care.

Unlike unilineal descent systems in which formal norms buttress personal feelings of obligation to particular kin, bilateral systems require more active efforts by individuals to create a sense of obligation among their kin. This phenomenon is clearly visible among Polynesian societies which are largely bilateral and in which fosterage is highly regarded and seen as beneficial to all concerned. For example, in his study of Sikaiana, a Solomon Islands community, Donner (1987) found that 48% of the children on the atoll were residing in the households of foster parents. In this bilateral society fosterage can be understood as a mechanism for reinforcing extended kinship ties. "By fostering a child, the foster parent demonstrates his/her commitment to the child's biological parents, and the foster parent establishes an important relationship with the child" (Donner, 1987: 47–48). The Mende, a nominally patrilineal people living in Sierra Leone, also practice high rates of fosterage. Among a sample of 154 households in a market town in Mende country, Bledsoe and Isiugo-Abanihe (1989) report that 39% of the children under 18 were foster children. Concurrently the same 154 households had fostered out 34% of their biological children. The Mende foster children to others for a variety of reasons most of which reflect a desire to improve their or their children's life chances. Children are often sent to distant or highly placed kin or to prestigious patrons to enhance parental social networks. Children are also sent away from home to obtain an education or to learn a trade or domestic skills in a more modern setting. Nonparental caretakers are viewed as more capable of disciplining rather than indulging the children. Once someone has fostered a child, he or she has the right forevermore to lay claims to the child's support. Mende grannies, who may or may not be biologically related to their foster (grand)children, frequently use the fact of fosterage to secure support in the here and now from their charges' parents by stating their own needs for foodstuffs or cash as those of the children.

As social institutions, adoption and fosterage do not appear to be obviously linked to any particular form of kinship system. As the above cases illustrate, they are found among societies with patrilineal (the Irigwe), matrilineal (the Navajo), and bilateral (Polynesia) descent. On the other hand, they are absent among patrilineal groups such as the Tiriki, and until fairly recently their practice was regarded as a family secret among bilateral middle-class Euro-Americans. Descent systems do play a role in defining the range of kin within which it is appropriate to enact adoption or fosterage. Specifically children should normally be fostered within the unilineal descent group, but much more broadly in societies with bilateral descent. In either case adoption and fosterage present additional opportunities for the practice of grandparenthood.

Household Organization and Residence Patterns

The enactment of the grandparent role is greatly influenced by the ease of access to grandchildren. Obviously if grandparents and grandchildren share a common residence, access is maximized. While there is no one-to-one correspondence between household organization and residence patterns on the one hand and descent systems on the other, some generalizations are nevertheless possible. In societies characterized by bilateral kinship, young people are likely to practice some form of neolocal residence, that is, at marriage a couple sets up a household that is physically and economically independent of their parental households. Individual preferences or calculations of advantage rather than prescriptive norms determine whether they live near the husband's kin, the wife's kin, or far away from both. Under these circumstances the grandparent's access to the grandchildren is very much mediated by the parents. If parents and grandparents are on bad terms or live great distances apart, it is more difficult to actualize the grandparent role (King & Elder, 1995a; Kivett, 1991b). In societies practicing unilineal descent, there are often more explicit norms regarding household organization and residential placement. At a minimum even if a couple establishes an independent household, they are most likely to continue to reside in the immediate vicinity of the husband's kin in the patrilineal case and, though to a lesser degree, the wife's kin in the matrilineal one.

But many unilineal societies have much more stringent rules regarding residence. They may require the adult children of the appropriate sex to continue to reside in the parental homestead following their marriage and to remain members of a single economic unit, cultivating their fields or running their business collectively so long as the senior male (usually) survived. In both traditional China (Freedman 1966; Harrell, 1982) and traditional Hindu India (Madan, 1989), patrilineal kinship norms dictated that the sons of a man remain subordinate in his household until his death at which time they divided the property more or less equally among themselves. Ethnographic evidence suggests, however, that, at least in the case of China, division frequently occurred before the senior male's death (see Cohen, 1976).

Such living arrangements clearly disadvantage the access of maternal grandparents, but they are further disadvantaged by the fact that both rural Chinese and rural Indians continue to practice village exogamy, that is, daughters leave their natal villages at marriage to join their husband's family. In the case of Rampur, a village of 1,095 inhabitants, located about 15 miles west of Delhi, Lewis found that

A bridegroom must never be chosen from the same village in which the prospective bride lives. This rule is extended further to include any village whose lands touch the lands of the bride's village, or the lands of the four-village unit of which Rampur is a part. Moreover, any village in which one's own clan is well represented must also be avoided. One should even shun villages in which the other clans of one's own village are well represented. In effect this means that villagers of Rampur cannot marry into any of twenty nearby villages. (Lewis, 1958: 160–161)

As a consequence of these rules, the married women living in Rampur at the time of the research had their origins in about 200 different villages with the average distances falling between 12 and 24 miles. Madan (1989) encountered a less extreme case of exogamy in the larger Kashmiri village of Utrassu-Umanagri where 28% of marriages were endogamous while most exogamous marriages were contracted with villages within a 15-mile radius. When one considers that these distances were usually traversed on foot, one can appreciate the nature of the constraints facing maternal grandparents.

Village exogamy in China remains the norm, but it has been declining since the introduction of rural economic reform in the late 1970s (Chan, Madsen, & Unger, 1992; Yan, 1996). With increasing disparities in wealth among neighboring villages, young women from more affluent villages tend to resist marriage into poorer ones. In either case, regardless of distance, marriage does not terminate a woman's ties to her natal family. She is entitled, that is, her in-laws dare not interfere with her right, to visit her own parents on particular occasions, for example, holidays, weddings, parental illness, and funerals. Unless her parents live very close by, a married woman should not indulge in casual visiting as it would indicate that she is not keeping herself busy at her in-laws' residence. Under these circumstances, it is not easy for maternal grandparents to interact frequently with their grandchildren and to have the intimate relationship characteristic of most coresident grandparents. In China's cities there is no concept analogous to village exogamy, and nuclear families predominate. In the case of the elderly, however, the modal type of living arrangement remains with the patrilineal stem family, and newly married couples are far more likely to move in with the husband's family rather than with the wife's (Davis, 1993; Ikels, 1996).

The benefits to grandparents of living in a community in which one's neighbors are also one's relatives are substantial. For one thing, it is more difficult for adult children to violate kinship norms when the number of potentially concerned parties, who might intervene on the grandparents' behalf, is large. More importantly, the proximity of many of one's grandchildren (as well as grandnieces and grandnephews) can mean that there is almost always someone available to provide companionship, run errands, help out with chores, or otherwise assist an older person whose energy level is declining. The inauguration of primary and especially of secondary education in many rural parts of the world has set limits on the amount of time youngsters are available but has not freed them completely from providing services and companionship to proximate grandparents. Similarly, it is much easier for grandchildren to seek the comfort and support of local grandparents than of distant grandparents.

THE STATUS OF THE AGED

While the transition to grandparenthood most often occurs in middle age, occupancy of the status is usually associated with old age. Given this association researchers have speculated about the nature of the relationship between the status of the aged and the meaning or performance of grandparental roles. Much of this speculation has occurred in the context of the debate about the impact of modernization on the status of the aged. In its most simplistic form, modernization theory holds that in contrast to the elderly in modern industrialized societies, who are allegedly marginalized, impoverished, denied any meaningful roles in the family and wider society, neglected by their children, and generally devalued, the elderly in the past were allegedly fully integrated into society, controlling wealth, occupying important roles in both the public and the familial domains, receiving both love and respect, and valued for their wisdom and experience (Cowgill & Holmes, 1972). To test this theory, a host of cross-cultural studies, some exploratory, such as Simmons's 1945 pioneering work, and some hypothesis testing, such as the works of Cowgill and Holmes (1972), Glascock and Feinman (1981), Maxwell and Silverman (1970), Palmore and Manton (1974), Press and McKool (1972), and Silverman and Maxwell (1983) was undertaken. Two kinds of variables have emerged from these studies as especially influential with regard to the status of the elderly; broadly speaking, these are economic (or utilitarian) and ideological variables.

In the cross-cultural literature, economic variables are usually discussed under the rubric of "resource control." According to the basic argument, when the elderly control scarce resources to which others need access (and especially when the young have no alternative means of acquiring these resources), their status will be high. Resources refer to anything that has subsistence value or contributes directly to well-being, for example, herds, land, social contacts, esoteric knowledge, and healing powers. When something happens that leads to the devaluation of these resources or undercuts their monopolization, the elderly will suffer a loss of status (see Chapter 7). Thus, when land parcels become too small to support a family, when employment in factories becomes an alternative to farming, when the spread of literacy allows people of any age to acquire esoteric knowledge, or when modern pharmaceuticals displace local medicinal herbs, the position of the elderly will decline.

Not everyone has accepted the inevitability of this scenario. Palmore (1975), Palmore and Maeda (1985), and Olson (1990) have all argued that ideological variables can intervene between the processes associated with modernization and the status of the elderly. Palmore maintains that Japan's emphases on filial piety within the family and on seniority in both the public and private domains insulate the elderly from the forces that elsewhere might undermine their status. Others, for example, Plath (1983), are less sanguine about the circumstances of the elderly in Japan. In the case of China, Olson points out that we have completely overlooked the role of the state in mediating the impact of social change on the elderly. In the 1950's, the new Communist government instituted a generous pension scheme for urban workers and provided them with health care and housing as well. The more China industrialized, the more urban workers gained coverage. Far from being economic burdens, the cohort of workers retiring in the 1980's were regarded as assets—being available for baby-sitting and household chores and continuing to contribute financially to the household at the same time.

Møller and Sotshongaye (1996) offer another example of the role of the modern state in advantaging older people by providing them with special financial resources. They point out that in South Africa the noncontributory state old-age pension is one of the main sources of income for poor Zulu households and that

Many of the women in the study identified themselves as the sole breadwinner in the family. In a number of such cases the households which depended exclusively on pension income were above average in size. The finding that many older women supported large numbers of unemployed children and their illegitimate offspring is supportive of the idea that pensions act as a magnet for economically-weaker family members who form multigenerational households around female pensioners. (Møller & Sotshangaye, 1996: 17)

Indeed many of these Zulu grandmothers feared that their families would be destitute if they died and their pensions were no longer paid out.

As the Zulu case reveals, not all young people are able to participate successfully in the cash economy. In these situations older people can become important resources in themselves—less because of pensions (in most developing societies the elderly who have not engaged in waged work are not eligible for pensions) but because of their familiarity with the old way of life, for example, they are able to fall back on traditional subsistence patterns to support themselves and their dependents. Bahr (1994) notes the important role played by Apache grandmothers in the lives of their unemployed children as well as their grandchildren. She estimates that about 20% of Apache grandchildren live with grandmothers, partly because of the traditional view of the grandmother as an essential part of normal family life but perhaps even more because the employment of younger women, single parenthood, and alcoholism preclude a stable life in their natal family. Far from lamenting their re-occupied nests, these Apache grandmothers worried most about not being able to do enough for their descendants. They manage to scrape by on a combination of resources, for example, food stamps, the informal economy, and traditional skills. This last category includes making traditional handicrafts, such as dolls, cradle boards, and garments, and various forms of "gathering," such as harvesting worms for fishermen, gathering cattails from which pollen is shaken, and, in a modern adaptation, collecting discarded aluminum cans. In addition to helping out with the above activities, their grandchildren also contribute to the household economy by fishing. Bahr concludes that

> Despite multiple disadvantages, these Apache grandmothers were among the most influential and active participants in community life. Occupying the respected role of grandmother, enacting a tribal role definition that includes wisdom, energy, and resourcefulness, they stand out as the effective "managers" of much of the local economy and models of independence, courage, and strength in contexts where dependence, frustration, and resignation might be seen as more realistic adjustments. . . . Looking at their lives and challenges, one may conclude that Apache grandmothering is very hard on the grandmother. On the other hand, it plainly is very good for the Apache community as a whole, and for the Apache posterity. (Bahr, 1994: 247)

Researchers have also investigated the contemporary significance for grandparenthood of another resource that has frequently been linked with high status for the aged—possession of valued knowledge (Cattell, 1989, 1994; Weibel-Orlando, 1990). In a discussion of the role of elders among Native Americans, Weibel-Orlando argues that the role of grandparents as cultural conservators is not limited to Native Americans but characteristic of ethnic minority groups fearing loss of identity through the relentless pressures of assimilation. The importance of this role was particularly visible in the 1970s and 1980s when there was a sudden efflorescence of interest in minority and ethnic studies and in one's personal ethnic heritage among many groups in the United States (see Chapter 7). Whether the motives were to instill self-esteem, a quest to discover the past, or the development of a profitable tourist industry, elders who lived in communities where this movement was strong found themselves sought after for their knowledge of traditional ritual and lore. Amoss (1981) noted the importance of elderly Coast Salish Indians in perpetuating an Indian identity, while Cool (1980), conducting research in a Corsican community in Paris, found the younger generation, which had no direct experience of Corsica, actively seeking knowledge about the traditional way of life from the older emigrants.

In the absence of a conservative ethic, however, grandparents may encounter less enthusiasm among their young charges for learning about traditional folkways and proper comportment. Cattell (1994) notes that Samia women in Kenya admit to being confused about how best to carry out their traditional role as guides to the young.

Advising—in the sense of imparting knowledge and providing moral and social guidance—has been a preeminent duty of older Samia. But now "it isn't easy to advise," because young people want the knowledge of schools and books, which grandmothers lack. . . . Often older women do not know what younger women want to know. For instance, preventing pregnancy is a topic of great interest to most young people. When grandmothers were young, a bride was expected to be a virgin (with a wedding night test of virginity) and a lengthy postpartum sex taboo was the norm. (Cattell, 1994: 169–170)

Even though sexual behavior is a proper topic for grandmothers and granddaughters to discuss, it is a rare Samia grandmother who is familiar with modern modes of contraception.

As the above examples illustrate, there is no simple one-to-one correspondence between modernization (or economic development) and the status of the aged. Both concepts are too broad and multifactorial to be easily subject to analysis. To understand how subsistence patterns and resource control (to consider just two factors) affect community perceptions of the elderly and how these, in turn, shape the experience of grandparenthood requires long-term, onsite investigation. Social scientists cannot construct their theories solely on the basis of normative attitudes and behaviors.

CONCLUSIONS

The nature of grandparenthood—how one attains the status, enacts the role, and the meaning one ascribes to it—cannot be grasped in the abstract. Grandparenthood is first and foremost a kinship status and as such cannot be examined without regard to the norms and structure of the kinship system of which it is a part. Similarly grandparenthood is a relationship between the (relatively) old and the (relatively) young, and as such cannot be understood without regard to how older people are perceived and treated by the community as a whole. For these reasons comparative research is critical to our understanding of grandparenthood not only in exotic sites but in our very own backyard.

The studies presented in this chapter have for the most part represented steps in the right direction. They demonstrate a steady movement away from testing hypotheses with secondary data based on generalized norms towards an examination of the actual expression of behavior and attitudes in particular contexts, but as researchers we still have a long way to go. I will take up just two of the limitations of the cross-cultural research conducted so far. The first is that with very few exceptions, for example, Nahemow (1983), Van Ranst, Verschueren, and Marcoen (1995), grandparenthood tends to be treated as either a genderless phenomenon or an essentially female one. Grandfathers are conspicuous by their absence. Indeed, they often *are* absent. In a recent national survey carried out in the United States by Hodgson (1995), adult respondents reported exactly half as many surviving grandfathers as grandmothers. Maternal grandmothers, the most frequently surviving grandparent, outnumbered paternal grandfathers, the least frequently surviving grandparent, by a factor of 2.5. In societies that have lower life expectancies than does the United States, grandparents in general and grandfathers in particular are probably even less common. Madan (1989) reports that in the North Indian village which he studied, there were only three grandmothers with adult grandchildren and no grandfathers. Nevertheless, the relative scarcity of grandfathers cannot serve as an excuse for acting as if they do not exist and excluding them from studies—not, at least, if we are interested in theory construction.

The second limitation of much of the cross-cultural research is that it approaches grandparenthood from too narrow a perspective, for example, grandparents as care providers (or recipients), as transmitters of knowledge, as sources of intimacy, and does not adequately attend to the modifying effects of such critical variables as the sex of the grandparent (or the grandchild), age, health status, personality, lineage (maternal or paternal), and so on. We need more differentiated studies, and we especially need longitudinal ones that track change over time. We further need to distinguish the extent to which changes in the nature of the grandparent-grandchild relationship reflect the influence of life-course stages from how they reflect particular cohort characteristics. We have not yet exhausted this topic.

NOTE

1. The HRAF is a systematized corpus of knowledge about a large number of societies (or "cultures" in HRAF terminology) as well as of many of the ethnic groups found within them. The database includes information on historical, traditional, and (relatively) contemporary societies organized under 79 major headings and 637 subheadings.

Chapter 4

Grandparenting in Family Systems: An Ecological Perspective

Valarie King, Stephen T. Russell, and Glen H. Elder, Jr.

Ecological theory focuses on the interaction and interdependence of individuals and the environment. The environment provides the context for individual behavior and is broadly defined to include the physical, social, cultural, biological, economic, political, aesthetic, and structural surroundings in which individuals live. It also includes the broader contemporary and historical context in which these surroundings are embedded (Bubolz & Sontag, 1993; Moen, 1995). The most notable premise of ecological theory is that individuals are placed in context with behavior examined as a joint function of the characteristics of the person and the environment.

Ecological approaches have emerged across the social sciences, as well as in the arts and humanities (Bubolz & Sontag, 1993). Urie Bronfenbrenner's (1986) ecology of human development is a prominent example. His model attends to the interplay between characteristics of the individual and the social context (e.g., families, schools, neighborhoods) in affecting developmental processes (Moen, 1995). Research on grandparenting would also benefit from an ecological approach and its attention to the ways in which intrafamilial processes are influenced by extrafamilial conditions and environments.

An ecology of grandparenting focuses attention on the contexts within which grandparenting takes place. In this sense, it has much in common with the core principles of life-course theory (Elder, 1995), such as linked lives, life timing as context, and sensitivity to historical time and place. The contexts in which families live and interact are many and varied, including historical and societal (see Chapters 1 and 2), racial or ethnic (see Chapters 5, 6, and 7), and differentiated by social class or family structure (see Chapter 3). In this chapter we focus on the influence of one context that has received little attention: rural-urban environments.

Why would we expect to find differences in the experience of being or having a grandparent by the urban or rural environment in which people live? Coward and Smith (1981: 2) assert that the "rural environment is sufficiently different from the urban environment . . . to impose significant effects on certain aspects of family life." An ecological account of rural-urban differences views these differences as arising out of people's cultural adaptation to environmental circumstances. As long as the environmental milieu of the city is different from that of rural areas, differences in social life will persist (Ford, 1978).

The grandparent-grandchild relationship is one facet of social life that may be affected, although little research has been done in this area. Much of the published research on grandparenting is based on samples of college students or alternatively on small samples in one geographic region. Because so little is known about the influence of rural-urban contexts on grandparenting, we speculate about possible influences that might arise given what we know about rural and urban places and based on prior research that has examined and demonstrated the importance of the rural-urban comparison for understanding family life and family relationships.

It is important to consider the conceptualization and operationalization of rural-urban boundaries in current research. As McCulloch (1995: 344) notes, no consensus exists regarding the definition of a rural area. One common definition is that employed by the Bureau of the Census which designates rural areas as having fewer than 2,500 residents. Urbanized areas are defined as those having a minimum of 50,000 inhabitants. Alternatively, Standard Metropolitan Statistical Area (SMSA) definitions have been used to distinguish between metropolitan and nonmetropolitan areas (McCulloch, 1995; Van Nostrand, 1993). Such gross distinctions, however, run the risk of obscuring much of the variation that exists between and within environmental ecologies.

Size-of-place definitions conceptualize rural-urban distinctions on a continuum with farm/open country at one end to large urban centers at the other, although the degree of distinction varies from study to study. Furthermore, although farm life is often at one end of the continuum, even here families can fall into various ecological niches. Distinctions can be made between full-time farming and part-time farming, although exactly where to draw the line between them is not so clear. Families involved in farming differ in the amount of land they farm and own, the amount of income they derive from farming and from off-farm employment, and the amount of time spent running the farm relative to time spent in off-farm work. Even finer distinctions can be made, for example, between persistent part-time farmers, part-time sporadic farmers, and hobby farmers (Fuller, 1984). Displaced farm families and families with farm backgrounds (grandparent generation farmed) are further distinctions that are often relevant for understanding family dynamics (Elder & Conger, forthcoming). All of these definitions have their limitations and can affect research findings.

Figure 4.1
Ecologies of Grandparenting

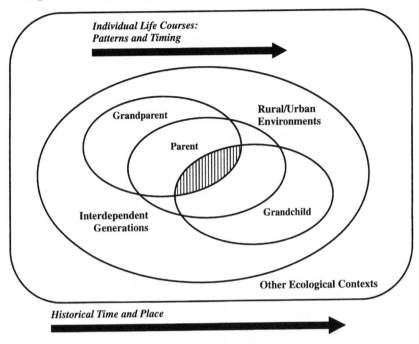

FAMILY SYSTEMS AND ECOLOGIES: SOME ANALYTICAL DISTINCTIONS

Before turning to a more general discussion of urban and rural influences, we will consider other pertinent aspects of family ecology that are central to grandparenting and give meaning to social contexts. Figure 4.1 serves as an illustration for the discussion that follows. As the figure indicates, each of the family ecological factors discussed below may interact with the urban and rural environment, as well as with other ecological forces that shape the lives of individuals and their communities.

We first consider the interdependence of generations within a family, as indicated by the interlocking ovals that represent each member of a three-generational family structure; a shaded area represents the linked lives of grandparents and grandchildren. Second, we explore the importance of life-course patterns and timing for understanding the role played by grandparents. Each member of the family system experiences his or her own unique pattern and timing of life-course events; the timing and patterning of the individual life course has consequences as individuals make the transition to grandparenthood. Third, we examine the relevance of historical time and place for the ways in which individuals take on and develop roles, particularly the grandparent role.

The life courses of individual family members are played out within the broader picture of historical change in local urban or rural environments. We consider each of these aspects of family ecology in detail.

Interdependence across Three Generations

Grandparenthood is embedded in a social system of interlocking generations (Hagestad, 1985; Kivnick, 1984). Thus to understand the grandparent-grandchild relationship, we must investigate its contingency on other important relationships, particularly grandparent-parent and parent-child.

The parent generation shapes relations between grandparents and grandchildren by either facilitating or hindering interactions between them. Parents who do not get along with their own parents are unlikely to foster close ties between their parents and their children (see King & Elder, 1995a). The grandparent-parent bond has been found to have significant positive effects on contact and closeness between grandparents and grandchildren (Cherlin & Furstenberg, 1986a; Hodgson, 1992; Johnson, 1985; King & Elder, 1995a; Matthews & Sprey, 1985; Rossi & Rossi, 1990; Thompson & Walker, 1987; Whitbeck, Hoyt, & Huck, 1993). King and Elder (1995b) also report the strong influence of parent-grandparent relationship quality on the type of roles grandparents play, such as instrumental assistance, mentoring, companionship, and joint activities with grandchildren. Relationships between grandparents and grandchildren are also enhanced when the grandchild has strong bonds to his or her parents (King & Elder, 1995a; Rossi & Rossi, 1990).

In what ways is the distinction between urban and rural family life relevant to the interdependence of the three generations? It is possible that the influence of parents on grandparent-grandchild interactions might be qualitatively different in urban versus rural settings. The instrumental assistance, mentoring, and companionship that grandparents provide for children, as well as the activities in which they participate with children, will likely vary in urban and rural contexts. For example, parents in a rural setting who farm may share economic production with their own parents; in these families, grandparents can play important everyday roles in the lives of their grandchildren (Elder & King, forthcoming; King & Elder 1995a, 1995b). Close proximity and a shared economy between the parent generation and their own parents tend to instill strong ties to grandparents. This type of family life may be less common in urban centers. However, multigenerational ethnic families in urban areas often share a common economic base, as in the case of a family business, and thereby experience the blending of family and occupation in much the same way that rural farming families do.

There are multiple grandparents and grandchildren in any family system. However most studies of grandparenthood focus on the relationship of grandparents with one grandchild, or alternatively, on the relationship of grandchildren with one grandparent. This approach ignores how the presence of other grandparents and grandchildren within a family influences particular dyadic relationships. For grandchildren, relations with grandparents can be affected by the characteristics of other grandparents in the same family. Chan and Elder (1996) report that within a family, grandchildren are drawn toward those grandparents who are physically accessible, close to the middle generation, part of family exchange networks, and who share similar interests. For grandchildren who have grandparents living in rural and urban areas, interaction and proximity are likely to be greatest where grandparents and grandchildren share ecological contexts.

A grandparent's relationship with a grandchild is also likely to be affected not only by the characteristics of that grandchild but also by the characteristics of other grandchildren in the family. King and Elder (1995b) found that an elderly person's involvement with a grandchild is significantly constrained by the sheer number of grandchildren who are close at hand. The more grandchildren a grandparent has, the less he or she will be able to interact individually with each grandchild. This constraint may be experienced more by rural grandparents who have had higher fertility rates than their urban peers.

The involvement of grandparents within families can also be viewed as a form of social capital as described by James Coleman (1988). Coleman distinguishes between social capital in the family, based on relations between parents and children (as in the amount of time they spend together), and social capital outside the household, based on family member's relations with institutions in the community, such as the church. In theory, investments in social capital, whether outside or inside the household, play a role in successful adolescent development. They do so by empowering parents, developing effective social norms, providing lines of communication, and promoting expertise.

Children's relationships with grandparents are another form of social capital which may benefit them directly or indirectly through their parents. Grandparents may also serve a "redundant" function in families characterized by close intergenerational relations; they reinforce an already strong family situation (Tinsley & Parke, 1984). Children who have greater access to these forms of social capital are more likely to succeed socially and psychologically, and in making the transition to adult roles (Elder & Conger, forthcoming; Furstenberg & Hughes, 1995; Schneider & Coleman, 1993).

Rural and urban grandparents may differ in the types of social capital they can provide for grandchildren. The closer proximity of rural grandparents to their adult children and grandchildren may create more capital in the form of day-to-day involvement and exchanges. The greater incomes of the urban elderly may enable them to serve as a more influential financial resource. The interdependent lives so characteristic of the family world of farm children ensures a notable measure of social capital, as do the multiple connections between farm households and community institutions (Elder & Conger, forthcoming; Salamon, 1992).

Rural communities can more easily serve as "functional communities" where members know each other and accept a common set of values (Coleman &

Hoffer, 1987). Residential proximity and common fields of involvement, as in church and community, bring members of the generations together, facilitating interactions between grandparents and their grandchildren (Elder, forthcoming).

In helping grandchildren negotiate their futures, grandparents may be most effective in providing resources for grandchildren who share their preference for rural or urban living. For example, ties within farming communities on the part of grandparents can benefit grandchildren who imagine their future in rural areas. Likewise, urban grandparents can draw upon their connections to urban institutions in guiding their grandchildren.

Life-Course Patterns and Timing

Life-course issues are also central to understanding the ecology of grandparenting. Where people are in their lives, where they are going, and where they have been will influence their experiences as a grandchild, parent, and grandparent. Important here is the intersection of individuals' life-course timing and their ecological experiences.

Attention needs to be paid to the age of both grandparents and grandchildren and how this relationship changes over time. The relationship between a 55-year-old grandmother and her 2-year-old granddaughter will differ from that between a 75-year-old grandmother and her 22-year-old granddaughter, and both of these relationships have and will continue to change over time. For example, activities such as mentoring and providing tangible aid are likely to be more common with older grandchildren. Early involvement by a grandparent in a grandchild's life can foster a continuing bond (King & Elder, 1995b). Unfortunately, most studies of the grandparent-grandchild relationship are cross-sectional and limited to grandparents and grandchildren in a narrow age range. Developmental processes in these relationships can only be inferred (King & Elder, 1995a).

How will these developmental processes vary according to the family's ecological context? Among farm families, for example, ties across the family generations are important for the economic operation of the farm. Early involvement by grandparents in the everyday lives of farm children will shape that relationship as children grow up, and will also shape the child's understanding of what it means for her or him to be a grandparent decades later. It may also lead to greater reciprocity in later years by rural grandchildren who remain in close proximity, especially since rural elders have fewer social services outside of the family available to them.

Another important issue involves the compression or extension of lineages. Compressed lineages result when generational succession occurs relatively rapidly through the early timing of first births. Lineages are extended when births are delayed and individuals pass more slowly through generational roles, increasing the time spread between the generations. The timing of family lineages has consequences for the ages at which individuals experience grandparenthood, as well as for the overlap of the grandparent and parent role. Generational boundaries may become blurred as parents and children become more similar in age (Nock, 1988). In the case of compressed lineages, it may be the grandparent, not the parent, who provides the family with a hierarchical authority structure.

A related distinction is whether individuals experience grandparenthood ''on time'' or ''off time'' which, in turn, has consequences for how they view and enact their role. Burton and Bengtson (1985) compared multigenerational black families where individuals became mothers and grandmothers at very early ages with families who experienced these events at more normative ages. They discovered that the new grandmothers who were early or ''off-time'' (median age = 32) reacted quite negatively to their new role and voiced discomfort at acquiring this ''old-age'' role. These younger grandmothers were overloaded with both parenting and grandparenting demands as well as demands from work and other family members. The majority of these early grandmothers avoided engaging in grandparent-role behavior because they associated the role with old age and because the role demands came at a time in their lives when they were overcommitted. In contrast, most of the ''on-time'' grandmothers (median age = 46) did not experience this type of role strain and felt positive about when they had become a grandparent.

Burton's (1994) comparison of semirural and urban African American grandmothers suggests that the timeliness of grandparental roles depends on the cultural context; young urban grandmothers often felt that they were too young for that role, while in the rural setting, early grandmotherhood was expected and eagerly anticipated. For rural grandmothers, teen motherhood was found to be valued and expected. The rural families showed a pattern of nonadjacent role responsibilities, in which teen girls were expected to have children young so that their grandmothers would have an opportunity to raise a child. All members of the family lineage expected that the grandmother would provide daily care for the grandchild. The same was not true for those in the urban study; for them there were clear tensions relating to becoming grandparents early in life. Generally, the timing of grandmotherhood was problematic for the young urban grandmothers.

Why did the grandmothers feel differently about the grandmother role in the two contexts, even though the family lineage patterns were similar? It seems likely that nonadjacent parenting patterns were acceptable in a rural setting where employment and partnership were not realistic options for the women in any of the family generations. In the urban setting, very young grandmothers were often employed and developing or maintaining intimate relationships—the role of grandmother did not fit with their occupational or relational role (Burton, 1994).

Connections between the life-course timing of grandparenthood and family lineage have implications for the sequencing of grandparenthood with other family and nonfamily roles. The experience of grandparenthood is also likely to differ according to its timing relative to educational or occupational roles, such as full-time employment or retirement. The relatively new pattern of early retirement places many urban grandparents in a leisure stage of their lives when they might invest more time in their role as grandparents. Meanwhile, although rural grandparents living in a farming tradition may delegate more of the responsibility of the family farm to younger generations, many continue the daily business of operating a farm as long as they are able. They may not have as much time to spend in leisure activities with grandchildren, but rather spend time with their grandchildren doing the work of living on a farm.

Historical Time and Place

Many historical, demographic, and family changes have shaped grandparenting over time (see Chapter 2). For example, declining mortality has resulted in an increase in the number and proportion of people who reach grandparenthood. Most adults now live long enough to get to know their grandchildren and watch them develop into adulthood, and most contemporary children have the opportunity to know most of their grandparents.

Thus grandparents today may be able to play an increasingly important role in the lives of grandchildren. This influence may even extend into future generations. King and Elder (1997) report that having known one's grandparents and learning about them through multiple aspects of intergenerational history (i.e., photos, stories) is associated with the degree to which rural elders are involved as grandparents and the types of roles they play with their grandchildren. Kivnick (1982/1980) found that several aspects of recalled experiences with grandparents (how well they knew a grandparent, how important a grandparent was, and feelings toward a grandparent) were positively associated with how grandmothers viewed the grandparent role (i.e., as being central to their lives, as providing feelings of immortality).

Grandparents who grew up in rural areas may have different feelings about what it means to be a grandparent than those who experienced childhood in the city. Historically, grandparents are likely to have played a more important role in the lives of their children in rural areas, given the interdependence of the generations in farm and agricultural work.

Historical time refers to a person's location in history, often indicated by membership in a birth cohort. Unique historical events and changes are experienced by different cohorts of grandparents, giving rise to variations in grandparenthood. In this century alone, major events such as the Great Depression, World War I, and World War II shaped the lives of those who lived through them, including grandparents and grandchildren. For example, living with a grandparent was a more common experience during the 1930's and 1940's than either earlier or later in this century, indicating that this type of household arrangement may have been formed in response to family crises brought about by the Great Depression and World War II (Szinovacz, 1996).

Different cohort experiences can lead to actual changes in the grandparent role (Bengtson, 1985). Older cohorts of grandparents, for example, might have more traditional views about grandparenting (Peterson, 1989). Certainly contemporary grandparents feel their role is much different from that of their own grandparents. They describe their grandparents as respected but more emotionally distant figures and believe they have a more companionate and emotion-laden relationship with their own grandchildren (Cherlin & Furstenberg, 1986a). Part of this change has arisen out of industrialization and the shift from a household-based economy to the market place. The influence and authority of the older generation weakened when members lost their economic hold over the family. In its place emerged an emphasis on bonds of sentiment and affection between family members.

A focus on historical time and place may lead to fruitful studies of grandparents in varying environmental niches. We can expect the experience of the grandparent role, both by older and younger generations, to be shaped by recent historical changes relating to rural and urban life. The increased prevalence of divorce, substance abuse, and HIV and AIDS, which are particularly prevalent in urban centers, have changed the nature of the grandparenting role for many individuals; more urban grandparents are helping out and some are even acting as primary caregivers in situations where parenting fails (see Chapter 14).

The historic decline of the rural farm population in the United States has produced changes across the generations in rural lives. A century ago, most Americans had ties to the land through their own lives and those of immediate kin. Only 2% of all Americans are living on farms in the 1990's. The end of an era is in sight across the span of three generations, from grandparent to grandchild. Many rural families have moved from a life in farming to a world in which the young must look elsewhere to make their living (Elder & Conger, forthcoming; Elder, King, and Conger, 1996). Hernandez and Myer (1993) refer to the movement of families out of farming as one of the "revolutionary changes" in the family experience of children during this century.

Thus cohort differences in the experiences of the generations have been dramatic and fewer families have experienced continuity in farming. The younger generations find themselves following very different life paths from their parents, which may result in a weakening of intergenerational bonds or a rise intergenerational conflicts. Given the importance of the middle generation as mediators, such conflict could interfere with connections between grandparents and grandchildren. The prevalent outmigration of the young in rural areas is also increasingly separating some grandchildren from the lives of their grandparents, socially, occupationally, and geographically.

To the extent that grandparents play a different role in the lives of farm children when compared with those in nonfarming communities, the social consequences of the substantial population decline in rural society would be expected to feature corresponding changes in intergenerational relationships. We explore this issue further in our review of research on grandparenting in farm families.

RURAL AND URBAN ECOLOGIES OF GRANDPARENTING

Rural Communities

Rural communities are characterized by low population density, smaller size, and extractive types of industries such as agriculture. Compared to urban areas, rural sectors have proportionately more families living in poverty, lower levels of female employment, and a greater proportion of elderly when compared to urban areas (Van Nostrand, 1993; Willits, Bealer, & Crider, 1982). Rural families also tend to be somewhat larger than urban families and experience lower divorce rates (McCulloch, 1995).

Rural elders (hence grandparents) are disproportionately disadvantaged on a variety of social and economic dimensions in comparison to urban elders; they have lower income, less education, poorer health, fewer medical services, more limited transportation, and lower housing quality (Lee & Lassey, 1982; McCulloch, 1995; Van Nostrand, 1993). For example, one-half of the nonmetropolitan elderly were in poor, near-poor, or low-income families in 1987 compared with 37% of the metropolitan elderly. At the other extreme, 18% of the nonmetropolitan elderly were in high-income families compared with 27% of the metropolitan elderly (Van Nostrand, 1993).

The greater economic disadvantage faced by rural elders may mean that their older grandchildren are called upon more often for assistance. Previous research has virtually ignored the role that older grandchildren play in the lives of their grandparents. Attention is often limited to affective dimensions of the relationship or to contact. When other types of roles are considered, it is usually examined from the vantage point of what the grandparent does for the grandchild and not the other way around. Younger grandchildren may not be able to provide much assistance to their grandparents; if it is needed, the parent is a more likely candidate to provide such help. But as grandchildren become older, they may be able to increasingly help out a grandparent in need, for example, by driving the grandparent to a doctor's appointment, mowing the lawn, or helping with housework. Rural grandchildren may be more likely to provide such types of assistance because there is a greater need for it. However, one countertrend which can mitigate greater involvement by older grandchildren is outmigration.

Rural outmigration of the young has been a long and continuing trend, but the agricultural crisis of the 1980's markedly increased the incentive to migrate from rural areas through a stunning collapse of land values and declining wage rates for rural workers (Lichter, Johnston, & McLaughlin, 1994). This continuing decline is producing greater economic inequality between rural and urban America. As noted previously, the continuing outmigration of rural youth is separating some grandchildren from the lives of their grandparents who remain behind. For these rural families, connections between the generations are loosened by geographical separation.

Another area where a number of rural-urban differences have been reported concerns beliefs and attitudes. Studies have generally found that, compared with urbanites, rural dwellers tend to be more conservative and traditional, particularly with regard to family values and attitudes toward gender roles. Rural residents also place greater importance on family and community interaction and tend to be more religious (Chalfant & Heller, 1991; Fischer, 1982; Glenn & Hill, 1977; Larson, 1978; McCulloch, 1995; Willits, Bealer, & Crider, 1982). Furthermore, these differences usually persist when demographic differences such as age or education are taken into account.

Lee, Coward, and Netzer (1994) found that older persons who were raised in rural areas, particularly on farms, have significantly higher expectations for filial assistance (expectations regarding assistance and care from adult children for elderly parents) than do older persons from urban backgrounds. An interesting aspect of this study was that current residence had no impact on expectations—where one had grown up was the determining factor. The authors hypothesized that such values develop early in life and develop out of rural experiences, such as the need for greater intrafamily cooperation and assistance due to the requirements of rural occupations and lack of public services. Such a context encourages family members to rely upon one another and creates expectations for assistance which do not disappear with a later change of residence.

Such beliefs about filial assistance, combined with more traditional family values and a greater emphasis on family interaction in rural settings may further differentiate the grandparent-grandchild relationship in rural and urban settings. If rural grandparents expect more help from adult children, they may also expect more help from grandchildren, or accept it more easily. If rural grandchildren have stronger familial ties, grandparents may play a larger role in their lives.

Studies of kinship and exchange have produced mixed findings. Some find few differences between rural and urban residents (e.g., Lee & Cassidy, 1982; Lee, Dwyer, & Coward, 1990), but many others reveal somewhat higher levels of interaction and exchange among rural residents, and these differences are often most pronounced for rural elders who tend to have more contact with, and receive more help from, family and friends (e.g., Amato, 1993; Lee & Lassey, 1982; Lee & Whitbeck, 1987; McCulloch, 1995). Fischer (1982) found urban and rural residents to be similar on the amount and quality of social ties, but they differed on the composition of their networks and drew on different types of people for support. Small-town residents were more involved with kin while city residents depended more on nonkin. The lower kin involvement of city residents was not due to kin being unavailable or living further away. Fischer concludes that urbanism tends to produce a different style of life rather than a different quality of life.

In the only national study to examine rural-urban differences in contacts between grandparents and grandchildren, Cherlin and Furstenberg (1986a) show that grandparents living in rural areas see their grandchildren more often than urban grandparents, even after controlling for proximity. They hypothesize that rural families hold values that lead to more social contact and mutual assistance compared to urban families.

Many of the characteristics of rural settings, such as the greater needs of rural elderly, stronger familial values, and higher levels of grandparent-grandchild contact, would seem to promote stronger grandparent-grandchild bonds in rural contexts when compared to urban ones. Other characteristics, such as the out-migration of rural youth, can hinder the maintenance of such bonds. Whether stronger or not, the types of relationships between grandparents and grandchildren are likely to be shaped by the contextual differences between rural and urban settings.

Farm Families

The study of family relationships in contemporary rural settings must account for the historical changes that have occurred during the last century in the economic and family lives of rural Americans (Elder & Conger, forthcoming). Within this time period, household economies based in family farming have been replaced by industry and commercial farming. With each successive generation, fewer and fewer family members continue the tradition of farming. The study of grandparent-grandchild relationships in rural settings offers the opportunity to study intergenerational relationships within the larger picture of economic and historical change.

In rural areas, it is important to distinguish between farm and other rural families; evidence of the historical transformation of rural life can often be seen when comparing farm to nonfarm families. Farm families are differentiated from other households by a close connection between family and work, and by interdependence among family members. Rural farm elderly interact more and live closer to their adult children than elders living in rural nonfarm areas and small towns. These differences are particularly pronounced on the paternal side (Elder, Rudkin, & Conger, 1994; King & Elder, 1995a; McCulloch, 1995; Powers, Keith, & Goudy, 1981; Wilkening, Guerrero, & Ginsberg, 1972). Farmers often hold the most traditional and conservative values in comparison to other rural residents or urbanites (Glenn & Hill, 1977; Larson, 1978).

Farm children live closer to their grandparents, report more frequent contacts with them, and rate the quality of their relationship higher than other rural children, particularly in regard to paternal grandparents (King & Elder, 1995a). Similarly, grandparents in farm families report higher levels of contact, better quality relationships, more involvement in activities, greater instrumental assistance, and a greater likelihood of serving as mentors and companions with their grandchildren than do other rural grandparents (Elder & King, forthcoming). Again these differences mainly occur for paternal grandparents such that paternal grandparents in farm families are significantly more involved with their grandchildren than paternal grandparents in rural families who do not farm. The closer proximity of farm grandparents explains part, but not all, of these differences. Two other factors that link paternal grandparents to their grandchildren in farm families include the strength of the grandparent-parent bond and the grandparent's level of church attendance. Both are positively related to farming and grandparent involvement.

The greater prominence of paternal grandparents in farm families than in other rural families undoubtedly reflects the more interdependent nature of farm family life and serves as a striking contrast to the general pattern in American society. Farm families are male centered, with residence, work, and inheritance patterns acting together to promote a patrilineal emphasis. For example, fathers and sons are the most common work team on the farm, and land, the most valuable resource in farming, is usually passed down through the male line (Salamon, 1992). Extended kin living in the surrounding community, such as paternal grandparents, find themselves drawn into the farm cycle as helpers, even if they themselves are involved in off-farm employment (Colman & Elbert, 1984). Labor provided by grandfathers varies from hauling crops to running errands during planting and harvesting. By preparing meals and baby-sitting, grandmothers enable other family members to do field work without interruptions (Salamon & Lockhart, 1980). Thus for children, contact with grandparents is not limited to occasional visits, vacations, or holidays. Grandparents are relatively accessible in the farm child's everyday life.

Differences in grandparent-grandchild relationships between rural families that farm and those that do not can be traced to the historical transformation of agriculture in the United States. The continuing historic decline of the rural farm population will continue to have consequences for intergenerational relationships.

Urban Families

What makes urban family life distinct? A traditional sociological view of urban life, based on work from the Chicago school, holds that urban living weakens families; institutions develop in urban centers that overtake many of the functions performed by families (Wirth, 1938). In urban areas, persons are less likely to marry, are more likely to divorce, are less likely to live with extended family or to share common households. Further, the kin of urbanites are more geographically dispersed than the kin of people living in rural areas (Fischer, 1984). These distinctive characteristics of urban families have implications for intergenerational relationships. If families are weaker in urban areas, we would expect grandparent/grandchild relationships to be weaker than in rural areas. How do these urban characteristics shape the grandparent/grandchild relationship, and the role of the grandparent?

DeFrain, LeMasters, and Schroff (1991) have suggested that urban families are influenced by the impersonality and anonymity of urban areas, the pluralistic nature of the city, and the increased leisure time and importance of the peer group for urban youth. These factors shape parent-child relationships, and thereby may have quite strong influences on ties across three generations. These characteristics of urban life may erode shared values within families, particularly those between grandparents and grandchildren.

In rural communities, most people know one another. It is more difficult in urban areas for parents to know their children's friends, much less to know the friends' parents. In addition, families live in close proximity to persons of diverse racial, ethnic, and religious backgrounds; this pluralism of urban areas offers many opportunities for families, but also can become a source of family conflict. Younger generations often gain exposure and develop attachments to ethnic and religious values and traditions that are often unknown or different from those of parents and grandparents. These issues are compounded by the comparatively increased leisure time of urban youth in comparison to youth in rural communities, and the focus of that leisure time on the peer group (DeFrain, LeMasters, & Schroff, 1991).

The anonymity of pluralistic environments in which the peer group is a major force in the lives of youth will likely enable gaps to form between the generations in the values that they share. When parents and children share fewer values over time, the values shared between children and their grandparents are likely to be even more differentiated. Certainly, many urban grandparents overcome potential value differences by focusing on an affectional relationship with their grandchildren. However, grandparents for whom traditional religious or ethnic values and practices remain important may feel a widening gap in the set of common values that they share with their grandchildren.

A study of rural grandchildren in Iowa revealed that shared values are an important factor in grandparent-grandchild relationships (King & Elder, 1995b). When these adolescent grandchildren were asked what the most important thing they learned from a grandparent was, the most common response focused on moral character and values—over one-third of the grandchildren mentioned this. By contrast, discontinuity across generations in common values may distinguish relationships between urban grandparents and grandchildren. However, we should not suggest that all urban families suffer from this discontinuity.

Urban grandparents often play instrumental roles in the lives of their grandchildren. As with rural farm and nonfarm families, important ecological variations also exist within urban families in terms of the roles grandparents play, due in part to many of the social problems evident in central cities. One example comes from research on grandparents who serve as primary caregivers for grandchildren because of drug problems among their children (Minkler & Roe, 1993). Rates of grandparental caregiving are particularly high in urban inner-city areas, especially among low-income African American families. Minkler and Roe (1993) attribute much of the rise in grandparent caregiving over the past decade to the crack cocaine epidemic. Grandparenting in such a context is very different, with grandparents assuming more of a parent-like role than their peers in other contexts.

Problems of grandparenting in response to their children's drug use interact with the adults' own life course. Many of these grandparents face stress that they never anticipated at this stage in their lives (Burton, Dilworth-Anderson, & Merriwether-de Vries, 1995). The stress of being the primary caregiver to a child is compounded by several other factors (Burton, 1992a). First, contextual influences, such as neighborhood crime, make the job of grandparenting difficult. Second, familial stress, involving the breakdown of the family network due to having a drug-addicted child, will further complicate the grandparent's caregiving role. Finally, there are individual factors that will add to the stress of taking over primary caregiving responsibilities for members of older generations. These include giving up personal needs and goals (Burton, 1992a), as well as declines in marital satisfaction and the loss of contact with supportive family and friends (Minkler, Roe, & Robertson-Beckley, 1994; see also Chapter 14).

NEW DIRECTIONS

An obvious gap in the research literature on grandparenthood is that so few studies have directly examined the influence of different environments on grandparent-grandchild relationships. Studies that specifically address issues of rural-urban variation in grandparenting will contribute to our understanding of context in patterning grandparent-grandchild relationships. Nationally representative data would be particularly welcome but should move beyond including simple measures of contact and relationship quality.

Research on rural-urban differences in grandparenting would also benefit from closer attention to how these environmental contexts are measured. Do different measures yield the same findings? Which distinctions are most important? Are size-of-place trends always linear? For individuals who cross ecological contexts, is current residence more or less important than prior residence?

Three central elements of family ecology—generational interdependence, life-course patterns and timing, and historical time and place—each shape the environmental context and the grandparental role. Future work should expand the study of family ecologies, and the degree to which these factors are shaped by environmental context.

An important aspect of family ecology—the interdependence of the generations—is well suited to studies of urban and rural variation in grandparenthood. King and Elder (1995a, 1995b) have illustrated the differences between farm and nonfarming families in the salience of grandparents in children's lives; this has to do in large part with having a shared economic base across the generations. Future research should compare family economies in rural and urban settings. Is farming a unique family and economic system? Or are similar family relationships found in ethnic enclaves in large urban settings, where all members in each generation often participate in the operation of a family business? In addition to economic interdependence, what other types of interdependence (i.e., cultural or normative) bring the generations together in ways that influence grandparent-grandchild relationships? Are certain forms of family interdependence more characteristic of rural or urban areas?

With regard to the intersection between life-course patterns and environmental ecologies, it should be noted that rural-urban differences in grandparent-grandchild relations can vary over the life course. For example, rural grandchildren may enjoy stronger bonds to grandparents than urban grandchildren when they are younger owing to closer proximity and greater levels of contact. But the outmigration of older rural youth may remove this advantage. At what stages of the life course are ecological differences in grandparent-grandchild relations the most or least pronounced? What happens to such relationships when individuals move across contexts? Of course, issues of historical time and place are also important here in influencing the context in which grandparent-grandchild relationships are played out.

Previous generational studies have been largely ahistorical. Attention needs to focus on the fact that many different cohorts are represented in every generation of three-generation families. For example, studies of grandparents often include individuals somewhere between 50 and 90 years old with many years separating the oldest and youngest grandparents. These grandparents were born at very different historical periods and represent a heterogeneous and diffuse group, a point which is rarely taken into account. How do cohort differences influence grandparenting? Are cohort differences more pronounced among urban grandparents or those who migrated to urban areas and experienced more rapid social changes in comparison to their rural counterparts?

What recent historical or current trends are influencing grandparenting in rural and urban areas? How do modes of grandparent support and guidance differ in these contexts, both generally and in times of crisis when grandparents are most likely to be called upon to help. For example, what is the role of rural grandparents in families who experienced the loss of a farm during the farm crisis of the 1980's? Did this crisis prompt rural grandparents to become more active participants in ways that have been reported for other families undergoing crises such as divorce or in economically disadvantaged African American families?

Attention to other contexts and their interdependence with environmental ecologies is also needed. Variations by race, ethnicity, social class, gender, and lineage are important to consider when examining grandparent-grandchild relationships; such factors can also influence grandparent-grandchild relationships differentially in urban and rural environments. For example, as noted earlier, lineage differences in grandparent-grandchild relationships vary across ecological contexts. Paternal grandparents in farm families are distinguished from paternal grandparents in other contexts by their greater involvement with their grandchildren.

In what other ways does the influence of factors such as gender on grandparent-grandchild relations vary in rural and urban contexts? Do the more traditional values and lower socioeconomic status of rural grandparents lead them to engage in more stereotypically gendered activities with their grandchildren than their urban peers? If family networks are more active in rural areas, does this lead to a stronger process of intergenerational transmission (i.e., of values and behaviors) from grandparent to grandchild in such contexts? Does the greater social differentiation of the city, with its economic and ethnic heterogeneity, result in greater variability in grandparent-grandchild relationships in urban than in rural families?

Finally, studies of rural-urban differences (in grandparenting and other areas) must move beyond a social address model which ignores the consideration of process (Bronfenbrenner, 1986; Bronfenbrenner & Crouter, 1983). What are the processes that lead to rural-urban differences, or to differences within rural and urban contexts? Although prior research has documented a variety of ways in which rural and urban dwellers differ, explanations for why this is so have been poorly developed. For example, some authors have speculated that rural-urban differences in kinship patterns are shaped by differences in values, but few have directly tested this assumption. To what extent do the beliefs and attitudes of rural and urban dwellers shape their family behavior? Under what conditions is the link between values and behaviors strongest (distance, for example, may impede even strong desires for frequent kin contact)? How do such values develop, and how is this process different in rural and urban ecologies?

Chapter 5

Grandparenthood in African American Families

Andrea G. Hunter and Robert J. Taylor

Grandparents have played a crucial role in the survival and functioning of African American families. Unfortunately, research on black grandparents has historically been couched within the public discourse on black families and social policy. This work has been defined by two interrelated issues: (1) debates about the inherent health and integrity of African American families and (2) the impact of culture and social structural factors (e.g., economic hardship, racial stratification, discrimination) on black-white differences in family patterns. Black grandparents are only emphasized to the degree that they help ameliorate family crises or as a focus on explanations of black-white differences in family life. This is in contrast to studies of grandparenthood in white families that have primarily been noncomparative and focused on noncrisis contexts (e.g., Bengtson & Roberts, 1991; Johnson, 1983a; King & Elder, 1995a; Roberto & Stroes, 1992; Robertson, 1977; Thompson & Walker, 1987). Although work on African American grandparents has to some degree been constrained by its linkages to the discourse on race and social policy, it does address issues that are fundamental in grandparent research—that of meaning(s), context, and behavior.

The aim of this chapter is three-fold. First, to review the lines of research that have been central points of inquiry in studies of African American grandparenthood. These research foci include (1) symbolic meaning and role expectations of grandparenthood, (2) grandparenthood in family context (i.e., family lineage, kinship systems, and living arrangements), and (3) the parenting, economic, and social support provided by grandparents. The chapter concludes with a discussion of directions for future research on African American grandparenthood.

SYMBOLIC MEANING AND ROLE EXPECTATIONS OF GRANDPARENTHOOD

Many of the basic issues concerned with grandparenthood have yet to be investigated among African Americans. Conceptualizations of grandparenthood among African Americans have not been the topic of intensive qualitative studies, like those of Kivnick (1982, 1983) and Neugarten and Weinstein (1964). Further, the varied typologies of grandparent roles or dimensions of grandparenthood have not been validated among African Americans (see Cherlin & Furstenberg, 1986a, for a notable exception). The symbolic meanings of black grandparenthood were, however, articulated in some of the earliest works on African American families (DuBois, 1899, 1908; Frazier, 1939). E. Franklin Frazier, in his groundbreaking monograph *The Negro Family in the United States* (1939), described the role of black grandmothers as the "guardian of the generations." He identified a core African American cultural archetype that has been described as both mythic and real (Hill-Lubin, 1991; Jones, 1973). In African American personal narratives and autobiographies, African American grandmothers are often described as persons of "action, involvement, hope, and dignity" (Collins, 1990; Gwaltney, 1980; Hill-Lubin, 1991; White, 1992). Hill-Lubin (1991: 174) argues that in African American autobiographies, grandmothers' roles are represented in three focal areas: (1) preservation of extended families; (2) repository and distributor of history, wisdom, and folk beliefs; and (3) a source and communication of values and ideals.

Grandchildren's expectations of their grandparents provides some insight into how African Americans construct the grandparent role. Kennedy's (1990) study of black and white college students found racial differences in expectations of grandparent role behaviors. African Americans were more likely than whites to agree that (1) grandparents hold a position of authority and provide discipline and guidance, (2) grandparents help with parenting and provide financial assistance, and (3) grandchildren should follow the guidance of grandparents. In contrast, white young adults were more likely to agree that it was important to visit grandparents and to share information about their activities with grandparents. White young adults were also more likely to endorse the idea that there were barriers between parent and grandparent roles (e.g., grandparents should not spoil grandchildren, and grandparents should maintain contact but leave parenting to parents). In sum, African American young adults were more likely to endorse role expectations that were consistent with an integrated and central role of grandparents, in which the boundaries between parents and grandparents were more malleable. In contrast, white young adults endorsed attitudes that reflected the norm of noninterference and supported a companionate relationship with grandparents, as opposed to a parent-like one.

Timberlake and Chipungu (1992) examined the symbolic meaning(s) of grandchildren and grandparenthood among middle-class African American grandmothers. Based on women's rating of values, they found "expansion of self'' (e.g., after death one lives on in one's grandchildren), ''morality or altruism'' (e.g., grandchildren provide an opportunity to give of one's self), and ''power, influence or effectance'' (e.g., having grandchildren is one way to have an effect on one's own life and the lives of others) were the most highly valued symbolic meanings of grandchildren. These domains overlap with Kivnick's (1982, 1983) dimensions of grandparenthood, including centrality, immortality through clan, and valued elder. The least valued areas were ''creativity, accomplishment, or competence'' (e.g., grandchildren provide a goal in life) and ''social comparison or competition'' (e.g., grandchildren's accomplishments reflect on grandparents). The lower rating found for these views of grandchildren may reflect African American grandparents' emphasis on what they are, bring, and give to the next generation.

Strom and colleagues (1993) investigated grandparents' and grandchildren's perceptions of the grandparent role. They found that black grandparents viewed their roles as teachers as being one of their major strengths. Grandchildren also agreed that their grandparents' roles as teachers were important to them. Central lessons focused on teaching grandchildren to care about the feelings of others, to have good manners, a sense of what is right and wrong, the importance of learning, and religious faith. Both black grandparents and grandchildren perceived this role as more important than did their white counterparts.

These few empirical studies on grandparent role expectations and role meanings among African Americans suggest that cultural notions of the ''traditional'' black grandparenthood, in some way, inform contemporary grandparenthood. However, African American families and grandparents are not homogeneous, and there is enormous variability in grandparenting practices. Unfortunately, we know little about the diverse ways African Americans may view the symbolic meaning of grandparenthood and how these meanings inform role expectations and behavior of grandparents, parents, and grandchildren.

GRANDPARENTHOOD IN FAMILY CONTEXT

African American grandparenthood is negotiated in multiple and simultaneous family contexts: (1) intergenerational family structure (e.g., age-structure and depth of family lineages); (2) extended families, personal kindreds, and domestic networks; and (3) household family structure. These family contexts are shaped by an intersection of individual lives that collectively form, reconfigure, and extend family lineages through marriages, births, death, marital dissolution, and fictive family ties (Aldous, 1990; Elder 1978b, 1991; Hareven, 1977; Stack, 1974). Kinship positions and family responsibilities expand and contract as individuals move through varied marital and family careers across the life span. The intergenerational family life cycle, a product of overlapping life course and family trajectories, highlights the continuity in family systems and accommodates normative and non-normative family transitions (e.g., early childbearing) and family events (e.g, nonmarital childbearing) that may occur within multigeneration family lineages. The structure of family lineages (e.g., age-structure, number of surviving generations) and generational positions held by its members (e.g., mother, grandmother, great-grandmother) shape the social organization of multigeneration family systems within which grandparenting practices are negotiated (Elder, 1978b, 1985; Hagestad & Burton, 1986).

Intergenerational Family Structures

Over the last three decades, changes in family demography and patterns of mortality have led to greater diversity in the structure and age composition of multigeneration family lineages (Burton & Dilworth-Anderson, 1991; Hagestead & Burton, 1986). Burton and Dilworth-Anderson (1991) describe three central types of intergenerational family structures that are characteristic of African American families: (1) vertical or beanpole (Bengtson, Rosenthal, & Burton, 1990; Hagestad & Burton, 1986); (2) age-condensed; and (3) fictive or substitutional (George & Gold, 1991). Studies of the linkages between intergenerational family structure and black grandparenthood have focused largely on age-condensed family lineages which are a product of one or more generations of early childbearing (e.g., Burton, 1990; Burton & Bengtson, 1985; Furstenberg, Brooks-Gunn, & Morgan, 1987). Although it has been argued that the vertical or beanpole structure will be increasingly characteristic of contemporary American family lineages (Bengtson et al., 1990), there has been little research on how it may shape intergenerational relationships and grandparenting in African American families (Bengtson et al., 1995; Burton & Dilworth-Anderson, 1991; George & Gold, 1991).

The broadest investigations of diverse multigeneration family structures among African Americans are based on the three-generational family study (TGFS) (Jackson & Hatchett, 1986; Jackson, Jayakody, & Antonucci, 1996; Taylor, Chatters, & Jackson, 1993). This study is the only one to use a national sample of three-generation families. All of the other major studies of three-generation families are based on a particular geographical area (i.e., Bengtson's Los Angeles-based sample, Markides' Texas-based sample of Hispanics, and Rossi's Boston-based sample). In the TGFS members of all three generations were interviewed, and the identified respondents in the youngest generation had to be a minimum of 14 years of age.

Taylor, Chatters, and Jackson's (1993) profile of three-generation black families documented the existence of heterogenous age patterns in the generational configurations of black families. Although there were instances of age-condensed family structures, this configuration was not representative of three-generation black families. Evidence of four- and five-generation black families was present. Although the three-generation family study is based on an exclusively African American sample, this information can be used for the purposes of basic comparisons in the demographic structures of black and white families. Probably the major difference between black and white three-generation families is the higher percentages of women in black families. This is particularly evident in the grandparent generation and is due to the much higher rates of widowhood among blacks (see Taylor, Chatters, & Jackson, 1993, for a more complete discussion of this issue). Younger generations of black families should increasingly become more female-headed as a result of the lower rates of marriage and remarriage, coupled with higher rates of divorce and separation (Taylor et al., 1997). In addition, consistent with research on older blacks, members of the grandparent generation, in contrast with the parent and child generations, had fairly low levels of income and education and were more likely to reside in the South (Taylor, Chatters, & Jackson, 1993).

Burton's program of research (Burton, 1990, 1995; Burton & Bengtson, 1985) documents the impact of age-condensed intergenerational family structures on grandparenting. Her work indicates that the timing of the transition to grandparenthood impacts the degree to which women are satisfied with the grandparent role. Burton and Bengtson (1985) investigated the differences in role perceptions and concerns of black women who experienced in a normative sense, early (median age 32 years) versus on-time (median age 46 years) entry into the grandmother role. Early grandmothers expressed significant discomfort in their role as a result of the inordinate child-rearing responsibilities of raising both their adolescent child and grandchild coupled with the role incongruity arising from being young and a grandmother. Future work on early grandparenting should investigate how early timing influences (1) the perceptions of grandparenting, and (2) the grandparent-grandchild relationship over time.

Burton (1990), in a study of an impoverished northeastern community also found that generational continuities in early childbearing resulted in the development of adaptive patterns of intergenerational caregiving responsibilities. For example, adolescent mothers turned over the care of infants to their own mothers, while they provided support to their aging grandmothers who raised them. Within this unique community, Burton suggests adolescent childbearing emerged as an alternative life-course strategy wherein grandmotherhood was equivalent to parenting. Burton's work is provocative in that it highlights the emergence of grandparent role definitions that are community-specific. While interesting, the findings from this 1990 study have not been replicated in any other ethnographic or survey-based study. More recently, Burton (1995) has identified diverse family and caregiving systems within age-condensed intergenerational family structures. Across these family systems, the roles of grandmothers and grandfathers vary dramatically. The major contributions of this body of work are (1) the documentation of the existence of families characterized by multiple generations of adolescent childbearing, (2) the effects of such generational arrangements on both the definition and roles of grandparents and the distribution of family caregiving responsibilities, and (3) verification of the existence of relatively young grandparents (i.e., middle aged or younger).

Ethnographic research on African American families suggests that the extension of lineage through fictive kin ties is not an uncommon occurrence (Aschenbrenner, 1975; Dilworth-Anderson, 1992; Jarrett, 1994; Martin & Martin, 1978; Stack, 1974). Fictive kin relationships are voluntary and non-institutionalized and build on the symbolic roles of biological kin (Aschenbrenner, 1973; Stack, 1974). Further, because fictive ties are bonds of choice, they are maintained through a system of mutual aid and obligation (Chatters, Taylor, & Jayakody (1994). In a national study of African Americans, Chatters, Taylor, and Jayakody (1994) found that two out of three adults indicated there was someone in their family who was regarded as fictive kin. The substitutional intergenerational family structure described by Burton and Dilworth-Anderson (1991) refers to family lineages that extend through fictive kin ties, specifically under conditions of childlessness or delayed childbearing. However, fictive grandparents and grandchildren relationships may also develop even when biological kin are available.

Extended Families, Personal Kindreds, and Domestic Networks

Ethnographic studies of black extended families provide insights into the social organization and family processes within multigeneration family systems (Aschenbrenner, 1975; Burton, 1990; Martin & Martin, 1978; Shimkin, Shimkin, & Frate, 1978; Stack, 1974). Although the structure of the extended kinship systems varies by community and kin network, these family systems have distinctive properties (Martin & Martin, 1978; Shimkin, Shimkin, & Frate, 1978). Extended kinship systems are interdependent and characterized by a sharing of resources across households and generations. Multiple generations are organized around a home base and headed by a central family figure, usually an elder (Martin & Martin, 1978). Further, nuclear family units (one- or two-parent) are linked together as satellites of the core household unit from which they grew.

A key family role in extended families is the dominant family figure(s) who serves as the family linchpin (Martin & Martin, 1978). It is a role that emphasizes intergenerational care and obligation, family legacy and continuity, and expressive and instrumental functions. Dominant family figures are usually family elders (e.g., grandparents, great-grandparents), and either women and men alone or married couples may assume this role. However, women are more likely to hold this central family position because of higher rates of male mortality and single parenthood, as well as the larger role that women play in kin-keeping. Extended-family systems are not static entities; they reconfigure, generate new family systems, and dissolve (Martin & Martin, 1978; Shimkin, Shimkin, & Frate, 1978). In extended families, family members often hold multiple generational positions. Shifts in generational position (e.g., from parent to grandparent, to oldest surviving generation) are fueled by events in the family life cycle (i.e., marriages, births) and family deaths whose effects ripple throughout the family lineage (Hareven, 1977; Mogey, 1991). These shifts can have different implications for family members that vary in relation to the extent of family lineages (e.g., three, four, or five generations) and intergenerational family structure.

Ethnographic studies of personal kindreds provide the most comprehensive look at substitutional intergenerational family structures where male and female elders may take on a fictive grandparenting role. Anthropologists exploring poor non-Southern urban communities highlight the malleability of household boundaries, family-like relationships, and the web of kin networks that people use to survive difficult circumstances (e.g., Aschenbrenner, 1975; Jarrett, 1994; Stack, 1974). Stack (1974) describes these networks as personal kindreds and domestic networks. Both personal kindreds and domestic networks mirror the social organization of black extended families, which are built on both biological and fictive kin ties.

Extended-Family Living Arrangements

One of the most consistent findings in family research indicates that, across the life span, African Americans are more likely to live in extended-family households than are white Americans (Beck & Beck, 1984, 1989; Chevan & Sutton, 1985; Farley & Allen, 1987; Hays et al., 1995; Hofferth, 1985; Kivett, 1991a; Raley, 1995; Richards, White, & Tsui, 1987). Similarly, research has consistently found that black children are more likely to live with grandparents than white children (Hernandez & Myer, 1993; Taylor, Tucker et. al, 1997). As a consequence, African American grandparenthood is often studied within the context of extended-family living arrangements. Indeed, 12% of African American children live with a grandparent (U.S. Bureau of the Census, 1991) compared to 3.6% of white children. Longitudinal studies of children's living arrangements suggest that even more children will spend some part of their childhood years with extended kin, who are most frequently grandparents (Hofferth, 1985; Hunter & Ensminger, 1992). These patterns are mirrored in the living arrangements of middle-aged and older black adults (Beck & Beck, 1984, 1989; Hays et al., 1995; Richards, Whire, & Tsui, 1987).

Based on the Panel Study of Income Dynamics (PSID), Beck and Beck (1989) estimate that six out of ten African American women live with extended kin, primarily grandchildren, at some point during mid-life and their elder years. Although most studies examining grandparent coresidence and family processes focus on grandmothers, African American men also live in multigeneration households. A community study by Pearson, Hunter, Cook, Ialongo and Kellam (1997) found that 24.6% of sixth graders who lived with their grandmothers also lived with grandfathers. Beck and Beck (1984) estimate that 50% of married black men will spend part of the middle and elder years living in extended-family households. African American men are also more likely than white men to head multiperson households (Mutchler & Burr, 1991) and share a residence with their grandchildren (Beck & Beck, 1984; Kivett, 1985a). Szinovacz's

(1996) analysis of the National Survey of Families and Households indicates that among blacks adults 18% spent some time during their childhood in their grandparents' household (downward extension), whereas 11% indicated that at some point during their childhood a grandparent lived with them (upward extension). For both grandmothers and grandfathers, extended-family living arrangements result in greater contact and involvement with grandchildren (Kivett, 1985a; Pearson et al., 1990).

Coresidential grandparents are more likely to be involved in key child-rearing activities (e.g., rule setting, routine child management, discipline, behavior monitoring) than their nonresidential counterparts (Pearson et al., 1990; Pearson et al., 1994; Timberlake & Chipungu, 1992; Wilson, 1984; Wilson, 1987). However, coresidential grandparents' involvement in parenting varies by family structure. Grandparents who are parent surrogates are the most involved, followed by households where only one parent is present (Pearson et al., 1990; Pearson, et al., 1997; Wilson, 1984). However, grandmothers in single-father households still maintain a prominent role in parenting (Pearson et al., 1990; Pearson et al., 1994).

Coresidential grandparenting among African Americans has been fairly extensively studied in families of adolescent mothers. Grandmothers are a critical source of parenting advice, child care, and economic and housing assistance for teenage mothers and fathers (Johnson, 1995b; Marsiglio, 1995; Miller, 1994; Stevens, 1984; Unger & Cooley, 1992). There are, however, significant variations in the participation of grandmothers in the parenting of grandchildren (Apfel & Seitz, 1991; Burton & Bengtson, 1985; Chase-Lansdale, Brooks-Gunn, & Zamsky, 1994). Generally, parenting support provided by grandmothers is associated with more positive developmental outcomes for adolescent mothers and their children (Furstenberg, Brooks-Gunn, & Morgan, 1987; Kellam, Ensminger, & Turner, 1977). Extended coresidence with grandmothers, however, is related to poorer long-term outcomes for young mothers (Chase-Lansdale, Brooks-Gunn, & Zamsky, 1994; Furstenberg, Brooks-Gunn, & Morgan, 1987). Studies of grandfathers are rarer; however, grandfather presence and involvement is associated with positive developmental outcomes for teenage mothers and their babies (Oyserman, Radin, & Benn, 1993; see also Chapter 11).

The impact of grandparent coresidence on children's development outcomes in families with adult mothers has been examined as well. Early work by Kellam, Ensminger, and Turner (1977) indicates that second nonparent adults, most frequently grandparents, who lived in single-parent family households, functioned to mediate the developmental risks associated with single parenting. Subsequent studies, however, have been inconclusive on the impact of grandparent coresidence on African American children's developmental outcomes (e.g., Astone & Washington, 1994; Chase-Landsdale, Brooks-Gunn, & Zaniesky, 1994; Pearson, Ialongo, Hunter, & Kellam, 1994; Soloman & Marx, 1995; Vaden-Kiernan et al., 1995; Chapter 11).

GRANDPARENTAL INVOLVEMENT AND THE PROVISION OF ECONOMIC AND SOCIAL SUPPORT

Early studies of African American families viewed grandparents, particularly grandmothers, as a rather peculiar satellite of nuclear families that was endemic of the social disorganization of black families (Kardiner & Oversey, 1951; Moynihan, 1965; Pettigrew, 1964; see Allen, 1978; Staples, 1971 for reviews). In response to the paradigm introduced by Frazier, subsequent African American family research and theory (e.g., Billingsley, 1968; Blassingame, 1972; Gutman, 1976; Martin & Martin, 1978) highlighted the role of extended-kin relationships and multigenerational family systems. In contrast to characterizations of extended-family networks as examples of social pathology, this research viewed extended-family networks as an alternative to the isolated nuclear family and as a form of family adaptation. In both of these perspectives, grandparents are viewed as playing a critical role that is based upon African American cultural traditions and the economic and social realities of black life (Gutman, 1976).

During the last 15 years, empirical research on African American grandparenthood has been dominated by a focus on social problems affecting the family. This work emphasizes the reaction of grandparents to family troubles such as early childbearing (Burton & deVries, 1992; Colletta & Lee, 1983; Stevens, 1984), single parenthood and poverty (Chase-Landsdale, Brooks-Gunn, & Zamsky, 1994; Hogan, Hao & Parish, 1990); and drug addiction of adult children (Burton, 1992; Minkler & Roe, 1993). Studies of white grandparents, in contrast, have primarily focused on noncrisis contexts, the meaning of grandparenthood, and intergenerational family processes (e.g., Bengtson & Roberts, 1991; Johnson, 1983a; King & Elder, 1995a; Roberto & Stroes, 1992; Robertson, 1977; Thompson & Walker, 1987). In general, studies of African American grandparenthood have focused almost exclusively on their parenting roles and functions, including the provision of economic and social support to children and grandchildren.

Parental Involvement: From Parenting Support to Parenting Surrogacy

Cherlin and Furstenberg (1985) found that African Americans rarely demonstrate a passive grandparenting style. Rather, the majority of black grandparents (63%) had either an "authoritative" or "influential" grandparenting style that involved high levels of support and parent-like influence. Similar patterns of grandparent involvement have been found in several studies (Burton, 1990; Hogan, Hao, & Parish, 1990; Kivett, 1991a, 1993; Pearson et al., 1990; Pearson et al., 1997; Strom et al., 1993; Wilson et al., 1990). In particular, parents often view grandmothers as a primary source of parenting support and guidance (Hunter, 1997). African American grandmothers and grandfathers also characterize themselves as being close to their grandchildren in both affect and ideology

(Cherlin & Furstenberg, 1985; Jackson, 1986; Kivett, 1991a, 1993; Taylor, Chatters, & Jackson, 1993).

African American grandparents frequently take on important and central roles in the family. However, the grandparent role remains malleable, contingent, and varied (Burton & Bengtson, 1985; Robertson, 1975; Tinsley & Parke, 1984). Demographic characteristics of parents (e.g., age, marital status, economic need) and households (nuclear or extended); the kin group (e.g., proximity, intergenerational family structure); the quality (e.g., relationship history, closeness) of intergenerational relationships; and characteristics of the grandparent (e.g., age, health, timing of role transition) and children (e.g., age, gender), all affect grandparent behaviors and their views of their role (Tinsley & Parke, 1984; Troll, 1985).

Demographic and economic characteristics of both parents and households predict intergenerational assistance patterns and support across race and ethnicity (Aldous, 1995; Chatters & Taylor, 1993; Hofferth, 1985; Hogan, Hao, & Parish 1990; Jackson, Jayakody, & Antonucci, 1996). In African American families, grandparents may assume primary responsibility for parenting or augmented parenting in situations involving early childbearing, single parenthood, and parental crisis (e.g., drug addiction, illness, incarceration). Adolescent and unmarried mothers are more likely than are older and married mothers to rely on grandmothers to provide parenting in key child-rearing domains (Chase-Lansdale, Brooks-Gunn, & Zamsky 1994; Hogan, Hao, & Parish, 1990; Pearson et al., 1990, Wilson, 1984). When parents are unable to parent due to drug addiction, incarceration, or mental or physical illness, grandparents, grandmothers and grandfathers, step in as parenting surrogates (Burton, Dilworth-Anderson, & Merriwether-deVries, 1995). Women with inadequate financial resources are also more likely to rely on unpaid child care provided by grandmothers and other relatives than are more affluent mothers (Hogan, Hao, & Parish, 1990; Jarrett, 1994; Martin & Martin, 1978; Stack, 1974).

Kin proximity is related to contact, relationship quality, and emotional closeness in intergenerational relationships (Taylor & Chatters, 1991). Black grandparents are more likely to be involved in parenting, give help to grandchildren, and be involved in activities with their grandchildren if they live in close proximity to grandchildren (Hogan, Hao, & Parish, 1990; Hunter, 1997; Kivett, 1993; Wilson, 1987; Wilson, 1984). Timberlake and Chipungu (1992) found that coresidential grandmothers placed higher values on the symbolic meaning of grandchildren. However, Strom and colleagues (1993) note that distance did not affect black grandparents' view of their role or how effective they felt they were. Further, black grandchildren also felt they could count on grandparents regardless of whether they lived far away or close by.

Single parenthoood, being a young parent, and having fewer resources are all factors associated with involvement with grandparents. However, the mobilization of grandparents also depends on cultural-based social norms and the social organization of intergenerational families (Hill-Lubin, 1991; Martin &

Martin, 1978; Robertson, 1975; Stack, 1974). For example, Hunter (1997) found that kinship ties, intergenerational family structure and relationships, and residence in the rural South predicted mothers' reliance on grandmothers for parenting support. Factors associated with receipt of grandparent assistance that have been identified in other studies were unrelated to parents' view that they could count on grandmothers for parenting support.

The level of grandparent involvement is also shaped by the intersection of the life courses of family members, the timing and sequencing of family events, and the developmental tasks of families (e.g., family formation, reproduction, and child rearing) and individuals (e.g., generativity) (Aldous, 1995; Burton, 1990; Elder, 1978b; Hareven, 1977). In addition, off-time family transitions and non-normative sequencing of family events add to the complexities of family relationships (Burton, 1990; Burton, & Bengston, 1985; Hunter & Ensminger, 1992).

Both the age of grandparents and grandchildren shape cross-generational interactions and role perceptions. Strom, Collinsworth, Strom, and Griswold (1993) found that older black grandparents (age 60 and older) felt successful in their role, an assessment that grandchildren agreed with. In contrast, white younger grandparents perceived themselves more positively, as did their grandchildren. Black grandparents also felt more successful in relationships with younger grandchildren, as compared to older grandchildren (i.e., ages 12–18). However, there were no age differences in how black grandchildren perceived grandparents. In terms of perceptions of grandchildren, Timberlake and Chipungu (1992) found that among middle-class women, early grandmothers (30–41 years) rated the generative symbolic meanings of their grandchildren less highly than did on-time grandmothers (i.e., women 65–80 years of age).

Family roles and intergenerational family relationships vary by gender (Cooney & Uhlenberg, 1992; Thompson & Walker, 1987). Grandmothers are more likely to be involved in parenting activities than are grandfathers (e.g., Pearson et al., 1990). Kivett (1993) found rural black grandmothers were more likely to give help to granddaughters; however, the grandchild's gender did not affect the degree of help exchanged with grandfathers (Kivett, 1991a). With respect to family structure, Pearson and colleagues (1990) found that when boys lived with grandmothers, the households were more likely to include adult male relatives, either fathers or grandfathers, than when girls lived with grandmothers. In contrast, girls were more likely to live with grandmothers in parent-absent households with no other adult relatives present.

Custodial Grandparents

Since 1980, there has been a substantial increase in the number of grandchildren living with grandparents (see Chapter 2). Presently, about 35% of black children who reside with their grandparents live there without either parent present (Taylor et al., 1997). Historically, grandparents rearing grandchildren has been a response to parental mortality and illness, unmarried parenthood, and migration (Angelou, 1969; Frazier, 1939; Gutman, 1976; Stack & Burton, 1993). Today's custodial grandparents are most likely to take on full-time parenting to handle parental crises. Jendrek (1993), in her study of custodial grandparents, found that the leading catalysts for grandparent custody of grandchildren were (1) mother's emotional problems; (2) prevention of foster-care placement of grandchildren; (3) mother's drug problems; (4) mother's mental illness; and (5) mother's alcohol dependency. Although grandchildren most often come into the care of grandparents as a result of parental crisis, Soloman and Marx (1995) found children being raised by grandparents were not more likely to exhibit school adjustment or health problems than children being reared in other family types.

Recent studies of custodial black grandparents have focused on the difficulties faced by grandparents who took on guardianship because of parental drug addiction. (Burton, 1992; Minkler, Roe, & Price, 1992). Burton's (1992) study of 60 grandparents found that 86% of grandmothers were anxious or depressed. Almost one-half of grandparents had heightened medical problems or experienced a serious heath problem (i.e., minor stroke, mild heart attack) since they assumed care of their grandchildren. Although grandparents valued their grandchildren and felt there were rewards associated with caregiving, 41% reported multiple stressful outcomes. Minkler, Roe, and Price's (1992) study of 71 black grandmothers found that 36% felt their physical health had worsened and 46.6% felt their emotional health had worsened since caregiving began. A minority of grandmothers felt their physical and mental well-being changed for the better. Most women dealt with periods of depression, exhaustion, and/or isolation. Despite these challenges, most women felt their efforts were appreciated and that they were meeting their responsibilities adequately.

Burton (1992) and Minkler, Roe, and Price (1992) provide important insights into the challenges and burdens of custodial grandparenting in multiple-problem families where there are limited personal, economic, and community resources. However, there are few investigations of black custodial grandparents based on national or diverse community samples. Yet, there is considerable diversity in characteristics (e.g., age, employment, marital status, income) of custodial grandparents which may affect their adaptation to parenting. For example, Pearson and colleagues (1997), examining grandmother parenting involvement in a community-defined sample, found that custodial grandmothers who headed households alone had the least parenting support and the lowest household incomes. Grandmother grandfather families were the most affluent. In addition, custodial grandmothers in these households had more parenting help than grandmothers who were raising grandchildren alone.

Due to the high levels of stress and health problems suffered by surrogate grandmothers and great-grandmothers they have a variety of unmet social-service needs. Some of these needs have been met by the recent growth of several major self-help groups such as "Grandparents Raising Grandkids" (see

Chapter 17). Burton (1992) provides one of the more extensive discussions of the types of services that black grandparents and great-grandparents who were surrogate parents indicate that they need. Respite care from parenting responsibilities was a frequently mentioned need. Many surrogate parents reported that they could not afford the costs of high quality child care or baby-sitting. Being concerned that child protective services would remove the grandchild if there was any question about the quality of child care, these women chose to forgo the opportunity to have a break from caregiving (Burton, 1992). Additional services required by surrogate parents include legal counseling that addresses issues of guardianship and foster care, financial guidance and assistance, substance-abuse seminars, counseling for depression and anxiety, and access to appropriate resources and care for their own health concerns. (Burton, 1992).

Black Grandparents' Receipt of Informal Social Support

Presently only a limited amount of research addresses the assistance that black grandparents receive from their informal social-support networks. The general research on support networks of black Americans indicates that older blacks have strong supportive networks consisting of family, friends, and church members (Taylor, 1985; Taylor & Chatters, 1986a, 1986b). Older blacks with children have a distinct support advantage relative to their childless counterparts; they are more likely to receive assistance from both family (Taylor, 1985) and church members (Taylor & Chatters, 1986a) and have a larger network of people that they can draw upon for assistance when confronting a health (Chatters, Taylor, & Jackson, 1985) or mental health problem (Chatters, Taylor, & Neighbors, 1989). In addition, older blacks with children indicated that they were affectively closer to their families and engaged in more frequent interactions with their family members (Taylor, Chatters, & Jackson, 1993).

Taylor, Chatters, and Jackson (1993) provide one of the few analyses of the support networks of black grandparents. Consistent with the general research on the importance of kin ties among black Americans, black grandparents were well integrated in informal social-support networks. Grandparents interacted with their family members on a frequent basis, displayed a higher degree of family affection, and were fairly frequent recipients of informal help from extended kin. Grandparents indicated that they were affectively closer to their intergenerational family members than the members of the parent or child generations. In addition, the type of assistance received by grandparents tended to reflect the salient needs of this generation. Members of the grandparent generation indicated that goods and services (e.g., cooking, housekeeping, small repairs), companionship, and transportation were the most important types of assistance received from family members.

CONCLUSION AND DIRECTIONS FOR FUTURE RESEARCH

Since 1960, there have been significant changes in the marital status of black adults and shifts in family structure. These changes in family demography increase the likelihood that parents and grandchildren will require the assistance of grandparents to provide parenting support, economic resources, and housing. However, despite the continued role of grandparents in African American families, it is important to note that black grandparenthood is in transition (Burton & Dilworth-Anderson, 1991). Changes in black family demography and mortality have led to greater diversity in the structure and age composition of multigeneration family lineages. These demographic shifts will increase the complexity of cross-generation relationships and the functioning of multigeneration family systems. Attempts to adequately assess and understand the diversity and complexity of African American grandparenthood must build on what we have learned and integrate the theoretical and methodological traditions that have emerged from population-specific research. The sections below highlight directions for future research and theory building for the main topics of inquiry addressed in this chapter.

Culture and Symbolic Meaning of Grandparenthood

The impact of culture versus structural (e.g., racism, discrimination) and demographic (e.g., socioeconomic status, marriage patterns) factors on racial differences in intergenerational family patterns or processes is a frequently revisited topic. A number of studies find that economic factors and demographic characteristics are predictors of intergenerational support and assistance (Chatters & Taylor, 1993; Hofferth, 1984; Hogan, Hao, & Parish, 1990). African Americans are more likely to be poor and have higher rates of single parenthood and unmarried child bearing than do white Americans, but these factors alone do not explain racial differences in intergenerational family patterns (e.g., living arrangements, exchange, support networks) (Mutran, 1985; Raley, 1995; Richards, White, & Tsui, 1987; Tienda & Angel, 1982). To view intergenerational family patterns as primarily a reaction to demographic or economic circumstances ignores meanings, expectations, or belief systems that may underlie specific responses to family crises or non-normative events. Cultural background does produce organizing principles that inform its members, and it is important to recognize that heterogeneity in individual/family beliefs within racial/ethnic groups, life history, and experience, and that demographic characteristics are important sources of within-group variation.

African American family research has been shaped by debates about culture and its impact on the evolution and contemporary status of black families (Allen, 1978; Hunter, 1993; McDaniel, 1990; Staples, 1971). Grandparenting, particularly the involved grandparenting role, is both the subject of folklore and a matter of tradition in many African American families. Perhaps there have been so few quantitative and qualitative investigations of the grandparent role among African Americans because the nature of grandparenthood in black families has been largely assumed. The few studies that have examined role perceptions find racial differences in grandchildren's and grandparents' perceptions of the grandparent role, with African Americans placing greater emphasis on involvement and integration. However, we know little about the configuration of role meanings among African Americans and how they map onto those found in other populations. Similarly, there is little information on how role meanings and expectations vary by class, region, community, residence, intergenerational family structure, or other measures of family context (Burton & Bengtson, 1985; Timberlake & Chipchungu, 1992). Timing of the transition to grandparenthood is associated with variations in role meanings and the desire to fulfill a role. For example, younger grandmothers appear to perceive aspects of the grandparenting role (e.g., generative functions) differently than older grandmothers (Timberlake & Chipungu, 1992). No study to our knowledge examines continuities and discontinuities in role perceptions of early and on-time grandparents as they age and/or as characteristics of grandchildren shift (i.e., number, age, and gender composition).

Family Context of Grandparenthood

The impact of family structure and the organization of kinship systems on grandparenting in African American families has, historically, been a central issue. However, the interpretive lens has varied over time—that is, family pathology or family strengths. As a result, research traditions have focused either on viewing the unique features of black grandparenthood (1) against the backdrop of single parenthood and family crisis or (2) as an outgrowth of the centrality of extended kin groups in African American family systems. The former line of inquiry tell us something about under what conditions grandparenting is likely to take specific forms (e.g., as parental surrogate). The latter directs attention to the social organization of families, the diveristy and complexity of kinship, and to the cultural foundations of families.

Currently, one direction of grandparenthood research focuses on understanding grandparenting roles and behaviors within the context of emergent intergenerational family structures. Of particular interest is the impact of shifts in mortality and fertility, as well as the diversity that results from non-normative (off-time or early) childbearing. Ethnographic descriptions of African American families provide a conceptual lens that complements and extends current thinking about intergenerational family contexts. Hence, in addition to intergenerational family structure, African American research has highlighted the importance of extended kinship systems, personal kindreds and networks, and extended-family living arrangements as contexts for intergenerational family relationships and grandparent involvement. It also directs attention to not only structure and form, but the content (e.g., system of mutual aid, nature, and quality of relationships) of these network relationships. However, driven largely by concerns about early childbearing in African American families, age-condensed intergenerational family structures in poor communities have received the most attention. Although an important line of inquiry, it does not represent the diversity in African American family lineages. This is a critical oversight in the study of African American grandparenthood. In addition, the increasingly diverse landscape of American families and the rise in the reliance on fictive and nonfictive kindreds across ethnicity, class, and sexual orientation suggest the integration of the theoretical and methodological traditions of studies of African grandparenthood and intergenerational family relationships.

Grandparental Involvement and the Provision of Social Support

The most extensive literature on grandparenthood in African American families addresses what grandparents do—including parenting activities and providing economic and social support to parents and grandchildren. This work clearly indicates that grandparents, both male and female, are often an invaluable resource for African American parents and grandchildren. Work in this area has emphasized the conditions (e.g., single parenthood, early childbearing, parental crisis) under which grandparents are mobilized to provide help. However, the effect of factors such as relationship quality (e.g., closeness, conflict, history), intergenerational solidarity, or personality are less frequently examined. Beyond the fact that African American grandparents provide various types of assistance when needed, we know little about the processes involved in support mobilization.

Given the extensiveness of the literature on grandparent behaviors, some attention to methodological issues is warranted. As noted in recent reviews (Aldous, 1995), studies of grandparenthood are often based on small and nonrepresentative samples. Despite the sampling biases associated with small samples, intensive studies of African American families and intergenerational relationships remain an important tool for exploring grandparenthood. In the case of African American families, exploratory methodologies (focus groups, intensive interviews) may be particularly useful for addressing the many questions that have yet to be posed. A number of current national studies that include African Americans provide baseline data for the study of grandparenthood and intergenerational relationships. The National Survey of Black Americans, however, is the only national study that is culturally grounded in the experiences of African Americans. Community studies that combine large-scale survey methods with more intensive ethnographic techniques provide a synthesis of qualitative and quantitative approaches that can address the need for both breadth and specificity in research on African American grandparenthood (Chatters & Jayakody, 1995).

In conclusion, empirical evidence indicates that grandparents are an important resource for the functioning of black families. Although the last decade has seen a considerable increase in research on black grandparents, this body of work is still small in comparison to the literature on white grandparents. Research and theory on African American families has historically been linked to a broader political discourse on race which tended to emphasize the functioning and roles of grandparents in relation to the challenges and difficulties faced by black families (e.g., single motherhood, poverty). As a consequence, studies of African American grandparents have largely addressed separate and distinct research questions and/or demonstrated a preoccupation with the investigation of simple race differences in the behaviors and attitudes of grandparents. To a much lesser degree, work on black grandparents has been concerned with the types of substantive issues that are comparable to those represented in the literature on white grandparenthood. The goal of future research should be an understanding of black grandparents in their own right, as opposed to a focus which only views African American grandparents in a strictly comparative sense (i.e., to their white counterparts) or in relation to the specific social and economic barriers faced by black families.

Chapter 6

Grandparenthood among Hispanics

Norma Williams and Diana J. Torrez

This chapter synthesizes the existing literature on grandparenthood among Hispanics and in the process points to the need for more focused research on the role of Hispanic grandparents within the family and within the larger society. Although the study of grandparenthood dates back a number of decades, it is only recently that this topic has received considerable attention. Even so, one neglected area of research is that of Hispanic grandparenthood.

In examining Hispanic grandparenthood, we immediately encounter problems in defining the concept of Hispanic. Some social scientists prefer the term Latino to the term Hispanic; we shall use these terms interchangeably. And, as we shall observe, the concept of Hispanic or Latino refers to a group of people who are far more diverse than many students of the family, or of grandparenthood in particular, often recognize. The label Hispanic includes Mexican Americans, Mexicans, Puerto Ricans, Cubans, Central and South Americans, and Other Hispanics.

In this chapter we will first briefly discuss selected demographic patterns with respect to the Hispanic population in the United States. Then we shall discuss the historical origins of various Hispanic groups. Having sketched out their demographic and historical backgrounds, we then examine existing research on Hispanic grandparents, especially within the context of changing familial relationships. Of necessity, most of the attention is given to Mexican Americans. This is the largest sector of the Hispanic population, and most of the research on grandparenthood has been carried out on this group.

SELECTED DEMOGRAPHIC CHARACTERISTICS OF THE HISPANIC POPULATION

The U.S. Bureau of the Census defines a person as of Hispanic origin if she or he identifies his or her ancestry as Mexican, Puerto Rican, Cuban, Central and South American, or Other Hispanic cultural origin, regardless of race (Moore & Pachon, 1985). The origin or descent can be viewed as a nationality group, lineage, or country in which a person or a person's parents or ancestors were born. Thus, a person can identify him or herself as Hispanic based on the origin of his or her parents, grandparents, or some far-removed ancestors. These persons share a common language—Spanish—but they differ in terms of their historical and cultural traditions.

According to the Current Population Survey, March 1994, there were approximately 26.6 million Hispanics in the United States, constituting 9.8% of the total U.S. population (U.S. Bureau of Census, 1994a; Garcia, 1993). Of the Hispanic population, 64.1% were of Mexican origin, 10.4% Puerto Rican, 4.2% Cuban, and 14% Central and South American. The remainder fell into the category of Other Hispanic.

The Hispanic or Latino population is growing rapidly. It increased 53% during the 1980's, and some projections indicate that by the year 2050 one in five residents in the United States will be Hispanic (Tienda, 1995).

The current Hispanic population is concentrated in ten states. The largest number live in California, the second largest in Texas. Other states in the Southwest with large Hispanic populations are Arizona, New Mexico, and Colorado. In the Northeast, New York, New Jersey, and Massachusetts have sizeable Hispanic populations. In the South, it is Florida, and in the Midwest, it is Illinois (especially Chicago). It is also important to remember that the Hispanic population is largely urban, not rural, in character. This population is typically poor when compared to non-Hispanic whites. "The data show that in 1995, median household income rose for every other ethnic and racial group, but for the nation's 27 million Hispanic residents it dropped 5.1%" (Goldberg, 1997).

The Hispanic population is younger than the non-Hispanic white population and younger than the black population. In March 1994, 32.4% of all Hispanic persons were under 16-years-old, compared to 23.1% for the non-Hispanic white population. By contrast, 5.1% of Hispanics and 12.7% of non-Hispanic whites were age 65 years and over. There are important variations in the age patterns within subgroupings of the Hispanic population. For instance, the median age for Cubans was 41 in 1994, for the Mexican origin population it was 23 (U.S. Bureau of Census, 1994c). Yet, it is evident that the number of Hispanic elderly will increase in the years to come. One projection indicates that the number of Hispanic elderly will increase from 1 million to 2.5 million by 2010 and to about 5.6 million by 2050 (Angel & Hogan, 1992). As a result we can expect a considerable increase in the absolute number of grandparents (Gelfand, 1994).

Extended-living arrangements, including grandparents and grandchildren, are somewhat more common among Hispanics than among non-Hispanic whites, but less frequent than among either African Americans or Asians. In 1993, 5.9% of all Hispanic children lived in the home of their grandparents, compared with 3.3% for non-Hispanic whites and 12.1 for blacks (Saluter, 1994b; see also Szinovacz, 1998; Chapter 7). However, social scientists know little from these data about the actual familial arrangements as defined by those persons who are interacting in these relationships.

HISTORICAL DEVELOPMENT OF HISPANIC SUBGROUPS

We cannot conduct research on grandparenthood among Hispanics effectively without taking into account the different historical and cultural experiences that have shaped the lives of various Hispanic subgroups (Moore & Pachon, 1985; Moore & Pinderhughes, 1993). These groups differ significantly from one another, a fact social researchers must take into account (Aponte, 1991).

To put matters somewhat differently, the cultural traditions of Mexican Americans are not the same as those of Cuban Americans, and these, in turn differ from the cultural traditions of Puerto Ricans. Moreover, these groups occupy different social positions in the U.S. social order, and the positions they occupy have been strongly shaped by the way particular minority groups have come to be defined within the larger society. Although we cannot trace out the complexity of the historical and cultural relationships within this chapter, we suggest that researchers need to consider this social and cultural diversity within the Hispanic or Latino population when they study grandparent roles.

We begin with Mexican Americans (often referred to as Chicanos). Spanish explorers came into the Southwest as early as the sixteenth century. This area was once part of Mexico's northern frontier. In the early 1800's Anglos began moving into the region, and one of the consequences of the Anglo incursion was the Mexican American War. The United States defeated Mexico, and this led to the Treaty of Guadalupe Hidalgo (1848). Thus, what is now Texas, New Mexico, Arizona, and California became part of the United States, and the Mexican American minority group was initially created as a result of conquest (Montejano, 1987).

Early on there were important regional differences among Mexican Americans. The Mexican Americans in Texas differed from those in New Mexico, and these groups differed from those in California. Also, there were class distinctions among Mexican Americans in each of these regions (Moore & Pachon, 1985).

The complexity of the Mexican American population has been compounded by various waves of immigration of Mexicans into the United States. For instance, during the 1980's even in the face of increased restrictions on immigration, the number of immigrants from Mexico into the United States was considerable. Unlike Cubans or many Central Americans, the immigration from Mexico to the United States was primarily for economic reasons.

Puerto Ricans began arriving in the aftermath of the Spanish American War when the United States took possession of Puerto Rico (Sanchez-Ayendez, 1988). Puerto Rico became a commonwealth in 1952, and this facilitated increased migration from the island.

The first migration wave of Puerto Ricans was in the period 1900–1945; the second wave, known as "the great migration," occurred between 1946 and 1964. These migrants settled primarily in New York City. The third wave of migrants, from 1965 to the present, is termed "the revolving door migration," and these persons have been more dispersed and are settling in cities in the Northeast and the Midwest (Rodriguez, 1997).

A striking feature of the Puerto Rican population is its overall poverty. They are the poorest of the Hispanic population groups; they are poorer than blacks. Explaining this pattern poses significant problems for scholars (Tienda, 1995).

The third group of Hispanics are Cubans. Although some Cubans trickled into the United States after the Spanish American War, the main migration of Cubans came as a result of the rise of the Castro regime. Since then, four waves of immigrants have been delineated (Garcia, 1996). The first wave, and perhaps the most important one, consisted of a privileged educated and professional group. They were largely white, and they were treated as bonafide refugees. They secured state and federal assistance and established a significant political, social, and economic presence in, for example, Miami. More recent waves have been less privileged.

The fourth group of Hispanics includes persons escaping from political repression in El Salvador and Guatemala, who typically have not been accorded bonafide refugee status. Also, included in this fourth group are Dominicans and others from Latin America. The fifth group—Other Hispanics—is a residual category.

THE ROLE OF HISPANIC GRANDPARENTS

Against this brief demographic and historical background, we can examine grandparenthood among Hispanics or Latinos. We have located a few studies of grandparenthood for Cubans, Puerto Ricans, and Central and South Americans. Markides and Mindel's (1987) observation that research on Hispanic families and Hispanic elderly is lacking and focused primarily on Mexican Americans still holds true today. We shall first describe the few existing studies on Hispanic grandparents who are not of Mexican American origin and then proceed to a more detailed discussion of grandparenthood among Mexican Americans.

Raphael (1989) conducted interviews with ten Hispanic grandparents in a senior center in a low-income area of New York. In the main, Raphael's study suggests rather close bonds between grandparents and grandchildren. Rogler and Cooney (1991) studied intergenerational relationships between parents and their children in a Puerto Rican community in New York, and they also emphasized the importance of intergenerational familial ties (see also Bastida 1988; Bastida & Gonzalez, 1993). Also, Hernandez's (1992) discussion of Cuban elderly might be useful to some students of grandparenthood.

Most of the published research on Hispanic grandparents, however, has been carried out on Mexican Americans. But before surveying this literature, we must place the problem of grandparenthood in a larger social context, in particular with respect to the debates concerning familism and ethnicity.

A number of social scientists have long held the view that Mexican Americans have strong familistic (especially extended-family) bonds. Such an emphasis has resulted from the confluence of a number of social factors. One is the stereotype regarding Mexican Americans held by Anglo scholars. Second, the public at large and even many social scientists confuse Mexican immigrants with Mexican Americans. Familistic patterns in Mexico cannot be equated with the familistic patterns of Mexican Americans. That differences between Mexican immigrants and Mexican Americans exist finds support in recent research (Angel, Angel, McClellan, & Markides, 1996). Third, a number of the early and highly influential studies of Mexican Americans—notably those by Madsen (1964) and Rubel (1966)—were carried out in small towns in South Texas. These small communities should not be taken as the basis for generalizing about family life in contemporary urban settings (Williams, 1990).

Grebler, Moore, and Guzman (1970), in their major work on Mexican Americans, questioned the views of social scientists regarding familism (particularly extended-family ties) among Mexican Americans. Moore (1971) was even more pointed in her criticisms with respect to overstating familial bonds among the Mexican American elderly (see also Gratton, 1987). Sotomayor (1973), in her early research on Mexican American grandparents, took note of the debate about familism. This debate continues to permeate the literature (cf. Vega, 1991). The dangers of overemphasizing familistic ties has been raised by Maldonado (1978) who contended that the emphasis on the extended family may serve to undermine the need for social services which the Mexican American elderly, for instance, can rightly claim as citizens.

More generally, the problem of familism becomes linked to the researcher's assumptions regarding the process of assimilation (Williams et al., 1995). Hispanics are acculturated, but typically not assimilated. Acculturation occurs when members of the minority group acquire social and cultural patterns that permit them to participate within certain sectors of the majority society; assimilation occurs when the minority group is socially and culturally accepted by the majority sector of the society. A number of researchers employ the "Anglo model" as a standard when studying Mexican American family life, for they assume that Mexican Americans are becoming like Anglos. That many Hispanics because of discrimination are excluded from full participation in the society is often not taken into account when researchers analyze their data. In addition, both Anglo American and Mexican American familial patterns have been undergoing rapid change for decades (Williams, 1990). What are the ideal or actual familial patterns even among Anglos is the subject of considerable debate. Thus, researchers must carefully consider which standard they employ when evaluating their research findings.

In reviewing the literature on Mexican American grandparents, we shall emphasize those publications that report original research. One of the pioneering efforts was carried out by Sotomayor (1973, 1989). In her unpublished doctoral dissertation (1973), she analyzed the research that she carried out in a barrio in Denver, Colorado. She interviewed 38 grandparents in a poor neighborhood. They were 55 years of age and older, with only four under 60 years of age. She was interested in understanding the perceptions that both grandfathers and grandmothers had of their roles. First, most of the grandparents believed that they had an important function in helping to rear their grandchildren. Many of the respondents believed that they should stand ready to rear their grandchildren if anything happened to the parents of the children. Second, they viewed themselves as having responsibility for grandchildren in times of crises, especially economic ones. A number saw themselves as a source of support in times of sorrow. Third, they perceived themselves as having credible authority and influence in the decision-making process with respect to grandchildren. Fourth, the grandparents also perceived the grandmother as having religious influence. However, as Sotomayor indicated, there was a "falling away" of this function for grandmothers. Fifth, the question of responsibility for transmitting the cultural heritage was raised. In this realm, the grandparents who were interviewed seemed to view themselves as having declining influence—for example, with regard to the transmission of the Spanish language.

A second body of findings has resulted from the research conducted by Bengtson and his colleagues (Bengtson, 1985; Dowd & Bengtson, 1978) in Los Angeles County in 1975. They surveyed intergenerational relationships among blacks, Mexican Americans, and whites.

Bengtson and his colleagues concluded that minorities in the sample were quite heterogenous. In fact, there were no "minority versus white" patterns. By that they meant that Mexican Americans clearly had a different pattern from blacks and whites, and the last two groups were closer to one another than they were to Mexican Americans.

With respect to intergenerational connections, Mexican Americans, in comparison to blacks and whites, had many more children, grandchildren, and great-grandchildren who might serve as a potential source of social support. Compared to blacks and whites, they derived greater satisfaction from contacts with their grandchildren. Mexican Americans also reported more frequent contact across generations, and they had greater expectations of intergenerational assistance than did blacks and whites.

In addition, 66% of Mexican Americans wanted to live in the same neighborhood as did their children, whereas only one-third of blacks and one-fifth of whites expressed this desire. Fifty percent of Mexican Americans in the survey reported that they wanted to live with a child, whereas only 10% of the blacks and 4% of the whites wanted to do so.

A third body of data is provided by Schmidt and Padilla (1983). They conducted telephone interviews with Mexican American grandparents. The respondents, who lived in the Los Angeles area, were selected via a snowball sample. The focus of the study was on the interaction behavior of these grandparents with their grandchildren between ages 3 and 12 who did not live in the same household. The unit of analysis was the "dyad" (grandparent and grandchild).

In a more specific sense, Schmidt and Padilla studied the reported interaction of grandfathers and grandmothers (ages 43 to 76) with grandchildren. One hypothesis was that interaction would increase along the sex-blood line. The data partially supported this thesis. Thus, grandmothers, in contrast to grandfathers, reported that they spoke Spanish more often with their grandchildren, and they did this more often with children of daughters, especially when the grandchildren were female. A second hypothesis was that grandmothers and grandfathers reacted differently and that they varied their actions with the sex of the grandchild. The data did not support this thesis. "Both grandmothers and grandfathers reported being involved in the socialization of grandchildren, and this involvement is not significantly different" (Schmidt & Padilla, 1983: 196).

A fourth body of data that related to the grandparent role is the result of research carried out by Markides and his colleagues in San Antonio, Texas. They first conducted a series of studies on the aged Mexican American population of San Antonio (Markides, Martin, & Gomez, 1983); this was followed by an investigation in the early 1980's of three generations of Mexican Americans. Their sample included older Mexican Americans (aged 65–80) living in San Antonio who had a child in the metropolitan area. This child, in turn, had to have an adult (18-years-old or over) married or previously married child who resided within a 50–mile radius of San Antonio (Markides, Boldt, & Ray, 1986; Markides & Krause, 1985). A summary of selected findings of these early studies can be found in Markides and Martin (1990). Currently Markides and colleagues are beginning to publish findings from a follow-up investigation of their intergenerational study of the early 1980's, but the full results of this recent research have yet to appear (Levin, Markides, & Ray, 1996).

In their earlier work on the Mexican American aged, Markides, Martin, and Gomez (1983) found that the elderly did not have a privileged position in the extended family. Their findings challenged the conclusions of many previous researchers. With respect to their three-generations study, they discovered a highly supportive and interdependent network of relationships, especially between parents and their children. Mexican Americans relied upon advice and help from members of the family, not from friends and nonrelatives (Markides, Boldt, & Ray, 1986; Markides & Martin, 1990). At the same time, they observed that grandparents did not rely upon grandchildren for advice and help (Markides, Boldt, & Ray, 1986).

The patterns of help and advice indicate that grandparents relied on their children and these patterns tended to be gender specific. The women typically carried out expressive roles and the men carried out instrumental ones. For example, women were relied upon in health matters and men were relied upon in house repairs and upkeep.

Another finding that bears, at least indirectly, on the role of grandparents relates to the association between solidarity and psychological well-being. High levels of association with children were significantly related to higher levels of depressive symptoms among the elderly, leading to the speculation that the dependency role may be the source of distress (Markides & Martin, 1990).

Another research study that bears on the patterns of Mexican American grandparenthood—in this instance grandmothers—is that carried out by Facio (1996, chapter 5). Unlike much of the other research, Facio's study is qualitative in nature. She interviewed 30 Chicanas that were 50 years of age and older who were contacted through a senior center located in a suburban area of northern California. Of the 30 interviewees, 28 were grandmothers; some were greatgrandmothers. Facio concentrates on the cultural expectations placed on grandmothers. From her discussion of grandmothers, we have identified four types of roles that they carried out. A few were alienated from their grandchildren, but the other grandmothers functioned as caregivers, in a parental role or as cultural teachers. However, some of the grandmothers, according to Facio, were reluctant to take on the role of serving as a parent.

Research by Williams (1993) on elderly Mexican Americans in Dallas, Texas, provides some additional clues concerning the roles of grandparents. She conducted in-depth interviews with 60 Mexican American elderly in 1991, using a snowball sample. In addition, participant observation was used. Except for seven persons, the elderly were in the age group 60–85; five were under 60 years of age, and two were over 85. Most of the respondents were grandparents and provided information on relationships with their children and grandchildren.

Several characteristics of the sample should be noted. In general the respondents were poor; some were very poor. They had suffered from discrimination throughout their life course, and some specifically observed how past discrimination had shaped their present circumstances. The bulk of the respondents had moved into Dallas from elsewhere, primarily from other regions of the state. They were products of the urbanization, industrialization, and bureaucratization that has dramatically changed the landscape of the Southwest during the period they had lived.

As for their roles as grandparents, a few were alienated from their children and grandchildren. A few were functioning in a parental role. For example, some grandparents were helping their daughters in raising their grandchildren. Most of the grandparents served as providers for their children and grandchildren. The research carried out in Dallas suggests that there is considerable asymmetry in the relationship between grandparents and their children and grandchildren. With respect to reciprocity, the grandparents, despite their poverty, appear to be contributing more to the general well-being of their children and grandchildren than the latter are assisting the grandparents. The children and grandchildren were busy with their own lives, and inasmuch as they, too, were also struggling to make ends meet, they could do very little to assist their grandparents economically and socially.

The research conducted in Dallas indicates that the elderly lacked knowledge about how to secure social services (Sotomayor, 1973). The elderly do not have children or grandchildren who could assist them in acquiring such services as health care; however, these are essential for a minimum quality of life (Williams, 1994). The children and grandchildren do not have the necessary education to serve as brokers between grandparents and the social service organizations within the community. Many of the respondents lacked the educational background to interact directly with social-service agencies. The Mexican Americans often spoke Spanish as their first language, and the staff of social-service agencies typically did not speak or understand Spanish.

CONCLUSIONS AND IMPLICATIONS

This chapter has surveyed the limited literature on Hispanic grandparents. Cherlin and Furstenberg (1986a), in their major study of grandparents, observed that the numbers of Hispanics and Asian Americans were too small to enable them to draw any conclusions. The neglect of Hispanics is symptomatic of the fact that many social researchers continue to ignore this group.

In generalizing about Hispanics or Latinos we must consistently be aware of the fact that the Hispanic population is culturally diverse. As noted earlier, the cultural traditions of Mexican Americans, Puerto Ricans, Cuban Americans, and Central and South Americans differ significantly from one another, and these groups occupy different social positions in the society. Because of the limited amount of data on Hispanic grandparents and because of the differences among various groups of Hispanics, social scientists have only scratched the surface of this important problem area.

At this point we are able to step back and consider some of the main patterns that run through the research efforts to date. One group of scholars (Raphael, 1989; Rogler & Cooney, 1991) stresses the importance of cultural traditions such as familism in their analysis of these findings. At the same time, social and cultural changes are occurring, and social scientists should realize that Hispanic grandparents are engaged in shaping their roles not only within their own cultural frame of reference but also within the larger society. Thus, the research conducted by Williams (1993) indicates that grandparents were being called upon to engage in a great deal of role making, and consequently they were reconstituting their own cultural heritage. They engaged in role making to cope with the problems that they encounter within contemporary U.S. society. Hispanic grandparents are proactive in reshaping their roles not only with regard to their children and grandchildren but also with regard to their interactions with organizational structures, but they face major obstacles in their efforts.

Scholars who study intergenerational relationships among parents, children, and grandchildren tend to study the family as a self-contained unit. However, this is an unsatisfactory orientation for studying minority grandparent relationships among Hispanics. Scholars should examine the grandparent role within a larger social context for a number of reasons.

First, as noted above, historical and cultural data indicate that Mexican American families differ from Cuban and Puerto Rican families (Tran & Dhooper, 1996). These differences can be considerable. However, few studies that discuss the social and cultural dynamics of familial relationships have compared these three groups. Instead, researchers often focus on how Hispanics differ from Anglos and how Hispanics differ from Anglos and blacks. Social scientists need to carry out more comparisons among Hispanic groups, while keeping in mind that these groups differ along class and gender lines.

Second, with respect to Hispanics, grandparent relationships are affected by the group's position in the larger society. Students of the family, including those who study grandparents, tend to sidestep the issue of how ethnicity affects the relationships among grandparents, children, and grandchildren. One might surmise that the patterns of acculturation differ for grandparents, children, and grandchildren. For example, grandchildren are likely to be more fluent in English, but we do not have careful studies of the consequences of this difference.

Third, we require more detailed research on how grandparent relationships with children, grandchildren, and great-grandchildren are embedded in the organizational context of the community. The stability of family relationships is to a considerable extent related to the amount of community support—for example, education and social services—that family members are able to secure. Thus, if contemporary urban families are to remain stable, they require considerable community and organizational support.

The issues we have raised point to a sizeable agenda for students who carry out research on Hispanic grandparenthood in the United States. If scholars are to understand family life and grandparenthood among Mexican Americans, Puerto Ricans, Cubans, and Central and South Americans, they must carry out far more in-depth investigations of these groups.

NOTE

We thank Gideon Sjoberg and Hiram J. Friedsam for their helpful critical comments on earlier versions of this chapter.

Chapter 7

Asian Grandparents

Yoshinori Kamo

Grandparents of Asian origins have diverse backgrounds. They come from different countries of origin; some were born in the United States and many others immigrated; some grandparents have strong ties with their countries of origin while others do not. Although there is diversity among Asian grandparents, they still have much in common. Most, if not all, come from Confucian backgrounds and many are Buddhists. Past research has found that both elderly Japanese and Chinese Americans are more likely to live with their adult children than their non-Hispanic white counterparts (Kamo & Zhou, 1994), and this pattern may be common to elderly Asians of many different countries of origins.

Research on grandparenthood entails diverse aspects of grandparent-grandchild contacts, including association, affection and consensus, exchange of services, and kin expectations (Bengtson & Harootyan, 1994; Kamo, 1995a; Kivett, 1993; Mancini & Blieszner, 1989; see also Chapter 10). This chapter will focus on demographic and social psychological factors surrounding Asian grandparents. They include immigration and assimilation history, the notion of filial piety based on Confucianism, living arrangements, interaction styles between grandparents and grandchildren, and socialization of grandchildren.

HISTORICAL AND CULTURAL BACKGROUNDS OF ASIAN FAMILIES

To examine issues surrounding Asian grandparents, we need to look at cultural backgrounds in their countries of origin. While Buddhism has been widely practiced in East Asian countries such as China, Japan, Korea, and Vietnam, Christianity has been popular in the Philippines, Vietnam, and Korea, and Hinduism has been dominant in India. These religions, however, have not contributed much to form unique characteristics and social norms among Asians. A more common influence was Confucianism, which originated in China as one of its moral codes. Many countries in East Asia such as China, Taiwan, Korea, and Japan adopted Confucianism. Expressed in books compiled for collections of sayings by Confucius (551–479 B.C.), Confucianism has become the center of ethics in many Asian countries.

Confucian ethics emphasize status differences among persons based on gender and age, and stress family life. One of the major parts in Confucianism is the notion of filial piety or filial responsibility. Filial responsibility is defined as "the responsibility for parents exercised by children. The term emphasizes duty rather than satisfaction and is usually connected with protection, care, or financial support" (Schorr, 1980: 1). Normatively, filial piety prescribes respect for and a sense of obligation toward one's parents and ancestors. The second verse of the Analects (or Lun Yü in Chinese), which is mostly a collection of Confucius' sayings, states "Those who in private life behave well towards their parents and elder brothers, in public life seldom show a disposition to resist the authority of their superiors" (Waley, 1971: 83).

When parents age, filial responsibility is enacted through personal contact with and financial and physical support for these elderly parents. Even in the Philippines, where Confucianism is not considered particularly strong among Asian countries, filial responsibility is emphasized and practiced (Blust & Scheidt, 1988).

Confucianism emphasizes not only filial responsibility but also hierarchy by gender. Thus, elderly fathers/grandfathers rather than mothers/grandmothers possess the final authority of the family. Family membership and family property are most often inherited through the paternal line, from father to son (called patrilineal descent). Married women belong to their husbands' family, rather than their own (see also Chapter 3).

Derived from filial responsibility and gender hierarchy, another related and dominant theme among Asians and Asian Americans is coresidence with elderly parents, particularly husband's parents (called patrilocality). Combined with patrilineal descent, this living arrangement has helped husbands or their mothers dominate their wives or daughters-in-law, strengthening gender hierarchy in Asian countries. These extended-family households often include grandchildren. De Vos and Lee, referring to Korean families, summarize the notion of filial piety and gender hierarchy among Asians which emphasize coresidence with the husband's parents as follows:

The traditional, agrarian-based Korean family was patriarchal, extended, and dominated by the Confucian ethic of filial piety. Marriage did not herald in a new family but, rather, helped insure the continuation of the patrilineal, patrilocal stem family. Coresidence of old people with adult sons was the ideal and norm. It was a matter of prestige for an older parent to reside with an adult son. Attention to needs related to health care and financial support were considered normal parts of the filial relationship. This was strongest between the oldest son and his parents, since the other sons were expected to maintain separate households upon marriage. Daughters were expected to marry into other families. (1993: 377)

The expectation and practice of coresidence with elderly parents seem to vary by countries and time periods. While coresidence seems to be less commonly practiced in such industrial countries as Japan, it is far from having disappeared (Kojima, 1989; Tsuya & Martin, 1992). Parental coresidence with adult children is probably most strictly enforced in Korea (De Vos & Lee, 1993; Martin, 1989; Min, 1988), but it also is widely practiced in China (Tu, Liang, & Li, 1989), Taiwan (Freedman, Chang, & Sun, 1982; Tu, Liang, & Li, 1989), the Philippines (Martin, 1989), Vietnam (Gold, 1993), and India (Ram & Wong, 1994). The above description of coresidence with parents more or less applies to all Asian countries from which immigrants came to the United States.

For coresidence with elderly parents, whether the adult child is married or not is irrelevant, and whether the elderly parent is still married, widowed, or divorced is not relevant either. Coresidence is usually not for any tangible needs such as caretaking of the elderly parents or assisting the adult children in their economic insufficiency; rather it is a normative arrangement, derived from patrilocal residence rules.

Elderly parent-adult child (and grandchild) coresidence, however, is not entirely the result of filial responsibility. It is facilitated by economic factors also. Retirement pensions are either very small or nonexistent in Asian countries, and this often forces elderly parents to depend on their adult children. Yang and Chandler (1992) describe elderly parents' financial dependence on their married sons and resulting intergenerational tensions in rural China. On the other hand, grandparents in Asian countries may play an active role in their three-generation households in household work and child care. Olson (1990: 144), for example, quotes an elderly Chinese man as follows: "She (my wife) does all the cooking and also takes care of the two grandchildren while my daughter-in-law goes off to work. . . . I usually spend a little time playing with the grandson who is three."

IMMIGRATION AND ASSIMILATION OF ASIAN GRANDPARENTS

Immigrations from Asian countries have fluctuated in the past century due to internal and external reasons (Kitano & Daniels, 1995). During the late nineteenth century, Asian immigrants were primarily Chinese males who were seeking gold or hired for physical labor such as railroad construction and farm jobs. Japanese immigrants soon joined them, followed by Filipinos (at that time Filipino workers were not immigrants since their land was a U.S. territory). Due to various anti-Asian legislations in the early 1920's, legal immigrations from

Asian countries (again, except the Philippines) halted except for family reunion purposes until 1965.

A new immigration law in that year provided opportunities for immigration among people from Asia. A large number of Chinese immigrated following the new immigration law, while the immigration from Japan never rebounded to the level of the pre-1920 period. In the meantime, the Vietnam War and the subsequent Communist takeover in 1975 prompted the first wave of Vietnamese immigrants to the United States, estimated at 130,000 (Gold, 1993). The second wave of immigrants from Vietnam of more than 400,000 followed the Vietnam-China conflict of 1978 (Gold, 1993). The recent political turmoil in Southeast Asia led to a flood of new immigrants from Cambodia and Laos. Primarily due to its political and economic instability, South Korea sent a large number of immigrants to the United States after the 1965 immigration law came into effect. The Korean population in the United States increased from 69,000 in 1970 to 350,000 in 1980, and to 800,000 in 1990 (Min, 1993). Thus, "Asian immigrants" or "Asian grandparents" do not consist of a homogeneous group. They not only came from various countries but also had different immigration histories.

Because several immigration waves occurred fairly recently, many Asian and Hispanic elderly were born outside the United States. Many others are children of immigrants. Before they immigrated to the United States or when they were raised by immigrant parents, their life styles and/or cultural values were much different from those of mainstream Americans. Even now, many Asian grandparents speak languages other than English, eat their traditional foods, believe in non-Christian religions, and/or have different values from white grandparents on many issues (Ishii-Kuntz, forthcoming; Kitano & Daniels, 1995). This is particularly true among Korean, Vietnamese, Cambodian, and Laotian grandparents who came to the United States recently. Even among such "traditional" Asian Americans as Chinese and Japanese, many grandparents are immigrants themselves or children of immigrants (second-generation Asian Americans). In sum, many Asian grandparents are not fully acculturated to the American society.

On the other hand, some young Asians, particularly Japanese, Filipino, and Asian Indians, have been well assimilated into the mainstream society through education, occupation, residential assimilation, and intermarriages (Kitano & Daniels, 1995). Thus, normative and/or cultural changes associated with modernization (Goode, 1963) may be reflected within each immigrant's family as grandparents live by more traditional values while their grandchildren are more attuned to "modern" American values. Such value and life style differences most likely have profound effects on the interaction between grandparents and grandchildren as we will see later.

The 1990 Census data on the immigration status of older and younger Asian Americans demonstrate these generational differences.[1] Moreover, many grandparents of Asian Americans are not in the United States but rather, in their

Table 7.1
Proportions of Foreign-Born Persons among Various Ethnic/Racial Groups

	Total	Foreign-Born	
55 Years or Older			
Non-Hispanic White	44,529,852	2,399,522	5.39%*
Black	4,496,389	159,549	3.55%*
Hispanic	2,222,293	1,037,484	46.69%
All Asians	875,874	652,368	74.48%
Chinese	254,683	212,697	83.51%
Japanese	214,287	62,495	29.16%
Filipino	194,987	177,074	90.81%
Korean	77,066	72,299	93.81%
Asian Indian	54,656	52,478	96.02%
Vietnamese	38,955	38,134	97.89%
19 Years or Younger			
Non-Hispanic White	49,275,787	369,140	0.75%*
Black	10,673,253	163,519	1.53%*
Hispanic	8,474,669	1,342,676	15.84%
All Asians	2,163,471	742,311	34.31%
Chinese	439,940	150,662	34.25%
Japanese	178,911	38,554	21.55%
Filipino	437,648	108,110	24.70%
Korean	277,789	91,634	32.99%
Asian Indian	256,142	87,333	34.10%
Vietnamese	227,487	117,028	51.44%

*Since exact numbers are not available from published sources, these numbers are estimated from
  Public Use Microdata Samples.

Sources: U.S. Bureau of the Census (1993), 1990 Census of Population, Social and Economic
  Characteristics, United States (1990 CP-2-1, table 40); 1990 Census of Population, Asians and
  Pacific Islanders in the United States (1990 CP-3-5, table 1); 1990 Census of Population,
  Persons of Hispanic Origin in the United States (1990 CP-3-3, table 1).

countries of origin. Table 7.1 shows the proportions of foreign-born persons
among the elderly population (55 years or older) and young population (19 years
or younger) for the six largest Asian American groups (Chinese, Filipino, Japanese, Asian Indian, Korean, and Vietnamese), non-Hispanic whites, blacks, and

Hispanics. The majority of elderly Asian Americans (except for Japanese Americans) were born outside the United States. Only a minority of Asian Americans in the grandchildren's generation share this characteristic of foreign birth. Except for Vietnamese Americans, the majority of young Asian persons were born in the United States.

These data show that among Asian Americans (and some Hispanic Americans), grandparent-grandchild relationships will not only be characterized by the "generation gap," but also by differences in immigration status. Once again, there are pronounced differences among the various Asian groups. Comparison of the percentages of foreign-born individuals in grandparents' and grandchildren's generations indicates that Japanese American families are least likely to experience differences in immigration status between the two generations. Only a minority of both older and younger Japanese Americans were born in Japan. Among all other Asian American groups there are large differences in the percentages of foreign-born persons between the old and young generations, suggesting that two-fifths to two-thirds of non-Japanese Asian families include foreign-born grandparents and U.S.-born grandchildren.

How much grandparents' foreign-born status impacts on their relationships with grandchildren may vary for different Asian American groups. I would expect that Chinese, Korean, and Vietnamese grandparents have a tougher time dealing with their grandchildren due to cultural differences than do their Japanese, Filipino, and Asian Indian counterparts. Most of Vietnamese Americans are political refugees who may have been forced to emigrate from their country. They thus may not have prepared to assimilate to American society, unlike some other immigrants who chose to come to the United States. Koreans and Chinese, on the other hand, chose to come to this country, but they strongly adhere to their traditional cultures which are quite different from the American mainstream culture. In their own country, they probably practiced filial responsibility more strictly than did Japanese, Filipino, and Asian Indians. Given larger gaps between their own culture and American culture, Chinese and Korean grandparents are likely to have more difficulty with their grandchildren, many of whom are completely assimilated. Poor command of English language may also contribute to difficulty in their relationships with grandchildren among Chinese, Korean, and Vietnamese grandparents. When percentages of people 55 years or older who speak English only, very well, or well (rather than not well or not at all) are calculated from the census data, they are 33% for Vietnamese, 37% for Korean, and 49% for Chinese, compared to 73% for Asian Indians, 82% for Filipinos, and 88% for Japanese.

Setting these inter-ethnic differences in assimilation and relationships with grandchildren aside, there are a couple of characteristics common to most Asian Americans that distinguish them from non-Hispanic whites. These are the notion of filial piety and coresidence between grandparents and grandchildren. These two characteristics may help facilitate interactions and enhance value consensus between grandparents and grandchildren. I will discuss these in the next sections.

spouses. Except for Japanese Americans, the majority (60%-85%) of Asian grandparents who live with their grandchildren do so in their children's households, and young Asian Americans who live with their grandparents are more likely to do so in their parents' households (in 75%-92% of these cases) rather than their grandparents'. Once again, Japanese Americans are an exception. This is in stark contrast to other racial/ethnic groups, particularly blacks, whose grandchildren are more likely to live in "downward extended households" (i.e., households headed by the grandparents). This unique pattern among Asian Americans reflects Confucian ideals and patrilocal norms of coresidence. Once they have established themselves, adult children of Asian origins often bring their elderly parents into their households. Confucian ethics, which stresses age and gender hierarchy, would suggest that most of these adult children are sons, particularly the oldest son in the family, but census data do not allow us to confirm this point.

On the other hand, coresidence between grandparents and grandchildren among Japanese Americans and other racial/ethnic groups is more likely to occur in the grandparents' household (Kamo, 1995b). In many of these cases, adult children's or grandchildren's needs are the primary reason for coresidence (Ward, Logan, & Spitze, 1992), and it is often a temporary arrangement. In these coresidence arrangements, adult children are often daughters, many of them single mothers. This pattern is particularly common among black households (Flaherty, Facteau, & Garver, 1987; Szinovacz, 1996, 1998).

While young Japanese Americans and Vietnamese Americans are both less likely to live with their grandparents, there is a clear difference when they do so. Grandparent-grandchild coresidence is much more likely to occur in the grandparents' house (downward extension) among Japanese Americans, but it is much more likely to occur in the parents' house (upward extension) among Vietnamese Americans as is the case with all other Asian American groups. While Japanese Americans seem to closely follow the pattern of non-Hispanic whites, Vietnamese Americans still adhere to the "traditionally Asian" pattern of coresidence.

INTERACTION BETWEEN GRANDPARENTS AND GRANDCHILDREN

As noted above, many young Asian Americans such as Vietnamese, Cambodians, and Laotians (see Table 7.1 for the case of Vietnamese) were born outside the United States and have their grandparents living in their home countries. In these cases, it is obvious that grandparent-grandchildren interactions have become minimal. This is exacerbated by the fact that many Asian Americans are political refugees, and, therefore, cannot communicate with family members still living in their countries of origin, including their grandparents (Gold, 1993; Uba, 1994). Likewise, many Asian grandparents, particularly those from Southeast Asia, left their grandchildren in their countries of origin in the turmoil of fleeing (Detzner, 1996).

In contrast, when grandparents live with their grandchildren in the same household (in the United States), there must be some interactions between them. Confucian ethics stress age seniority, that grandparents are to be respected and honored by their offspring, including their grandchildren. Asian grandchildren are thus expected to interact with their grandparents in a more deferential manner, use a more formal conversational style, and use more polite language (Uba, 1994). Describing Asian Americans' interactions between family members, Uba states "they (many Asian Americans) can not remember the last time that one of their parents hugged or kissed their grandchildren" (Uba, 1994: 38). Thus, expected among Asian Americans are more formal interactions between grandparents and grandchildren than among other racial/ethnic groups.

When Asian grandparents do not live with their grandchildren, do they maintain more frequent interactions than do grandparents of other races/ethnicities? Frequent interactions could be expected, given the emphasis on filial piety among Asian cultures. Lubben and Becerra (1987), however, show that elderly Chinese in California are not more likely to see their grandchildren on a regular basis, particularly compared to Mexican and black Americans. This may suggest that enactment of filial responsibility may not be as common as it used to be, or it may be in effect only in more formal aspects such as coresidence. There is a possibility that Asian Americans do not practice filial responsibility when it comes to such spontaneous behaviors as visiting and/or keeping in contact with elderly family members including grandparents.

Even when grandparents and grandchildren see each other, their primary languages may differ. Table 7.3 indicates proportions of elderly (55 or older) and young (between 5 and 19) persons who primarily speak languages other than English at home. The majority of Asian Americans of both young and old generations primarily speak non-English languages at home, except for young people of Filipino and Japanese origins. Nonetheless, there are intergenerational differences in the proportions of young and old people who primarily speak non-English languages among each Asian American group. These differences are particularly pronounced among Filipinos, followed by Asian Indians and Japanese. Thus, many Asian grandparents and their grandchildren may not share the most fundamental method of communication, language. Such language barriers will inevitably affect communication between grandparents and grandchildren in an adverse fashion. This situation parallels that among immigrant families from Europe at the turn of century. For example, in Cherlin and Furstenberg (1986a: 37) a Polish grandmother describes the relationship with her own grandmother as follows: "Well, see, my grandmother was Polish, and she couldn't speak English. But she used to come every Sunday. . . . And she'd try to speak to us—it was hard. It was hard for her to speak to us, because we all spoke English and she was Polish."

Kennedy (1992a) has shown that grandchildren's feelings that they are known

Table 7.3
Percent Who Speak Non-English Languages at Home

	55 or Older	Between 5 and 19
Non-Hispanic White	7.61	8.41
Black	3.87	6.30
Hispanic	86.71	71.15
All Asians	80.96	70.17
Chinese	88.29	77.12
Japanese	92.72	41.20
Filipino	51.59	36.59
Korean	88.15	66.84
Asian Indian	93.21	83.14
Vietnamese	98.85	92.53

Sources: 1990 Census of Population and Housing; Public Use Microdata Samples; U.S. Bureau of the Census (1992).

and understood by the grandparents and that they know and understand the grandparents are critical for successful relationships between grandparents and grandchildren. If they do not share the same language, it is rather difficult to "know" each other. Thus, speaking different languages most likely inhibits the development of close relationships between grandparents and grandchildren.

The content of grandparent-grandchild communications among Asian Americans may also differ from that of non-Hispanic white Americans as a result of the immigration history of both generations. We may conceptualize the effect of modernization on grandparent-grandchild relationships as a shift from bonds of obligation to bonds of sentiment (Cherlin & Furstenberg, 1986a). Burgess and Locke (1960) characterize this shift as that from "family as institution" to "family as companionship." They describe these two ideal types of family as follows:

In the past the important factors unifying the family have been external, formal, and authoritarian, such as the law, the mores, public opinion, tradition, the authority of the family head, rigid discipline, and elaborate ritual. In the new emerging form of the companionship family, its unity inheres less and less in community pressures and more and more in such interpersonal relations as the mutual affection, the sympathetic understanding, and the comradeship of its members. (Burgess & Locke, 1960: vii)

Filial responsibility clearly belongs to the former ideal type (family as institution) and may have prevented or delayed this shift among Asian Americans. Due to the notion of filial responsibility, relationships between Asian grandparents and grandchildren are likely to be characterized by bonds of obligation to a greater extent than are found among white Americans. Furthermore, many Asian American grandparents are immigrants themselves, and they may possess an insufficient English-speaking ability and thus may not have acquired enough retirement income or pension, rendering them economically dependent. As shown by Anderson (1977), economic dependence of one generation on the other promotes bonds of obligation, and their economic dependence might be an extra factor leading to more formal relationships between Asian grandparents and their grandchildren.

Cherlin and Furstenberg (1986a) distinguish three styles of grandparent-grandchild relationships: remote, companionate, and involved. They argue that the companionate style is the most common among American grandparents, followed by the remote, and then involved ones. Out of the respect to the parent-child relationship, grandparents usually adhere to the "norm of noninterference" and do not get involved in raising, socializing, and disciplining their grandchildren. They, however, prefer to maintain their relationships with grandchildren and thus the companionate relationship becomes the most prevalent. This is a useful classification system to describe Asian grandparents. As discussed above, many Asian grandparents live outside the United States, and this inevitably leads to the remote style of grandparenting. As Cherlin and Furstenberg claim, great geographical distance is the most common cause for the remote grandparenting style.

At the other extreme, many Asian grandparents live in the same household as their grandchildren, as shown above. In addition, under the Confucian ethics, children (and grandchildren) belong to the entire extended family, not just to their parents, as is the case among white American households. The "norm of noninterference," described by Cherlin and Furstenberg, which inhibits many grandparents from playing a surrogate parent's role, may not be as strong among Asian Americans. The combination of these factors probably leads to more "involved" grandparents among Asian Americans than among their white counterparts.

Although the companionate style is the most common type of relationship among white Americans, this style may be less common among Asian grandparents. For one thing, this type may be squeezed by the two other types, remote and involved, which are more prevalent among Asian than white American families. Also, this type of relationship requires good communication skills, affectionate expressions, and the notion of equal status between grandparents and grandchildren. Asian grandparents may not be the best candidates for these qualities. Due to the insufficient English language skills, they may not be able to communicate well with their grandchildren. Traditionally, more reserved expressions among Asians may prohibit Asian grandparents from expressing love and affection to their grandchildren (Ishii-Kuntz, forthcoming), and Confucian ethics and age seniority may lead them to regard their grandchildren as unequals. Thus, companionate relationships between Asian grandparents and their grandchildren are probably less common than among their white counterparts. However, there are as yet no reliable data to support this claim.

It should be noted that some studies suggest that the moderate levels of contact between grandparents and grandchildren typical for the companionate style may be better for the quality of the relationship than either high or low levels of contact (Tinsley & Parke, 1984). For this reason also the relationship between Asian grandparents and their grandchildren may suffer since they often live either in separate countries or in the same household.

Whereas Asian grandparents may ignore the "norm of noninterference" because of their adherence to extended-family ideals and norms of filial piety, this norm may be cherished by their children, who are more assimilated to American society (Holmes & Holmes, 1995). This disagreement may also contribute to a more strenuous and perhaps remote relationship between Asian grandparents and their children and grandchildren.

Cowgill (1974: 129) argues that "modernization results in . . . a relatively lower status of older people in society" (also see Williams & Domingo, 1993: Chapter 3). This is primarily because knowledge or wisdom possessed by elderly people is not as useful or relevant in modern society. If we conceptualize the process of immigration and assimilation as an accelerated process of modernization at the individual level, basic tenets of modernization theory on aging may apply to Asian immigrants and their families (see also Markides, Liang, & Jackson, 1990, for a different application of the modernization theory to minority aging).

Different intergenerational exposure to modernization processes is likely to result from grandparents' and grandchildren's divergent immigration status, the difference in their English skills, and the rapid assimilation of the younger generation into American society. This may lead to a pronounced generation gap and take a toll on intergenerational relationships among Asian Americans. Grandparents often do not speak English, do not communicate well with people outside their own ethnic group, and are generally less assimilated than their grandchildren. Being better assimilated into mainstream society, children and grandchildren acquire better education and better-paying, more prestigious jobs. They also know more about mainstream American culture and values. These factors may erode Asian grandparents' authority. Asian grandparents often feel they are not given the respect by grandchildren which they think is their due, rendering interactions between grandparents and grandchildren more strenuous (Detzner, 1996; Holmes & Holmes, 1995; Markides, Liang, & Jackson, 1990; Min, 1988).

SOCIALIZATION OF GRANDCHILDREN

One of the possible roles grandparents may play is that of "historians" (Kornhaber & Woodward, 1985: Chapters 1 and 3). They may transmit "values, ethnic heritage, and family traditions" (Tinsley & Parke,1984: 172) to their grandchildren either through the middle generation or through direct contacts. This is particularly important among ethnic minorities who face the duality between the adopted culture of American society and their traditional culture. Foreign-born grandparents may be able to tell their grandchildren what their countries of origin were like and what kind of life they lived before immigrating to this country.

Among Asian Americans, however, grandparents' role as family historians may differ from that of other ethnic groups. First, given their limitations in English language ability and communication skills, Asian grandparents may not transmit their values and traditional culture to their grandchildren well. Nevertheless, it is absurd to assume that there is no transmission of ethnic values, culture, and heritage from grandparents to grandchildren, particularly given the strong notion of filial piety among Asian Americans.

Second, among whites and some minorities, if certain values are transmitted from grandparents to grandchildren, this transmission often occurs through the middle generation. In contrast, anecdotal evidence indicates that the third-generation Asian Americans learned Asian culture directly from their grandparents (Ishii-Kuntz, forthcoming; Phinney, 1990). This generation-skipping value transfer occurred in historical context among Japanese Americans. After the second-generation Japanese tried hard to fully assimilate themselves into the mainstream American society during the 1930's and 1940's, the third-generation Japanese Americans wanted to restore their cultural identity during the 1960's and 1970's, probably affected by general sentiments to preserve cultural heritages.

Asian American grandparents' role in the socialization of grandchildren may be limited to that of family historians. Many Asian American grandparents may not be able to contribute to the general socialization of their grandchildren because their cultural values are based on their original society rather than on American society. To the extent that grandchildren are immersed in mainstream society, their grandparents' perspectives may be irrelevant. On the other hand, their knowledge of the Asian culture and its heritage may be cherished, and grandparents may become a specialized source of knowledge about the traditional Asian culture. In so doing, Asian grandparents play a role in developing and preserving ethnic identity among young Asian Americans. Their cultural heritages, both tangible and intangible, and the history of struggles in the past often serve to solidify ethnic identity among Asian Americans. While grandparents' values, norms, and even behaviors may be out of touch, they still offer a reference point for their young family members, including grandchildren. Thus, Asian American grandchildren learn to be Asians mostly from their family members including grandparents, while they learn to be Americans mostly from people outside their family.

CONCLUSION

The unique immigration history of Asian grandparents leads to their unique positions regarding their relationship with grandchildren. Compared to non-Hispanic white grandparents, they are much more likely to be foreign born, to speak non-English languages (except Japanese Americans), and to live with grandchildren. Many grandparents of Asian Americans reside outside the United Sates, and communications and interactions with them are either nonexistent or very scarce. When Asian Americans have their grandparents in this country, however, they are more likely to coreside with them. Young Asian Americans' primary language is more likely to be English, and this may render their communications and interactions with grandparents rather difficult. The fact that many Asian grandparents are not assimilated into the American culture may minimize their role in the socialization of their grandchildren. However, many Asian grandparents play the role of family historian and help solidify ethnic identity of young family members, including their grandchildren. The unique normative characteristic of filial piety among Asian Americans also may help to preserve ties between the two generations.

Little research has been done on Asian grandparents and the relationships with their grandchildren. As Ou and McAdoo (1993: 248) suggest, there is "a need for empirical research that looks at family interaction patterns and conflicts in parent-child relationships in (Asian American) families where the children have chosen to integrate into the mainstream of society." This is also true for grandparent-grandchild relationships. We further need more empirical research on differences among Asian groups in grandparent-grandchild relationships, the extent to which Asian culture is maintained and transferred by Asian grandparents, and whether traditional Asian cultures and their manifestations, including family authority structure, formal interactions, or coresidence between grandparents and grandchildren, disappear after several generations in the United States.

NOTE

1. All analyses rely on 1990 U.S. Census data, both in published and electronic forms. I used the public use microdata sample (PUMS-A, or 5% sample) of the 1990 Census of Population and Housing. These are the only available data that contain a sufficient number of elderly people of various Asian American groups. I first identified Asian Americans 55 years or older and those 19 or younger. Then, for each elderly and young person, I examined coresidence with grandchilren or grandparents as well as foreign language use. The latter analyses exclude grandchildren under age five.

For purposes of comparison, non-Hispanic white, black, and Hispanic persons 55 years or older and 19 years or younger were chosen from the same data set. To keep the computing time manageable, I drew a 5% random sample of households in which the head of household is an Asian. Then, to allow roughly equal statistical power, I randomly chose similar numbers of non-Hispanic white, black, and Hispanic persons. The six largest Asian groups (Chinese, Japanese, Filipino, Korean, Asian Indian, and Vietnamese) were separately examined. It should be noted that the percentages in Table 7.3 do not indicate who *can* speak the non-English language. Thus, it is conceivable, and common, that grandparents speak English when they talk with grandchildren, or grandchildren speak non-English languages when they talk with grandparents. It is also common that an older member of a household talks to a younger member in his/her native language and the latter replies in English.

Chapter 8

Gender Variations

Glenna Spitze and Russell A. Ward

Gender is an organizing feature of many family roles and relationships. This is reflected in intergenerational relations between parents and adult children as well as between grandparents and grandchildren, including stronger ties along the female line. Differences are less consistent in the grandchild generation, however, and apparent differences in the grandparent generation may be exaggerated by a tendency to ignore grandfathers and their concerns in past research. Further, this literature tends not to focus explicitly on theoretical and conceptual issues, with a resultant lack of attention to the specific processes through which gender differences may be produced or the conditions under which they might be expected to change.

In this chapter we aim to enhance understanding of gender differences in the experiences of grandparents and grandchildren in several ways. First, we present a multigenerational framework for studying gender differences in grandparent/grandchild relationships. Second, we discuss theoretical explanations of gender differences in grandparent/grandchild relations, as well as recent demographic and social trends that may have implications for gender differences in these relations. We then summarize major research findings on gender differences, organized according to a multigenerational framework. Finally, we evaluate methodological issues and data needs and suggest future theoretical and research directions for this topic.

CONCEPTUALIZING GENDER DIFFERENCES IN GRANDPARENT-GRANDCHILD RELATIONSHIPS

Because three generations are involved (grandparent, adult child, grandchild), with the adult child often seen as mediator (e.g., Matthews & Sprey, 1985;

Thompson & Walker, 1987; Tinsley & Parke, 1984; Whitbeck, Hoyt, & Huck, 1993), gender differences can manifest themselves at three levels: (1) in relations of grandfathers and grandmothers to their grandchildren, (2) in relations of grandsons and granddaughters to their grandparents, and (3) in differences between maternal and paternal grandparents. The latter reflect differences in adult sons' and daughters' relations with their parents.

Perhaps in keeping with a greater focus on the grandparents' perspective in the general literature, there is more empirical research on gender differences in the grandparent (and to some extent the adult child) than in the grandchild generation. There are also more theoretical reasons for expecting gender differences in the grandparent and adult child generations than in the grandchild generation. Thus, as we discuss theoretical perspectives and the research literature, we will attend to these three levels of analysis.

THEORETICAL PERSPECTIVES ON GENDER

Most research on gender differences in grandparent/grandchild relationships lacks a theoretical foundation. However, explanations for gender differences in grandparenting can be derived from the more general literature on gender and aging or on intergenerational relationships (e.g., Arber and Ginn, 1991; Cherlin & Furstenberg, 1986a; Kivett, 1991b; Thomas, 1989, 1995). We discuss three theoretical perspectives that can be applied to gender differences at one or more of the three generational levels we have noted. These can be characterized as social, bioevolutionary, and social-psychological.

Social Theories

The dominant perspective in this area focuses on socially constructed gender differences in family roles: women are socialized into a stronger orientation toward family relationships (Cherlin & Furstenberg, 1986a; Eisenberg, 1988) and are expected to function as "kinkeepers" (see, e.g., Arber & Ginn, 1991; Rosenthal, 1985). Women are viewed as responsible for maintaining kin relations, arranging gatherings, and keeping kin in touch with each other. Rossi and Rossi (1990: 355) point to the "more precarious nature of men's family relations," and conclude that "mothers and daughters and grandmothers and granddaughters share special bonds that persist through time and across personal crises" (p. 358). The "work" of kinkeeping is viewed as part of the gendered division of labor in society (Hagestad, 1985; Lee, 1992; Rossi & Rossi, 1990; Thomas, 1989; 1995; Troll, 1971). This division of labor is consistent with greater involvement of men in paid employment and women in child care, and with patterns favoring maternal child custody following divorce.

This view predicts *strongest* ties between grandmothers and granddaughters and mediation of grandparent-grandchild relations along the maternal line if adult daughters favor their own parents in their kinkeeping activities. It also implies greater salience of the grandparent role for grandmothers; some have suggested that the grandparent role is viewed as "essentially a maternal one" (Hagestad, 1981) and grandfathers as "feminized" if they become involved (Troll, 1983). It has also been argued that the grandmother role is the *only* legitimate and socially valued role for older women (Arber & Ginn, 1991).

A focus on female ties and gender-stereotyped child rearing would also imply gender differences in the experiences of grandchildren. Granddaughters would be socialized into familial roles and prepared for bonds among adult female kin. It is not clear whether this perspective would predict weakest ties between grandfathers and grandsons, there being no female involved to "work on" the relationship, or whether grandfathers might have a special role in socialization of grandsons. Kornhaber and Woodward (1981; see also Kornhaber, 1996) refer to the role of grandparents as helping to develop sexual identity in the same-sex grandchild, working with the materials of life, and developing gender-typed skills.

A variation on this perspective stems from Gutmann's (1975) discussion of "the normal unisex of later life." He argues that the "parental imperative" creates sharply differentiated gender roles while children are present, but that once children leave, men will become less aggressive and more diffusely sensual, while women will become less sentimental and more aggressive. (While Gutmann argues that these patterns have an evolutionary basis, the transition to less polarized gender roles is assumed to follow from changes in other roles, and this explanation has been used by others who clearly view the transition as social. Thus we include it in our discussion of socially based theories.)

Others have developed these ideas further. Kivett (1991b: 274) argues that grandparenthood "offers individuals, especially men who were busily involved in earlier years, a second chance at parenting." Being a grandfather may be a particularly important vehicle for personal growth and fulfillment of nurturance needs, assisting in resolution of important psychosocial issues for older men (Kivett, 1991b; Thomas, 1994). And changes in other roles besides parenthood, such as retirement, may produce a similar movement toward uni-sex roles (Thomas 1989; 1994; 1995).

Thus, in more general terms, roles may become less differentiated with age, with retirement, and the end of parenting of young children (Kivett, 1991b; see also Moen, 1996). This implies that grandmothers and grandfathers would relate to grandchildren in increasingly similar ways as they age and as their other life roles become more similar. It would have no implication for gender differences in the other two generations as discussed above.

Evolutionary Theory

A second theoretical perspective focuses on biological differences and evolutionary processes. For example, M. S. Smith (1991) suggests that grandmothers are more certain of their biological connection to grandchildren than are grandfathers, and that both are more certain of connections to daughters' than sons' children. Consequently, they would be motivated to "invest" more in these relations. (Smith also suggests more situational reasons for expecting differences between maternal and paternal grandparents that bridge social and biological perspectives. For example, if daughters are more often home with their children, their parents may be more comfortable visiting them.)

Rossi (1984) has argued that women have a biological advantage in parenting, and she finds stronger ties between mothers and their children than between fathers and their children (Rossi & Rossi, 1990). This implies stronger ties between grandmothers and grandchildren if this difference in nurturant qualities continues into the older years, and between grandchildren and their maternal grandparents to the extent that children are closer to their mothers, who mediate these ties.

These bioevolutionary perspectives would generally predict gender differences for the grandparent and the adult child generation, but are not clearly related to the level of the grandchild. While they imply similar patterns to those predicted by the social explanations, bioevolutionary perspectives seem to predict differences that would not vary with changes in social roles. For example, changing patterns of women's employment might moderate expectations based on social roles, but not those rooted in biologically based gender differences.

Exchange Theory

Third, expectations about grandparenting may be derived from exchange theory. While this has rarely been applied directly to grandparent-grandchild relations (Kivett, 1991b), it has been used to analyze intergenerational relationships (Mancini & Benson, 1989; Nye, 1979). This explanation, which focuses on reciprocity and/or a calculation of costs and benefits of relationships, implies that adult children maintain closer ties with mothers than fathers due to feelings of indebtedness from childhood nurturance. These differences might, in turn, lead to closer ties to maternal than paternal grandparents and to grandmothers than grandfathers.

Exchange theory seems applicable at the level of the grandparent and the adult child, but is less clearly relevant to gender differences among grandchildren. Indeed, with the exception of the "uni-sex" perspective, all three major perspectives predict stronger relations with grandmothers and with maternal grandparents, making it necessary to look for other ways to distinguish findings that would support one over the other. Of the three perspectives discussed here, only the socially based perspective makes a prediction about gender differences in grandchildren's experiences, focusing on gender-role socialization by grandparents.

EFFECTS OF DEMOGRAPHIC CHANGE ON GENDER DIFFERENCES

A number of demographic and historical changes that affect intergenerational relations, including changes in mortality, divorce, and gender relations, may affect gendered patterns of grandparenting. First, increased longevity during this century has been accompanied by an increased gender gap in life expectancy (Chapter 2). All persons now have a greater chance of becoming grandparents, but this trend also exacerbates differences in the experiences of grandmothers and grandfathers. Women are somewhat more likely than men to become grandparents and likely to live more of their lives as grandparents (Hagestad & Burton, 1986: Chapter 2); they are also more likely to experience grandparenthood as widowed persons. Grandmothers may draw particular strength from intergenerational continuity, as grandchildren compensate for other losses (Kivnick, 1981).

Similarly, children are more likely to have (or to have for a longer time) living grandmothers than living grandfathers (Hoffman 1979; Matthews & Sprey, 1985; Chapter 2). Continuing age differences between husbands and wives (Hagestad, 1985) may influence grandchildren's access to maternal and paternal grandparents. Grandchildren are somewhat more likely to have living maternal than paternal grandparents, and surviving maternal grandparents may be slightly younger (and also less frail) than surviving paternal grandparents (Cherlin & Furstenberg, 1986a; Hagestad, 1985; Sprey & Matthews, 1982).

Gender differences in ties to maternal and paternal grandparents are also likely to be reinforced by trends in divorce. Due to preference for maternal custody, children of divorce are likely to have stronger ties with maternal than paternal grandparents (see Chapter 13).

Counteracting the impact of demographic and family structural changes are societal trends toward less differentiated gender roles. As women become more involved in the labor force and men participate more in household activities and especially child-rearing activities, they may perform increasingly similar grandparental roles. Men in the middle generation who are increasingly pressured to perform housework and parenting may also do more of the management activities involved in kinkeeping, and thus may mediate relations between their children and their parents to a greater extent. Some commentators do not expect gender roles to fade away soon (e.g., Cherlin & Furstenberg, 1986a), but even the older generation may feel some pressure to treat sons and daughters, grandsons and granddaughters, in more similar ways. This might be reinforced by decreased fertility; when there are few grandchildren, one may be less inclined to differentiate among them by gender.

RESEARCH ON GRANDPARENT-GRANDCHILD RELATIONS

Our discussion of research findings is organized around the generational levels noted earlier—grandparents (grandmothers versus grandfathers), adult children (maternal versus paternal grandparents), and grandchildren (granddaughters versus grandsons). Within each level a variety of dimensions of grandparent-grandchild relations are of interest, including styles and perceptions of grandparenting, contact and assistance patterns, and such outcomes as satisfaction and well-being.

Grandmothers and Grandfathers

Grandfathers have been considered the "forgotten men" in the family, as the maternal and expressive nature of grandparenting is presumed to make grandfather a peripheral role that offers little of interest or importance (Baranowski, 1990). Indeed, there are indications that the "nurturant grandmother" is perceived as a distinctive subtype of older persons (Brewer, Dull, & Lui, 1981; Turner & Turner, 1994), with images of the "perfect grandparent" associated primarily with women (Hummert, 1991). There are some indications that grandfathers are less involved in the lives of grandchildren and less expressive about the role (Brubaker, 1990; Cunningham-Burley, 1984b; Hagestad & Lang, 1986; Kivett, 1985b, 1991b). However, differences are not large and may reflect sampling or measurement (as we discuss later). Other studies report no gender difference in the "centrality" of grandparenting (Thomas, 1995) or in feeling close to grandchildren (Bengtson & Harootyan, 1994), and indicate that grandfathers are not generally detached or passive (Cherlin & Furstenberg, 1985, 1986a; Tinsley & Parke, 1987).

Regarding role content, it is commonly argued that activities of grandmothers and grandfathers reflect traditional gender roles, with grandfathers engaging in instrumental activities and grandmothers in "warmer," more expressive activities (Baranowski, 1990; Cherlin & Furstenberg, 1985, 1986a; Thomas, 1995; Tinsley & Parke, 1987; Troll, 1983). Fischer (1983), for example, found that grandmothers emphasized emotional and symbolic significance, with less attention to interactional or instrumental dimensions. Grandfathers may lack child-rearing skills to be surrogate parents or engage in direct child care (Baranowski, 1985). Other studies report that grandfathers focus more on nonfamily issues (e.g., schooling, jobs, money) in their relations with grandchildren, whereas grandmothers deal with more emotional and interpersonal issues that are often family-related (Eisenberg, 1988; Hagestad, 1985). Grandmothers provide more emotional support to parents (their adult children) and more advice and modeling on child rearing, whereas grandfathers provide more financial assistance (Tinsley & Parke, 1984); grandmothers are also likely to have greater influence on grandchildren because they are more likely to coreside or act as surrogate parents. Others have cited the particular importance of grandmother-mother-granddaughter relations for family cohesion and emotional well-being (Hagestad, 1985; Halperin, 1989). However, a nurturing grandfather may have particular value as a nontraditional role model, and such nurturance can contribute to fulfillment of the grandfather's developmental needs (Thomas, 1986b).

Gender differences in activities may reflect styles and meanings attached to being a grandparent; for example, grandfathers may be more formal and grandmothers more informal and affect-oriented (McCready, 1985). Neugarten and

Weinstein (1964) reported that grandmothers were more likely to emphasize "parent surrogate" and "biological renewal" dimensions of grandparenthood, whereas grandfathers emphasized "reservoir of family wisdom" and "emotional fulfillment." Other studies also find that grandmothers emphasize continuation of the family line and reliving parenthood, whereas grandfathers emphasize assistance to grandchildren (Hagestad & Lang, 1986). Thomas (1989, 1995), however, found that grandfathers emphasized "immortality through clan" (suggesting the tradition of patrilineal descent) and indulgence (perhaps reflecting male expressivity needs in later life).

Although some studies report gender differences in styles and meanings of grandparenting, others find weak or no differences between grandmothers and grandfathers (e.g., Shore & Hayslip, 1994; Strom et al., 1993; Thomas, 1989, 1995); for example, they have found that the most important functions of grandchildren for grandfathers are symbolic (reinvolvement with one's past and linkages to life review), patterns that are similar to reports of grandmothers (Baranowski, 1990). Cherlin and Furstenberg (1986a) found only modest gender differences in grandparenting styles that are weaker than differences between mothers and fathers, who are involved in day-to-day child rearing. Similarly, studies of contact have produced mixed results. Some report more contact by grandmothers than grandfathers (e.g., Roberto & Stroes, 1992), but others find no difference by gender of grandparent (Bengtson & Harootyan, 1994; Cherlin & Furstenberg, 1986a; Field & Minkler, 1988).

A few studies explore gender differences in the implications of grandparenting for well-being. There is some evidence that grandmothers express greater satisfaction with being a grandparent, perhaps because of greater continuity of experiences in family caregiving roles (Brubaker, 1990; Thomas, 1986a, 1986b, 1989, 1995); however, the differences are small, and one panel study found no gender differences, with stable satisfaction for both grandmothers and grandfathers (Field & Minkler, 1988). Other studies suggest similar predictors of satisfaction for grandmothers and grandfathers. Grandfathers can be satisfied if they value the role, have opportunities to interact, and have positive interactions with grandchildren (Shore & Hayslip, 1994), but this seems likely for grandmothers as well. Similarly, Thomas (1986b) found that although grandparents may not desire parental responsibilities, perceived responsibility for helping grandchildren and for their care is associated with higher satisfaction for both grandfathers and grandmothers.

Gender differences in the implications of grandparenting for mental health have been investigated by Kivnick (1981, 1982). Centrality and reinvolvement were associated with mental health among grandmothers. These meanings were more common when grandparents had role deprivations, such as widowhood, suggesting a compensatory value of grandmotherhood. Grandmothers may derive self-expression and identity from opportunities for creativity and accomplishment (Kivett, 1991b; Timberlake, 1980). Mental health of grandfathers was associated with indulgence, immortality, and being a "valued elder"; Kivnick attributes the latter to an emphasis on competence, control, and success in the lives of men.

The "costs" of grandparenting may also be greater for grandmothers. The multifaceted networks and obligations associated with kinkeeping by women have both benefits and costs (Antonucci, 1990), and mothers are more likely than fathers to experience stress from problems in the lives of their adult children (Greenberg, Becker, & Dessonville-Hill, 1988). More specifically, grandmothers are more likely than grandfathers to take on surrogate parent responsibilities and the potential burdens they entail (Chapter 14); however, studies have not directly compared grandmothers and grandfathers in such circumstances.

Maternal and Paternal Grandparents

As noted earlier, grandparent-grandchild relations are likely to be mediated through the middle (adult child) generation. Gender differences in grandparenting may reflect patterns of relations with daughters and sons; grandparents may have stronger ties with same-sex grandchildren from same-sex children (Hagestad, 1985), for example. The mother-daughter-granddaughter linkage may be particularly significant (Halperin, 1989). Becoming a grandmother may strengthen the mother-daughter tie, with greater sharing and perceptions of continuity among women of different generations because of the shared salience of family roles (Brubaker, 1991; Fischer, 1983; Hagestad, 1985; Hagestad & Lang, 1986; Troll, 1983). However, other studies have failed to find differences in perceptions, meanings, and satisfaction between maternal and paternal grandparents (Johnson, 1985; Thomas 1989, 1995).

Older parents have more contact with daughters than sons (Rossi & Rossi, 1990), implying that they may also see daughters' children more often. The greater frequency of interacting with daughters is supported by several studies, though more consistently for telephone contact than in-person visiting (Cherlin & Furstenberg, 1986a; Eisenberg, 1988; Hodgson, 1995; Hoffman, 1979; Logan & Spitze 1996). Grandfathers appear to see the sons of their daughters the least among their grandchildren (Baranowski, 1990). Some studies have reported more contact with maternal grandmothers in particular (Eisenberg, 1988; Hodgson, 1995), perhaps reflecting both female longevity and younger average age of maternal grandmothers. Eisenberg also found that maternal grandmothers engaged in a greater variety of activities. However, others report no difference in contact between maternal and paternal grandparents (Johnson, 1985; Roberto & Stroes, 1992).

Young mothers frequently rely on their own mothers for assistance with child care (Parish, Hao, & Hogan, 1991; Presser, 1989; Thomas, 1989), and parents tend to help adult daughters more than they help sons (Cooney & Uhlenberg, 1992; Kivett, 1991b). Three-generation households more often involve daughters rather than sons (Coward & Cutler, 1991), which may reflect assistance to daughters who are divorced (Aldous, 1985; Cherlin & Furstenberg, 1986a). Indeed, the clearest evidence of maternal/paternal variation involves divorce. The likelihood that divorced mothers have custody favors maternal grandparents (Ahrons & Bowman, 1982; Johnson, 1983a, 1988c; Spanier & Thompson, 1984). This may occur even without divorce, as "marital discord weakens the ties between men and their children, especially sons, and between children and their paternal grandparents . . . well in advance of any parental divorce" (Rossi & Rossi, 1990: 355). Post-divorce differences may be partially offset by a tendency for paternal grandmothers to maintain contact with former daughters-in-law more than maternal grandmothers with former sons-in-law (Johnson, 1985; Johnson & Barer, 1987).

Granddaughters and Grandsons

Gender patterns may also be evident for grandchildren. Reflecting the interconnections among generations, we assess the implications of grandchild gender from several perspectives: whether grandparents report differences in their involvements with granddaughters and grandsons, whether grandchildren report different relations with grandmothers and grandfathers, and whether granddaughters and grandsons differ in their orientations toward grandparents. Differences between granddaughters and grandsons may also be related to the maternal/paternal distinction, as noted in the previous section.

Evidence is limited and mixed on whether grandfathers or grandmothers differentiate between grandsons and granddaughters; Tinsley and Parke (1984), for example, indicate that grandmothers are more likely to do so, but Hagestad (1978, 1985) reports that grandfathers are more likely. Others have focused on the distinctiveness of the grandfather-grandson relationship, particularly on the paternal side, with more frequent instrumental exchanges that may involve male-typed household chores (Cherlin & Furstenberg, 1986a; Kivett, 1991b). Grandfathers, especially paternal grandfathers, may focus on grandsons, but Baranowski's (1990) sample of grandfathers mostly disagreed with a statement that they could be of greater help and value to grandsons and mentioned granddaughters as often as grandsons in the interviews. Other studies find little significance for grandparents of the gender of their grandchild with regard to perceived responsibilities and meanings, contact, and satisfaction (King & Elder, 1995a; Kivett, 1993; Thomas, 1995), though Shore and Hayslip (1994) found that grandparents reported more positive relations and higher satisfaction when they had granddaughters.

Does grandparent gender matter to grandchildren? Some studies indicate that college students feel closer to grandmothers than grandfathers (though males more often identify a grandfather as "most close"), have more activities with grandmothers, and perceive grandmothers as having greater influence on their values (Kennedy, 1992a; Roberto & Stroes, 1995); the latter may reflect interpersonal issues traditionally associated with women, as well as sex-role beliefs about appropriate topics of conversation. In particular, maternal grandmothers appear to be distinctive. There is evidence that grandchildren feel closer to and have more activities with maternal than paternal grandparents (Eisenberg, 1988; Hodgson, 1995; Kahana & Kahana, 1970; Kennedy, 1990; Rossi & Rossi, 1990; Thomas, 1989) and that kin position may be more important than gender of grandparent (Hoffman, 1979; Matthews & Sprey, 1985; but see Creasy & Koblewski, 1991). Rossi and Rossi (1990) indicate that feelings of obligation are highest toward mothers' mothers and lowest toward fathers' fathers. However, others find little difference in perceptions about maternal and paternal grandparents (Roberto & Stroes, 1995) or little relationship between grandchild-grandparent gender and the importance or influence of grandparents (e.g., Hagestad, 1978, 1982; Kivett, 1985b).

Do granddaughters and grandsons differ in their relations with grandparents? Ponzetti and Folkrod (1989) found that young girls focused more on emotional attachment and less on exchanges and shared activities, whereas boys focused more on doing things together. There have also been reports that granddaughters are more concerned with and feel closer to grandparents (Kennedy, 1990; Peterson, 1989). However, others have found no differences in such feelings by gender of grandchild (Bengtson & Harootyan, 1994; Eisenberg, 1988; Hodgson, 1995; Whitbeck, Hoyt, & Huck, 1993). Studies report no differences between grandson and granddaughter contact (Bengtson & Harootyan, 1994; Roberto & Stroes, 1995); parents would likely arrange contact between their parents and their children without regard to the gender of those children, and often in activities involving the whole family. There are also mixed results on differences by gender of grandchild in help to grandparents (Creasey & Koblewski, 1991; Kivett, 1993), and we found no specific evidence of different consequences for grandsons compared with granddaughters.

Interactions of Gender with Other Factors

Implications of the gender of grandparents and grandchildren may depend in part on other characteristics that shape family ties and the meanings of family roles.

Roles and expectations are likely to change as grandparents age, and the effects of age and timing may differ for grandmothers and grandfathers. Some have suggested particular discomfort for grandmothers who are "off-time" (early or late in becoming a grandparent) (Aldous, 1995; Brubaker, 1991; Burton & Bengtson, 1985). This may reflect problems of younger grandmothers who provide child care or more comprehensive surrogate parenting, and confront overload from their other role responsibilities as mothers, wives, children, and employees (Brubaker, 1991; Burton & Bengtson, 1985; Burton & Dilworth-Anderson, 1991; Presser, 1989; Chapter 14). However, age is also relevant for grandfathers. "Early" grandfathers (in their 40's) may also feel uneasy (Baranowski, 1990), and other studies suggest similar changes with age in the views of grandmothers and grandfathers; for example, older grandfathers may have a more formal style and attach greater symbolic meaning to grandparenthood (e.g., as part of life review and validation of family history) (Baranowski, 1990), similar to Roberto's (1990) finding of greater remoteness and symbolic significance on the part of great-grandmothers. However, evidence of greater satisfaction among grandfathers who are older and whose grandchildren are younger suggests the value of opportunities for nurturance and expressivity among older men (Thomas, 1986b).

Gender patterns in grandparent-grandchild relations may also depend on the age of grandchildren. Grandmothers appear to have greater involvement than grandfathers with younger grandchildren, a view expressed and supported by both grandmothers and grandfathers reflecting their common-sense beliefs about gender roles (Cunningham-Burley, 1984b). However, there appear to be few differences between young adult granddaughters and grandsons, perhaps because these granddaughters are still too young to assume kinkeeping roles (Eisenberg, 1988). Gender differences may change or emerge later as grandchildren age and interact with grandparents independently (Baranowski, 1985; Thomas, 1995), with greater contact by adult granddaughters (Hodgson, 1995). Weakening of the mediating influence of the middle (child) generation as grandchildren enter adulthood (Roberto & Stroes, 1992) may alter gender patterns in other ways, however. In contrast to findings for younger grandchildren, Cooney and Smith (1996) found that parental divorce did not affect the solidarity of adult grandchildren with either maternal or paternal grandparents, as young adults from divorced families were more likely than those from intact families to take the lead in initiating visits with grandparents.

Racial and ethnic differences in family norms may also assign varying roles to grandfathers and grandmothers (Burton & Bengtson, 1985; Burton, Dilworth-Anderson, & Merriwether-DeVries, 1995). Black grandparents, especially grandmothers, are much more likely to share households with grandchildren than are whites (Pearson et al., 1990; Szinovacz, 1996; and see Chapters 2 and 5), often as surrogate parents. The role of black grandmothers as family matriarchs is often idealized, but it is also a burdensome role that they may not desire and that carries a potential for resentment, conflict, and adverse effects on well-being (Burton & Bengtson, 1985; Burton & Dilworth-Anderson, 1991; Minkler, Roe, & Price, 1992; Chapters 14 and 16); however, other than noting that black grandfathers are less likely to be in coresident and surrogate parent situations, few comparisons have been made of black grandmothers and grandfathers.

There are scattered indications that factors other than age and race may interact with gender in shaping grandparent-grandchild relations. The significance of grandparent roles for both men and women may depend on marital or employment status (Wood & Robertson, 1976), for example, and grandfathers may view their roles as more important if other male role models are lacking in the family (Kivett, 1991a). Paternal grandparents also appear to be more salient in rural farm families, reflecting patrilineal families (King & Elder, 1995a: Chapter 4).

Summary

The three perspectives with which we began—social, bioevolutionary, and exchange—yield predictions that grandparent-grandchild relations would be strengthened by female ties, whether involving grandmothers, maternal grandparents, or granddaughters. However, research on the role of gender in grandparent-grandchild relations has yielded decidedly mixed results. There are both similarities and differences between grandmothers and grandfathers, between maternal and paternal grandparents, and between granddaughters and grandsons. Some studies find that gender matters, and others do not, and gender differences that are found are often small. There are some indications that grandparent-grandchild relations are more significant and active for grandmothers, especially maternal grandmothers, but it is not clear to what extent these are due to demographic patterns of life expectancy, widowhood, divorce, and remarriage. Thus, it is premature to make definitive conclusions about gender differences in grandparent-grandchild relations.

Where there are gender differences, they are consistent with socially constructed gender roles emphasized by the social and exchange perspectives. For example, the kinkeeping role (and its attendant costs) is evident among grandmothers, especially with surrogate parenting; gender patterns of divorce are associated with differences between maternal and paternal grandparents; and the mediating role of adult daughters seems reflected in closer ties between grandchildren and maternal grandmothers. A bioevolutionary view seems less supported empirically, given the inconsistency of gender differences and variation associated with race and other factors that bear on social norms and behaviors. And aside from the often insubstantial gender differences, there is little evidence that they become more similar in response to broader personality changes. However, research has not been conducted in ways that allow us to clearly distinguish among the theoretical frameworks. Further, without earlier baseline data for comparison, we cannot determine whether demographic trends are shrinking or enlarging gender differences in grandparenting.

EMPIRICAL AND METHODOLOGICAL ISSUES

The mixed evidence on gender differences in grandparent-grandchild relations may reflect sampling or measurement. Studies are frequently based on small, nonrandom, selective, or convenience samples that overrepresent or are restricted to grandmothers. We lack even basic demographic information about grandparent characteristics and the intergenerational structure of families (Aldous, 1995). Many studies pay no attention to the gender of grandparents or grandchildren, and it has been common to discuss grandparenting without reference to gender or to generalize from samples that are all or nearly all female. Grandfathers have been overlooked, either in comparisons with grandmothers or in their own right, perhaps because grandfathers are presumed less willing to participate in such research because they are less involved and interested in grandparenting (Baranowski, 1990). The focus on grandmothers also to some extent reflects differences in life expectancy; grandfathers are fewer in number, and their health is more likely to interfere with study participation. Except for the relatively large number of convenience samples of college students, there has also been little attention to the perspectives of grandchildren, especially adult grandchildren.

There is only limited available data on some dimensions of grandparent-grandchild relations in which gender may play a role. For example, family assistance patterns tend to have a gender-based division of labor, but studies of assistance between grandparents and grandchildren are rare (frequently subsuming them under "other kin"). There has also been little research on the potential outcomes of grandparent-grandchild relations—in terms of family stability and individual well-being for any of the three generations—and whether those outcomes vary by gender.

Inconsistent findings on gender differences also reflect measurement issues. The role of gender and lineage may depend on what specific aspects of grandparent-grandchild relations—which behaviors and attitudes—are being addressed (Baranowski, 1990; Pearson et al., 1990; Roberto & Stroes, 1992); in particular, grandfathers may appear to be less involved if dimensions important to them are not measured. Studies focusing on mothers and child care may emphasize the involvement of grandmothers and understate the role of grandfathers. Family roles of older men are overlooked when topics, samples, and measures give little attention to men who do "women's work" (such as caregiving) and rely on gender-biased measures reflecting female conceptions of familial behavior (e.g., "emotional closeness") (Bengtson, Rosenthal, & Burton, 1996). Help *from* grandfathers, for example, may be underestimated because it is not expected and respondents do not think of men when asked who helps (Wilson, 1987). Survey research needs to be sensitive to gender differences in response patterns (Cunningham-Burley, 1984b; Kivett, 1991b). Grandfathers may appear to be uninvolved and uninterested because men and women express themselves differently in interviews.

We also need studies that incorporate new variables and that gather information about entire families. Issues of family structure have begun to be addressed in studies of parent-adult child relations (e.g., Aldous & Klein, 1991; Coward & Dwyer, 1990; Matthews & Rosner, 1988; Spitze & Logan, 1990; 1991) but are absent from the literature on grandparenting (see Peterson, 1989). We do not know the distribution of grandchildren for those who are grandparents, and to our knowledge no study has gathered specific information about relations with each of a respondent's grandchildren (as Matthews & Sprey [1985] did for all living grandparents of a sample of college students). Relevant questions include how relations with specific grandchildren vary by number and gender distribution of grandchildren; for example, are relations different with firstborn or only grandchildren, and are relations more or less gender stereotyped when all grandchildren are of one gender?

In order to conduct tests that allow comparison among theoretical perspectives, we need information regarding theoretically relevant variables. We need to know the history of gender-related familial behavior experienced by current grandparents and who in their family has performed the kinkeeping role. We also need to know the employment history of grandmothers, other current roles and activities of grandparents (such as employment, volunteer work, and other family involvement), men's history of participation in other family roles such as household labor and child care, and histories of parent-adult child contact in families of divorce. Only with such information can we distinguish among theories that focus on differences arising from biology, current or past family situation, or the history of exchange within a family.

THEORETICAL ISSUES AND RESEARCH DIRECTIONS

Ambiguity and weak socialization for the grandparent role give grandparents considerable discretion and yield a wide variety of roles and styles. The choices of grandparents will be shaped by factors that mold other dimensions of life, so it is reasonable to expect gender-based experiences and roles to be reflected in differences between grandmothers and grandfathers. However, the research and theoretical perspectives we have reviewed have failed to account for gender differences in a convincing manner. Grandparent research has been characterized as atheoretical and descriptive (Aldous, 1995; Robertson, 1995). In particular for our focus on gender, there is a need to place grandparent–adult child–grandchild relations within the more general context of family structure and roles, and to incorporate sources of diversity and change. That is, we need to better account for the influence of social context as it shapes and interacts with gender differences (Chapter 4). Further, we need to better understand the ways in which grandmothers and grandfathers respond to past roles and relationships, as well as to current circumstances in their lives and in the lives of their children and grandchildren.

This suggests the usefulness of incorporating a life-course perspective that emphasizes the intersection of social and historical factors and heterogeneity in the transitions and trajectories of individual lives (George & Gold, 1991). Others have noted what Troll (1985) has called the "contingencies" of grandparenthood, including timing, sequencing, and synchronization with other family and nonfamily roles, and intraindividual developmental concerns (Burton, Dilworth-Anderson, & Merriwether-deVries, 1995; Hagestad & Lang, 1986; Thomas, 1994). It can be expected that these will be linked to gender and gender differences. Further, gender is likely to interact with race, class, age-cohort, and other dimensions relevant to grandparent roles.

While theories discussed earlier in this chapter tend to imply relatively static sources of gender differences in these relations, a life-course perspective underlines the value of a longitudinal and dynamic view of grandparenting. Longitudinal research will facilitate understanding of stability and change in the meanings, styles, and activities associated with grandparenting, the relationship between styles of grandparenting and earlier styles of parenting, and what it means to become a grandparent (Baranowski, 1985). Cross-sectional research that gathers information on family histories is also useful in promoting such understanding.

There is also a need to attend to social change and cohort flow in gender roles. Hagestad (1986, 1987), for example, notes that divorce is more disruptive of the family networks of men, so increased divorce rates in recent cohorts are likely to weaken their intergenerational ties; she also notes the need to investigate the outcomes for children of divorce and remarriage in their later years. On a more positive note, Baranowski (1985) suggests that cohort flow may reduce gender differences; for example, today's grandfathers may feel more comfortable as advisors and confidants to granddaughters than did grandfathers in the past.

The foregoing comments are most relevant to understanding gender differences in the grandparent generation, and are also somewhat relevant to differences in the mediating role of adult children, which is likely to be influenced by factors reflecting social change and family history. At the level of the grandchild, gender differences are more likely to reflect gender-differentiated socialization by their parents and grandparents, but here too a life-course perspective can provide a useful focus. There is suggestive evidence of changes in the salience of gender with the transition to adult roles by the grandchild. This should be investigated further with attention to grandchildren's exit from the student role and entry into the labor force, family-building activities, and independent living.

Thus, we urge that future research incorporate more theoretically motivated information on family relations and family structure, and on the variety of factors relevant to understanding issues of gender and social change. To understand gender differences in grandparent-grandchild relationships, we need to place them in a familial, historical, and societal context.

NOTE

The authors contributed equally to this chapter. The names of the authors are listed in alphabetical order.

Part II

Grandparenting—
Dynamics and Contingencies

Chapter 9

Transitions in Grandparents' Lives: Effects on the Grandparent Role

Vira R. Kivett

It has been noted that, "whereas parenting tends to shape and alter all other parts of life, grandparenting tends to be shaped by other events going on in life . . . Grandparenting is a contingent process" (Troll, 1985: 135). Transitions, or life changes or events, are key elements shaping the structure, function, and quality of the grandparent role. They may be prompted by biological, sociological, historical, or other phenomena, and their effects may be sudden, delayed, noticed or unnoticed, and positive or negative (Spierer, 1977). Often these effects are less a matter of objective change than of the individual's perception of the change (Schlossberg, 1984). Considerable research has addressed events in the lives of grandparents. Few studies, however, have explicitly operationalized or conceptualized these events as transitions.

The majority of research on transitions influencing the grandparent role has been based upon the effect of alterations in institutions, including the family. Considerable attention, for example, has been given to the effects of child divorce and the legal system (primarily custody issues) on the role (see Chapter 13). Areas of moderate attention include the influence of social movements on grandparents' involvement (cohort analyses), children's off-time pregnancy, developmental stage of the grandchild, and surrogate parenting (see Chapter 14). Studies relative to age and gender of the grandparent, primacy of the grandparent role, and the developmental stage of the grandparent are largely lacking (Hagestad & Burton, 1986).

The purpose of this chapter is to provide an overview of the impact of transitions on the dynamics of the grandparent-grandchild relationship. The first part of this chapter will provide a brief review of leading theoretical perspectives related to changes. Second, the influence of transitions on grandparent involvement and satisfaction according to type and context will be examined. Finally, factors moderating the effects of transitions on the role will be addressed, followed by a discussion of implications for the grandparent role and research voids.

THEORETICAL EXPLANATIONS

Several perspectives from psychological and sociological traditions hold particular relevance for studies of transitions. The first group, from a psychological legacy, forms a continuum of theoretical perspectives of adult development. These include age and stage positions (Erikson, 1950; Gilligan, 1982; Gould, 1978; Levinson et al., 1978; Loeringer, 1976; Vaillant, 1977), life event and transitions views (Brim & Kagan, 1980; Lowenthal, Thurnher, & Chiriboga, 1975; Pearlin, 1980), and individual timing and variability perspectives (Neugarten, 1979; Pearlin, 1980; Vaillant, 1977).

The age and stage theories deal with the sequence of development, the unfolding of life and the resolving of inner issues. These theories suggest that the consequences of transitions on the grandparent role are related to their timing and compatibility with the developmental needs of the grandparent and grandchild. For example, it is thought that grandparenting assists adults in meeting important psychosocial needs such as postmaintenance generativity and grandgenerativity (Kivnick, 1985). That is, the grandparent experience provides additional opportunities following parenthood for meeting continuing developmental needs to care for and to nuture. The life event and transition perspectives address the centrality of life events, coping, stress, the importance of stage over age, and adjustment. Thus, the effect of transitions on the grandparent role is contingent on life events, their associated stresses, and grandparents' attitudes. A life event of increasing frequency among older adults is retirement relocation. Lack of proximity to grandchildren created through moving can modify or decrease grandparenting behaviors. As a result, stress may be placed on the grandparent-grandchild relationship.

Individual timing and variability perspectives speak to the relationship between the timing of events and their outcomes, the concept of the social clock, and the differential distribution of strains. These perspectives suggest that the relationship between transitions and grandparent behaviors and satisfaction can be explained through generational differences, social timing, or the differences in which individuals react to stress. Burton and Bengtson (1985) found that early grandmotherhood in a sample of black maternal grandmothers resulted in disassociation with the role. "Off-time" grandmothers expressed less comfort with their role and sensed that the role was inappropriate in its timing.

In addition to these adult development perspectives, a family development framework, with a similar emphasis on timely sequences of roles and family behaviors, has been a useful paradigm for the examination of transitions and family outcomes (Hagestad & Burton, 1986). A family-development framework proposes that grandparenthood is a sequential stage in the family, occurring in the context of interlocking roles and interacting timetables. For example, if a woman is in a caregiving role to her mother, she is less likely to have significant time and energy to put into the grandparent role than if she were not a caregiver. Moreover, large age differences between grandmother and grandchild can add further complexities to the relationship. Family transitions are of theoretical importance because they are regulated by the process norms of the institution of marriage and family (Rodgers & White, 1993).

Three theories from the sociological tradition have particular relevance for studies of life transitions. These include role theory, social stress theory, and life-course perspectives (George, 1993). Role theory deals with transitions through the concepts of status and role entrances and exits. Role theory presumes that grandparenthood is experienced most smoothly when it occurs on time according to normative expectations and when there has been socialization to the role. Therefore, an individual becoming a grandparent at the approximate age as their peers and who has observed others in the role will experience the role with more success.

The major emphasis in stress theory is on both the singular and accumulative effects of stress on outcomes and the factors mediating or moderating consequences of stress (George, 1993). From a stress theory perspective, the amount of stress generated in grandparenthood by transitions would be influenced by the number, type, and context of the transitions and moderated by social indicators such as gender, education, income, and race. For example, grandparents might be expected to be marginally involved in the role if they were experiencing poor health and the loss of peer support complicated by financial difficulties.

A newer perspective, life course, evolved over the last two decades, has been found to be especially appropriate in the study of the origins of transitions and their personal and social consequences (Bengtson & Allen, 1993; George, 1993). The life course perspective focuses on "age-differentiated" sequences of transitions and the manner in which social and historical contexts configure lives. It incorporates transitions as a key concept. This perspective allows for the examination of transitions in the context of interacting time tables on the life-course trajectory (Elder, 1975). That is, grandparents whose cohort values an active and companionate relationship with grandchildren, whose life stage is relatively unencumbered with commitment, and whose grandchildren's stage is similarly characterized, will have higher role involvement than others in the role.

TYPES OF TRANSITIONS IMPACTING THE GRANDPARENT ROLE

Transitions typically fall into four classifications: anticipated, unanticipated, chronic "hassle," and nonevent categories (Schlossberg, 1984). *Anticipated transitions* predictably occur in the course of the unfolding life cycle. Individuals can rehearse and prepare for them. When the transition into the grandparent role is developmentally appropriate for both the grandparent and the adult child, greater identification and satisfaction are derived from the status. Anticipated transitions among older adults possibly influencing the grandparent behaviors and attitudes include retirement, expansion of nonfamily activities such as volunteerism, relocation, and great-grandparenthood. Anticipated transitions in the lives of grandchildren with potential for altering the grandparent role include leaving the paternal home, mobility through occupation, marriage, and, increasingly, the development of ''significant other'' relationships.

Unanticipated transitions are those ''nonscheduled'' events or nonpredictable events that may have consequences for grandparenthood. Examples include some changes in work patterns, sickness or death of a family member, or the divorce or remarriage of a child. Becoming a grandparent ''off time'' can lead to numerous problems and stresses, including role overload, the infraction of life plans, conflict of developmental imperatives between generations, and a lack of age-appropriate peer groups (Burton, Dilworth-Anderson, & Merriwether-deVries, 1995; see Chapter 14). Other unanticipated events also can have negative consequences for grandparent-grandchild relations, including national crises such as wars or conflicts and natural disasters. Increasingly, foster placement of grandchildren may be an unanticipated event prompting changes in the grandparent role.

Chronic hassle transitions are identified by their continuous and pervasive nature. The effect of persistent hassles comes through their erosion of self-confidence and the subsequent inability to make necessary changes in roles or relationships. Chronic hassles may include continuous unharmonious relationships. An incompatible relationship between a grandmother and a daughter-in-law, for example, can lead to a tenuous, erratic, and limited relationship with a grandchild (Hansson & Carpenter, 1994). Other chronic hassles include personal concerns regarding health, finances, health of others, or crime (Schlossberg, 1984). Grandparents living in a high-crime area might restrict the type and range of activities in which they can engage with a grandchild. Few studies have examined the influence of chronic hassles on grandparent involvement and satisfaction. This void may, in part, be related to the perceived nature of hassles and to the necessity, but difficulty, of examining their unbounded and accumulative effects.

Nonevent transitions are those transitions that were counted upon but never occurred. Unrealized expectations may alter self-image, life satisfaction, and relationships. Few studies have examined and addressed the consequences of nonevent transitions. The grandparent role may fail to be initialized because of grandchildren with special needs, disabilities, or chronic illnesses; bicultural grandchildren; geographically dispersed grandchildren; or no grandchildren. Increasingly, the grandparent role may not be realized because of children's options of career over childbearing or to large age differences between children and their spouses. Other nonevents that alter the grandparent role include the grandparents' postponement of retirement and children's decisions not to visit or live in proximity to grandparents.

THE CONTEXT OF TRANSITIONS

The setting of transitions is central to understanding their effect on the grandparent role (Elder, 1994; Schlossberg, 1984). Transitions occur within life arenas that are personal, interpersonal, or societal in nature. Each of these contexts may be further delineated as relating to self, family, health, work, or economics. Most research on grandparenthood and transitions has been cross-sectional, quantitative, and noncontextual. An increasing number of qualitative studies are providing insights into the influence of transitions on grandparent commitment and satisfaction from a contextual perspective (Burton & Bengtson, 1985; Johnson, 1983a; 1988c). These studies show the embedded and interactive nature of individual lives and the complex environment in which family roles are performed (Hagestad & Burton, 1986).

Personal Context

Transitions in a personal context have their genesis in the grandparent. Examples of transitions that may affect the grandparent role within a personal context include age, developmental stage, physical and mental health, socioeconomic status, leisure, institutionalization, work and retirement, and housing. The literature, however, is sparse on the influence of these factors on grandparent involvement and fulfillment.

The structure of the grandparent role changes with age. Older grandparents, for example, have more lineages of grandchildren (e.g., great- and great-great-grandchildren) than younger grandparents (Hagestad, 1985). Research indicates, however, that expanded grandparent structures do not necessarily contribute to significant increases in grandparenting behaviors (Cherlin & Furstenberg, 1986a). By illustration, great-grandparent roles are usually commandeered by the grandparents, thus leaving an unclear role for the oldest generation (Wentowski, 1985). Developmental changes in the centrality and function of the grandparent role have also been found. Decreases in energy level and physical mobility, for example, can contribute to a decline in active involvement with grandchildren (Johnson, 1988c).

Developmental changes in attachment in late-late life can heighten or diminish the grandparent role (Bengtson, 1985; Johnson, 1994). The very old may distance themselves from children and grandchildren in an effort to conserve energy by decreasing or limiting their involvement in family conflicts. In contrast, as some adults age and divest themselves of various social responsibilities, they may put more energy into the grandparent role (Troll, 1985). Older men may be more involved with grandparenthood than are younger men because of the developmental need for increased expression of nurturance and an increased capacity for intimacy with age (Gutmann, 1977).

A number of age-related events, such as changes in physical and mental health, can influence the saliency and function of grandparenthood. Examples include the onset of Alzheimer's disease and other dementias, depression, poor physical health, and decreased vigor (Troll, 1985). The lack of good health can interfere with constructing, accessing, or maintaining a relationship with a grandchild (Hansson & Carpenter, 1994). Kivett (1993) observed that association between older rural white grandmothers and grandchildren declined with the health of the grandmother. Some research, however, has shown little correspondence between health of grandparents and grandchild-grandparent functional and associational solidarity after controlling for proximity (Cherlin & Furstenberg, 1986a; Troll, 1985). In other words, if grandparents and grandchildren live in proximity, the health of the grandparent is of little consequence to the extent to which they affiliate or assist one another.

Financial problems or limited income associated with age can potentially affect the instrumental dimensions of the grandparent role. Furthermore, loss of income in later life can have important implications for the status of grandparents among grandchildren. For example, the cost of travel or telephone calls may be prohibitive for some older adults, thus limiting the maintenance of strong grandparent-grandchild bonds when families do not live in proximity. In some cases, grandchildren's perceived status of grandparents may decline with decreases in older adults' income (Troll, 1985).

The geographic relocation of grandparents has been found to alter the extent to which they associate and exchange assistance with grandchildren (Barranti, 1985; Cherlin & Furstenberg, 1986a; Gladstone, 1988; Hodgson, 1992; Kivett, 1991b) but not the quality of the relationship (Kivett, Dugan, & Moxley, 1994). Cherlin and Furstenberg (1986a) found geographic proximity to be especially interfering to relationships with great-great-grandchildren. For example, what are the role implications for a great-grandmother not living in proximity to a great-grandchild, whose relationship to the child is mediated through two generations, and who has few normative guidelines for the role? Others have addressed the increased role ambiguity often associated with decreased proximity to grandchildren (Fischer, 1983).

Frequency of contact with grandchildren is not necessarily related to marital status (Cherlin & Furstenberg, 1986a). The extent to which grandparenthood is affected by changes in marital status, especially widowhood, depends upon other factors in the relationship and simultaneous events (Kivnick, 1985). A widowed grandmother, for example, who is highly involved with a widow's peer group, travel, and volunteerism might have less involvement in the grandmother role than another widowed grandmother with few outside interests and friends. Remarriage of the grandparent, most predictably among grandfathers, may distract from grandparental feelings and interests, especially if new infants are involved (Troll, 1985).

Finally, synchronous events may work within a personal context to produce changes in the structure and function of the grandparent role (Troll, 1985). For example, the event of grandparenthood may coincide with a mid-life career change of the grandparent. As a result, the occupational change may "shape" the grandparenting experience. Because of simultaneous events converging on the grandparent role and, hence, its distinct stages, grandparenthood has been compared to a "career" (Cherlin & Furstenberg, 1986a). That is, the stages follow the developmental transformations in the child and grandparent and reflect changing content and relationships.

Interpersonal Context

Transitions within an interpersonal context are countertransitions or ripple effects brought about by other individuals' transitions (Hagestad & Burton, 1986). Individuals whose life events affect the grandparent role include spouses, other family members, and friends. Because of the lack of control over another's transition, few transitions can be anticipated within an interpersonal context. Additionally, internally generated transitions are thought to be better assimilated than those forced by others (Schlossberg, 1984).

There is some support for functional changes in the grandparent role according to the developmental stage of the grandchild. Findings are equivocal, however. Several studies have reported more grandparent involvement among older than younger grandchildren. Cunningham-Burley (1984b) observed grandfathers' delayed involvement in the role until the grandchild had "grown up a bit." Powers and Kivett (1992) found older rural grandparents received more assistance from older grandchildren than from younger ones, suggesting heightened associational and functional solidarity. Hodgson (1992) found a decrease in grandparent-grandchild interaction with the age of the grandchild. That is, there was less association as the age of the grandchild increased. Others have observed no effect of the grandchild's pubertal level on the grandparent-grandchild relationship (Clingempeel et al., 1992). Some researchers have reported increasing variability in styles and patterns of grandparent-grandchild behavior with the passage of time. Bengtson (1985) noted that grandparents and grandchildren may become "consociates" as bonds develop over time. Cherlin and Furstenberg (1986a) found that the grandparent role changed to a largely symbolic one as the grandchild moved from childhood to adolescence. Opportunities for role enactment by grandparents have been found to decrease as the identity needs of adolescent grandchildren increase (Baranowski, 1982). That is, with adolescents' increased interest in friends and peer-related activities, less time is available for grandparent-grandchild interaction.

Most transitions impacting the grandparent role are unanticipated changes and occur within an interpersonal context. They may be family or "other" related. Several unanticipated transitions triggered by the grandchild can influence grandparenthood. Discontinuities of culture and traditions spurred by acculturation of the grandchild, for example, may affect the content and meaning of the grandparent role (Hansen & Jacob, 1992). Van Tran (1988) found that young Vietnamese who abandoned their language created barriers between themselves and grandparents, therefore, reducing the quality and function of the grandparent role. Similarly, the changing nature of socioeconomic conditions for Korean immigrants has been found to strain their intergenerational relationships (Levitt, Guacci, & Weber, 1992). The health of the grandchild also may have consequences for the grandparent role. Chronically ill grandchildren may heighten grandparent roles through caregiving and the provision of other resources (Dilworth-Anderson, 1994).

Most of the unanticipated transitions within an interpersonal context are initiated by the middle generation (Aldous, 1985). Two of the most frequent events influencing the grandparent role are "off-time" pregnancy of daughters (see Chapter 14) and child separation and divorce (see Chapter 13). The effect of early grandparenthood on the grandparent role is well documented (Burton & Bengtson, 1985; Burton, Dilworth-Anderson, & Merriwether-deVries, 1995). Heightened grandmother roles due to "off-time" pregnancies may extend across generations. Burton and Bengtson (1985) found numerous incidences of great-grandmothers providing care for the offspring of their adolescent granddaughters. While many grandparents willingly accept these heightened roles, others do not.

The child's remarriage can affect the grandparent role functionally, qualitatively, and structurally. When the child remarries, grandparents are less likely to be involved in custody situations and to provide financial assistance to the grandchild (Cherlin & Furstenberg, 1986a). Remarriage and the formation of blended families can largely expand the grandparent role, greatly increasing its complexity. The addition of stepgrandchildren and great step-grandchildren also increases the ambiguity of the role (e.g., normative expectations are vague if they exist at all). It has been noted that the process of "recycling" the family through divorce, remarriage, and cohabitation has contributed to the complexity of defining family roles and responsibilities including that of a grandparent (Cherlin & Furstenberg, 1994).

A number of contemporary social problems among adult children produce transitions affecting the grandparent role. Socially and economically induced unanticipated roles create considerable stress on the grandparent. Alcoholism among adult children can expand the grandparent role (Bahr, 1994). The role is often heightened by economic problems of children such as marginal employment or unemployment (Dressel & Barnhill, 1994). Few studies have examined the effect of the increasing number of employment "lay offs" and business "buy outs" on the grandparent role. Two increasing social phenomena important to the grandparent role are drug-addicted children and children with AIDS (Burton, 1992a; Minkler & Roe, 1993). While many grandparents are coping with surrogate parenting, they must also deal with problems associated with drug-exposed grandchildren. It has been estimated that between 20% and 50%

of children in the inner city whose parents were victims of the crack cocaine epidemic in the early 1990's may be living with grandparents (Minkler et al., 1993). The transition of the grandparent role to one of surrogate parent has prompted community interventions to support grandparent caregivers (see Chapters 16 and 17).

Incarceration is yet another transition mobilizing the grandparent role. This transition is primarily due to the increasing numbers of imprisoned women, up nearly 20% during the last decade (Dressel & Barnhill, 1994). Approximately 53% of children of incarcerated mothers live with grandparents. Here, two critical transition points occur, each characterized by serious issues with implications for the grandparent role. The first transition is at the point of arrest and usually has short-term implications for the role. The second transition is at the time of conviction, which usually has long-term implications such as caregiving. Data suggest that psychological response to role stress created by these grave transitions is a function of ethnicity interacting with socioeconomic level. Some minority grandmothers, for example, have been found to be reconciled to a "conflict" orientation to life and, consequently, accept the conflict and stress better than others (Bahr, 1994).

Chronic difficulties within an interpersonal context can abrade the grandparent role. Examples include social, economic, physical, and psychological hassles. Similar to hassles in a personal context, these erode the dimensions of the grandparent role over time, and are interactive and cyclical in their effect upon the role. Chronic hassles frequently stimulate grandparents to serve as "stress buffers," "national guards," "arbitrators," and roots to counteract negative forces (Denham & Smith, 1989; Kivett, 1991b). While some chronic hassles may enlarge the grandparent role, their persistent nature may affect role satisfaction. On the other side of the coin, the grandparent-grandchild relationship may be influenced negatively because of the continual diversion of family resources to a chronically ill or financially disadvantaged grandparent (Denham & Smith, 1989).

A number of nonoccurring events within an interpersonal context are related to the status or full realization of the grandparent role. Many of these events overlap with unanticipated transitions. The most obvious nonevent in an interpersonal context relates to grandparent status (e.g., never having had a grandchild). Miscarriages, abortions, stillbirths, and the giving up of infants for adoption might be considered nonevents affecting the grandparent role.

Societal Context

A number of events occurring at the societal level have important effects upon individuals and families. In many cases, grandparents assist in ameliorating the negative affect of such events on the younger generation (Denham & Smith, 1989). Events potentially influencing the grandparent role include natural and contrived disasters—such as floods and wars (Kivett, 1991b); economic declines

(Bahr, 1994; Kornhaber, 1985); justice system issues—including custody and visitation rights (Foster & Freed, 1984; J. George, 1987), crime (Schlossberg, 1984), sociohistorical processes (Bengtson, 1985; Cherlin & Furstenberg, 1986a; Kearl & Hermes, 1984); social policies (Cherlin & Furstenberg, 1986a); demography (Bengtson, 1985); and social movements (Bengtson, 1989). Permanent and temporary surrogate parenting can result from parents' military activation, fires and floods, and increasing crime rates, for example.

Societal changes in the image and normative expectations of the grandparent role have important implications for the role. Guttman (1985), by illustration, addressed the eroding effect of the new individualism, or hedonism, among grandparents on the grandparent-grandchild relationship. He maintained that grandparent-grandchild relations have been undermined by contemporary grandparents' self-indulgence and general lack of concern for the collective experience. Similarly, Kornhaber (1985) spoke to an increasing emotional distance between grandparents and grandchildren based upon a "new social contract" between parents and grandparents which places mutually agreed upon contingencies on the grandparent role.

Societal efforts through legislation and grandparent programs can have positive outcomes for grandparents (see Chapters 16 and 17). Grandparent visitation rights, currently established in most states, assist in maintaining the grandparent role. Grandparents of divorced children who otherwise might not have contact, or systematic association, with grandchildren are assured this prerogative. Societal recognition of grandparents through the declaration of a special day of the year, grandparents' day, can also heighten the role. This symbolic recognition can serve as a "prompt" for grandchild-grandparent contact and convey the message of the significance of grandparents.

Society's efforts to address issues surrounding the grandparent role through grandparent support groups and educational programs can enhance the grandparent role. Successful programs can contribute to a higher quality of life for the adult and contribute to a fuller realization of the developmental benefits from the role (see Chapter 17).

FACTORS MODIFYING THE IMPACT OF TRANSITIONS

The extent to which transitions affect the grandparent role is modified by the normative significance of the role, its personal significance, the amount of change caused by the transition, and the extent of socialization to the role (George, 1980). The more normatively significant the role, the greater the effect of the transition on role outcomes. The normative expectations of the grandparent role vary widely according to ethnicity. While Anglo Americans generally have unspecific grandparent norms except in family crises (Johnson, 1988c), groups such as Native Americans, Korean immigrants, and Mexican Americans have highly specified grandparent norms (Bahr, 1994; Bengtson, 1985; Kim, Kim, & Hurh, 1991). For example, the remarriage of a Mexican American grandmother will likely have less effect upon the extent to which she is involved in grandparenting than a corresponding white, middle-class grandmother. Severe social sanctions or rewards are associated with strong normative expectations (Bahr, 1994). As a result, transitions may be critical to the mental and social adjustment of some older adults.

The greater the personal significance of the grandparent role (e.g., identity with the role), the greater the effect of a transition on the role. A grandfather experiencing debilitating health problems who previously met important developmental needs of nurturance through grandparenting will likely experience a greater change in role satisfaction than a corresponding man for whom the role has less personal significance. Personal resources such as social supports, economic assets, and physical and mental well-being influence the personal significance of grandparenthood. Grandparents who are in relatively good health and who can afford to travel to distant grandchildren and telephone them frequently will probably find the role to be of more personal importance than similar grandparents in poor health with few financial resources.

The more a transition interferes with established patterns of behavior, the greater the effect on the grandparent role (George, 1980). For example, if a grandparent who had daily contact with a grandchild becomes institutionalized, more disruption will occur in the role than if previous contact had been infrequent. Established patterns of behavior in the grandparent role can also modify role outcomes with the relocation of a grandchild, increases in volunteering, and retirement. In the case of the latter event, a charitable grandparent who has to reduce or eliminate gift giving to grandchildren following retirement can experience more disappointment in the fulfillment of the role than similar individuals whose relationship with grandchildren is less predicated on materialism. Similarly, changes may result in the grandchild's relationship to the grandparent. Outcomes of a transition are related to the individual's extent and perception of the change in behavior.

The degree to which the individual has been socialized to the grandparent role affects the impact of transitions. Both intense and gradual socialization (anticipatory) enhance role identity and performance (George, 1980). In the case of a child's divorce, grandparents whose peers have experienced similar family crises will have clearer perceptions of their role than grandparents who have not been exposed to child divorce. Similarly, first time grandparents better understand the dynamics of the role if they have age peers who have experienced the role. Quite in contrast to this view, Johnson (1983a) suggests that weak socialization to the role of grandmother leaves more opportunity, in the case of child divorce, for the grandparent to fit the role to her own lifestyle. That is, the grandmother has more control over the impact of the transition than if she has to follow a socially prescribed role. It is generally concluded that the greater the number of transitions experienced, the lesser the effect of additional transitions.

CONCLUSIONS

Transitions have important implications for relationships and patterns of behavior (Hansson & Carpenter, 1994). Transitions in the lives of contemporary grandparents, their families, and society require that the grandparent role be revisited in relation to its saliency, normative guidelines, and dynamics. Although numerous studies have addressed events potentially influencing the grandparent-grandchild relationship, few researchers conceptualized these events as transitions. Part of this problem may be related to the absence of a unified theory of transitions, to the weaknesses in available theories in addressing issues of heterogeneity, and to the genesis and timing of transitions (George, 1993). Currently, the most promising approach to the study of how transitions impact life roles would seem to be the convergence of role theory, social stress theory, and life-course theory (George, 1993). A number of theoretical perspectives of adult development also appear to be important in the explanation of grandparent outcomes as a result of life changes.

There are three important voids in research on transitions affecting the grandparent role. First, there is the lack of longitudinal research addressing the processes and outcomes of transitions. For example, what are the mechanisms used by families to facilitate grandparenting at a distance? What is the stability of the grandparent-grandchild relationship over time in "distance" grandparenting? Second, there is a paucity of information on the relational outcomes for grandchildren, grandparents, and parents resulting from transitions. Third, little data exists on various grandparent groups and transition types. Little is known, for example, on the effects of transitions on the stepgrandparent, great-grandparent, or "fictive" grandparent roles. Information is also scarce on the differential impact of transitions according to ethnicity and gender (Kivett, 1991a). Additionally, a number of transitions occurring in middle and later adulthood with potential for influencing the grandparent role have seldom been addressed. Examples include death of friends, chronic illness of a spouse or significant other, births of additional grandchildren, marriage or cohabitation of a grandchild, and grandchildren with a socially stigmatized disease such as AIDS.

The saliency and function of the grandparent role is inexorably related to transitions in their lives. Research on the effects of transitions on the grandparent role can inform families, practitioners, and policy makers. Examples can be seen in the need to provide counseling intervention for grandparents in families with divorced and dysfunctional adult children (Myers & Perrin, 1993); to promote grandparents' adjustment to disabled or chronically ill grandchildren (Seligman, 1991); or to assist grandparents in ascension to the grandparent role (Strom & Strom, 1987). Research can also advise housing and economic policies that accommodate surrogate parenting and promote legal rights for grandparents in the case of child divorce or family dysfunction (George, 1987; Shandling, 1986; Chapter 16).

Transitions in the lives of older adults and families are inevitable and have important implications for the structure, function, and saliency of the grandparent role. The major charges to researchers and practitioners are to identify and interpret transitions in the context of their type and occurrence and to assist individuals and families undergoing transitions in the fullest utilization and gratification of the grandparent role.

Chapter 10

Intergenerational Solidarity and the Grandparent Role

Merril Silverstein, Roseann Giarrusso, and Vern L. Bengtson

Over the past quarter century research on intergenerational relationships in adult families has been guided by the theoretical construct of intergenerational solidarity (Atkinson, Kivett, & Campbell, 1986; Markides & Krause, 1985; Roberts, Richards, & Bengtson, 1991; Rossi & Rossi, 1990). As originally formulated by Durkheim (1933), solidarity describes the structural forms by which individuals are integrated within groups. In applying this concept to contemporary intergenerational family relationships, researchers have codified the principal sentiments and behaviors that link family members across generations (Bengtson & Black, 1973).

The development of the intergenerational solidarity model represents one of the few long-term efforts in the sociology of the aging family to develop theory that is informed by the results of empirical investigations (Mancini & Blieszner, 1989). There have been substantial advances in establishing the measurement properties of the principal dimensions that comprise the construct of intergenerational solidarity, as well as examining the linear relationships among them (Bengtson & Roberts, 1991; Mangen, Bengtson, & Landry, 1988). Tests of the solidarity model have demonstrated that it represents a valid and reliable multidimensional tool for assessing the strength of intergenerational family bonds (Mangen, Bengtson, & Landry, 1988). However, the majority of empirical investigations based on the solidarity model have focused on adjacent—parent-child—intergenerational family relationships; few efforts have explicitly drawn on the solidarity paradigm to describe cohesion in grandparent-grandchild relationships.

In this chapter, we (1) demonstrate that intergenerational solidarity—a conceptual and empirical model of intergenerational relationships—can describe nonadjacent intergenerational relationships as effectively as it does adjacent intergenerational relationships, (2) identify unique aspects of the adult grandchild-grandparent relationship that are informed by the application of the solidarity model to nonadjacent generations, (3) describe promising empirical applications of the solidarity model to grandparenting, and (4) discuss the need for conceptual and methodological development in this area of research.

THE INTERGENERATIONAL SOLIDARITY MODEL

One of the most important issues related to grandparenting is the extent of relational bonds or connectedness. The lives of grandparents and their grandchildren are linked in a number of ways: through roles, through interactions, through sentiments, and through exchanges of support. Therefore, connectedness between grandparents and grandchildren must be considered along multiple dimensions. Bengtson and colleagues suggest that six dimensions adequately describe the solidarity between generations: affectual, consensual, structural, associational, functional, and normative solidarity (Bengtson & Schrader, 1982; Mangen, Bengtson & Landry, 1988).

We begin by describing the six principal dimensions of the construct of intergenerational solidarity and illustrate how each has been used in empirical investigations of grandparent-grandchild relations.

Affectual solidarity involves the degree of emotional closeness that is felt between grandparents and grandchildren. Generally grandparents and grandchildren report feeling close to one another; however, there are variations in intimacy depending on the generational perspective being considered, the gender of each generation, and the middle generation's relation to the grandparent.

Studies of linked generations reveal a generational bias where grandparents report a greater degree of closeness in the relationship than do grandchildren (R. Miller, 1989). This perceptual difference has been identified as the ''intergenerational stake phenomenon''—the tendency for older generations, parents as well as grandparents, to view joint relations more favorably than younger generations (Giarrusso, Stallings, & Bengtson, 1995).

Second, gender influences the degree of affectual solidarity between grandparents and grandchildren (see Chapter 8). Of all gender pairings, grandmothers and granddaughters have the closest relationships (Hagestad 1985; Roberto & Stroes, 1992), suggesting that maternal bridges between the generations produce the most emotionally intimate intergenerational relationships (Creasey & Koblewski, 1991; Eisenberg, 1988; Hoffman, 1979) and affirming in another context the ''kinkeeper'' role that women play in the family (see Troll, Miller, & Atchley, 1979). Further, the tendency for grandchildren to have a closer relationship with their maternal grandparents suggests the ''matrifocal tilt'' of two-generation families extends through the matrilineal line of at least three generations (Hagestad, 1985). This is not to say that grandfathers do not also report close relationships with their grandchildren. One study found that 88% of grandfathers felt close to the grandchild with whom they had the most contact (Kivett, 1985b).

Affectual solidarity between grandparents and grandchildren is also influenced by members of the middle generation, since they provide a bridge between nonadjacent generations. Consequently, if parents are emotionally closer to grandparents, grandparents and grandchildren are more likely to be closer as well (Cherlin & Furstenberg, 1986a). However, in absolute terms, grandchildren continue to feel close to grandparents, even after they leave their parental house. The majority of young adult grandchildren who no longer coreside with their parents describe their relationship with their grandparent as intimate to close (Kennedy, 1992a). Further, young adult grandchildren's relationships with grandparents remain close, even when there has been a divorce in the parental generation (Cooney & Smith, 1996).

Consensual solidarity indicates the amount of intergenerational similarity or agreement in beliefs and values. This form of solidarity has long been regarded by social theorists as an important source of stability in society. Insofar as they are agents of socialization, grandparents transmit to their grandchildren the values and norms of social order. Similarity in beliefs and values between parents and children, and between grandparents and grandchildren, is often taken as evidence of successful socialization to the social structure of adult life (Troll & Bengtson, 1979). Grandparents in particular are considered as "wardens of culture" guarding against deculturation and generational discontinuity (Gutmann, 1985). Structural-functional social theorists have suggested that without such intergenerational continuity, the stage is set for conflict and disruptive change, not only within the family but also within the broader society (Chodorow, 1978; Parsons & Bales, 1955; Thomas & Znaniecki, 1958).

Studies of young adult grandchildren indicate that consensual solidarity between grandparents and grandchildren remains high even after grandchildren reach adulthood. Nearly nine out of ten post-adolescent grandchildren feel their grandparents influence their values and behaviors (G. Kennedy, 1992a). However, both maternal and paternal grandmothers seem to have a stronger sway over their grandchildren; grandsons as well as granddaughters indicate that their values are more greatly influenced by their grandmothers than their grandfathers (Roberto & Stroes, 1992). Surprisingly, young adult grandchildren from divorced and stepfamilies perceive their grandparents to be more similar to them, and to have a greater influence on them, than do grandchildren from intact-parent families, suggesting that relations with grandparents may help buffer the disruption caused by parental divorce (Kennedy & Kennedy, 1993).

However, little is known about intergenerational continuity in beliefs and values between grandparents and grandchildren over longer periods of time (Miller & Glass, 1989). Does the influence of grandparents on grandchildren end when grandchildren become adults and start families of their own? Or does it continue throughout life? Questions regarding the occurrence of intergenerational transmission across the entire life course are only beginning to be addressed since most previous research has been limited by cross-sectional designs and samples restricted to pre-adolescent, adolescent, or young adult children.

Structural solidarity refers to factors that enhance or reduce the opportunity for social interaction between grandparents and grandchildren. Foremost among these is geographic distance between the generations, followed by factors such as the marital status, gender, age, and health of each generation.

Structural solidarity in many families has changed over the last quarter century as evidenced by increases in divorce, single-parenting, and dual-earner marriages. Such changes in family composition and household structures may limit or enhance opportunities for social interaction between grandparents and grandchildren (Cherlin & Furstenberg, 1986a), and they indirectly influence such opportunities by affecting how geographically close the grandparents live to their grandchildren's parents (Baranowski, 1987; see Chapter 2).

Structural solidarity, though conceptually distinct from affectual, associational, and functional dimensions of solidarity, predisposes cohesion between generations based on other dimensions. For instance, greater structural solidarity increases the opportunity for social contact, which leads to a stronger sense of intimacy and greater functional exchanges between parents and adult children (Roberts & Bengtson, 1990). Similarly, the greater the proximity of grandparents to their young adult grandchildren, the higher their levels of association and their mutual exchange of assistance (Kivett, 1985b).

Indeed, the majority of young adult grandchildren who live independently from their parents live in close proximity to grandparents. One study found that two-thirds of young adult grandchildren lived within 50 miles of their grandparents (Kennedy, 1992a). Further, there was no difference between distance to grandmothers and distance to grandfathers. In spite of this equivalence in proximity, grandchildren had greater social contact with grandmothers than with grandfathers, suggesting that the gender of the grandparent may be more important than proximity in determining other forms of solidarity.

Associational solidarity refers to the frequency of social contact and shared activities between the grandparent and grandchild. As a result of changes in structural solidarity (such as increased divorce rates), it has now become necessary to make greater efforts to maintain intergenerational contact between grandparents and grandchildren. Increasingly, the grandparent-grandchild relationship develops outside the purview of the middle generation, and is, therefore, less bound by the directives of the wider family. As Hagestad expresses it: "In a complex, heterogeneous society, families need to build their own bridges between the old and the young. A 'common ground' is not provided by the surrounding community, but has to be developed through family interaction" (1985: 37).

For the most part, grandparents and grandchildren do stay in regular contact (Kivett, 1985b), at least when their contact is not impeded by the divorce of the parents. Divorce has a particularly harsh affect on contact between grandparents and grandchildren whose parents have not been given custody—usually the father. Some research suggests that contact with grandchildren may be further reduced when the parent remarries (Gladstone, 1991). Even though all states now have Grandparent's Rights legislation, which gives grandparents the power to go to court to secure their right to visit with their grandchildren (Wilson & DeShane, 1982), associational solidarity with grandchildren will probably remain higher for the matrilineal grandparent (see Chapter 16).

Once they leave the parental home grandchildren still keep in touch with their grandparents (see Chapter 12). Although contact with grandmothers is greater than with grandfathers, young adult grandchildren interact with their grandparents on average once a month (Hodgson, 1992; Roberto & Stroes, 1992), and more than eight out of ten young adult grandchildren have had phone contact with their grandparents within the past six months (Creasey & Koblewski, 1991). However, these high levels of interaction appear to decline with the age of the grandparent (Field & Minkler, 1988).

Functional solidarity is the help and assistance that is transferred between grandparents and grandchildren. When grandchildren are young, many grandparents babysit them (Robertson, 1977), and a growing percentage of grandparents are assuming the role of parent when the middle generation is unable to fulfill their parental responsibilities (Chalfie, 1994; Chapter 14). However, grandparents typically adhere to the "norm of noninterference," which stipulates that grandparents should not interfere with the activities of the nuclear family (Cherlin & Furstenberg, 1986a).

In most families, the real values of grandparents "can be felt simply from their presence, not their actions" (Hagestad, 1985: 44). Grandparents serve as a stabilizing force and act as a resource for their children and grandchildren. Hence, just "being there" is an important function for grandparents in their relationship with their grandchildren (Bengtson, 1985). Yet grandparents do provide a variety of concrete services to their grandchildren, primarily when the grandchildren are young. About half of young adult grandchildren retrospectively reported that their grandparents had provided them with emotional, instrumental, and financial support during childhood (Eisenberg, 1988). However, the balance of support changes after grandchildren achieve adulthood; grandparents report that they receive more expressive and instrumental support from adult grandchildren than they provide to them (Langer, 1990).

Normative solidarity concerns the perceptions of obligations and expectations about intergenerational connections. The sense of familial duty among grandparents is evidenced by the increasing numbers of grandparents who are raising their grandchildren because of problems within the parental generation, such as drug and alcohol addiction, AIDS, divorce, and unemployment (Chalfie, 1994). That some grandparents accept the role of "surrogate parent" to their grandchildren is probably the most dramatic example of normative intergenerational solidarity (see Chapter 14). In fact, grandparents who "parent" or "coparent" their grandchildren (in conjunction with their children) tend to report higher levels of normative solidarity than do grandparents who do not provide such extensive care for their grandchildren (Giarrusso et al., 1996).

However, even grandparents who do not take on full or partial caregiving responsibilities for their grandchildren report family obligations—although they differ with the age of the grandchild. Both maternal and paternal grandparents feel responsible for disciplining and advising younger grandchildren while they feel responsible for sharing wisdom with older grandchildren (Thomas, 1989). Conversely, grandparents also feel that grandchildren have obligations toward them. A study of grandfathers found that three-quarters felt that their grandchildren are responsible for providing them with financial and instrumental help during times of need (Kivett, 1985b).

SPECIAL ISSUES IN THE APPLICATION OF SOLIDARITY TO GRANDPARENT STUDIES

For more than a quarter century, the solidarity paradigm has effectively guided research on adult parent-child relations (for example, see Atkinson, Kivett, & Campbell, 1986; Lee, Netzer, & Coward, 1994; Markides & Krause, 1985; Rosenthal, 1987; Rossi & Rossi, 1990; Starrels et al., 1995). While the solidarity model has also been applied in the study of grandparent-grandchild relations, the application has been implicit rather than explicit. That is, researchers use the concepts of the model but rarely use the nomenclature or the overarching framework of solidarity in devising empirical specifications. Consequently, few studies on this topic acknowledge that grandparent-grandchild relationships are multidimensional in character; when they do, few treat dimensions of the relationship as mutually interdependent components or examine their causal ordering. Finally, there has been little work on the measurement properties of these dimensions within grandparent-grandchild relationships. Do the same six dimensions that characterize parent-child relations also characterize grandparent-grandchild relations?

Thus, basic questions concerning the utility of the solidarity model for understanding relations between nonadjacent generations remain unanswered at this time. However, we suggest that there are intriguing features of the grandparent role that will be informed by the intergenerational solidarity paradigm. In this section we focus on the utility of the solidarity model for understanding three aspects of the grandparenting role that distinguish it from the parenting role: (1) the normative ambiguity of the grandparent role, (2) the mediation of grandparent-grandchild relations by the middle (parental) generation and by the wider spectrum of roles available to today's grandparents, and (3) dynamic approaches to grandparenting including developmental and historical aspects of grandparent-grandchild relationships.

Normative Ambiguity

Previous research has demonstrated that grandparent roles are most noteworthy for their large variance in both form and function (see Bengtson & Robertson, 1985). Since there are few normatively explicit expectations placed on the role behavior of grandparents, the appropriate type and level of family involvement of grandparents is often a matter of negotiation. Indeed, previous descriptions of grandparenting styles range from "surrogate parenthood" to being little more than a stranger to grandchildren (Cherlin & Furstenberg, 1986a; Neugarten & Weinstein, 1964).

Today grandparents may range in age from 30 to 110, and grandchildren range from newborns to retirees (Hagestad, 1985). With this demographic and functional diversity has come a corresponding diversity in the enactment of the grandparent role (Bengtson, 1985). Consequently, some scholars have suggested that the role of grandparent is ill-defined and is a social status without clear normative expectations attached to it. Fischer and Silverman (1982) and Wood (1982) refer to the grandparent role as "tenuous" or "ambiguous," without clear prescriptions regarding the rights and duties of grandparents. Given the literature that discusses the wide range of possible grandparenting styles, the question remains whether the grandparent role is so amorphous and individuated that no generalizations can be drawn or whether the role, however diverse, has identifiable and recognizable forms.

Multidimensional Structure

We argue that the same dimensions that characterize parent-child relations also represent the dimensions of grandparent-grandchild relations. Consequently, the solidarity model represents a useful tool for identifying the multidimensional structure of grandparenting and for describing the range of possible grandparenting styles.

Research by Silverstein, Lawton, and Bengtson (1994) investigated the factor structure of six measures reflecting five dimensions of intergenerational solidarity in both adjacent and nonadjacent adult intergenerational relations. This analysis yielded a similar factor solution for both parent-child and grandparent-grandchild relationships. In both sets of relationships the dimensions of solidarity are divided into three clusters: structural and associational solidarity comprised an *interactive-opportunity* cluster, affectual and consensual solidarity comprised an *affective-cognitive* cluster, and providing and receiving social support comprised an *instrumental* cluster. The affective-cognitive cluster represents a latent form of solidarity—the affinity of one generation for another. The interactive-opportunity and instrumental clusters represent manifest or enacted forms of solidarity—potential or overt action of one generation toward another. These results suggest not only that it may be possible to reduce the construct of intergenerational solidarity to three underlying meta-dimensions, but also that this more parsimonious factor structure is characteristic of parent-child and grandparent-grandchild relations. Such comparability implies that the solidarity model may be generalizable to nonadjacent intergenerational relationships.

Given the multidimensional structure of solidarity, we maintain that to adequately describe intergenerational relationships it is necessary to consider several dimensions of solidarity *simultaneously*. Adhering to this simple but powerful strategy will allow researchers to represent the central characteristics of inter-generational relations and to contrast characterizations of adjacent and nonad-jacent generations. For instance, scholars have long considered grandparenting to be a "symbolic" role that revolves more around affective states and the perception of family continuity than around overt behavioral manifestations. Are grandparent-grandchild relations characterized more by latent than by enacted forms of solidarity? Is this characterization a defining feature of grandparent-grandchild relations that differentiates them from parent-child relations? In order to answer these questions, it is necessary to simultaneously contrast several dimensions of solidarity—an approach that requires the use of classification analysis—or *typologies*.

Typologies cluster relationships by their joint standing on several measures, thereby simplifying an unwieldy number of interdependent variables into a re-duced set of meaningful types. Clustering relationships based on a combination of attributes makes evident the nuances and anomalies of intergenerational fam-ily relations—a goal that remains elusive to models that treat solidarity on a variable-by-variable basis or as simple additive composite (Mangen, 1995). Typologies can lead to insights about the grandparent role in several ways. First, they effectively demonstrate diversity in this role by clustering, or sorting, peo-ple with similar grandparenting experiences into groups. Each group—or type of grandparenting style—consists of grandparents with roughly the same profile on multiple solidarity dimensions, and the relative size of each type represents its prevalence in the population. Second, the distribution of grandparenting types can be compared across subpopulations (such as ethnic or gender groups) or different kinds of family relationships.

In an innovative application of typologies to grandparent-grandchild relation-ships, Cherlin and Furstenberg (1985) classified grandparenting styles into five types: (1) the detached, (2) the passive, (3) the influential, (4) the supportive, and (5) the authoritative. Their analysis suggested that none of the five styles are dominant, and they concluded that grandparenting styles are quite diverse in contemporary American society. However, Cherlin and Furstenberg's clas-sification scheme did not systematically take into account all possible dimen-sions of grandparent-grandchild relations.

On the other hand, the intergenerational solidarity paradigm offers a system-atic and rigorously tested model to advance research on grandparent relations. One benefit of classifying grandparenting styles along the same dimensions of solidarity used in classifying parent-child relations is that direct comparisons between the two relationships would be possible. For example, five underlying types of parent-child relations have been identified along the dimensions of solidarity by Silverstein, Lawton, and Bengtson (1994): (1) the tight-knit (strong on all dimensions); (2) the detached (weak on all dimensions); (3) the sociable (strong interactive-opportunity and affective-cognitive, but weak instrumental); (4) intimate-at-a-distance (weak interactive-opportunity and instrumental, but strong affective-cognitive); and (5) obligatory (strong interactive-opportunity and instrumental, but weak affective-cognitive). Do grandparent-grandchild relations fall into the same groupings as parent-child relations, and, if yes, how differently are they distributed? The answer to these questions awaits the results of current and future investigations that contrast both kinds of family relationships.

Mediation by the Middle Generation and a Wider Spectrum of Roles

The role played by the middle or parental generation in mediating grandparent-grandchild relations has been conceived of as a bridge between the two generations (Barranti, 1985; Hagestad 1985; Robertson, 1976, 1977; see Chapter 12). Parents may set the tone for grandparent-grandchild relations over the entire life course by how they performed their earlier function as gatekeepers to grandparents and as regulators of appropriate grandparent role behavior (Robertson, 1975). Grandchildren also model the behavior of their parents toward grandparents or maintain the same close or distant relationship with grandparents that they experienced when they were living in the parental home (Matthews & Sprey, 1985). Even as adults, grandchildren tend to interact with grandparents in the context of wider family activities, often involving the parents (Kennedy, 1992a). These dynamics may explain Hodgson's (1992) finding that greater emotional closeness between parents and grandparents is associated with greater emotional closeness and greater frequency of contact between adult grandchildren and grandparents.

Events and transitions in the parental generation—including divorce, drug addiction, and death—have profound implications for the evolution of grandparenting styles. Research has shown that when parents divorce, the quality of the grandparent-grandchild relationship may change, but interestingly it may either suffer or strengthen depending on custody decisions. Divorce generally weakens grandparent-grandchild relations on the noncustodial (usually paternal) side of the family but strengthens those relations on the custodial (usually maternal) side of the family (Clingempeel et al., 1992; Creasey, 1993; Matthews & Sprey, 1984). Custodial parents effectively prevent the grandparents of an estranged spouse from seeing their grandchildren (Gladstone, 1989).

Marital disruptions of the grandparents' adult children may have indirect consequences for the well-being of the grandparent by blocking enactment of intergenerational roles (see Chapter 13). Especially, for grandparents with greater investment in the grandparent role, a decline in contact with grandchildren following the divorce of an adult child may cause emotional distress (Myers & Perrin, 1993). If the divorced parent remarries and takes on other children, then grandparents may enter a new role of stepgrandparenting that is fraught with even more ambiguous expectations (Cherlin, 1978; Henry, Ceglian, & Ostrander, 1993).

Grandparent roles are also mediated by wider family and nonfamily relationships. For instance, Troll (1985) observes that while some grandparents have nobody in the world to whom they are important save their grandchildren, others are actively involved with other relatives, coworkers, neighbors, friends, and club members. Thus, there are consequences, as well, to the relative importance attributed to the grandparent role compared to other roles. Krause and Borawski-Clark (1994) find that among older adults, stressors arising in salient social roles reduce feelings of self-esteem and control more than stressors that occur in nonsalient roles. The notion that roles are arranged in a salience hierarchy (Burke, 1991; Stryker, 1987; Thoits, 1991) implies that roles compete with each other for the time and attention of the role incumbent. If, for example, several roles are assessed as highly salient, such as family roles and work roles, then the forced trade-off between the two conflicting roles may lead to emotional distress. The grandparent role operates within a constellation of other roles enacted by the elderly, such as work, volunteer, leisure, friendship, as well as other family roles such as spouse, sibling, and parent. If many of these roles are simultaneously salient, then they may interfere with each other and compromise the ability to engage in ''successful'' grandparenting.

Developmental and Historical Aspects of Grandparent-Grandchild Relations

Like all family relationships, grandparent-grandchild relations evolve over time. Evidence from cross-sectional research suggests that the relationship between grandparents and grandchildren weakens with increasing age; older grandchildren are less involved with their grandparents than are younger grandchildren (Hodgson, 1992; Johnson, 1983b; Kivett, 1985b; Sprey & Matthews, 1982; Thomas, 1986a). At least one longitudinal study of grandparents supports this conclusion, by demonstrating that frequency of contact with grandchildren declined over a 14-year period (Field & Minkler, 1988). That the authors found no corresponding decline in level of satisfaction with grandchildren suggests that growing autonomy between grandparents and grandchildren may be a normative and accepted change in this relationship over the life course.

However, some research suggests that grandparent-grandchild relations are characterized more by continuity than by change over the life course. Retrospective reports by adult grandchildren about the degree to which their childhood was influenced by grandparents strongly predict the emotional closeness in their contemporary intergenerational relationships (Lawton, Silverstein, & Bengtson, 1994b; Matthews & Sprey, 1985). These findings demonstrate that the quality of early attachments to grandparents is sustained into the later adult stages of the relationship (Kornhaber & Woodward, 1981). Nevertheless, the long-term consequence of relationships between grandparents and grandchildren—including those disrupted by parental divorce and remarriage—for the well-being of both generations is a subject about which little is known.

The study of *adult* grandchild-grandparent relationships represents a frontier area in social gerontology. Given the wealth of studies of adult child-parent relations, it is indeed surprising that only scant attention has been devoted to studying relationships between grandparents and their adult grandchildren. Due to dramatic increases in longevity over the last century, it has become more likely that a parent will eventually become a grandparent and survive long enough to have long-term relationships with adolescent and adult grandchildren (see Chapter 2). Where fewer than half of the adolescents living in 1900 had two or more grandparents alive, by 1976 that figure had grown to almost 90% (Uhlenberg, 1980). As the median age of grandparenthood has remained constant over the past century at 45 years (Hagestad, 1985), gains in life expectancy imply that grandparents are spending more years in the grandparent role.

Evidence reveals that it is now more the rule than the exception for grandparents to have at least one grandchild who has reached adulthood. Farkas and Hogan (1994) in a study of intergenerational family structure in seven economically developed nations (including the United States) find that more than half (50.6%) of people 65 years of age and older have a grandchild who is at least 18 years old. This percentage is consistent with a study of intergenerational relations conducted in the United States by the American Association of Retired Persons (AARP) (Bengtson & Harootyan, 1994), which shows that 56% of those 65 years of age and older have at least one adult grandchild. Yet we know relatively little about the characteristics and dynamics of this increasingly more common intergenerational relationship. Do grandchildren represent an overlooked but potentially important source of emotional meaning and practical social support to grandparents, or do they recede into the background of the grandparents' family life?

The exchange dynamics between generations in the family represent a promising line of inquiry for understanding how early family attachments influence the enactment of intergenerational roles in the older family. Research on parent-child relationships suggests that past family experiences have an enduring influence on intergenerational behavior such that the quality of the early relationship influences whether the child will provide assistance to parents when they are aged (Cicirelli, 1983; Rossi & Rossi, 1990; Whitbeck, Simons, & Conger, 1991). One useful paradigm for viewing serial patterns of reciprocity in adjacent generations over the life course is the "support bank." In this paradigm early investments in children are withdrawn later in life when the parent requires social support due to old-age dependencies (Antonucci, 1990). However the life course exchange dynamics that govern reciprocity between grandparents and grandchildren are less obvious and the model of lagged reciprocity has yet to be tested with respect to grandparent-grandchild relationships. What degree of obligation do adult grandchildren have for their grandparents, and how are they tied to earlier family experiences?

The proliferation of grandparents raising their grandchildren (see Chalfie, 1994; Dressel & Barnhill, 1994; Giarrusso et al., 1996; Jendrek, 1993, 1994;

Minkler, Roe, & Price, 1992; Roe, Minkler, & Barnwell, 1994; Roe, Minkler, & Saunders, 1995; Shore & Hayslip, 1994; Solomon & Marx, 1995) raises the intriguing possibility that surrogate parenting by grandparents is compensated by social support from grandchildren in much the same way as parents are reciprocated. There remain more questions than answers. Will the dynamic of reciprocity occur among grandchildren who were emotionally close with their grandparents? Will grandchildren who were only casually acquainted with their grandparents establish an independent adult relationship with their grandparents following departure from the parental home? Does the mechanism of *indirect* reciprocity result in even detached grandchildren serving the needs of grandparents by supplementing care delivered principally by their middle-aged parents? Conversely, do grandparents help grandchildren they barely know to fulfill an obligation to their adult children? And what about the responsibility to stepgrandparents? As a result of marital disruption and reformation, adult grandchildren may have multiple grandparents and multiple stepgrandparents. Our understanding of these relationships requires consideration of idiosyncratic childhood experiences with their grandparents, including the timing of the divorce and the nature of the relationship between the two older generations.

Another aspect of temporal dynamics in grandparent-grandchild solidarity has to do with the role that historical time plays in grandparenting styles. Research has demonstrated that sociohistorical context profoundly influences family processes by structuring options available to family members (Elder, 1974, 1984; Chapters 2, 3, 4). If grandparents act as contingent resources—or "safety valves"—that buffer the distress caused by economic downturns and marital disruptions (Hagestad, 1985; Troll, 1983), then we may witness elevated rates of solidarity between grandparents and grandchildren over recent historical times, when wages have stagnated and divorce rates have risen for younger generations.

If, on the other hand, growing individualism, divorce, and economic stressors have caused the family to abdicate its functions (Popenoe, 1993), then grandparents may play a reduced role over time. Other historical changes such as the increase in the relative wealth of the elderly, earlier retirement, and better health in later life have expanded the social alternatives available to grandparents for a fulfilling social life. Kornhaber (1985, 1996) has been among the most vocal critics of what he perceives as a weakening grandparent role. He asserts that grandparents have abdicated their responsibility by "turning their backs" on grandchildren (both in terms of emotional and practical support), as they pursue their "selfish" goals (see also Gutmann, 1985).

Evidence for a "declining-grandparent-role" hypothesis is refuted by the high levels of affection, obligation, and helping behavior reported by many surveys of grandparent-grandchild relationships (Cherlin & Furstenberg, 1986a; Robertson, 1976). In a rare attempt to compare data from two periods of time, Kennedy (1990) found that compared to Robertson's (1976) findings 12 years earlier, contemporary young adult grandchildren were *more* likely than their earlier counterparts to turn to grandparents for advice and support. This study suggests that grandparents are becoming increasingly more valuable in serving as a resource to grandchildren who are making the sometimes difficult transition to adulthood.

CONCEPTUAL AND METHODOLOGICAL DEVELOPMENT IN GRANDPARENTING STUDIES

Before empirical researchers can begin answering the questions raised above, conceptual groundwork needs to be laid to guide these new efforts. Conceptual models in the social and behavioral sciences are important because they serve to alternatively focus or deflect attention from potentially promising areas of inquiry. We suggest that conceptual models are especially valuable in areas where complexity makes it difficult to fully understand the phenomenon of interest. It has been suggested that models used to understand the nature of grandparent-grandchild relations have lagged behind the rapid social changes that have increased the heterogeneity of these relationships and the contexts in which they are enacted (Cohler & Altergott, 1995). For instance, social science models that focus only on grandparents who are raising grandchildren have little basis for understanding the myriad conditions under which the grandparent role is enacted. Similarly, models of grandparent-grandchild relations have tended to focus on interactional dynamics (associational solidarity) to the exclusion of other forms of cohesion, such as value consensus (consensual solidarity) and financial exchanges (functional solidarity) (Aldous, 1995).

An important component of developmental analysis is the investigation of changes and trajectories of grandparent-grandchild relations across the course of later life of the grandparent and across the transition from adolescence to adulthood of the grandchild. Cross-sectional studies of grandparent-grandchild relations generally find that older grandparents and older grandchildren are more likely than their younger counterparts to have lower affectual solidarity, suggesting a pattern of withdrawal over the life course (for example, Cherlin & Furstenberg, 1986a). The use of age as a proxy for the passage of time and its concomitants, however, confounds birth cohort/historical and maturational factors, thereby presenting problems in the interpretation of such results. Analyses of longitudinal data are clearly needed. Without such data is it is not possible to answer many intriguing questions about grandparent-grandchild relations. Do grandchildren interact as often with grandparents (associational solidarity) after they gain residential autonomy? Do adult grandchildren get involved with the care of dependent grandparents (functional solidarity)? Do they live nearby (structural solidarity), feel close (affectual solidarity), or share view points (consensual solidarity) with their aging grandparents, and how much do the answers to these questions depend on earlier—including childhood—patterns of intergenerational solidarity? Is there a structured ''career'' in these relations over the life course? As grandparents and grandchildren are spending more years as contemporaries of each other, answers to these question have become increasingly important. The solidarity paradigm offers a useful lens that brings into focus the salient relational dimensions that need to be measured and tracked over time in order to address these issues.

The analysis of grandparent-grandchild dyads is an innovation that extends our understanding of the relationship over time by considering dimensions of solidarity from the point of view of *both* generations. Models that consider only one perspective ignore *interdependence* between grandparents and adult grandchildren over the life course. For example, disruptive life events, such as widowhood and the onset of disability, may interfere with the ability of grandparents to visit with grandchildren (limiting associational solidarity), but may induce grandchildren to provide social support (enhancing functional solidarity). However, such dynamics are contingent on life-course events experienced by grandchildren. For instance, after leaving the parental nest, grandchildren often renegotiate their relationships with grandparents—some may develop stronger affectual and normative solidarity, and others weaker. In addition, the obligations of career, marriage, and family formation felt by adult grandchildren may interfere with associational, structural, and functional solidarity with their grandparents. The study of dyads allows the consideration of how the unique but mutually interacting developmental trajectories of both generations influence life-course patterns of solidarity.

Tracing the grandparent-grandchild relationship—as it toggles between latency and activity over the life course—also requires that longitudinal data be available and longitudinal methods be used to study the temporal dynamics of solidarity. For example, while at any one point in time the relationship between grandparents and their adult grandchildren may appear to have little functional solidarity, when considered over a longer time frame the relationship may be punctuated by functional exchanges as the needs of each generation dictate. Such episodic, but important, forms of functional solidarity include grandparents helping with a down payment when grandchildren are buying their first house, and grandchildren aiding the transition of grandparents to a nursing home. These overt forms of intergenerational solidarity, though sometimes rare and intermittent, are of crucial importance when triggered and usually have latent forms of solidarity (for example, affectual and normative) as their antecedents.

The solidarity paradigm is particularly useful in providing an interpretive scheme and nomenclature for investigations on the frontier of intergenerational family relations—such as the study of great-grandparenting. Indeed, the only three published studies to examine the experiences of great-grandparents (Doka & Mertz, 1988; Roberto & Skoglund, 1996; Wentowski, 1985; see also Chapter 12) found a great deal of similarity with the experiences of grandparents. In an emerging area of investigation there is an even greater need to rely on a well-grounded theory in model specification and testing. Use of the solidarity model can provide conceptual consistency across studies and enhance our understanding of the experience of grandparenting under assorted conditions and contexts, as well as in relation to other intergenerational ties.

Finally, we suggest that family theory and methodology have not kept pace with the increasing complexity in grandparent-grandchild relations. Divorce and remarriage have created legions of stepgrandparent-grandchild relations—about which we know very little—as well as grandparents related to their biological grandchildren through a noncustodial divorced parent (usually a son). Given the growing structural heterogeneity of intergenerational families, we predict that it will become ever more difficult to describe a "normative" career of grandparenting. Nevertheless, we anticipate that grandparents and grandchildren will continue to be important resources to each other—but within relationships that are less obligatory and more voluntaristic in nature. These changes make it more important that researchers use a *multidimensional* framework, such as that provided by the intergenerational solidarity model, to better understand the evolving contingencies and complexities of the grandparent role.

Chapter 11

Grandparents' Influences on Grandchildren

Angela M. Tomlin

Although the grandparent-grandchild connection plays a primary role in spanning generations, it is less defined and understood than other family relations (Kivett, 1991b). Research examining the scope, intensity, quality, and mechanism of grandparents' influences on grandchildren has been conducted for at least 50 years. Despite this long history of interest in the topic, evidence both about the processes of grandparents' influences on grandchildren as well as about grandchildren outcomes remains limited and often inconsistent and lacks a clear theoretical foundation (Denham & Smith, 1989; Kivett, 1991b).

One reason for the lack of a unifying theory is that research about grandparents has reflected the major theoretical frameworks of the time. The earliest efforts were often psychodynamically based case studies, which typically offered a negative view of grandparents' influence on grandchildren. Grandparents, and particularly grandmothers, were portrayed as intrusive and meddlesome—or worse, as Strauss's (1943) contribution, "Grandma made Johnny delinquent," makes apparent.

By the 1960's, researchers were more positive in their treatment of grandparents' influence on grandchildren. Focusing on the grandparent-grandchild dyad, several studies document that grandparents can directly influence their grandchildren's development, attitudes, or behaviors (Tinsley & Parke, 1984; Smith, 1995). These studies most often involved interviews or surveys of grandparents or adolescent and college-aged grandchildren (Fischer, 1983; Kahana & Kahana, 1971; Kivnick, 1983; Neugarten & Weinstein, 1964), retrospective accounts of the childhood interactions with grandparents (Hartshorne & Manaster, 1982; Robertson, 1975) or more rarely, direct investigation of young children (Kahana & Kahana, 1970).

Beginning in the 1970's and continuing today, increasingly sophisticated re-

Figure 11.1
Influence Processes among Grandparents, Grandchildren, and Parents

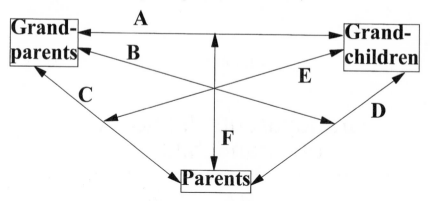

search recognizes that grandparents are able to influence grandchildren in *indirect* as well as direct ways. Grandparents can influence grandchildren through the middle generation by acting as a source of support or role model to parents (Denham & Smith, 1989; Levitt, Weber, & Clark, 1986). Tinsley and Parke further describe these "indirect effects" of grandparents on grandchildren's behavior as occurring through "advice, information, and modeling of child-rearing skills" given to parents (1984: 174). At present, the study of direct effects takes a back seat to work examining indirect effects, which may be the major method by which grandparents influence grandchildren (Kivett, 1991b). The popularity of the indirect approach is probably a result of beliefs that grandparents should not "interfere" and that parents have primary responsibility for their children.

Researchers have also become more aware that grandparents' influences are contingent on a variety of factors, including grandparents' age, gender, health, or their ethnic/racial background (Barranti, 1985). Likewise, grandchildren vary widely in these factors, which also may lead to differences in the impact grandparents have on them. In addition to factors stemming from variations within the grandparent-grandchild dyad, grandparents' influences on grandchildren's outcomes can be affected by the child's family configuration and other contextual factors. Grandparental influences are mitigated by parental divorce and custody arrangements, geographical distance, the grandparent's relationship with the parents, or household composition. Socioeconomic status or rural/urban residence also impinge on grandparents' influence on their grandchildren (see Chapter 4).

GRANDPARENTS' INFLUENCES ON GRANDCHILDREN: OVERVIEW

A proposed model of the process of grandparental influences on grandchild outcomes is presented in Figure 11.1. The model allows for *direct* and *indirect* effects of grandparents as well as *reciprocal* effects of grandchildren on grandparents (Denham & Smith, 1989; Robertson, 1975; Tinsley and Parke, 1984).

Grandparents *directly* influence grandchildren through activities that involve interactions between grandparents and grandchildren (path A), such as transmitting family values, teaching specific skills, or even surrogate parenting. Such direct influences can be affected by parental characteristics and interventions (path F). *Indirect* influence occurs when grandparents' interaction is mediated through grandparent-parent or parent-grandchild interactions or relationships (paths B, E; C-D chain). For example, the grandparents' parenting of the middle generation may impact the middle generation's later parenting of the third generation (C-D chain). In addition, current grandparent interactions with the middle generation may influence grandchildren by providing role models for intergenerational relationships (E). Grandparents can also indirectly influence grandchildren by intervening in relationships between the grandchildren and their parents, for example, when teenage parents lack parenting skills (B). The model further allows for *reciprocal* influences (Shore & Hayslip, 1994), in which actions of the grandchildren directed toward parents or grandparents circle back to inform and change grandparent and parent behaviors (indicated by the two-directional arrows in the figure).

The outcomes of grandparents' direct and indirect influences on grandchildren are far-reaching. Grandparents impact their grandchildren's cognitive, social, and emotional development, attitudes and values, and behaviors in both positive and negative ways; these effects can be short term or long lasting. In addition, the influence itself can be perceived by the recipient as beneficial or detrimental. This chapter will separately address the processes by which grandparents affect grandchildren's development and the specific grandchild outcomes that result from grandparental influences (for grandparent influences under selected conditions, see Chapters 12, 13, 14, and 15).

GRANDPARENTS' INFLUENCES ON GRANDCHILDREN'S DEVELOPMENT: PROCESS

A variety of survey, interview, and laboratory studies regarding the relations of grandparents with young adult, adolescent, and school-aged grandchildren demonstrate many ways in which grandparents directly impact their grandchildren's development. Grandparents' influence grandchildren through various processes and roles including surrogate parent, buddy, storyteller, and confidant (Franks et al., 1993).

An important vehicle for grandparental influence is the role of advocate or advisor (Franks et al., 1993). Similarly influential is the role of mentor or motivator, who is capable of "providing inspiration and encouragement" to the grandchild. Grandchildren who report being influenced in this way often wish to imitate the personal attributes of their elders, such as risk-taking, patience, and tenacity (Franks et al., 1993).

The influence process may vary with the age of the grandchild. For example, younger children conceptualize their relationship with their grandparents in terms of what the grandparent does for them, whereas adolescents find in the grandparent someone willing to listen to them and maintain their trust (Tyszkowa, 1993). Young adults, with somewhat more perspective and life experience, begin to better convey the grandparents' influence in their lives, particularly with regard to such value-laden topics as politics and religion. Grandparents' role as a teacher of values, rules, and mores, including religious, sexual, political, moral and educational beliefs, family ideals, work ethic, and personal identity is highlighted in research with college students (Franks et al., 1983; Kennedy, 1992a; Lawton, Silverstein, & Bengtson, 1994; Roberto & Stroes, 1992). Among some racial and ethnic minorities grandparents also serve as transmitters and translators of their culture (see Chapters 3 and 7). As adults, grandchildren's recollections of the grandparents' influences during childhood are linked to current levels of shared opinions and values (Lawton, Silverstein, & Bengtson, 1994b). In general, grandmothers may be more influential than grandfathers, with the exception of values surrounding beliefs about work ethics, which appear to be equally influenced by grandmothers and grandfathers (Roberto & Stroes, 1992). Often these values are transmitted through three generations, with young women, their mothers, and their maternal grandmothers endorsing similar social and political attitudes, for example (Kalish & Visher, 1982).

Grandparents' ability to influence grandchildren's values appears to be itself contingent on family configuration, race/ethnicity, and grandparent and grandchild characteristics, such as gender. For example, agreement about values tends to be higher among African American families than Caucasian families (Lawton, Silverstein, & Bengtson, 1994b). African-American grandchildren see their grandparents as more influential in teaching life skills and providing direction about values and morals than do Caucasian grandchildren (Strom, Collinsworth, Strom et al., 1993). In a Finnish sample, strong correlations between grandparent and parent child-rearing attitudes were found, with the grandmother-mother connection stronger than that between the grandfather-father pairs (Ruoppila, 1991). Grandparenting style has an impact on influence, with those falling in the apportioned group having more influence than remote grandparents (Roberto & Stroes, 1982). Women, only and firstborn children, and those in blended families tend to report increased grandparental influence (Kennedy & Kennedy, 1993). Grandparents' involvement in disciplining grandchildren appears to depend on their overall responsibility for the grandchildren. For example, Blackwelder and Passman (1986) found that amount of discipline administered by the grandmother in an experimental situation was strongly related to the amount of responsibility she felt for the grandchild in several areas, including personal authority, teaching and socialization, emotional needs, child rearing, and discipline.

Besides helping grandchildren directly, grandparents can indirectly have an impact on their grandchildren's lives by providing assistance to their own children, the grandchildren's parents. The supportive activities include emotional support (Levitt, Weber, & Clark, 1986; Tinsley & Parke, 1987), financial assistance or maintenance of living standards (G. Wilson, 1987), and child-care help (Jendrek, 1994). These functions are especially likely to occur during times of family crisis, such as divorce and remarriage, parental job loss, or need to perform military service (Franks et al., 1993). In such difficult times, grandparents can provide grandchildren with a stable adult presence when other important figures are unavailable (Kennedy & Kennedy, 1993). Often parental job responsibilities or problems such as drug abuse in the middle generation provide an impetus for the grandparent to take partial or complete care of the grandchild (Jendrek, 1994). Although these child-care situations appear to be increasing, limited information is available regarding the effects of such arrangements, especially on the grandchildren (Minkler, Roe, Robertson-Beckley, 1994; see also Chapter 14).

Most of these studies focus on grandmothers' support to mothers, especially teen mothers (M. Wilson, 1989). At least one study, however, demonstrated that grandfather support can positively impact a teen mother's nurturance toward her young child (Oyserman, Radin, & Benn, 1993). Furthermore, fathers can benefit from grandparent support, especially with regard to paternal adjustment to a child with a disability who has been associated with receiving financial and child-care support from grandparents (Sandler, Warren, & Raver, 1995).

In general, grandparents' influence may be enhanced in nonintact families. Grandparents may serve as "resistance resources" for grandchildren in single-parent and blended families; these youngsters benefit from the continuity and support a grandparent may provide (Werner & Smith, 1982: 160). Specifically, single-parent and blended-family households report a more involved and influential role for grandparents, including giving gifts and money and taking an active role in child rearing, significantly more than in intact families, in which the grandparents' importance in transmitting family heritage and stability is emphasized (Kennedy & Kennedy, 1993; Thomas, 1990a). Ethnic differences in grandparent support have also been found, with African American grandparents more directly involved in raising grandchildren, including providing direct discipline, guidance, and support to grandchildren than grandparents from other ethnic groups (Kennedy, 1990; Strom et al., 1993).

Grandparents' impact on child outcomes are not always positive, however. The perception that members of one's social network, including grandparents, provide both support and interference is shared by married and single, adult and adolescent mothers (Richardson, Barbour, & Bubenzer, 1991; Thomas, 1990a). Concerns include grandparents' possible interference in child rearing, for example, the giving of unsolicited advice about parenting. Thomas (1990a) reviews the "double bind" to grandparents when the single mother expects the grandparents to simultaneously provide support in child rearing without being too intrusive.

Grandparent support may also be detrimental to fathers, although the effects may be transmitted through their spouses. Men with unstable work histories were reported to be more punitive toward their children than other men when their wives received support from friends and relatives (Robertson et al., 1991). Parents who are in the process of divorcing may be especially sensitive to unwanted parental advice, whereas grandparents tend to feel that voicing child-rearing concerns is appropriate at this time (Johnson, 1988d).

Although adolescent parents receive positive support from various sources, including their own parents, negative interference is frequently present in the same relationship. For example, among African American families, high levels of grandmother support to a teen mother were associated with negative consequences for the teen. Teen mothers who received the most grandparent support reported lower self-esteem, were less likely to work outside the home, and tended to have received less prenatal care (Voran & Phillips, 1993).

One common result of teen pregnancy or divorce is a three-generational household. The impact of coresidence on both mothers' and grandmothers' parenting skills may be modulated by the age of the mother and the child (Chase-Lansdale, Brooks-Gunn, & Zamsky, 1994; Harrigan, 1992). For older mothers, both mothers' and grandmothers' parenting skills are enhanced when they do not share a residence. Grandmothers and mothers are most similar in negative parenting practices when sharing housing and most alike in positive practices when living separately (Harrigan, 1992). Conflicts such as disagreements about parenting, household stress, as well as a tendency for diffusion of parenting responsibility may occur in such three-generational homes (Harrigan, 1992).

In contrast, children of very young mothers are likely to benefit from coresidence with grandmothers. When living in this three-generational configuration, grandmothers are more involved, supportive, and have better parenting skills (Harrigan, 1992). For example, knowledge about child development is enhanced in teen mothers who live with grandmothers, when grandmothers also provide a model of appropriate parenting skills. These teen mothers consider the grandmother a good source of help with child-rearing concerns (Stevens, 1984). Laboratory studies by Oyserman and her colleagues further reveal that teen mothers' nurturance seems to be enhanced by grandfathers' nurturance, whereas grandmothers' supports tend to inhibit nurturant behaviors among teenage mothers (Oyserman, Radin, & Saltz, 1994). In addition, less conflict is reported by young mothers when the grandmother helps with child care (Oyserman, Radin, & Benn, 1993). Despite the potential for emotional, material, and child-rearing support from family members, the likelihood of interference in these areas suggests that "it is unwise to assume that the family of origin is necessarily the optimal residential arrangement for the adolescent mother and her child" (Richardson, Barbour, & Bubenzer, 1991: 434).

The effect of child care provided by grandparents or other extended-family members on parent employment and school attendance is unclear. Overall, kin-provided child care does not increase a young mother's chances of entering the workforce, although among kin, grandmothers were the most facilitating of working mothers (Parish, Hao, & Hogan, 1991). Within the three-generational household, financial and child-care support to a teen mother facilitates school attendance and work force participation, factors which can improve the grandchild's standard of living (Trent & Harlan, 1994). Grandchildren in this family configuration may have lower poverty rates and less dependence on public assistance than children in single-parent families (Trent & Harlan, 1994).

Family ethnicity may also be a factor in expectations for the grandparent role with regard to indirect forms of support (Wilson, 1989). For example, African American grandparents are seen as more active in helping parents with parenting than are Caucasian grandparents (Kennedy, 1990). In contrast, grandparent support in Caucasian families tends to be in the form of financial assistance to parents (Parish, Hao, & Hogan, 1991). Increased support to parents in African American families may be especially likely when the mother is single and shares housing with the grandmother (Wilson, 1987).

In addition to current practices, grandparents, by acting as parents themselves, influence their children's subsequent parenting behaviors (Smith, 1995) and the grandchildren's perceptions of their relationships with grandparents (Whitbeck, Hoyt, & Huck, 1993). For instance, adults who recall nonoptimal childhood relations with their parents continue to experience strained family interactions. Furthermore, their children's current relationship with the grandparents is affected directly and indirectly by a history of negative family relations (Whitbeck, Hoyt, & Huck, 1993). In a longitudinal study, women who recalled their parents as hostile and their mothers as unstable were likely to display hostile attitudes toward their own children (Elder, Caspi, & Downey, 1986). Similarly, in a Dutch study, about one-third of the variation in mothers' parental functioning was attributable to the maternal grandmother's earlier parental functioning (Vermulst, de Brock, & van Zutphen, 1991).

GRANDPARENTS' INFLUENCES ON GRANDCHILDREN'S DEVELOPMENT: OUTCOMES

Grandparents' actions within the family systems have wide-ranging impact on grandchildren's outcomes, including social, emotional, cognitive and identity development, behavior, and family relations. Both positive and negative effects are generated through these interactions.

Grandparent child rearing, whether jointly with parents or alone, appears to be fairly successful in terms of child outcomes. With the exception of academic performance, outcomes of children raised by grandparents are remarkably similar to outcomes of children from intact families (Solomon & Marx, 1995). Children raised by grandparents and parents were rated as similar in school behaviors and in susceptibility to illness and frequency of problems such as headaches, asthma, accidents, and enuresis. Both groups have fewer concerns in these areas than did children in single-parent families. Furthermore, children being raised in intact families had a higher level of academic success (more were defined as being better students and fewer had to repeat a grade) than those raised by grandparents only or by single parents, which were equal (Solomon & Marx, 1995).

In general, outcomes for children being raised by single mothers can be enhanced by the presence of another adult in the household, including a grandparent (Dornbusch et al., 1985; Stolba & Amato, 1993). For example, adolescents living with single mothers had better behavior when a grandparent was also in the home. The child's age appears to modulate grandparents' effects, as children in middle childhood did not benefit from the grandparents' presence. For these children, behavior ratings were worse with a grandparent present than without (Stolba & Amato, 1993).

Although most studies of three-generational families focus on the mother-grandmother-child triad, effects of grandfathers have been documented. For example, very young grandchildren's compliance with their teenage mothers' requests are enhanced by the presence of a nurturing grandfather in the household. In addition, the more the grandfather participates in child-rearing activities, the less negative affect is shown by the child (Oyserman, Radin, & Benn, 1993).

Collaborative caregiving in a three-generational household has positive effects on the grandchild's concept development, an important factor in cognitive development (Furstenberg, 1976). Emotional development and self-esteem are also enhanced by the addition of a grandparent to a single-parent home. Kellam, Ensminger, and Turner (1977) found that children in a low-income population showed as good social adaptation and psychological well-being when they belonged to a mother-grandmother family as when they came from intact mother-father families. The pattern of an additional adult improving child functioning in single-mother-headed homes continues through adolescence (Dornbusch et al., 1985). Adolescent males experience lower levels of deviant behavior, including fewer contacts with legal authorities and fewer episodes of truancy when their mothers receive this type of in-home support. Female adolescents also benefit, with less smoking and fewer arrests noted in the extended-family households. Generally, an improved relationship with parents is a positive result of a strong teen-grandparent relationship (Baranowski, 1982).

Grandparents' impact on their grandchildren's conduct is not always positive, however. Aggressive and antisocial behaviors in children have also been attributed to intergenerational influences, for example, drug use by the mother and developmental and behavioral problems in the third generation (Stein, Newcomb, & Bentler, 1993). Grandchildren whose mothers reported feeling burdened by caring for a grandparent with Alzheimer's disease reported poorer relations with their fathers (Creasey & Jarvis, 1989).

Grandparents' behaviors have been shown to impact one of the most consequential tasks in the young child's emotional life: the development of an attachment to caregivers (Ainsworth & Eichenberg, 1981). The importance of infant-caregiver attachment cannot be overestimated. Infant-caregiver attachment is positively related to the child's future self-esteem, self-effectiveness, and ability to forge later connections. (Ainsworth et al., 1978).

Comparison of maternal scores on a measure of adult attachment (the Adult Attachment Interview; Main, Kaplan, & Cassidy, 1985) with child behaviors in the Strange Situation demonstrates that security of 12- to 18-month-old infants' attachment to their mothers relates to the mothers' attachment to their own mothers. Mothers with autonomous adult attachment to their own mothers (i.e., those who recalled both favorable and unfavorable attachment experiences openly and objectively) were more likely to have infants with secure attachments. Similarly, dismissive adult attachment (i.e., those who placed little value or importance on previous attachment experiences) related to avoidant infant attachment and preoccupied adult attachment (i.e., those who remain dependent on parents and involved with pleasing them) is related to ambivalent infant attachment (Ainsworth & Eichenberg, 1981). In addition, current grandparent behaviors can facilitate or hinder child-parent attachment. For example, unsatisfactory mother-grandmother relations have been shown to relate to an avoidant attachment between mother and (grand)child (Levitt, Weber, & Clark, 1986).

The relationship between security of child attachment and grandmother behavior has also been documented with teen mothers, their mothers, and the babies of the teens (Benn & Saltz, 1989). The grandmother's behavior in taking over direct care of the infants and in being directive toward the mother was related to the security of the child's attachment to the mother.

In addition to facilitating the parent-child attachment, grandparent behavior can result in an attachment between themselves and the grandchild. Grandchildren show evidence of secure attachment to their grandmother when more contact occurs between grandmother and grandchild, the grandmother reports having more responsibility for the child, and the mother and grandmother have better agreement on child-rearing issues (Myers, Jarvis, & Creasey, 1987; Tomlin & Passman, 1989). The attachment or connection may be particularly evident in blended families (Kennedy & Kennedy, 1993). This ongoing relationship may be positive for the grandchild, but can impede the development of solidarity in the new blended family.

Other emotionally based behavior patterns or personality traits can also be influenced by grandparents' behavior. For example, child dependency, an emotional preference leading to striving for support and aid of others, has been shown to be transmitted principally by child-rearing attitudes (Fu, Hinkle, & Hanna, 1986). Grandmothers' dependency influences both the mothers' dependency and the grandmothers' parenting. These factors, in turn, affect mothers' parenting, which influences the child's dependency.

RECIPROCAL INFLUENCES

Even though reciprocal influences in intergenerational relations have been recognized for at least two decades (Hess & Waring, 1978; Shore & Hayslip,

1994), research that specifically addresses the ways in which child behavior influences adult behavior is relatively sparse. However, as we continue to move to more system-oriented research, the fact of bidirectional influence must be considered (Shore & Hayslip, 1994).

Research on discipline strategies may be the area in which investigation of reciprocal effects has received the most attention, especially with regard to parental discipline. Several experimental studies indicate that a child's reaction to discipline is one of the factors that influences subsequent parental discipline (Mulhern & Passman, 1977, 1981; Passman & Blackwelder, 1981). Mothers in these studies increased their discipline when presented with prepared data indicating that their children's performance on a task was worsening.

A few studies also provide initial support for parallel effects of grandchildren on grandparents' behaviors. For example, effects of a child not responding to discipline have been shown to be similar for grandmothers and mothers (Blackwelder & Passman, 1986). In a study that considered both reciprocal and indirect effects, the mother and grandmother administration of reward and punishment was affected by each other's apparent responses in addition to the child's apparent responses (Tomlin & Passman, 1991).

Another way to view the child's impact on the grandparent-grandchild relationship is to consider variations in such interactions due to specific grandchild characteristics such as gender, age, or physical and mental condition. There is limited evidence that grandparents may treat granddaugthers differently than grandsons (see Chapter 8). Grandchildren's age, on the other hand, does impact on grandparent-grandchild interactions. Specifically, grandchildren's age influences both the frequency of interaction between grandparents and grandchildren and the type of activities and roles grandparents assume vis-à-vis the grandchildren. Apparently, grandparents adjust their actions to the developmental stage of the grandchild and are affected by other commitments especially on the part of older grandchildren (Kahana & Kahana, 1970; Kornhaber & Woodward, 1981; Tyszkowa 1993). Research also shows that grandchildren's health impacts on grandparents. Grandparents of premature infants felt unprepared for their role and worried about the child's survival (Rempusheski, 1990), and grandparents of disabled grandchildren reacted with sadness, shock, and sometimes anger (Seligman, 1991).

More generally, grandparents have been shown to benefit from the relation with grandchildren in various ways. Several studies indicate that grandparents derive status and satisfaction from the transition to grandparenthood and derive meaning, enjoyment, and companionship from their interactions with grandchildren (Barranti, 1985; Cunningham-Burley, 1984a, 1986b; Kivnick, 1982, 1985, 1988; Russell, 1986; Thomas, 1990b). Within the multigenerational household, grandparents reported a variety of benefits including companionship and closeness, personal growth, and the exchange of knowledge among generations (Harrigan, 1992; Poe, 1992; see also Chapter 14).

Interaction with grandchildren can also be negative. The costs of raising grandchildren are numerous, ranging from financial, mental health, and overload problems to marital and physical health concerns among these grandparents (see Chapter 14). Furthermore, the extent and type of problems experienced by surrogate grandparents is contingent on whether or not the grandchildren exhibit physical, mental, or behavioral problems (Hayslip et al., forthcoming; Poe, 1992). Assimilation of minority grandchildren (e.g., Hispanic, Asian) into the mainstream culture also can lead to some distancing in grandparent-grandchild relationships (see Chapters 6 and 7).

FUTURE RESEARCH DIRECTIONS

The amount and quality of information available about grandparents' effects on grandchildren has increased dramatically as many researchers recognize the ubiquity of the role. Despite many well-conducted studies, the field remains fragmented (Kivett, 1991b). The continuing lack of cohesiveness can be attributed to the heterogeneity of both grandchildren and grandparents and the many competing mediating factors inherent in family research. For example, variation in grandparents, grandchildren, family configurations, ethnic and other social differences, and gender issues point to the need for broader and more sophisticated research models. Overarching research models that evaluate unique patterns of intergenerational solidarity and their impact on child behavioral and psychological outcomes are needed (Roberts, Richards, & Bengtson, 1991).

Future studies should utilize designs that allow for the multidimensional nature of family research. Studies will need to account for layers of effects within three- and even four-generational families. As indicated in Figure 11.1, it will be important for these research efforts to consider the direct and indirect effects of an extended family on child outcomes (Voran & Phillips, 1993; M. Wilson, 1989), as well as reciprocal influences among grandparents, parents, and grandchildren. Cohort effects and cross-cultural variations are other pieces of the puzzle to be considered.

It is especially important to consider theoretical frameworks that can account for the influence of grandparents on grandchildren at different points in development (Kivett, 1991b). Developmental studies that involve young children as direct participants and longitudinal designs may help researchers clarify competing ideas about the role and effects of grandparents in their grandchildren's lives. Both negative and positive impacts and short- and long-term effects of grandparents must be considered when evaluating their influence on grandchildren. Qualitative approaches may be helpful in assessing the impact of these types of variations on grandchild outcomes across the lifespan.

Finally, as our concept of family continues to expand, researchers will need to consider kinship relations beyond three generations and those that represent nonlinear connections (Roberts, Richards, & Bengtson, 1991). Investigators must include nontraditional family configurations, with evaluation of the impact of stepgrandparents and other extended-family members included. The development of an encompassing, cohesive theory to explain the evolving role of the grandparents in the development and life of grandchildren should be a priority (Kivett, 1991b).

Chapter 12

Grandparents and Older Grandchildren

Lynne Gershenson Hodgson

A GRANDCHILD'S STORY—TWICE TOLD

A is 22 years old and has just graduated from college. He lives three hours from his parents, who live in the same town as his maternal grandparents and his paternal grandmother. Until he went away to college, he saw both sets of grandparents at least once a week, but more often than not, he saw them even more frequently than that. Since both his parents worked outside the home as he was growing up, his grandparents often took over for them when needed—a ride home from school when he got sick, a lift to the local library to complete a class assignment, an adult to speak to the police when his car was stolen out of the high-school parking lot. Actually, even when he went away to college, his grandparents were still very much a part of his life, not just when he came home for vacations, but in a continued support role, like the time he needed his car up at school and his grandfather drove it up. Contact is not as frequent now that he has a job in another state. But he heads home every couple of weeks and always spends time with his grandparents. These days, A also provides help for his grandparents when it is necessary—last year, he accompanied his 92-year-old paternal grandmother out west to see her first great-grandchild. Her 30-year-old granddaughter had bestowed this new status on her and she wanted to meet her great-grandson face-to-face. She needed A as a companion to make the trip. A has grown to adulthood under the watchful eyes of his grandparents; they have grown into old age under his watchful eyes. A is just one of x million grandchildren in this country, but he hardly fits the image that is projected of the grandchild in the literature. That is because A is an adult grandchild.

B is 46 years old, married with two children. She's a health planner, working for a human service agency. B has one brother who lives 300 miles away. Her parents live in the next town, independently, but in failing health. Her mother, 75, who has been on kidney dialysis for ten years, suffers from an advanced case of osteoporosis. She is unable to walk unaided. Her father, at 80, continues to drive, cook, and keep up the house. B's 97-year-old grandmother, her mother's mother, lives in B's town, as do B's maternal aunt and uncle. B is her grandmother's court-appointed conservator and has been her primary chore support (transportation, home repair, etc.) for years. Though frail, she had lived independently until a week ago, when B had to place her grandmother permanently in a local nursing home. Why, you may ask, did B take on so much of the responsibility for her grandmother when there were two adult daughters (and two sons-in-law) still alive and in the area? She would answer that she took over the responsibility because neither her mother nor her aunt were capable of doing so. Is B extraordinary? Certainly, B's efforts on behalf of her grandmother are extraordinary, but her situation is not. B is just one of x million grandchildren in this country; but she hardly fits the image that is projected of the grandchild in the literature. That is because B is an adult grandchild.

"Grandchild." The very terminology focuses attention on the "child" aspect of the role. The image of the young grandchild coddled by the smiling grandparent pervades our thinking. Yet the statistics belie the common wisdom. Grandchildren today are, increasingly, not children at all. They are adults. And the relationships between these older grandchildren (defined commonly as 18 and over) and their grandparents are relationships between two generations of adults. More often than not, these older grandchildren are young adults, with stories something like that of A. But, some people remain grandchildren into their fifth decade of life, with stories more like that of B. Clearly, the changing demographics of family structure necessitate a reassessment of the way we look at grandparent-grandchild relationships. Although research published within the last 15 years acknowledges this fact, it has yet to catch up fully with the demographic reality.

In a time when the literature on grandparenthood is growing rapidly, few studies focus specifically on the contextual quality of the adult grandchild-grandparent bond. Yet, theoretically and practically, our picture of grandparents and grandchildren cannot be complete without this understanding. As increasingly sophisticated studies focus on the various dimensions of grandparent-grandchild relations, the question of change and development over time in these cross-generational relations becomes more critical. In every aspect of inquiry—association, affect, significance and meaning of the role, and exchange behavior—the age of the grandchild (and grandparent) is potentially important. This chapter offers a look at the present state of knowledge on adult grandchildren, the theoretical reasons for a new investment of effort in this direction, and a conceptual framework for future study.

THE DEMANDS OF DEMOGRAPHY

A growing body of literature confirms that shifting trends in family structure have major consequences for the grandparenthood career (Bengtson, Rosenthal, & Burton, 1990). In Chapter 2 in this volume, Uhlenberg establishes the importance of twentieth-century changes in fertility, mortality, and migration for the grandparent/grandchild experience. As he notes, one of the most critical sociodemographic trends has been the increase in life expectancy. This phenomenon has resulted in a major increase in the duration of the grandparent/grandchild relationship; more grandparents than ever before are living long enough to see their grandchildren grow into adulthood. According to Uhlenberg and Kirby (Chapter 2), in the year 2000, almost all of 20-year-olds, three-quarters of 30-year-olds, and one-fifth of 40-year-olds will have at least one living grandparent. Similarly, recent studies on intergenerational family structures, such as Farkas and Hogan (1994), have reached the conclusion that more than 50% of people aged 65 and over have at least one adult grandchild. Although Szinovacz (1998), in her analysis of the National Survey of Families and Households data, cautions not to overestimate the survival of grandparents into their grandchildren's adulthood, it is clear that increasing numbers of grandparents will know their grandchildren through infancy, school, college, job establishment, and family formation. Grandparents will live long enough to be turned into great-grandparents by their adult grandchildren. Conversely, increasing numbers of grandchildren will know their grandparents from middle age through retirement, and old age through frailty preceding death. Concomitant demographic patterns—high divorce rates, delayed fertility, childlessness, and a variety of structural differentials (such as race and ethnicity) in timing of family formation—may alter the actual numbers of older grandchildren in the future, but the trend is well established.

Theoretically, this reality necessitates an approach to grandparent/grandchild relationships that recognizes its dynamic quality. The context and characteristics of the relationship between an 8-year-old and her 55-year-old grandmother will be different from when that child becomes an 18-year-old college student and her grandmother, a 65-year-old new retiree, or when that grandchild, at age 30, has her first child and makes her 77-year-old grandmother a great-grandmother. As the contexts of the relationship change (e.g., changes in grandparents' and grandchildren's marital, employment, or health status), the dimensions of the relationship—association, affect, role significance, and exchange—are likely to change as well.

Additionally, the existence of large numbers of older grandchildren necessitates new research perspectives on current attitudes and behaviors regarding grandparents. Adult grandchildren become another potential thread in the fabric of support available to older men and women. Their attitudes and behaviors become important to the future of intergenerational solidarity and to the decisions that are made at the policy level. Thus, as we know and continue to learn more about the importance of young grandchildren in the lives of grandparents and vice versa, about the contacts between young grandchildren and their grandparents, and about their exchange behavior, the demographic facts demand that we know and learn as much about the older grandchild or our picture of grandparenthood will remain incomplete.

THE CURRENT STATE OF KNOWLEDGE ABOUT THE OLDER GRANDCHILD

Age has long been cited in the literature as an important mediating factor in the grandparent/grandchild relationship (Kivett, 1991b). In fact, age is a strong predictor in most intergenerational relationships within the family constellation, not just between the cross-generations. Until recently, though, much of what we knew about the adult grandchild came from information derived from general studies of grandparenting (Kahana & Kahana, 1970; Sprey & Matthews, 1982; Thomas, 1986a) or kinship relationships (Hagestad, 1985; Hill et al., 1970; Markides, Boldt, & Ray, 1986), rather than from research which was specifically focused on the older grandchild. One major exception is Robertson's (1976) study of the perceptions of young adults towards their grandparents, which serves as a model for much of the later research. Studies of grandparent/grandchild relationships often include speculation about the likely changes in the bond as the grandchild ages, based on developmental and socialization theories. For example, both Troll (1980) and Hagestad (1981) argued that achieving adulthood might strengthen the relationship between grandchildren and grandparents.

A few studies (Cherlin & Furstenberg, 1986a; Hill et al., 1970; Sprey & Matthews, 1982) offer tentative conclusions about older grandchildren, based on empirical evidence they had gathered on grandchildren of all ages, but the findings are inconclusive and often contradictory. Hill and colleagues (1970) seminal three-generation family study shows that older grandchildren renew and strengthen their relationships with grandparents after they move through the teenage years and into the adult stages of their lives, suggesting that grandparent/grandchild relationships follow a curvilinear trajectory. Sprey and Matthews (1982) concurred, finding that grandchildren who reside close to their grandparents enhance their involvement with the grandparents as they move from adolescence into adulthood. However, Cherlin and Furstenberg (1986a: 95) found that "for most grandparents, the entrance of grandchildren into adulthood . . . signals the end of the grandparental career in all but the symbolic sense" (p. 95). The common wisdom has leaned more towards the latter interpretation of the facts than the alternative explanation because it tends to fit in with our thinking about the normative development of independence in adulthood as well as our notions regarding cohort differences (or, more commonly, the "generation gap") at both a macro- and a microlevel. In the absence of research focused specifically on the adult grandchild and/or changes in grandparent-grandchild relations over time, then very little concrete evidence about the structure or texture and especially the dynamics of the relationship existed.

In the last 15 years, a small but growing number of studies have concentrated effort on the older grandchild. Several have specifically targeted the older grandchild (Hodgson, 1992; Hoffman, 1979; Kennedy, 1990; Langer, 1990; Roberto & Stroes, 1992) and others have included that age group in large-scale research on intergenerational connections (Bengtson & Harootyan, 1994; Markides,

Boldt, & Ray, 1986). Taken together, these studies have yielded new insights into the relationship but provide few definitive answers, partly because of conflicting conclusions that are linked to methodological limitations of the research. These limitations parallel the concerns about the general grandparenthood literature raised in other chapters (see especially Chapters 1 and 18) and serve to underscore the tentativeness of research on this aspect of the topic.

For the most part, studies are small scale and drawn from convenience samples of relatively homogeneous groups. They are largely atheoretical, descriptive studies based on cross-sectional data collected from one member of the dyad. Thus, they are best suited for hypothesis generation, not hypothesis testing. For example, most studies that focus on the adult grandchild/grandparent connection approach the topic from the perspective of the grandchild (Hodgson, 1992; Hoffman, 1979; Kennedy, 1990; Roberto & Stroes, 1992; Robertson, 1976). Most often and undoubtedly due to convenience of access, these samples are drawn from populations of college students (Hoffman, 1979; Kennedy 1990; Roberto & Stroes, 1992; Robertson, 1976), which minimizes diversity and skews the median age towards young adult grandchildren. The exception is national telephone surveys of adult grandchildren conducted in 1990 by Hodgson (1992) and, independently, by Bengtson and his colleagues (Bengtson & Harootyan, 1994), but, like the others, the sample sizes are small and thus limited in generalizability. Langer's (1990) research provides information about the adult grandchild/grandparent connection from the alternate perspective of the grandparent, but the ethnic homogeneity (an exclusively Jewish population) and the small size of her sample limit the degree to which her conclusions can be applied to the general population. At present, there also are few studies targeting the older grandchild that rely on evidence from both members of the dyad, though broader studies by Hagestad (1985), King and Elder (1995a), Markides, Boldt, and Ray (1986), and Rossi and Rossi (1990) are based on interviews with three generations of a family.

Another major limitation of the existing studies on adult grandchildren is that they are typically cross-sectional rather than longitudinal and, thus, can offer only a snapshot of the relationship rather than a dynamic picture of the developing bond. The only longitudinal research to offer conclusions about older grandchildren are studies (Field & Minkler, 1988; Hill et al., 1970; King & Elder, 1995a) that focus on the broader spectrum of intergenerational ties rather than on the specifics of the grandparent-grandchild bond.

Limitations noted, the current body of research does offer some tantalizing and suggestive conclusions regarding the relationship between older grandchildren and their grandparents. Findings from this research are discussed below.

Association. Speculation regarding the diminishing role of the grandparent in the life of the developing grandchild stems in part from the sense that older grandchildren infrequently associate with their grandparents. Do grandchildren stay in contact with their grandparents even as they move into adulthood? The perception is that peers and growing independence from the family of origin, coupled with college attendance and geographic mobility, work to keep grandparents and older grandchildren apart. The actual research findings are mixed but point to the persistence of associational ties even into adulthood. Although it is true that young grandchildren tend to see their grandparents more often and that face-to-face contacts tend to decline over the years (Cherlin & Furstenberg, 1985; Field & Minkler, 1988; Roberto & Stroes, 1992; Robertson, 1976), most older grandchildren maintain a regular contact—typically monthly, but some even weekly (Lawton, Silverstein, & Bengtson, 1994b; Hodgson, 1992). Those who remain in or near the parental home are more likely to have frequent contact, which would tend to indicate that the middle generation remains a bridge between older grandchildren and their grandparents (Hartshorne & Manaster, 1982; Hill et al., 1970; Hodgson, 1992; Hoffman, 1979; Robertson, 1976). But there is growing evidence to show that contact between the two adult generations is not simply ritualistic or obligatory; rather, it is substantive and voluntary (Hodgson, 1992; Roberto & Stroes, 1992; Robertson, 1976). Since proximity tends to play such an important role in the frequency with which face-to-face encounters occur between the generations and older grandchildren tend to live at a greater distance from their grandparents than their younger counterparts, contact is not always in person but may take the form of telephoning or letter writing (and, at least in the case of this author, sending e-mail). In terms of the dimension of association, then, the weight of the findings suggest that, though frequency may decline, adult grandchildren and grandparents are not isolated from each other but often maintain regular contact through the years.

Role Meaning, Significance, and Affect. Levels of association are just one indicator of the quality of bonds between adult grandchildren and their grandparents. The meaning and significance of the roles and the emotional strength of the bond speak to other, qualitative, dimensions of the relationship. What do adult grandchildren and their grandparents expect of each other and how important are they to each other? How would they characterize their relationship in terms of the closeness of affect? At different stages in their lives, children may perceive their grandparents differently, expect different things from them, and the substance of the relationship may change. At the same time, grandparents' expectations regarding their grandchildren may also change. Little has been written about these changes as they apply to the adult grandchild, partly because the research in this area tends to be cross-sectional, rather than longitudinal. Robertson (1976) found that young adults do not have established expectations for the roles that their grandparents should play, and subsequent studies have validated these findings (Roberto & Stroes, 1992). Much more has been written, though, about the significance of the roles and the affective level of the relationship. Studies of older grandchildren consistently find that grandparents are significant to their grandchildren (Field & Minkler, 1988; Hartshorne & Manaster, 1982; Kennedy, 1990; Roberto & Stroes, 1992; Robertson, 1976) and that the relationship is emotionally close (Hodgson, 1992; Hoffman, 1979; Lawton, Silverstein, & Bengtson, 1994b). Similarly, the majority of grandparents feel "very close" to their adult grandchildren (Lawton et al., 1994b). Moreover, grandparents can influence grandchildren in various ways, such as value development (Roberto & Stroes, 1992). For more information on the ways in which grandparents influence their grandchildren, see Chapter 11 in this volume. The quality of the ties between older grandchildren and their grandparents, then, appears to be strong and enduring though lacking in normative prescriptions.

Exchange. A final dimension of the relationship between adult grandchildren and their grandparents is that of exchange behavior or functional solidarity (Bengtson, Rosenthal, & Burton, 1990). Bonds that connect the generations often include various types of emotional and instrumental (physical and financial) assistance. There are two components of such support—the attitudinal and the behavioral—exactly what do adult grandchildren say about their obligations to support their elderly grandparents and what do they actually do in that arena? What do grandparents say that they are obliged to do for their older grandchildren and what do they actually do? And, what degree of reciprocity exists in these cross-generational relationships? Despite the scant literature, certain conclusions regarding grandfilial responsibility appear consistent. Adult grandchildren express the belief that they bear some responsibility—emotional and instrumental—for their grandparents (Brody, 1983; Hodgson, 1991, Robertson, 1976) and by the accounts of the two studies that include such data (Hodgson, 1991; Langer, 1990), the younger generation actually provides support, especially emotional support. Hodgson (1991) found that older grandchildren believe that their parents (and the middle generation in general) should be the first line of assistance for elderly grandparents, but that they, too, share the obligation to help when needed. Similarly, when asked about specific types of assistance actually provided, adult grandchildren report that although their parents are more likely to step in when aid is requested, they do provide certain types of instrumental and emotional help as part of the family support network. Financial help, however, flowing from the younger to the older generation does not seem to be a common pattern.

Langer's (1990) study offers the only evidence available on the beliefs of grandparents regarding what they consider to be appropriate levels of grandfilial responsibilities for adult grandchildren. Her conclusions point to expectations of expressive support, which are largely met, and very modest expectations of instrumental support, which are also congruent with actual behaviors. A broader, more general understanding of the degree to which exchange behavior from the grandchild to the grandparent is the reciprocal extension of earlier exchanges from grandparent to grandchild does not emerge from this literature. However, more broadly based studies of intergenerational exchanges indicate a pattern of lifelong aid passing from grandparents to grandchildren until such time as the older generation becomes disabled (Hogan, Eggebeen, & Clogg, 1993; Kronebusch & Schlesinger, 1994). At that point, grandchildren, as part of the convoy of support (Antonucci & Akiyama, 1991), do offer aid. They are rarely the first line of assistance (as in the case of B cited above), but they do become part of the wider social support network of their grandparents.

Mediating Factors. Several factors can mediate relationships between adult grandchildren and their grandparents. The mediating effects of lineage or kin position, gender, racial and ethnic diversity, and proximity for adult grandchildren appear to parallel the findings of studies of younger grandchildren and their grandparents. Specifically, maternal grandparents are more likely to be considered emotionally close, enjoy higher levels of contact, and greater exchange of support than the paternal side (Hartshorne & Manaster, 1982; Hodgson, 1992; Hoffman, 1979; Kennedy, 1990; Robertson, 1976). Additionally, the gender of the grandparent is associated with relationships reported—grandmothers are the closest, enjoy the highest levels of contact, and exhibit more and different types of exchanges than grandfathers. These findings with regard to lineage and gender of grandparent are not unexpected given the primacy of women as the kinkeepers in our society (see Chapter 8).

Very little is known about the racial and ethnic differentials that exist in the relationships of adult grandchildren and their grandparents because most of the studies were conducted with small, homogeneous samples drawn from the white, Anglo population. Extrapolating from the work of Markides, Boldt, and Ray (1986), Burton and Bengtson (1985) and Lawton, Silverstein, and Bengtson, 1994b), though, there is reason to believe that adult grandchildren who are Mexican Americans and African Americans exhibit different patterns than whites. The differences are attributable to both cultural factors and variations in the timing of family formation. Recent work by King and Elder (1995a) also points to farm/nonfarm differentials in cross-generational relationships.

Perhaps the most consistent finding, though, is the one that marks the association between geographical distance and the adult grandchild-grandparent bond. Older grandchildren who are in closer proximity to their grandparents are more likely to report a close relationship, maintain face-to-face contact, and exchange instrumental support (Hartshorne & Manaster, 1982; Hill et al., 1970; Hodgson, 1992; Hoffman, 1979; Kennedy, 1990; Robertson, 1976). This finding is entirely consistent with the evidence established in the vast literature on grandparent-grandchild relationships (see Chapter 10).

The Bridge Generation. One additional factor that plays a major role in the development of the grandparent/grandchild bond is that of the mediating role of the middle or parental generation (King & Elder, 1995a; Kivett, 1991b; Robertson, 1975). Although the power of a parent to mediate the cross-generational relationship when the grandchild is young has been demonstrated (Cherlin & Furstenberg, 1985; Hagestad, 1985; King & Elder, 1995a; Robertson, 1975; Thompson & Walker, 1987), the connection is much less apparent as the grandchild reaches adulthood (Sprey & Matthews, 1982). As grandchildren attain some degree of independence, they can rewrite the relationships that they share with their grandparents. But do they? Hodgson's 1990 national survey of adult grandchildren (the range of ages is 18–51) offers some insights into the question.

Hodgson (1995) found that, despite the adult status of the grandchild, the parental generation still plays a significant role in the cross-generational relationship. On each of the dimensions studied—association, affect, and exchange behavior—the continuing importance of the bridge generation was apparent. For example, men and women who perceive the relationship between their parent and grandparent as "close" report significantly higher levels of contact with their grandparents. They are also much more likely to report high levels of association if the middle generation stays in frequent contact with the oldest generation. In terms of affect, when these grandchildren perceive the bonds between their parents and grandparents to be positive, their own bonds are also significantly more likely to be perceived as positive. Data on the provision of support to the grandparental generation offer more evidence of the importance of the bridge generation. Consistently and significantly, the helping behavior of the parental generation is associated with the behavior of the grandchild. When parents are reported to offer either instrumental or expressive support to the oldest generation, the grandchild is more likely to offer support as well. So, despite speculation to the contrary, the findings of this study argue for the continued importance of the bridge generation to the adult grandchild-grandparent relationship.

The findings can be explained in several ways. One possibility is that there is still an active linkage formed by the middle generation. The bridge generation is still providing opportunities for contact, initiating visits, and physically bringing the cross-generations together. Even though the grandchildren have grown to adulthood, many in their late teens and twenties still live with or near their parents. Thus, the concept of family obligation would still be operational. Grandchildren interact with their grandparents because they are brought along on visits or are participating in family rituals, not in voluntary associations. In this interpretation of the data, parents are actively mediating the relationship between grandparents and grandchildren by initiating the contacts between the generations. An alternative explanation of the findings is that middle-aged parents who interact on a regular basis with their aging parents provide role models for their own children. They act as socializing agents for their sons and daughters who then go on to reenact, in adulthood, the behaviors and attitudes they have been taught in childhood. Some research evidence further suggests that the establishment of close grandparent-grandchild ties during childhood when parents are usually active mediators serves as a strong foundation for future relationships (Lawton, Silverstein, & Bengtson, 1994b; see also Chapter 10). Spending time with the grandparental generation during childhood may establish family norms or strengthen linkages which are played out between the cross-generations over an entire lifetime. These two explanations pose very different, though not mutually exclusive, explanations for the findings. It is beyond the limits of this study (or the other studies that have looked at this issue) to disentangle the active or passive nature of the mediation offered by the middle generation.

As the available literature is reviewed, several overall themes emerge. First, with a few notable exceptions, research has begun to focus specifically on the adult grandchild only very recently. Contrary to much of earlier speculation, these recent studies portray the relationship between adult grandchildren and their grandparents as often close, significant, and mutually beneficial. But these findings come primarily from small, homogeneous convenience samples with limited methodological sophistication, which categorizes their conclusions as exploratory rather than definitive and sample-specific rather than generalizable to the entire population. In the past, authors who have reviewed the research on grandparents and (young) grandchildren have pointed to the same shortcomings in the general grandparenting literature (Aldous, 1995; Barranti, 1985; Giarrusso, Silverstein, & Bengtson, 1996; Kivett, 1991b; Pruchno & Johnson, 1996; Robertson, 1995), and several have specifically cited the almost total lack of attention given to older grandchildren in the rapidly growing literature. Given the weight of demographic changes and the emerging reality of multigenerational adult relationships, future research on grandparenthood cannot afford to ignore the topic any longer.

GREAT-GRANDPARENTS AND GREAT-GRANDCHILDREN

A focus on the older grandchild brings up another intergenerational relationship that requires research attention—that of the four-generation family. As grandchildren grow to adulthood, marry, and begin families, they bestow a new status on their grandparents, that of a great-grandparent. Between 40% and 50% of all older people are great-grandparents (Roberto & Skoglund, 1996), but research specific to this status is limited to fewer than a handful of studies (Doka & Mertz, 1988; Roberto & Skoglund, 1996; Wentowski, 1985). Early research on grandparents raised questions about the salience of the great-grandparental role (Troll, Miller, & Atchley, 1979; Wood & Robertson, 1976) but it was not until the last decade that studies were initiated to answer those questions. Similar to methodological constraints of much of the grandparenting literature, the studies that focus on great-grandparents are of limited generalizability due to the size and homogeneity of their samples. They do not, for example, take into account the major demographic differentials among ethnic and racial groups in the great-grandparental experience (Szinovacz, 1998). They do, however, add to our understanding of the changing family constellation surrounding older people and they provide some initial findings from which future research can be generated.

If grandparenthood has been called the "roleless role" (McPherson, 1983), then great-grandparenthood extends the concept to another generation and level. Twice removed from the responsibility (for the great-grandchild) and the effects of structural change on the middle generations (divorce, remarriage, cohabitation), great-grandparents report symbolic and emotional significance in their role but with limited contact and only ritualistic exchange (Doka & Mertz, 1988; Wentowski, 1985). Wentowski (1985), who studied 19 great-grandmothers, concludes that women were pleased with their new status but quite removed from most social and instrumental contact with their great-grandchildren. Doka and Mertz (1988) further defined the significance of the great-grandparent role as providing a sense of personal and family renewal, providing a new and welcome diversion, and, finally, marking a milestone in longevity. Although the overwhelming majority of the 40 great-grandparents in their study report their relationships with great-grandchildren as "remote," they still feel emotionally close to them. Most recently, Roberto and Skoglund (1996) looked at the relationship from the perspective of the (young adult) great-grandchild. In their study of 52 college students who had living grandparents and great-grandparents, they found that most young adults have only limited contact with the oldest generation and see them as peripheral to their family network. The findings from this study draw a sharp distinction between the significance of contact with grandparents and great-grandparents, the farther removed generationally, the farther removed in thought and deed. Although the evidence is still tentative, the findings of these three studies are consistent. Great-grandparenthood adds to the network of generational bonds in some meaningful ways, but at the same time, it stretches those bonds rather thin.

FUTURE APPROACHES TO RESEARCH ON OLDER GRANDCHILDREN

A decade ago, this author wrote a personal account about the "graying grandchild" (Hodgson, 1987), emphasizing the way in which the relationships among three generations of adult family members evolved. As each generation experienced its own transitions and life events, the color and tenor of the relationships changed. There was nothing extraordinary about the personal account—the same story could have been written by countless other graying grandchildren. And, therein, lies the point; the story should be written by future research.

The concept of the aging grandchild speaks loudly for longitudinal studies to track the development of the relationship. If what we seek is the knowledge of changes and continuities in the bond over the life course—the tenacity and texture of the relationships from childhood through adulthood—then we need to follow a cohort of grandchildren through their grandchild careers and plot the trajectories. We need to follow them through their transitions (from early childhood to adolescence, to young adulthood, to career formation, to family formation) and their grandparents through their own transitions (from middle age, to career changes, to retirement, to widowhood, to disability). Imagine the questions we could ask—should ask: Are the life transitions of the grandchild or the grandparent more fundamental to the relationship (i.e., does the marriage of the grandchild have more of an effect than the sudden disability of a grandparent?)? Are the choices that grandparents make in terms of association, affect, and functional solidarity when their grandchildren are young, visited back upon them when their grandchildren are adults (i.e., does the grandmother who has served as a surrogate parent enjoy the help of an adult granddaughter when disability strikes in very old age?)? These types of questions are grounded in traditional, sociological theories as well as developmental, life-course perspectives. Much as the family literature plots normative marital and parenting careers, so should we work towards establishing baseline grandparent and grandchild careers, not as prescriptions to follow but as markers of change and continuity along which to plot the similarities and differences which diversity engenders.

In her review of historical changes in grandparenting, Hagestad (1985: 36) concludes the following: "In a society where grandparents range in age from 30 to 110, and grandchildren range from newborns to retirees, we should not be surprised to find a wide variety of grandparenting styles and few behavioral expectations regarding grandparenting." Herein lies another challenge for the future of research on adult grandchildren. Reviewers (note those from this handbook) have frequently pointed out that few normative prescriptions exist for grandparents and grandchildren; this is arguably more true for the relationships between older grandchildren and their grandparents (and certainly, for great-grandchildren and great-grandparents) since the phenomenon of multiple generations of adults is so new and tied up with the vagaries of the "alpha-omega chain" (Hagestad, 1982). We are now talking about three, and potentially four, adult generations coexisting. What happens, for instance, to the norm of the "birthday check," that birthday card with the money slipped inside, which is one of the behavioral expectations we do have of grandparents? At 18 that birthday check may still be part of the ritual between the generations; but what happens when that grandchild turns 21 or 30 or 45, has far exceeded the income level of the oldest generation, and has grandchildren of her own? Research will, thus, have to explore and appreciate the differences and not concentrate on developing one picture of the typical relationship. This is necessitated, of course, not just by the age range of grandparents and grandchildren, but by the increasing diversity among families economically, ethnically, racially, and structurally.

Diversity, both socially and structurally, demands that large-scale studies be part of the future of adult grandchild research. Past studies have primarily utilized small, homogeneous samples to generate hypotheses but with little claim to generalizability. To test hypotheses, size and heterogeneity are required. For example, social class, which is increasingly associated with race, is likely to be an influential factor in the cross-generational bond. Past studies have confirmed the effect of socioeconomic status on parent-child relationships (Rossi & Rossi, 1990), and it is highly likely that the differential will hold up in the grandparent/ older grandchild tie as well.

Having argued that longitudinal studies would enable us to learn much about the dynamics of the older grandchild-grandparent bond, large-scale, cross-sectional research can also contribute to our understanding of some basic facts. It has already been argued here that adult grandchildren are a potential resource to the social support networks of their grandparents; they can and do offer a variety of types of assistance. Program planners and policy analysts should be very interested in the attitudes and behaviors of adult grandchildren towards grandfilial responsibility. When all the trends converge—increasing verticalization of the family, reduced government spending on support programs, longevity, divorce—grandchildren may find themselves as primary players or co-caregivers in the care provided to the oldest generation. History may tell us that grandparents are reluctant to turn to the youngest generation for help (Antonucci & Akiyama, 1991), but circumstances may change that pattern. The tables on lifetime caring for dependent parents (Watkins, Menken, & Bongaarts, 1987) which so startled us a decade ago and forewarned us of the coming filial obligations of the twenty-first century, may give way to demographic statistics on equally startling grandfilial obligations. That is not to ignore the reverse flow of exchange, from grandparent to grandchild, which is also an important focus for research. Today's grandparents of adult grandchildren may still be the providers of more support than they are the recipients. High rates of divorce and unstable work histories among the third generation, for example, may necessitate reliance on the oldest generation for housing or economic support. Regardless of the direction of the flow of aid, policy planners will need to take into account the factor of adult grandchildren.

Have you ever looked closely at paintings from the Elizabethan period? Have you ever noted their portrayal of children? Tiny adults. Dressed in adult clothes, with adult faces, and adult attitudes. Today we smile at those depictions, those notions of children as miniature adults, because we have come to view children radically differently from our Elizabethan counterparts. It is possible that our persistence in portraying grandchildren only as young dependents will seem outmoded to future generations in much the same way. Demographic trends producing shifting family structures and constellations will necessitate a much more inclusive notion of the concept of grandchild. We will recognize as normative the existence of the "graying grandchild" (Hodgson, 1987). And, if future research bears out the tentative conclusions of current work, the strength of a lifelong grandparent/grandchild bond will not only be a possibility but a cultural reality. Much as the notion of the modified extended family came to replace our earlier "truths" regarding the predominance of the isolated nuclear family, so, then, might new truths about the durability of grandparent/grandchild bonds replace old notions that significant grandparent-grandchild relationships do not survive the adulthood of the grandchild. Change and development are endemic to all relationships, and so is continuity—the child who reaches up to take her grandmother's hand as they cross the street will be different than the woman who reaches down 30 years later to again take her grandmother's hand as they cross the street, but they will still be holding hands.

Chapter 13

Effects of Adult Children's Divorce on Grandparenthood

Colleen L. Johnson

Marital disruption is more common today than at any time in the history of the United States, so common in fact that our society seems to be rejecting norms of the traditional nuclear family (Popenoe, 1993). The norm that two parents should stay together for life contrasts markedly with the view of some family therapists that divorce is a normal process of family change or, for some couples, a successful conclusion to marital therapy (Ahrons & Rodgers, 1980). Consistent with these assumptions, the number of divorces has quadrupled since 1960, and future estimates indicate that the majority of the recently married will divorce (Bumpass, 1990; see also Chapter 2).

To this point, most research has centered upon the dissolving nuclear family and the adaptation of divorcing parents and their children. As divorcing families go through a process of reorganization, there are usually profound influences on the lives of divorcing parents and their children (Hetherington, 1989; Hetherington, Cox, & Cox, 1982). Divorces of children can also have far-reaching effects upon the kinship systems of large numbers of grandparents. An upstate New York survey indicated that one-half of those 60 years and older with an ever-married child can expect that child to divorce (Spitze et al., 1994). When children divorce, grandparents can become a potential family resource. While they may ease the strains their children and grandchildren are experiencing, their distracted divorcing children may be less able to assist them if the need arises (Cicirelli, 1983). Thus, divorce may affect not only the divorcing parents and grandchildren but also grandparents.

In the following, I will review the structural issues in the study of divorce and grandparenting by *first* exploring the grandparents' position during the post-divorce process of family reorganization, when one parent leaves the household.

Second, although the research is sparse, I will also examine the situation of grandparents whose children remarry. When grandparents become stepgrandparents, they acquire a new child-in-law and possibly stepgrandchildren who join the families of their own grandchildren. *Third*, the contemporary grandparent role following these marital changes will also be analyzed in terms of how grandparents redefine their role to take divorce into account and how they respond to the needs of children and grandchildren. Because research on minorities is lacking, this chapter is confined to the research literature on grandparenting during a child's divorce and remarriage among white families.

In areas where research findings are sparse, such as those on stepgrandparenting, I will draw upon my own study of Northern California divorcing families (Johnson, 1988d). This research followed the divorce process in 50 white, mostly middle-class suburban families. Both the grandparents and their divorcing children, who lived within the San Francisco Bay Area, were interviewed three times over five years, so processes of remarriage were also observed. Where possible, both maternal and parental sides in a kinship system were followed, so the situations of both sets of grandparents of a specific divorce were mapped.

FAMILY TRANSITIONS WITH MARITAL CHANGE

Marital Dissolution after Death versus Divorce

In the past, the transition from two-parent to one-parent households occurred with the death of a parent, while today most such transitions come after a divorce. The divorce-initiated transition differs markedly from a household change after a death in two major ways. *First*, with death, the society has rituals and institutional mechanisms that moderate the effects of losing a spouse as supports are mobilized for the bereaved (Lopata, 1973). Such processes are not well developed with marital disruption, so no one knows quite how to respond when a relation divorces, even in deciding whether they should act grieved or relieved (Goode, 1956). Moreover, obligations to a wider kin network tend to diminish after a divorce (Rossi & Rossi, 1990), while after a death, kinship involvements usually increase.

Second, any subsequent remarriage after divorce differs structurally from remarriage after the death of a parent. As Furstenberg and Spanier (1984) conclude, remarriage after a death entails one marriage being replaced by another, while a divorce rearranges existing family members. Matthews and Sprey (1984) suggest that divorce is a threat to the equilibrium and the resource balance of the family, a situation that particularly concerns economic factors. Unlike widowhood, when the estate is inherited by the surviving spouse, economic resources are stretched with divorce. Both spouses survive and must share the same assets that now must support two households rather than one.

The Cultural Context of Family Change

The reorganization of families after divorce and remarriage today is taking place in a different cultural and social context than in the past. In this era of "voluntary bonds" (Barranti, 1985), individuals play an important role in shaping their own families and social networks in a social environment with few normative sanctions against divorce and remarriage (Furstenberg, 1981). Recent decades are also noted for a rise in egocentric priorities over family responsibilities (Bellah et al., 1985; Lasch, 1978). Some speak of an impulse-directed character type that is quite different from the inner-directed or other-directed social character of the past (Riesman, Denney, & Glazer, 1950; Turner, 1976). This character is one who rejects institutional anchorages of self and endorses pleasure-seeking activities. Grandparents as products of our culture, consequently, may also be influenced by these normative changes, so they do not invariably endorse conventional nurturing conceptions of their role and may not respond willingly to the needs of grandchildren with traditional norms of responsibility and sacrifice (Kornhaber, 1996).

Nevertheless, grandparents usually have more conservative values than their adult children (Johnson, 1988d), so the parent-child relationship may be undermined by value conflicts, not only after the marriage breaks down, but also during the conflictual period leading up to the divorce. As a marriage is dissolving, a nuclear family that was once a private unit becomes more public (Laslett, 1978). As their help is enlisted, consequently, grandparents may learn more about their child's life than they want to know as new sexual liaisons are formed, substance abuse may be observed, or grandchildren develop behavioral problems. As their child's life becomes more open to their observations, grandparents may have to cross the once-private boundary around a child's nuclear family, if they are to actively intervene to serve the interests of their grandchildren.

This normative ambiguity compounds the conflict arising from the strong mandate about autonomy and independence of adult children in our culture. A child's marriage is a normative transition to a status independent from parents, so parents may have difficulty with an adult child's renewed dependency after divorce, particularly if they must incorporate a formerly married child back into their lives (Johnson & Barer, 1987). As a consequence, issues of power and dependency between generations may surface (Emerson, 1962).

A continual theme throughout the literature on marital changes, in fact, focuses on the process as being incompletely institutionalized and without clear guidelines on new norms that specify expectations about family roles (Cherlin, 1978). The conclusions of William Goode (1956), whose research took place in the 1950's, still apply today. He describes the post-divorce period as one of social limbo. In other words, our society permits divorce but does not provide for its consequences. There are no rules on which relatives one should relate to or who is even a relative after divorce. If divorce is an ambiguous situation, remarriage is even more so (Cherlin, 1978). Despite the high rates of marital changes over several decades, important questions about the impact of divorce have no socially mandated answers: where is home, who is family, and how is the incest taboo extended?

Since children have periodic life-cycle events that become occasions when all of these individuals must meet, some guidelines or rules of etiquette are needed to regulate relations among the formerly married and their spouse of remarriage. Such occasions as grandchildren's marriages, graduations, or bar mitzvahs bring together those who would rather not meet. If they are recently divorced, gatherings that include a former spouse's new spouse, new children of the remarriage, and stepchildren can be tension-filled, so new rules of etiquette are needed. The descriptions of these encounters have a ritualized quality, what I have labeled "socially-controlled civility" (Johnson, 1988b). While divorcing couples usually have a conflictual or at best strained relationship at least initially, grandparents are less emotionally involved and can potentially help to moderate these conflicts during periods when the formerly married must meet.

Post-Divorce Economic Strains

Not only does divorce undermine the social and emotional well-being of the individuals involved, but, as noted above, it also threatens the family's economic security (Wallerstein & Kelly, 1979; Weitzman, 1985). As a consequence, divorcing parents with custody of dependent children are likely to cope with these stressors by turning to their parents. Women have the most to lose after a divorce. They are less likely to remarry than are men, and they have fewer economic resources. Divorced men on the contrary fare better economically, even after they remarry (Weitzman, 1985). As a result of economic factors, Longino and Earle (1996) conclude that the high divorce rate of the baby-boom population has increased the size of our low-income population. Half the fathers no longer maintain contact with their children one year after the divorce (Furstenberg et al., 1983), so divorced women often have to perform parenting as well as work roles formerly performed by two people. Given the pervasive economic problems occurring after a divorce and the stress of single parenting, maternal grandparents may be asked to contribute more of their own financial and social resources than they had anticipated in their career or retirement planning (Johnson, 1988d).

GRANDPARENTING DURING STRUCTURAL CHANGES IN THE FAMILY

Researchers on grandparents usually focus on the grandmother and her style as she performs the role. Nevertheless, the dissolution of a marriage reverberates throughout the kinship system (Johnson, 1989b; Rossi & Rossi, 1990), so few grandparents are unaffected by the major changes in family structure when children divorce and remarry. The position of grandparents, consequently, cannot be fully understood without attention to the structural conditions in which that divorce process takes place (Johnson, 1989a; Matthews & Sprey, 1984; Sprey, 1991). Because the household is usually formed upon marriage in our society, the nuclear family rests upon that relationship. When the marriage breaks down and one spouse moves out, the household is no longer synonymous with the family. During the process of change, when negative effects are likely to occur with both divorcing parents and their children, contacts with consanguineal relatives increase, while those with former in-laws decrease (Gladstone, 1988; Spicer & Hampe, 1975).

Three common patterns of kinship reorientation with marital changes are described here. *First*, the matrifocal bias or the female linkages following divorce are more common than patrifocal or male linkages. With custody of the children, women turn to their parents, while their ex-husbands and their parents usually become more peripheral in the lives of his children (Bulcroft & Bulcroft, 1991). *Second*, matrifocal in-law linkages also occur as paternal grandmothers retain a relationship with former daughters-in-law in order to have easy access to their grandchildren. *Third*, with remarriage, the kinship group often expands as grandparents accrue new grandchildren and stepgrandchildren, while maintaining relationships with those of a child's first marriage.

Matrifocal Post-Divorce Kinship Ties

The matrifocal bias in the American kinship system (Yanigasako, 1977) in normal times becomes accentuated with divorce, because custody is usually awarded to mothers. Strong linkages can be observed after divorce between mothers and their divorced daughters and grandchildren (Gladstone, 1988; Johnson, 1989b; Johnson & Barer, 1987; Johnson, Klee, & Schmidt, 1988; see Figure 13.1). Women generally have the most to lose after a divorce, both economically and socially. Thus if women cannot maintain their marriage, they have a greater developmental stake in preserving and strengthening their ties to their parents (Rossi & Rossi, 1990). Consequently, maternal or custodial grandmothers are more active than paternal grandparents (Anspach, 1976; Gladstone, 1988; Johnson & Barer, 1987; Sprey & Matthews, 1982). In contrast, grandparents in either kinship position receive fewer supports from divorced children (Cicirelli, 1983).

Female In-law Links

Interventions to assist grandchildren may be particularly problematic for paternal grandmothers. Since they occupy a derived role, any contact with grandchildren must be mediated by the parents of their grandchildren. If the custodial parent is an adult child-in-law, then grandparents may not have direct access to grandchildren. Since custody is usually granted to mothers, paternal grand-

Figure 13.1
Maternal Bias after Divorce

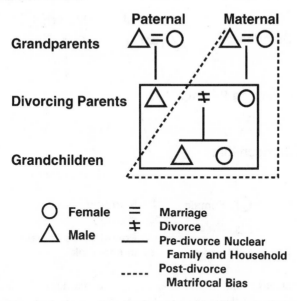

parents are most often in that situation. If the divorce is conflictual, their own son may not be able to provide such access. In such cases, they must rely upon someone who is no longer legally related to them, if they are to see their grandchildren (Furstenberg & Spanier, 1984; Johnson, 1989b). In many respects, they face very different problems than maternal grandparents when confronted with a child's divorce.

Because of the freedom of the system, however, grandparents are not required to sever the in-law relationship of their child's previous marriage (see Figure 13.2). The normative flexibility as well as the matrifocal bias of the kinship system are important in determining kinship reorganization following divorce (Furstenberg, 1981). Consequently, paternal grandparents can retain a relationship with a former child-in-law to assure their continuing relationship with their grandchildren and to further the best interests of a son's children. Most paternal grandparents conclude that a grandchild's mother may no longer be a daughter-in-law, yet they still share with her a biological tie to their grandchildren (Johnson, 1989a). She is usually viewed, not as "my son's ex-wife," but as "my grandson's mother." Most paternal grandmothers want to retain that affiliation and have easy access to grandchildren that some sons are unable to provide. From time to time, they also want to compensate for a son's deficiencies as a parent. Consistent with the blurring of kinship with friendship in our society (La Gaipa, 1981; Paine, 1974), grandmothers often refer to the relationship with a former daughter-in-law as a friendship. One study found that the paternal grandmother/ex-daughter-in-law relationship was retained only if the relation-

Figure 13.2
Post-Divorce Female-Linked In-Law Bond

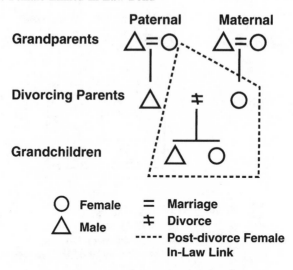

ship was satisfactory and friend-like during the marriage (Duran-Aydintug, 1991). In some cases, allegiances to a former daughter-in-law transcend in importance the relationships with a son (Johnson, 1989b).

Grandparents' Status with an Adult Child's Remarriage

From a grandparent's perspective, definitions of who is family and who is kin generally must be altered after divorce (Johnson, 1989a, 1989b). Their child's marital changes initiate revisions in the classification of kin, particularly of old and new in-laws, notions of closeness and distance, and the expectations and rules for regulating these relationships (Furstenberg, 1981). With remarriage also, grandparents and their children have a much more complicated extended family through which they must navigate than in the case of a death, for they have to sort out their own rights and responsibilities among an expanded pool of people. Since divorce and remarriage also entail major changes in inheritance rules and the redistribution of wealth, grandparents are particularly concerned.

Of the two million marriages annually contracted in the 1980's, around 40% were remarriages of one or both spouses (Wilson & Clarke, 1992). Since 61% of the divorced remarry divorced people, step and in-law relationships are likely to be added. While stepfamilies are not growing in numbers as fast as the one-parent family, in 1987, 12.7% of all dependent children were stepchildren, and one-third were predicted to be a stepchild before they reached age 18 (Glick, 1989; Popenoe, 1993). This new family form is attracting widespread interest, but from a wider kinship perspective, very little research has been done (Bulcroft & Bulcroft, 1991). For example, Ganong and Coleman (1984) reviewed 38 research projects on stepfamilies and not one dealt with the implications of the changes in the structure and functioning of the kinship network. Likewise their later review (Coleman & Ganong, 1990) had over 75 citations, none of which dealt with grandparents' role in a kinship network. Similarly, Pasley and Ihinger-Tallman's book (1987) on remarriage and stepfamilies does not refer to grandparents.

A few studies do indicate that biological ties seem to be more central than those acquired through multiple marriages. A college survey indicated that young people from reconstituted families show a strong preference for biological grandparents over stepgrandparents (Sanders & Trygstad, 1989). The strength of the blood tie is confirmed in a study of remarried families that found no difference in contacts between noncustodial fathers and their children over seven years (Bray & Berger, 1990). Contradictory findings come from Selzer and Bianchi (1988), however, who found that contact with the noncustodial spouse declines when a stepparent enters the household. Likewise, a study of adult step, half, and full siblings found that participants see their full siblings significantly more often (White & Riedmann, 1992). Finally, college students from divorced families feel closer to their grandparents compared to those in intact families, while those from stepfamilies are even closer to their grandparents than students from divorced or intact families (Kennedy & Kennedy, 1993).

When either a child and/or a former child-in-law remarries, noncustodial paternal grandparents continue to have problems of access. Consequently, they must still maintain a relationship with a former daughter-in-law to ensure continued contact with their grandchildren. A conflict of loyalties may develop, for they feel some responsibility to support a son's new marriage. As Furstenberg and Spanier (1984) point out, repudiating a former spouse strengthens the solidarity of the new marriage. The need for such allegiances also arises with grandparents. If the new daughter-in-law has children or children are born of the remarriage, the stepchildren and new children of a son's remarriage are added to an already dynamic kinship system. Understandably, the added categories of relatives may compete for grandparents' time and resources, as they attempt to maintain relationships with their biological grandchildren, who have membership in several families (Johnson, 1989b; Johnson & Barer, 1987).

Figure 13.3 portrays three types of structural emphasis after remarriage. Most common is the matrifocal emphasis now expanded to include a new son-in-law and perhaps new grandchildren. Paternal grandparents may become more distant from these grandchildren. Instead they may concentrate their energies on their son's new family. Nevertheless, some grandmothers in our research continued a strong kinship affiliation with their former daughter-in-law and were slow to transfer their allegiances to a son's new wife.

Kinship Expansion with Remarriage

While research studies on remarriage and step relationships are prolific, few report on how grandparents are affected by acquiring multiple step and in-law relationships through their children's marital changes. Structurally, however,

Figure 13.3
Divorce and Remarriage Linkages

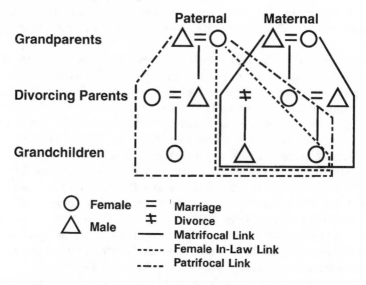

there are two broad categories of affinal relatives, the relatives of a child's divorce and the relatives of his or her remarriage. These individuals occupy positions along divorce and remarriage chains that have three generation's depth of grandparents, divorcing parents, and grandchildren (Bohannon, 1971; Furstenberg, 1981; Schneider, 1968). The children of divorce generally are the links between grandparents and the new kinship system because of their biological ties to a remarried parent.

If the Northern California families in my research are indicators or forerunners of broader changes, then one can expect that, as grandchildren retain and accumulate relationships, it can have a cumulative effect upon those grandparents who maintain close ties with their grandchildren. Of the 50 divorces tracked over three years in my research, the kinship systems of grandparents contracted in size in 38% of the divorced families. The majority of these were maternal grandparents who strengthened the consanguineal ties between generations after a child's divorce (Johnson, 1988a; Johnson & Barer, 1987). In those cases, little or no contact took place with former in-laws. In families of remarriage, contact ceased as the former in-laws were replaced by new in-laws of remarriage.

In the remainder, 48% of the divorces, the kinship systems of grandparents expanded with divorce by four processes: (1) Mostly paternal grandparents retained relationships with relatives of a child's divorce at the same time new in-law relatives were added with a child's remarriage. This coalition with a former daughter-in-law, as I have noted, can compete with the grandmother's transfer of affiliation to a new daughter-in-law. (2) When a relationship with a former child-in-law continues after his or her remarriage, then the new family of one's grandchildren can potentially contain half- and stepsiblings, who may join a pool of grandchildren. A grandmother who is in contact with a grandchild can become part of such a reconstituted family. (3) Grandparents also can witness the divorces and remarriages of multiple children, so they accrue multiple subsets of relatives. (4) Some grandparents themselves divorce and remarry, or they remarry after widowhood and in the process add another set of step and in-law relations.

Such expanding systems of divorce and remarriage are more common among paternal grandmothers, not only in Northern California, but also in a Midwestern sample of grandmothers (Ahrons & Bowman, 1982). It is unlikely that the expansive kinship networks would have occurred in more traditional and rule-bound kinship systems. Given the flexible rules of the American kinship system, it is not surprising that almost half of the Northern California sample have accepted these freedoms and constructed a kinship system that permits ready access to grandchildren. This emphasis in some cases takes place at the expense of consanguineal ties.

THE GRANDPARENTING ROLE DURING DIVORCE

With large numbers of children currently affected by divorce, attention has increasingly turned to grandparents as potential comforters and supporters of grandchildren during the stressful breakup of their parents' marriage. While the empirical and clinical research literature on divorce is prolific as is an increasingly informative literature on grandparenting (Kivett, 1991b), only a few studies have addressed grandparents' role during the divorce process (Cherlin & Furstenberger, 1986a; Gladstone, 1988; Henry, Ceglian, & Matthews, 1992; Johnson, 1983a, 1985, 1988d; Matthews & Sprey, 1984; Spitze et al., 1994; Sprey & Matthews, 1982).

The Divorced Child as Mediator

In both intact and disrupted families, parents in the middle generation usually function as mediators between their parents and their children. Consequently, they influence both the quality and quantity of the interactions between grandparents and grandchildren. If a parent has a close relationship with his or her parent, then their children are also likely to have a close relationship (Hodgson, 1992; Kennedy, 1992a). Such closeness is related to the age of grandchildren with younger grandparents and grandchildren being closer (Sprey & Matthews, 1982). A national survey found that the quality of intergenerational relationships is influenced by divorces of both parents and adult children (Umberson, 1992). When either a parent or adult child divorces, intergenerational relationships are substantially more strained, Umberson concludes, most often because of financial problems. Bulcroft and Bulcroft (1991) found that divorced parents are more likely than married parents to have a negative relationship with their adult children. Likewise, divorced parents extend significantly less support to divorced children (White, 1992). Apparently, a child's divorce is usually an upsetting experience to grandparents (Johnson, 1981).

With a strong matrifocal bias, bonds between mothers, daughters, and granddaughters are stronger and more enduring than those in the male line (Hagestad, 1990). More subtle family processes are also undoubtedly affected by divorce. Thompson and Walker (1987) in a study of mothers and daughters found that grandparents were most likely to have a global family sentiment where closeness to their daughter and granddaughter are indistinguishable. Granddaughters, on the contrary, differentiate between their feelings about their mother and grandmother. The authors conclude that family feeling may have something to do with the systemic rather than the interactional nature of family relationships. Grandparents' undifferentiated feelings toward descending generations may facilitate their role responsibilities in maintaining family continuity (Troll, 1983). Thus, the significance of grandparents during the divorce process may have more to do with maintaining family continuity than with their interactions and supports with their children and grandchildren. My research also shows that grandparents stress the importance of their maintaining family continuity, indicating that such continuity should descend to all generations. Continuity can also be observed in how the history of that relationship influences the relationship during the divorce process (Johnson, 1988a). For example, if an adult child has long had an interdependent role with parents, that bond was strengthened after a divorce. Other divorcing parents, who had always been independent from their parents, tended to have a distant relationship, so after their divorce, they still maintained a private family unit. Still others had divorce and remarriage networks that blurred family boundaries between relatives of blood, marriage, and divorce, so their parents were included along with relatives accumulated by marital changes.

The Grandparent Role During the Divorce Process

An analysis of divorce and grandparenting converges upon two socially ambiguous situations. As noted above, divorce initiates rearrangements in the family and kinship system without clear normative guidelines as to their impact, while remarriage results in even more uncharted situations. In our culture, the grandparenting role also has weak and confusing directives. Consequently, statistical findings about the role suggest patterns of diversity rather than central tendency (Troll, 1980).

In general, grandmothers are far more active with grandchildren than are grandfathers, younger grandparents with younger grandchildren are more active than older ones, and maternal grandparents are more active than paternal grandparents (Clingempeel et al., 1992; Kivett, 1991b; see Chapter 8). Spitze and her colleagues (1994) point out that the gender-based kinship position accounted for more closeness in general, with both maternal grandmothers and grandfathers being more important than grandparents on the paternal side. These gender and lineage differences continue when children divorce. Divorced daughters have more contact with their parents than do divorced sons, and they receive more aid from them (Johnson, 1988d). Likewise, late adolescents reported being closer to maternal grandparents than paternal grandparents after their parents' divorce, a situation possibly stemming from more frequent contact with them during childhood (Matthews & Sprey, 1984). Cherlin and Furstenberg (1986a) report that in the absence of divorce, maternal and paternal grandparents saw grandchildren with about the same frequency, while with disrupted marriages, maternal grandmothers had more contact and were more involved. Thus, divorce tends to strengthen the matrifocal bond.

The capacity of grandparents to meet the needs of grandchildren depends upon a number of factors. For example, it can be traced to geographic proximity. Hetherington, Cox, and Cox (1982) found that grandparents living nearby were important in the support network, but their help was never as central or as salient at that of a parent. Some of the diversity in grandparenting is also related to age; younger grandmothers with younger grandchildren are more active with grandchildren (Denham & Smith, 1989; Johnson, 1985; Kivett, 1991b; Sprey & Matthews, 1982). Younger grandparents, particularly maternal ones, are active baby-sitters for young grandchildren, and, in some cases, they make sacrifices in their own lives to meet their grandchildren's needs. Grandparents at all ages also help economically if they can afford to (Johnson, 1988c).

However much hesitance with which grandmothers conceptualize their role, in reality most grandparents rise to the occasion and extend assistance to their divorcing children and their children. In my study, three-quarters had at least weekly contact with their children after a divorce (Johnson, 1983a, 1985, 1988c, 1988d; Johnson & Barer, 1987). While these women tended to have less contact with their grandchildren than with their children, most extended considerable assistance to both generations in the period immediately following the divorce. Over two-thirds provided financial help, and most provided some services, at least intermittently. Nevertheless, there was considerable variation in their level of activity.

Constraints to Grandparenting During the Divorce Process

After such variables are accounted for, other sources of variation are more difficult to pinpoint. One source of variation are constraints experienced by grandparents. One constraint may be traced to the vagueness of the norms which regulate the role particularly after a divorce (Bengtson, 1985; Troll, 1980). Uncertainties may be accentuated because of innate qualities of the grandparent role that lead to the role being depicted in terms of styles—"the funseeker," "the formal," "the distant" or "the parent surrogate" grandmother (Neugarten & Weinstein, 1964; Robertson, 1995). According to some grandparents, the meanings of their role are more significant than their actual actions (Kivnick,

1982). The role has been described as having a ritualized quality and is often a "state of mind" rather than a functioning role (Kahana & Kahana, 1970). Perhaps the rise of grandparent rights groups and the frequent newsletters and popular writings on grandparenting (Brookdale Newletter, 1995–1996) all reflect and respond to grandparent's ambivalence about their role that is accentuated after adverse changes in their child's life.

When presented with the divorce of an offspring and the opportunity to substitute for parents in meeting the basic needs of the grandchildren, the grandmothers in my sample were somewhat confused about their potential functions. They tended to define their role in accordance with the situation and then determined the level of their involvement situationally depending on the needs of their children, grandchildren, and even children-in-law. Most grandparents were "close" to children but "intimate at a distance" to their child's family while their child's marriage was intact (Rosenmayr, 1972), and some prefer to preserve that distance.

A second constraint can be traced to the distracted parents' failure to mediate between grandparents and grandchildren. Grandparents in my study found it difficult to determine who was responsible for deciding what they should do for their children and grandchildren. They cannot step in uninvited or against the wishes of a child. Since their own norms center on noninterference in their child's family, grandmothers generally conclude that their relationship with a grandchild is voluntary, so it must be personally negotiated and situationally defined. Although a close, rewarding relationship with a grandchild is achieved through their own efforts, they do not generally see themselves as operating as free agents. Any actions they take are potentially constrained by the parents of their grandchildren, only one of whom is still related after a divorce (Johnson, 1983a, 1985, 1988c).

A third constraint may lie with competing priorities of grandparents. Given the high needs of their children and grandchildren, the major dilemma facing these grandmothers, when a child divorces, was commonly expressed with ambivalence, "If I do too much, I will have to do it all. If I do too little, I might lose grandchildren." During the divorce process when needs are high, this response reflects the quandary created by the voluntary character of the role. If the decision is made to take over parenting functions, grandmothers feel that they face the risk of becoming overburdened. Their explanations often entail a rationalization that the parent role should not be repeated: "I have paid my dues. It is time for me to think of myself."

Also among the people I have studied, those grandparents, who had initially taken on parental responsibilities for their grandchildren, no longer did so after three years. Their initial response was a stopgap measure intended to ease the immediate strains in their child's and grandchildren's lives (Johnson, 1988d). Thus, grandparents with such responsibilities rarely viewed the arrangement as permanent, but rather they looked forward to a time when they were free of such a commitment. If their responsibilities persisted, conflict with their children invariably arose, conflict often accentuated by an involuntary role reversal and often a regression on the child's part.

Since becoming surrogate parents was most incongruent with their expectations of grandparenting as a recreational role, not surprisingly these women expressed considerable ambivalence about their role. Many insisted, "I never wanted to repeat the parent role." They were particularly uncomfortable if they had to discipline grandchildren. They also complained about the boundaries between the roles of parent and grandparent becoming blurred. For example, in describing their full-time responsibilities for grandchildren of divorce, grandmothers make clear distinctions between their role as a parent and grandparent. They tend to conclude that merging the two roles is inconsistent with current social mandates (Johnson, 1988a, 1988c).

In any case, these more ethereal qualities result from the fact that most grandparents reject the authority and nurturing functions of parenting. Consequently, after a child's divorce, when asked to perform these functions, grandparents describe their responses as ad hoc: "I just roll with the punches." They no longer adhered to the image of a grandmother as a kindly old woman secluded in her home who bakes cookies, but instead see themselves as an "Auntie Mame," a lively, middle-aged woman, who leads an active and interesting life. It may be that grandmothers' attempts to reject instrumental or nurturing dimensions of their role and concentrate on expressive dimensions may be particularly frustrated after a child's divorce.

CONCLUSIONS

While the divorce rate in most countries decreased in the last few decades, only in the United States has the rate remained consistently high. Thus in a recent debate in the *Journal of Marriage and the Family*, Popenoe (1993) pointed out that even Mary Jo Bane, the respected demographer, had second thoughts about the American family being "here to stay." She concluded that the steady rise of one-parent households in combination with the increased numbers of new unwed mothers leave many dependent children particularly vulnerable (Bane, 1976; Bane & Jargowsky, 1988). Other critics have pointed out that such negative views arise out of outdated traditional definitions of the family that there should be two parents in a stable union (Stacy, 1993). While evidence is mixed on just how harmful divorce is for children (Morrison & Cherlin, 1995), economic strains alone, particularly for women with custody, affect the quality of children's lives. For this reason, some observers turn to grandparents as those who may alleviate distress.

With marital changes and processes of family reorganization, the focus expands beyond the nuclear family or an attenuated nuclear family, so a kinship model rather than a nuclear family model is needed. After five years of research on this subject, I have concluded that the kinship literature offers productive theoretical insights that go beyond the typical research reports today with counts of contacts and supports of grandparents with grandchildren. With this broader approach, important insights emerge on how the high rates of marital instability are affecting both the oldest and youngest generations in families. Research on black kinship networks confirm this stance. With the pediocentric emphasis in black kinship networks, for example, a host of kin, not necessarily a nuclear family, may be looking out for the best interests of dependent children (Crosby-Burnett & Lewis, 1993). Consequently, a nuclear bias in our thinking about families may overlook positive alternatives to the problems typical after divorce.

Stemming from their survey research on grandparenting, Cherlin and Furstenberg (1986a) posed the question, is the divorce process an indicator of family decline or is it merely a process of restructuring? Evidence suggests that the grandparents may ameliorate negative aspects of divorce even though their role is primarily symbolic and sentimental. They still function in a latent role as family watchdogs (Troll, 1983) that can be mobilized in times of need. Even if grandparents function as "family watchdogs" in any capacity (Troll, 1983), they conclude that it is an advance in social welfare for children and grandchildren as well as a source of a more functional role for grandparents.

In this chapter, I have devoted considerable space to the dramatic series of events when family and kinship relationships are reorganized, redefined, and rearranged with marital changes. These dynamic family changes are like a "fast-forward" on video cameras, where the processes of family breakdown and re-formation can be observed in a relatively short time. Thus, its study is a productive source of understanding about family processes in general that would otherwise require extensive longitudinal research.

To summarize the findings, I should first emphasize that the grandmothers' responses to their children's divorces are quite varied, not only because of the variables of age and lineage relationship, but also because the norms of grandparenting are somewhat blurred and open ended. The meanings or the cultural content of the role, however, were quite uniform in the literature; most grandmothers today deemphasize traditional conceptions of the role and its nurturing elements (Kornhaber, 1996; see also Chapters 1 and 10). Research findings suggest that active grandparenting is primarily a middle-aged activity, at least as evaluated by social contact and services. In some cases, the instrumental component of their role after a child divorces is quite prominent among those grandmothers who have responsibility for young grandchildren. The real decline in grandparents' involvement after divorce is found among paternal grandmothers, suggesting that in contrast to relationships with daughters, a grandmother's relationship with her son may not always provide access to to her grandchildren. In any case, grandparents are important family resources. They intervene in emergencies, and in normal times, they are there, not just as symbolic figures, but as an important latent family resource.

To avoid some of the pitfalls in research on grandparents, it is important to go beyond the sentimentality that so often colors discussions of this role. If they are labeled as the saviors of the family as they stem its decay, then most would be assigned such a status against their will, at least in the white middle-class families I studied. Nevertheless, when grandparents become custodial parents in general, the situation is so stressful that various support groups have arisen to assist them.

Future research also needs to go beyond the current literature related to divorce and grandparenting that largely ignores the great cultural diversity in family systems. As noted in other chapters in this book, the structure and functioning of the wider kinship group differs greatly among racial and ethnic groups, and kin from racial and ethnic minorities deal with marital instability differently than white middle-class families. Consequently, future studies on grandparenting also should be contextualized within a kinship model that may differ for diverse subgroups in this country.

Chapter 14

Grandparents as Caregivers

Barbara A. Hirshorn

Grandparents have long played the role of care providers to various family members. This is true, as well, of others who have assumed the role of "grandparent" in some families, such as great-grandparents, great-aunts and great-uncles, older cousins, and fictive kin.

In recent years there has been a growing awareness among both social analysts and the public at-large of the increasing numbers of such individuals (in this chapter referred to simply as "grandparents") who, for various reasons, provide care on a consistent basis for those considered grandchildren. Examples include routinely preparing grandchildren for school, providing full-time daycare for preschool grandchildren, and actually raising grandchildren in one's own home with no assistance from the parents of the children.

These activities move the grandparent out of the more traditional older-generation-in-the-family roles of mediator, provider of family cohesion and identity, and transmitter of family values, and into roles typically assumed by a child's parents. In so doing, grandparent caregiving stretches, reorganizes, and redefines the relationships between family members; redraws the boundaries of family and, often, of household units; and redirects the transfer of resources within the family.

This chapter explores the scope and context of grandparent caregiving—some basic and important parameters of the different care-provision roles a grandparent may assume; compelling reasons for being in these roles; the social context in which grandparent caregiving takes place; and the consequences of this care provision to the grandparents and the children they are raising. The chapter closes with some suggestions regarding theory and research methods that might be considered in future investigations of grandparent caregiving.

Table 14.1
Types of Care Provision by Time Frame and Level of Responsibility

Time Frame	Level of Responsibility		
	Helping	Coparenting	Surrogate Parenting
Occasional/ Emergency	1. Occasional helper	2. Occasional coparent	3. Occasional surrogate parent
Short-term	4. Short-term helper	5. Short-term coparent	6. Short-term surrogate parent
Routine/ Long-term	7. Long-term helper	8. Long-term coparent	9. Long-term surrogate parent

BASIC PARAMETERS: TIME FRAME AND LEVEL OF RESPONSIBILITY

What is the time frame for "grandparent caregiving"? It can vary along a continuum from circumstances where the nurturance of one or more grandchildren is done occasionally, or in response to an emergency or urgent situation; to on a short-term basis; or to a routine situation for the mid to long term. Level and type of responsibility can vary too. Grandparents can act as helpers to their adult children, coparents, or surrogate parents.

Table 14.1 distinguishes nine types of care provision according to these time frame and responsibility continuua. Helping refers to situations where grandparents perform some child-care tasks but with limited responsibility. Babysitting over a weekend for a few hours (cell 1) would be an example of *occasional helping*, while caring for grandchildren during mornings when an adult child is enrolled in a course or training program (cell 2) would be an example of *short-term helping* behavior. Assumption of daytime child-care responsibilities for a grandchild while an adult child works (cell 3) is typically a routine responsibility assumed for an extended period of time and constitutes an example of *long-term helping*.

The time frame for "coparenting" also varies. Caring for grandchildren while their parent recovers from an acute illness in the home (cell 4) usually implies the assumption of a broad range of parenting responsibilities (though not full care responsibility)—but in response to an emergency or crisis. It is an example of *occasional co-parenting*. Coparenting while the family unit undergoes a transition, such as a birth or a death in the extended family (cell 5) would be *short-term coparenting*. In contrast, coparenting when a child in her teenage years or early 20's becomes a parent yet lacks adequate parenting skills (cell 6) is likely to be routine and undertaken for a mid- to long-term duration. It thus exemplifies *routine coparenting*.

Surrogate parenting on an *occasional or emergent* basis entails circumstances where the grandparent assumes total care responsibilities during discrete instances of parental absence (cell 7), for example when parents take a trip or are hospitalized, while an example of *short-term surrogate parenting* (cell 8) would be when the adult child is overseas on active duty in the armed forces. Grandparents provide *long-term surrogate parenting* when adult children die, are seriously ill for an extended period of time, are employed permanently in another geographic area, are incarcerated, or are heavy substance abusers (cell 9).

In recent years some analysts have suggested different approaches for examining the child-raising roles grandparents undertake. For instance, Burton, Dilworth-Anderson, and Merriwether-deVries (1995) distinguish two types of "surrogate parenting" roles for grandparents. Those individuals who "coparent" assist adult children with their child-raising tasks. Other grandparents assume total responsibility for the care and socialization of grandchildren when adult children cannot fulfill these tasks themselves.

Jendrek, in research based upon a sample of 114 grandparents providing regular care to grandchildren in Butler County, Ohio, distinguishes between (a) "custodial" parenting, where grandparents go through the court system to seek the transfer of legal and physical custody from the grandchild's parents to themselves; (b) "day-care grandparents" whose daily provision of physical care extends for a considerable period of time, but with no assumption of legal responsibility; and (c) "living with" parenting, where grandparents provide from some to all of the daily physical care for a grandchild while authority for the grandchild remains with the parent. This last category further distinguishes environments where the grandchild's parents live in the same household with the grandparent/grandchild and those where they do not (Jendrek, 1993, 1994).

Occasional care (at any level of responsibility) as well as short-term helping and coparenting conform to the norm of noninterference in childrearing on the part of grandparents (Cherlin & Furstenberg, 1986a) and exemplify grandparents' role as "family watchdogs" (Troll, 1983). Many grandparents assume such care responsibilities. For example, data based on the National Survey of Families and Households conducted 1992–1994 indicate that two-fifths of grandfathers and over one-half of grandmothers with grandchildren age 10 or younger provide child care outside their adult children's work hours. These proportions increase to 56% and 74%, respectively, for grandparents with grandchildren residing within 25 miles (Szinovacz, 1997a).

Because routine care (at any level of responsibility) engenders considerably more investment on the part of the grandparent and most likely has more pronounced effects both on the grandparents and the grandchildren than other types of care, research to date has focused on such situations. When grandparents provide short-term or routine "help" in the form of daycare, they often are doing so for more than just a few hours per week (Table 14.1, cells 2, 3). By 1990, 19% of preschool children with employed mothers were cared for by family members "other than parents"—a figure that increased to 28% for low-income preschool children, with "the relation" primarily a grandmother (Hofferth et al., 1991; Brayfield, Deich, & Hofferth, 1993).

Indeed, some analysts consider daycare a major intergenerational economic transfer (Hogan, Hao, & Parish, 1990) which may be crucial for educational or occupational achievement for younger generations in the family (Furstenberg, 1976; Presser, 1980). In an analysis of nationally representative sample survey data during the 1980's, Presser (1989) determined that daycare provided to employed young mothers (mean age 23.7) by grandmothers accounted for 24% of all principal child care for preschool-age children. Using another national sample social survey from the late 1980's, Folk and Beller (1993) found that when grandmothers lived within 15 miles of adult children with offspring, the probability of these adult children choosing nonmarket child care increased from 42% to 59%. The juggling of roles may be complex for some grandparent daycare providers. For example, Presser discovered that one-third of grandparents helping out young, employed adult female children are, themselves, working for pay (Presser, 1989).

There is also considerable diversity *across* subpopulations in the use of grandparents as daycare provider, particularly according to race. For example, Hogan and colleagues (1990) found that African American mothers between 19 and 26 years of age were much more likely than their white counterparts (45.6% as compared with 33.9%) to utilize grandparents as child-care providers. Moreover, within the African American subpopulation, Jayakody, Chatters, and Taylor (1993) discovered that adult children living in the North were more likely to receive child care from "immediate family members" than were their counterparts in the South, and younger adult children (in their teens and twenties) were more prone to rely on family help than were older adult children.

Grandparents often assume a major role in or even sole responsibility for actually raising grandchildren (Table 14.1, cells 5, 6, 8, 9). Historically, the proportion of grandparents in the United States assuming these coparenting and surrogate-parenting responsibilities has varied considerably by cohort, ethnicity, and social class, and in response to national crises (e.g., wars, depressions), family structural change such as divorce, or conditions affecting parents' ability to care for their children (drugs, AIDS). Secular changes in childbearing patterns, such as recent increases in both early teenage pregnancy and mid-life family formation among career-oriented parents, also have affected the likelihood that grandparents assume these responsibilities (Albrecht, 1954; Streib, 1958; Szinovacz, 1996; Tinsley & Park, 1984; see also Chapters 2, 13, and 16).

Fuller-Thomson, Minkler, and Driver (1997), in their examination of National Survey of Families and Households 1992–1994 national social survey data, found that 10.9% of all grandparents indicated that they have had primary responsibility for raising a grandchild for a period of at least six months, and nearly half of these had assumed parenting responsibilities while the grandchild was still an infant (Fuller-Thompson, Minkler, and Driver, 1997). Using the same source of data, Szinovacz found that 3.9% of households headed by in-dividudals who were grandparents had grandchildren who lived there without either parent also coresident, and another 4.1% of households in which a grand-parent was not the head nevertheless had grandchildren residing there with nei-ther parent present (Szinovacz, 1998).

Recent U.S. Bureau of the Census data indicate that, over the last quarter century, the absolute number of children under 18 years of age and living in households headed by grandparents has increased by over 50%—from 2,214,000 in 1970 to 3,368,000 in 1993. In approximately two-thirds of these grandparent-headed households, at least one of the parents of these children is a resident, as well (Chalfie, 1994; Saluter, 1992, 1994a).

Some of the more remarkable patterns of change occured among those grand-parent-headed households in which the parent of the young children is not pres-ent. The number of such children raised in grandparent-headed households grew only marginally between 1970 and 1993 (6%). However, in the five-year period 1990–1994, the number of children 18 and younger in the United States who were raised in grandparent-headed households jumped nearly 45%—from 935,000 to 1,359,000 children. This increase can be attributed to a rise in the absolute number of dependent children as well as increased coresidence with grandparents among parent-absent grandchildren (Chalfie 1994; Saluter, 1994a, 1994b; Szinovacz, 1997a; see Chapter 2).

REASONS FOR GRANDPARENT CAREGIVING

What are the primary factors compelling grandparents to assume care-providing roles for grandchildren? The rationales are varied and numerous and may involve complex negotiations between grandparents and their adult chil-dren; between grandparent spouses; or between grandparents, adult children, and other members of the extended family. Moreover, interpersonal and family dy-namics in place over decades may play a large role in determining what level of care a grandparent feels comfortable offering or an adult child, accepting. The existence and availability of formal support resources, such as those pro-vided by health-care, social-service, religious, and civic organizations, and from government sources, also impact both the type of care grandparents provide and their time commitment to caregiving tasks.

Type of care provided and the timing of it are also affected by the particular reason why the grandparent assumes this responsibility. In some situations, such as the regular provision of daycare, establishing the grandparent as care provider may be a *necessary prerequisite* to undertaking the activity that is the rationale for that care—for example adult child's employment. In other cases the provi-sion of care may be a *mid-course* response to a particular circumstance or to a transition (e.g., when it is clear that an adult child needs "coaching" in par-enting skills; during or immediately after an adult child's divorce) or *after-the-fact* (e.g., after an adult child has been incarcerated).

Research suggests seven primary reasons for grandparent caregiving, ranging from providing relief to the adult child to surrogate parenting in cases of drug abuse by the adult child.

Giving Adult Children Relief. One reason grandparents care for grandchildren is to allow adult children some respite from parenting. Examples include activities such as baby-sitting on the weekend and caring for grandchildren when adult children go on a trip.

Responding to a Crisis Situation. Grandparents also provide care in crisis situations when adult children are temporarily unable to adequately fulfill their parenting responsibilities. Examples include coparenting while an adult child recuperates from illness, caring for grandchildren when an adult child has another child, and covering the "home front" while an adult child responds to a sudden misfortune such as death of a family member, job loss, bankruptcy, or natural disaster.

Providing "Give" in Transitional Circumstances that Threaten Overload for the Adult Child. These circumstances are more chronic than a "crisis," yet usually not interminable. Transitional "helping out" provides the boost an adult child may need when going through life phases that are particularly demanding or require temporary absence of the parent. Surrogate parenting while an adult child is on a short-term overseas assignment or is involved in intensive job retraining may enhance the adult child's career advancement opportunities and thereby benefit the larger family unit.

When an Adult Child Divorces. This is a common overload situation to which grandparents respond. Care provision, here, whether in the form of daycare, coparenting, surrogate parenting, or some mix of these, typically responds to the needs of an adult child trying to find a new equilibrium in the expenditure of her (or his) own time and energy, both at home and at work. There is some evidence that help by maternal grandparents in particular increases with the divorce of a child, especially since mothers are usually the parent awarded child custody. Cherlin and Furstenberg (1986a) found that, even controlling for race and age of the grandparent, maternal grandparents were more likely to exhibit such "parentlike behavior" toward a grandchild as disciplining, correcting something disapproved of, and not consulting the parent prior to making an important decision about the grandchild. Evidence regarding frequency of contact with the paternal grandparent, on the other hand, is mixed (e.g., Cherlin & Furstenberg, 1986a; Spicer & Hampe, 1975; Johnson, 1983a; Sprey & Matthews 1982; see also Chapter 13).

When an "Adult" Child is Immature. Another rationale for grandparents' provision of care is the immaturity of the child-bearing middle generation. Adult offspring of any age can evidence behavior that indicates that they are not prepared to competently or confidently handle parenting roles. Teenage mothers, in particular, often are emotionally not prepared to assume parenting responsibilities, especially when they remain unmarried. Under these circumstances, grandparents frequently either assist in child raising or assume the role of parent to the new child (Burton, 1990; Burton, Dilworth-Anderson, & Merriwether-deVries 1995; Flaherty, 1988; Furstenberg, 1980; Furstenberg, Brooks-Gunn, & Chase-Lansdale, 1989). They provide help with such tasks as managing of resources and activities, primary caretaking of infant, coaching about primary infant care and the maternal role, assessing the new mother's attitude about and competency in the maternal role, nurturing with emotional support, and overseeing the new mother's life style and goals (Flaherty, 1988; Flaherty, Facteau, & Garver, 1987).

Researchers have identified a number of different models of coparenting assistance to immature adult offspring. As early as 1980 Furstenberg noted that assistance with parenting responsibilities immediately after the birth of a grandchild to teenage parents often evolved into an "apprenticeship system" where the grandparent not only provided direction but also shielded the new parent from the full weight of child-care responsibilities (Furstenberg, 1980). Burton found a total of 14 multigenerational models of care in the family networks of African American teenage parents (Burton, 1995).

Smith discovered three types of family involvement in the lives of teenage parents: (a) those where family members "role shared" child-care tasks; (b) those where the teenage parent's child-care tasks were "role binding"; and (c) those where family members expropriated child-care tasks from the teenage parent through "role blocking" (Smith, 1983).

Finally, Apfel and Seitz (1991) identify four models of assistance by African American inner-city grandmothers to teenage daughters: (1) *parental replacement* in which grandmothers assume total responsibility for grandchildren, becoming, in effect, the "psychological parents"; (2) *parental supplement* in which mother and grandmother share child-rearing tasks, with the division of labor dependent upon the presence/absence of the teenage mother, the particular task, or the time of the day/week; (3) *parental apprentice* in which the goal is to enhance the young mother's confidence in her new role and skill in parenting tasks; and (4) a *supported primary parent* model in which the adult child is the primary caregiver while she receives baby-sitting or financial assistance from family members.

When an Adult Child is a Substance-Abuser. While it is difficult to obtain national prevalence estimates, there is widespread evidence on the local level that many grandparents assume the parenting role for grandchildren whose parents are substance abusing. In this situation many grandparents lack both personal and social resources that would facilitate their caregiving role. For example, many must relinquish organizational affiliations, such as social and church-related activities and, in many cases, paid employment to devote themselves full time to child raising (Burton, 1992; Minkler & Roe, 1993; Minkler, Roe, & Price, 1992). Moreover, informal support, even from other family members who provided resources during previous experiences requiring family assistance, often grows scarce in situations involving an addictive personality who is viewed as nonrecovering. Indeed, parent-adult child tensions concerning the substance abuse or household rules, including the presence of addictive substances on the premises, can have a uniquely destabilizing impact on the grandparent and family unit (Poe, 1992; Minkler & Roe, 1993).

At the same time, these grandparents are much more likely than are other grandparent caregivers to have assumed responsibility for grandchildren who bear the burden of their parent's behavior in the form of prenatal impacts (e.g., cocaine addiction, fetal alcohol syndrome, HIV/AIDS, attention deficit problems, and learning disabilities) and early childhood experiences (e.g., physical or sexual abuse, or neglect). Compounding these problems, with their attendant stresses and feelings of overburden, isolation, and uncertainty, is the formal support system's frequent antagonism toward or, at best, disregard of the grandparent's needs. Government social services departments, not-for-profit social-service agencies, school systems, and family and probate courts are frequently indifferent, uneducated, or even hostile to these grandparent caregivers. For example, school districts have been known to insist that the grandchild must be registered in the adult child's home district; courts often act as if they are ignoring "the best interests of the child" and return the grandchild to her substance-abusing parent; and local departments of social services sometimes suspect the grandparent's motives for raising her grandchildren (Burton, 1992; Minkler & Roe, 1993; Minkler et al., 1993).

When an Adult Child is Incarcerated. Grandparents are also sometimes called upon to raise the children of offspring who have been incarcerated. In a 1986 report based on the Survey of Inmates in State Correctional Facilities, 53% of incarcerated mothers with one or more children under the age of 18 reported that at least one of these children was living with a grandparent (Greenfield & Minor-Harper 1991). Dressel and Barnhill (1994) point out, moreover, that if the increased rate of female imprisonment continues to keep pace with its 202% rate over the last decade, between 60,000 and 75,000 grandmothers will be raising the offspring of incarcerated adult daughters by the year 2000—a figure that does not take into account the thousands of women on parole or probation who also rely on their parents for help with child care. Additionally, the linkage of incarceration to ongoing cycles of poverty and downward mobility and to substance abuse (Burton, 1992; Minkler & Roe, 1993) can lead to grandparents assuming child-raising responsibilities, whether by choice or by default (Dressel & Barnhill, 1994).

THE SOCIAL CONTEXT OF GRANDPARENT CAREGIVING

The context of the caregiving situation influences the care-providing tasks and responsibilities a grandparent assumes as well as how these impact the grandparent, the young children she or he cares for, and others in the social network. Typically, significant elements of social context range from the prevailing culture and any relevant subcultural factors, to specific components or networks of family and household structure, to consequent patterns of division of labor of care-giving tasks, to the "fit" of the grandparent with his or her roles (see Chapter 4).

Cultural and Racial/Ethnic Background. Cross-cultural and subcultural factors related to race or ethnicity affect how tasks are handled; which particular issues challenge family or personal development and which are handled easily; and even whether grandparents are viewed by others as legitimate in their care-providing roles.

For African Americans who consider themselves grandparents, three particular cultural factors may impact both the assumption and implementation of care provision. First membership in African American families often has been determined not only by lineage but also by the nature of the relationship between individuals, making fictive kin potentially as significant family members as those related by blood (Dilworth-Anderson, 1992; Gutman, 1976). Second, the extended African American family often has responded to the needs of its members by serving as a mutual aid system that frequently extends to the sharing of residences, especially intergenerationally (Franklin; Frazier 1939).

Third, black grandparents, particularly grandmothers, have performed a central role in family maintenance, often nurturing and raising younger generations (Frazier, 1939; Huling, 1978; White, 1985), and for many generations grandparents or grandparent figures (great-grandparents, great-aunts, fictive grandparents) frequently have assumed child-rearing responsibilities for grandchildren whose own parents faced change related to marital status, economic opportunity elsewhere, or poverty (Farley & Allen, 1987; Tinsley & Parke, 1984; see also Chapter 5).

Within families of Hispanic origin in the United States, there are variations in social norms and values among the different subcultures that may affect the assumption or implementation of care provision by grandparents. Universal among these groups, however, is the centrality of *familism*—the influence of the family as the principal social unit and, for the individual, a source of unconditional emotional and material support (Marin, 1989; Marin & Triandis, 1985; Sabogal et al., 1987). In many Hispanic subcultures, as well, the grandmother traditionally has been expected to provide nurturance and child care (Boswell & Curtis, 1984; Peres, 1986; see also Chapter 6).

The ethnographic perspective often focuses upon whether the provision of care by grandparents is normative or whether it is operant only under certain circumstances within a culture. Some examples illustrate the wide variety of such arrangements:

Accumulated information from a number of different studies of the Federal Republic of Germany during the mid-1980's indicated that a consistent minority of grandparents were surrogate parenting, particularly for grandchildren under ten years of age (Sticker, 1991).

Informal adoption by grandparents, long traditional in Polynesian island cultures, appears frequently today among Hawaiian families where grandparents *hanai,* or informally adopt, grandchildren. This practice is common in situations in which an adult child bears an out-of-wedlock baby, or is divorced, deserted, or widowed (1982; Werner, 1989; Werner & Smith, 1977). The intention with the *hanai* is for the child to have an *additional* parental relationship, while making every possible effort to retain the original parent-child bond (Werner, 1991).

In many American Indian subcultures, primary care provision for grandchildren is part of the grandparent's role as cultural conservator. Traditional Sioux women, for instance, consider this a mechanism for imparting cultural information to future generations (Schweitzer, 1987). However, there are completely practical considerations in American Indian subcultures as well. In the Apache culture, while parents are still the primary care providers for most children, the grandmother is the ''child caregiver'' of last resort—to at least one-fifth of Apache children on a continuing basis (Bahr, 1994; see also Chapter 3).

The Family/Household Structure of Grandparent Caregiving. The social environment in which grandparents provide care usually is attuned with the roles, tasks assumed within those roles, and temporal parameters of the circumstances for care provision. However, in most cases there are distinguishing family and household structural variations. For instance, ''grandparent'' care providers can be de facto lineal grandparents—the parents of the parents of the children they are raising. Yet, sometimes, ''Granny'' may actually be a young child's great-grandparent, aunt, great-aunt, cousin, or fictive kin (Minkler & Roe, 1993). Also, the caregiving experience may take place within the extended family but in more than one household; within different family/household environments; within the extended family and also within the same household; or within the ''skipped generation'' household—what Chalfie has referred to as the ''pure'' grandparent household headed by the grandparent/grandparent couple and with no other residents besides grandchildren (Chalfie, 1994).

The Division of Labor Regarding Caregiving Tasks. When grandparents provide daycare in their own homes and no one else lives in the household or is at home during the period of the activity, division of labor is not typically an issue. Nor is it, usually, regarding responsibility for parenting tasks in so-called ''pure'' grandparent households where there is no coresident middle generation. In these latter households, grandparents simply assume all or the great majority of parenting tasks (Burton 1992; Hirshorn & Van Meter, 1996).

However, in households that include other family members, especially the grandchildren's parent, the child-raising division of labor may be more complex. For example, in an investigation of the impact of household type on the various parenting roles of grandparents, Pearson, and colleagues (1990) looked at 130 multigenerational Southside Chicago households—some ''pure'' grandparent/grandchild households and some with the middle generation present, as well. Focusing on determining who, across household type, assumed the more ''authoritarian'' parenting roles (setting and enforcing rules) and who the nurturing and supportive ones, they found considerable differences across household structure in the roles played by grandparents. Not surprisingly, grandparents in households in which the grandchild's parents were not present were much more likely to assume control and punishment tasks—as well as nurturing tasks—while those in households where the grandchild's mother was also present were much more likely to confine their parenting tasks to "bedtime" and support activities.

The Life-Course Timing of Roles. Another contextual factor is the synchronization or dissynchronization between the caretaking roles grandparents assume and their own life-course developmental stage. Those grandparents whose major roles, especially regarding work and family, are congruent with what they had anticipated them to be at this point in the life course typically experience these roles as "on-time." As analysts Hagestad and Burton have noted: "individuals prepare for anticipated transitions, by reorienting their expectations and other role investments" (Hagestad & Burton, 1986: 473).

In contrast, "time-disordered" roles, such as becoming a grandparent at a point along the life course one considers "too early," are experienced "off-time" (Brim & Riff, 1980; Burton & Bengtson, 1985; Seltzer, 1976). Moreover, while roles experienced "on-time" usually are shared with peers, those experienced "off-time" may leave the individual feeling deviant, isolated, or lacking in social support (Hagestad & Burton, 1986; Hagestad & Lang, 1986).

Undertaking surrogate parenting responsibilities for grandchildren is often such an unanticipated and off-time event. Many grandparents not only anticipate involvement in other, more appropriate activities at this life stage, but also experience a disjuncture between their own activities as surrogate parents and those of their peers who do not have these responsibilities. Thus, grandparents whose lives have become "time-disordered" often must look elsewhere for social support, particularly to those whose own current experience is dominated by the same, unanticipated events (Hagestad & Neugarten, 1985; Jendrek, 1993).

Consequences of Grandparent Caregiving

When grandparents and grandparent figures actually raise grandchildren, there are immediate and long-term consequences for both the grandparents and the grandchildren they are raising.

Impact on the Grandparents

Research to date shows effects of grandchild-raising responsibilities on the grandparents' health, financial and emotional well-being, social networks, and daily activity. Most of the evidence indicating the impact of this caregiving experience on grandparents' physical and emotional health comes from small, nonrepresentative local population samples or studies that have not followed the individual or family unit over time. There is also a heavy reliance on the use of self-reported health measures in these studies, without clinical measures of specific health conditions. Moreover, there are likely interactions with demographic and other, mediating characteristics (e.g., age, prior health status, income). To date, these have not been explored in any systematic fashion.

Nevertheless, available information provides evidence that this child-raising role has both positive and negative impacts upon the well-being of grandparents. Emotional well-being is a central issue. Jendrek (1993) found, for example, that friendship networks changed considerably: nearly 40% of all of the grandparent care providers she studied changed their circle of friends after they began to regularly care for a grandchild, and at least one-half of grandparents seeking custody reported a decline in the following, resulting from child-related roles and responsibilities: less time for one's spouse (59.1%); less contact with friends (55.6%); less likely to do things for fun and recreation (55.6%); and less time for self (77.1%).

Much of the current research literature, again, focuses on the well-being of grandparents raising grandchildren when the middle generation is substance-abusing. These grandparent caregivers frequently struggle with feelings of self-blame, betrayal, an overwhelming sense of obligation, and ambivalence toward their responsibilities and charges (Poe, 1992). Many face continual and severe challenges to their sense of personal efficacy and self-esteem, especially when faced with problems that are difficult or even impossible to overcome. Burton (1992) found, in her study of 60 grandparents/great-grandparents raising the offspring of drug-abusing adult children, that 86% reported that they felt "depressed or anxious" most of the time. Focusing on the same type of population in their Oakland, California, study, Minkler and Roe (1993) described self-reports of changes in emotional health since care provision began where nearly equal proportions indicated enhanced, unchanged, worsened emotional health.

Researchers have studied the impact of care provision upon grandparents' physical health, as well. In a Washington, DC–based investigation of African American school-age children and the grandparents raising them (for all manner of reasons), only 6% of the 140 respondents rated their physical health as poor and another 26% as fair. Moreover, 90% of respondents self-reported their mental health as good or better (Brown, 1995). However, with the narrower focus upon grandparents where substance-abuse is the main cause for grandchild raising, Burton (1992) found that 61% had increased smoking; 36% increased alcohol consumption; and 35% accentuated problems with diabetes or arthritis. Likewise Minkler and Roe (1993) discovered that over one-third of their 72 respondents self-rated their physical health as worse than it was prior to undertaking grandchild-raising responsibilities as a result of substance abuse. For some, simply diminished contact with a substance-abusing adult child improved physical health. On the other hand, nearly half of their respondents reported no change in physical health status at all. The mixed findings of these authors regarding physical health suggest the importance of other covariates, such as pre-existing health conditions, availability of health care, and age as important risk factors that have both independent and interactive effects on physical health.

It is important to note that the child-raising experience has positive impacts on the well-being of many grandparents—even on those also experiencing negative outcomes. Feelings of satisfaction, accomplishment, and pride arising from the nurturing role and from seeing positive outcomes in the children are rewarding to many assuming this role (Minkler & Roe, 1993). Some are eager to use this experience as a ''second chance'' to ''do it right,'' in contrast with earlier child-raising experiences.

Impact on the Grandchildren

Evidence here is slim, since, over the years, the child-development literature mainly has focused on the impact of grandparental interactions in more traditional role situations (e.g. baby-sitting, daycare). Again, what research does exist is cross-sectional in design and, therefore, unable to distinguish the impact of antecedent factors upon the child (e.g., earlier home life, physical conditions existing since or even before birth). Recently, Solomon and Marx (1995), in an analysis of data from the 1988 National Child Health Supplement of the National Health Interview Survey, explored differences in health and school adjustment among children raised in traditional two-parent families, single-parent families, and grandparent-grandchild families. They found that membership in grandparent-grandchild families had no significantly different impact upon the health of these children. In Brown's (1995) study, 91% of the children were in good or better physical health and 81% in at least ''good'' emotional health. However, in nearly one-half of the 140 families, the emotional well-being of these school-age children was deemed negatively affected by the absence of parents in the household (Brown, 1995).

Regarding academic performance Solomon and Marx (1995) found that children raised in grandparent-grandchild households were less successful academically in school than were children raised in two-parent nuclear families but on a par with those raised by single parents. However, Aquilino found that children reared in grandparent-headed households had considerably less chance of completing high school than did their counterparts raised in single-parent households (Aquilino, 1996).

Research from other cultures provides a broader outlook. For example, Werner's landmark longitudinal study of a cohort of 698 physically or intellectually handicapped individuals born in 1955 on the Hawaiian island of Kauai indicates that those children who proved to be resilient in the handling of stress while growing up were particularly proficient at securing surrogate parents when biological parents were either nonexistent or incapacitated (Werner, 1989). Likewise, in the Sudan, cross-sectional data indicate that, in contrast with those living in Western-style nuclear families, Sudanese children brought up in the traditional extended family, with high levels of involvement by the *haboba* (grandmother) in child care and socialization, fared better on a number of behavioral, emotional, and physical dimensions (Al Awad & Sonuga-Barke, 1992; see also Chapter 11).

FUTURE RESEARCH ON GRANDPARENT CAREGIVING

Two primary concerns for future exploration of the provision of care by grandparents are (1) the need to regularly anchor future studies in theory and (2) the equally important need to expand the methodological horizon when considering how to design both basic and applied research on grandparent caregiver issues.

Potential Theoretical Frameworks

Family systems theory focuses on interactions among individual family members perceived as part of the larger unit (Hill & Klein, 1973; Kantor & Lehr, 1975; Minuchin, 1974). A major theoretical component is the concept of boundaries and their properties (e.g., clear, diffuse, rigid) to describe different dynamics between and expectations among family members regarding roles, norms, and rules (Boss, 1987, 1988; Minuchin, 1974). Boundary properties of the nuclear family units (the adult child's family and the grandparent's family) may define whether parents welcome grandparents' involvement in child care or merely accept it as necessary though problematic, whether grandparents themselves view their involvement in grandchildren's care as appropriate, and to what extent grandparents and parents experience conflicts over child-rearing issues (see also Chapter 15).

Conflict theory maintains that individuals in the family context, as elsewhere, act to further their own personal interests and that, insofar as this need to fulfill self-interest will conflict with similar needs of others, conflict arises (Bach & Deutsch, 1970; Davis, 1940). Conflict theory might be useful in the exploration of grandparent caregiving in populations undergoing fast-paced cultural change, such as those where first-generation immigrants and later-generations live in the same environment (Winton, 1995; see also Chapter 7).

Feminist theory views families as political institutions in which power, a scarce resource, is fought over and, typically, unequally distributed. From this perspective, the key and defining role of gender in distinguishing roles and power holders could be used to explore the division of labor between grandparent couples and the apparent preponderance of grandparent caregiving assumed by grandmothers, great-aunts, female cousins, and so forth (Campbell, 1995; Hooyman, 1995; Thompson & Walker, 1995).

Symbolic interactionism emphasizes the way in which individuals selectively perceive and process information regarding others to conform with previously established expectations (Mead, 1934; Stryker, 1959, 1972). Since a central concept here is "role reciprocity" (e.g., in families in which one individual is always the caregiver and another always the care-receiver), this theoretical perspective may be helpful in examining settings where grandparent caregivers have long been perceived by others in the family as "the caregiver."

Broadened Methodological Scope

Many of the studies cited or described in this chapter have utilized survey re-search techniques—either the personal interview or large- or small-scale social surveys of the noninstitutionalized U.S. population. Yet, for issues related to grandparent caregivers, the methodological scope could be broadened in order to consider a range of possible approaches or an amalgam of methodological ap-proaches.

Oral history techniques focus the research issue on particular individuals in a specific setting and thereby supply a level of detail or insight not readily available from other sources of information (Allen & Pickett, 1987; Schvaneveldt, Pickett, & Young, 1993). Possible uses include cross-ethnic comparisons of a grandparent caregiving issue or cross-generational comparisons within one family regarding values (e.g., reciprocity, familial obligation) or coping strategies (e.g., validity of seeking respite or other forms of assistance from the formal sector).

Ethnosemantic strategies, favored by anthropologists, are anchored in the use of native categories, definitions, and boundaries to those categories, and the use of "key informants" to derive those categories (Fry, 1986, 1995). These techniques could prove invaluable to the conceptually valid framing and measurement of is-sues surrounding care provision in a particular cultural context or across cultures.

Some researchers have begun to stress the importance of synthesizing qualita-tive and quantitative methodological approaches in the examination of intergen-erational issues. For example, Chatters and Jayakody (1995) suggest strategies that combine ethnographic research, such as the use of "kin maps," to determine patterns of involvement among family members, and secondary data analysis of large-scale social surveys to provide information about types of familial support and transfers.

Many investigations of grandparent caregiving also would benefit from a mar-riage of theory and application, particularly when social problems indicating so-cietal disorder, such as substance abuse or incarceration, are involved. For instance, the intervention research of Hirshorn and her associates exposes partici-pating grandparents to the family systems concept of boundary ambiguity and en-courages them to discuss how this concept figures in their lives as grandparents raising the offspring of substance abusing adult children (Hirshorn & Van Meter, 1996). Dressel and Barnhill's recent demonstration project to respond to the needs of three-generation families of imprisoned women also attempted to test the pri-macy of gender and race, rather than age, as predictors of life-course events for family members (Dressel & Barnhill, 1994). Lastly, the Grandparent Caregiver Study begun in 1991 in Oakland, California, not only documents the experience of grandmothers raising the offspring of crack-cocaine users and the health and so-cial impacts of this family formation but also tries to raise public awareness and support for these grandparents (Roe, Minkler, & Saunders, 1995).

Part III

Interventions in Grandparenting

Chapter 15

Clinical Interventions in Intergenerational Relations

Richard B. Miller and Jonathan G. Sandberg

The important role of grandparents in the functioning of intergenerational families has been recognized for more than 50 years. Early writers, most with a psychoanalytic orientation, focused on the negative impact of grandparents on the family (Borden, 1946; Fried & Stern, 1948). These writers emphasized the meddling role that some grandparents take with their children and grandchildren. Rappaport (1957) coined the term "the grandparent syndrome" to refer to this intrusive pattern of interacting.

More recent writers have emphasized the positive influence that grandparents often have in their families. For example, Barranti (1985) views grandparents as a family resource. They are available to help their children and grandchildren both emotionally and instrumentally. Many grandparents are in a position to help their children financially, if necessary, and they are usually willing to assist with child care. Descriptions of grandparents' roles as "family national guard" (Hagestad, 1985) and "family watchdog" (Troll, 1983) also symbolize the idea that grandparents function as a resource in family crises, to be available in case their children and grandchildren need their help. They can be a protective, stabilizing influence in a family, ready to provide support, comfort, and assistance in times of turmoil and crisis.

Although these two perspectives view grandparents quite differently, research suggests that both views have some validity. Numerous studies have demonstrated that most grandparents and grandchildren are satisfied with their relationship (Cherlin & Furstenberg, 1986a; Hoffman, 1979; Kennedy, 1990; Matthews & Sprey, 1985), but these studies also indicate that among a minority of multigenerational families, there is substantial conflict or angry detachment. Indeed, families develop different patterns of interaction between the generations, with grandparents forming a variety of styles of interacting with their children and grandchildren (Cherlin & Furstenberg, 1986a; Robertson, 1977). In some situations, these styles of interacting are helpful to the family system; in other cases, they detract from healthy functioning. In other words, this research suggests that, although most families have good relationships between the generations, there are some families that experience chronic conflict.

The challenges facing intergenerational families have been documented and described in the chapters throughout this volume. The issue at hand is how to help grandparents, their children, and their grandchildren live in a family environment that is mutually satisfying. In this chapter, we will examine the intergenerational family in a therapeutic context. Current approaches of working with conflicted intergenerational families will be described, and patterns of conflicted interaction between the generations will be examined.

CLINICAL THEORIES

Interventions aimed to help grandparents experience more satisfying relationships with their children and grandchildren are typically based on three major theoretical orientations. These are the developmental, psychodynamic, and family systems perspectives. Each theory, in addition to offering explanations for intergenerational family interaction, provides a set of interventions to facilitate improved relationships.

The Developmental Perspective

From the developmental perspective, individual psychosocial development occurs through the successful completion of tasks associated with stages of life. Erikson's eight stages of life (Erikson, 1963) are unique because the stages transcend childhood and adolescence, reaching into old age. As children become adults and begin their own families, the older generation makes the transition from the "generative" to the "integrity" phase of development. This final stage, striving for a balance between integrity and despair, requires the attainment of wisdom, as the older person reviews and accepts the accomplishments and disappointments in his or her life (Erikson, Erikson, & Kivnick, 1986).

Kivnick notes that during this period of review and reconciliation of earlier life, grandparents continue to have opportunities to extend their care to younger generations through "grand-generativity" (1988: 67). Reviewing one's earlier life plays a role in grandparents developing grand-generativity towards their grandchildren, and "active grandparenting stimulates further review which, in turn, continues to facilitate psychosocial integration" (1988: 68). Thus, the process of life review can facilitate active and positive interaction between grandparents and grandchildren.

This normal developmental task of life review has been adopted by psychotherapists as a clinical intervention (Butler, 1963), and various techniques have been developed to help older adults with the process of life review. The goal of life review, as an intervention, is to help the older adults recall past experiences, evaluate their motives and behavior, and resolve internal conflicts (Butler, 1996). In this way, the person is able to achieve the wisdom that comes from finding ego integrity.

There are a variety of techniques that have been developed to assist older people in their life review process (Hendricks, 1995). One set of techniques is clustered in the treatment modality called reminiscence (Burnside, 1996). The specific goal of reminiscence is to facilitate the recalling of past life events and experiences. Techniques include using scrapbooks, family picture albums, old newspapers, antiques, and music to help elicit significant memories. Helping a person write an autobiography is another technique of the recall process. Reminiscence can occur in either individual or group therapy.

The Psychodynamic Perspective

Psychodynamic theory has historically held a dominant place in understanding and changing intergenerational families. Indeed, the early writing about grandparent-grandchild relationships came almost exclusively from a psychodynamic perspective. However, in recent years, this perspective has become less popular among clinicians working with grandparents and their familial relationships (Butler, 1996; P. K. Smith, 1991).

More recent psychodynamic thinking about grandparenthood is more positive than earlier writing, giving most grandparents credit for having a positive influence on their grandchildren (Battistelli & Farnetti, 1991). The basic concepts of psychodynamic theory, though, are still used to explain psychopathology among grandparents and the resulting poor relationships that they experience with their grandchildren.

An application of the psychodynamic perspective to working with intergenerational families, "clinical grandparenting," was developed by Kornhaber (1986, 1996). He suggests that any evaluation of a family problem should include an assessment of the grandparents' functioning. Toward that end, Kornhaber has provided a description of normal and pathological grandparenting and has developed a classification system of grandparent disorders. He suggests that through the use of this classification system, a psychotherapist can better understand the pathology of the grandparent, which will be helpful in the treatment of the grandparent.

Kornhaber (1996) indicates that there are three major grandparent disorders. The first is the *Grandparent Identity Disorder*, which is "defined by the willful lack of involvement by a biological grandparent with a grandchild" (p. 156). These grandparents have a low drive to be a grandparent and little motivation to interact with their grandchildren. Also, these grandparents suffer from a developmental arrest, namely, they have not developed to a stage appropriate for grandparenthood. Kornhaber suggests that this disorder is most commonly caused by a personality disorder, such as narcissism.

The second disorder is the *Grandparent Activity Disorder.* In this category, "a strong grandparenting drive and identity may be present. However, grandparenting activity is dysfunctional and leads to conflicts, problems, and in extreme cases, alienation from children and grandchildren" (Kornhaber, 1996: 164). Examples of this disorder include grandparents not spending enough time with their grandchildren because they are not a priority in the grandparent's life and acting like a parent, rather than a grandparent, to the grandchildren. Also, these grandparents may lack the flexibility to adjust to the changing needs of their children and grandchildren.

The final category is the *Grandparent Communication Disorder,* which indicates a lack of effective communication among grandparents. Kornhaber (1996) states that two indications of this disorder are grandparents moving away from their grandchildren and grandparents "feuding" with their adult children. Additional symptoms include forgetting family events, last minute cancellations of visits, and noncommunication.

According to Kornhaber's approach, conflict between grandparents and their children or grandchildren is due to grandparents' intrapsychic problems. For example, he assumes that many intergenerational problems result from grandparents suffering from personality disorders, such as narcissistic and obsessive-compulsive personality disorders. Although there are older adults who suffer from personality disorders that impair their ability to maintain healthy and satisfying relationships, including those with their grandchildren, research indicates that they are far fewer than Kornhaber suggests (Sadavoy & Fogel, 1988). Tyrer and Seivewright (1988) present evidence that many of the personality disorders, including narcissism, diminish with age and become unusual among older adults. In short, research does not support Kornhaber's claim that grandparenting dysfunctions are commonly caused by personality disorders.

A major weakness of his approach is that his conceptualization of clinical grandparenting and grandparenting disorders is based on his own research projects, which have important methodological weaknesses. In his first major research project, the Grandparent Study, he and his wife interviewed 300 grandparents and grandchildren. The results of the study were published in 1981 (Kornhaber & Woodward, 1981). However, the methodology has never been adequately described. For example, the methods used to analyze the grandchildren's projective drawings were omitted. As Cherlin and Furstenberg (1986a) note, Kornhaber and Woodward seemed to ignore much of the data that was provided by the subjects, dismissing their responses as uninformed. Instead, the authors reached conclusions that were very different than what the data indicated. Their conclusions also are not consistent with the substantial body of grandparenting research that has been conducted in the past two decades.

Kornhaber mentions another study of 700 children, parents, and grandchildren, which also has a clinical component (Kornhaber, 1986). This is apparently what he later calls the Clinical Grandparenting Study (Kornhaber, 1996). Although this study, along with the earlier Grandparent Study, serves as the basis for the classification system of grandparenting disorders, only a paragraph is devoted to explaining the study in the two publications that address clinical grandparenting (Kornhaber, 1986, 1996). Because virtually nothing is known about the study, it is difficult to have confidence in the results that Kornhaber claims to have found regarding clinical grandparenting.

Family Systems Theory

A more common approach to dealing with intergenerational problems has been developed by a number of family therapists. Although each of them use different interventions, they share a common view of looking at intergenerational problems from a family systems perspective. When using this perspective, "attributions of linear cause and effect are replaced by notions of circular, simultaneous, and reciprocal cause and effect" (Walsh & McGraw, 1996: 5). This theory also posits that family members form a system in which each member is interconnected with the others. Because of this interconnection, change in one person affects all members as the system works to maintain its stability, a principle known as homeostasis. Therefore, because each person lives in the context of his or her family relationships, the behaviors and attitudes of each person can only be explained and understood in the context of the entire family system (Walsh & McGraw, 1996).

An important feature of family systems theory is its explanation of problems within the family. A common nonsystemic interpretation of family difficulties is that an individual is responsible for the problem(s). Usually, great effort is expended in finding the faulty cog in the system and taking him or her in for a tune up (clinical help), so this person can return to "normal." Systems theory, on the other hand, sees problems as occurring in a relational context. A significant feature of the theory is that it focuses on the *process* of interaction, not the *content*. The focus, then, shifts from individual pathology to relationship dynamics.

Family therapists have been using family systems theory to help families with intergenerational problems for over 30 years. When family therapy was still in its infancy, Minuchin and his colleagues (1967) and Haley (1976) recognized the important role that grandparents play in the healthy functioning of family members; therefore, they often included grandparents when they worked with families who came to therapy for a variety of problems. Framo (1976) also included the grandparent generation when working with couples who had marital problems. Bowen (1978) emphasized grandparents and their relationship with younger generations as an important key in understanding individual and family functioning. In addition, Boszormenyi-Nagy (Boszormenyi-Nagy & Sparks, 1973), as an early family therapist, worked with intergenerational family systems.

In summary, the focus of family systems theory–based therapy with multigenerational families is more concerned about patterns of interaction, rather than the topic of specific conflicts. For example, grandparents and their adult children may argue and disagree over parenting practices, in-law relationships, sexual lifestyles, religious affiliation, dress codes, or holiday observances. The content of the conflict is not as important as the way that they interact with each other before, during, and after the conflict. These patterns of interaction can best be understood by using a number of theoretical concepts that have been developed by leading family therapists. Equipped with these theoretical concepts, members of the helping profession can more effectively assist families with their intergenerational problems.

Boundaries

Boundaries can be seen as rules, most often implicit, about who participates in family processes and how (Minuchin, 1974). In our physical environment, boundaries are represented by fences, walls, and doors; in biology, cells are differentiated by membranes. Some of these various boundaries are rigid and impenetrable, while others are diffuse and easily penetrated. Similarly, the interactions between family members are largely determined by the rules that define boundaries within the family. Some family relationships are characterized by overinvolvement, often called enmeshment, while there is underinvolvement, or disengagement, in other relationships. The healthiest family relationships are those that have a balance of individuality and togetherness (Minuchin, 1974). Patterns of overinvolvement and underinvolvement are common sources of intergenerational conflict.

In a now-classic paper, James Framo (1976) describes four of these common intergenerational relationship patterns, both healthy and unhealthy. First, he outlines an "over-involved with family of origin pattern," where adult children, including spouses and children, fail to establish appropriate boundaries with parents (p. 194). This family pattern is often characterized by an emotionally enmeshed adult child-parent interaction, such as daily conversations regarding parenting, joint vacations, and/or close living arrangements. Not surprisingly, conflict between the adult child and his or her spouse over the involvement of grandparents in the day-to-day responsibilities of marriage and parenting can be frequent and heated.

Framo (1976) also describes a pattern at the other end of the boundary spectrum. This is typified by those who have completely and rigidly cut themselves off from their family of origin. Some individuals in this group are extremely angry and bitter at a parent, often forbidding spouses or children to visit or even speak to the offending party. Others, though less angry, still feel it best to avoid any interaction with their parents. Sadly, the grandparent-grandchild relationship in this case is sacrificed in behalf of ongoing resentment and bitterness. Framo (1976) points out that "these people have the greatest likelihood of repeating with their mates and children . . . the irrational patterns of the past" (p. 195). In other words, this standard of disconnectedness, if unaltered, will be the model for multigenerational functioning that children will most likely carry into and replicate in their adult relationships as well (Bowen, 1978; Framo, 1976).

The third pattern reflects a different type of disengagement. The "superficial, nonpersonal" pattern consists of "duty visits" to parents and joint attendance at events such as weddings and funerals (Framo, 1976: 195). Although there is contact between parents and grandparents, there is a lack of emotional connectedness in the relationship. The grandparent-grandchild relationship in this case, although existent, will likely be void of meaning and impact. Although this pattern is unlikely to produce high levels of conflict, intergenerational strain rooted in avoidance and denial of problems will still likely be present.

Framo's fourth pattern of intergenerational relationships characterizes functional families. He describes this pattern as "stemming from having established a self within the family of origin before separating from it. These people did not have a desperate need to stay with, or get away from, their parents; there is presently neither over-attachment nor angry distancing" (1976: 195). In this case, an adult-to-adult relationship, with flexible and clear boundaries, is formed between parent and grandparent which allows each to fulfill his or her distinct roles in the multigenerational family system. "Affection and a sense of obligation are still present, but not at the expense of one's present family or one's integrity of self" (Framo, 1976: 195). In these families, grandparents and grandchildren are free to develop voluntary bonds that respect the boundaries of other members of the family. Clearly, family-focused workers who are serving intergenerational families should assess for and treat ongoing boundary conflicts. Often, therapists can be most effective when helping families clarify and rework existing rules regarding troublesome boundaries, particularly those that encourage children to take on the responsibilities of adulthood or vice versa.

Triangulation

Triangulation is "the process which occurs when a third person is introduced into a dyadic relationship to balance either excessive intimacy, conflict, or distance and provide stability in the relationship" (Everett, Russell, & Keller, 1992: 32). In other words, a third party is brought into a two-person relationship to drain off mounting tension or anxiety (Bowen, 1978; Minuchin, 1974). The process of triangulation is often helpful for the original dyad because its relationship becomes stabilized with the introduction of the third member, but the third member almost always suffers. The stress of being in the middle of a triangle typically leads to symptoms such as depression, anxiety, or inappropriate behavior.

Some triangles are subtle. For example, feuding grandparents and their children may use the grandchildren as messengers. In this type of triangle, which Minuchin (1974) calls a detouring triangle, the grandparents ask their grandchildren questions about the parents, such as whether or not they have found a job or whom they are dating. The parents, in turn, ask their children questions about the lives of the grandparents. In many families, these questions are harmless, but they are inappropriate when the relationship between the grandparents and parents is strained and distant. Because of the tension, they use the grandchildren to "spy" on each other, which puts the grandchildren in the stressful role of being caught in the middle of the conflict.

Another triangle occurs when either the grandparents or the parents recruit the grandchildren to side with them against the other party. In these coalitions (Minuchin, 1974), one party, say the parents, criticizes the grandparents and encourages their children to join in the criticism. It is common, and even healthy, to have a particularly close relationship with some family members, but it becomes an unhealthy coalition when they join forces to attack, subtly or overtly, another family member. In both of these cases, family-focused workers can highlight troublesome communication patterns and foster conflict-resolution skills which can offset the need for triangulation.

Other triangles are more overt. In the case of custody and visitation disputes between grandparents and parents regarding the grandchildren, the grandchildren are caught in the middle of a powerful "tug-of-war." Even when the intentions of the parents and/or grandparents are based on their love of the grandchildren, the grandchildren suffer in these battles. They often feel torn by a perceived need to declare loyalty to only one party, when they would like everyone to "just get along" so that they can feel free to display loyalty to both their parents and grandparents. Therapist intervention in "tug-of wars" can free the grandchildren from the overwhelming responsibility of trying to "hold it all together." Once the grandchildren are out of the middle, therapists can then help parents and grandparents face difficult issues regarding separation and loss, and work toward a more amiable resolution.

Ledgers

Ledgers can be described as ongoing legacies of emotional commitments and obligations (Boszormenyi-Nagy & Spark, 1973; Everett, Russell, & Keller, 1992; Hargrave & Anderson, 1992). Simply put, multigenerational ledgers are accounts of relational charges (hurts) and credits (benefits) accrued by family members over time (Boszormenyi-Nagy, 1974). Symptoms of intergenerational conflict, therefore, can be seen as a sign of an unbalanced account.

To illustrate, when a family member is hurt or neglected, it goes down in an ongoing, implicit relational account. To avoid relational bankruptcy, this same member then attempts to rebalance his or her account through positive interactions (credits) with other family members. "For example, parents who were neglected as children may later contrive, even if unwittingly, to be nurtured by their own children to compensate for their deprivation" (Ingersoll-Dayton, Arndt, & Stevens; 1988: 283). However, the very attempt to rebalance one's own account may place unmanageable demands on another's. For this reason unbalanced ledgers are often reproduced across the generations.

Attempting to help families rebalance their ledgers is a delicate process. In order to gain a more complete understanding of the accounts in a given family, intergenerational therapists often begin with the grandparents (Spark, 1974). Imagine a case where an adult child, a mother, is struggling with feelings of neglect from her father, as well as the emotional problems of her own troubled son. The therapist, by exploring the grandfather's past in the presence of his daughter, would allow both parties to more clearly view the disappointments and sufferings of the elder's own childhood. Interestingly, as the mother is able to see and better understand the charges on her father's ledger, she will learn of his "human dignity and suffering" and view her relationship with him in a new light (Boszormenyi-Nagy, 1974: 267). As she reworks the account with her own father, additional assets are made available to this mother as she shifts her attention to the relationship with her son. She is now in a position to make deposits in the account of her struggling son. This therapeutic process frees up family members to identify with each other in new, healthier ways through the "rebalancing of indebtedness" and mutual appreciation and understanding (Spark, 1974: 229). Therefore, the objective of an intergenerational intervention that focuses on unbalanced ledgers is to develop action strategies for adjusting or repaying relational accounts in ways that reduce suffering and misunderstanding.

The concept of ledgers is illustrated in the following case study. Mrs. B came to therapy seeking help for her misbehaving son, who was struggling both at school and at home. At the therapist's request, Mrs. B invited her parents to attend the first session, as well as Mr. B and the son. During the first session, the family revealed that Mrs. B had been adopted and that she, in turn, had adopted her son. The therapist noted, as a key family theme, there was a common pattern of distancing that was present between both mothers and their children. Just as Mrs. B's mother had distanced herself from her child, Mrs. B was doing the same with her own son:

In a session that was particularly moving, Mrs. B and her mother met together with the therapist. The mother and daughter talked about their similar experiences as ungainly, awkward teenagers. As the daughter remembered these miserable "growing-up" years, she began to cry. Her mother reached out to comfort her, and Mrs. B wept in her arms. During the session, the two women reached a level they had never had before. After connecting with her mother in this meaningful way, Mrs. B found it easier to attain a close relationship with her son. His misbehavior at home subsequently decreased, and his school behavior improved. (Ingersoll-Dayton, Arndt, & Stevens, 1988: 287)

The case of Mrs. B and her family highlights the impact of unbalanced ledgers on family functioning. As demonstrated in this case example, children often show their loyalty to their parents by internalizing their parents' expectations and passing them on to their own children, even unwittingly. In this case, Mrs. B was carrying out the script of a mother-child relationship that her own mother had laid out for her. A balancing of ledgers occurred as mother and daughter were able to share an emotionally intimate moment around common teenage experiences. This sharing of suffering provided Mrs. B with an opportunity to better understand and exonerate (or vindicate) her mother of the wrongs she felt she had received from her. When Mrs. B was able to relate to her mother in a new way, she was also freed up to then rebalance her own ledger with her son. As a result, his conduct at home and school improved.

CLINICAL ISSUES OF GRANDPARENT-HEADED FAMILIES

Many grandparents are now assuming primary caregiving responsibilities for grandchildren whose parents are unable to care for them (Burton, 1992; Ehrle & Day, 1994; see also Chapters 2, and 14). In these cases, grandparents are often taxed to their financial, emotional, and physical limits as they care for their grandchildren, while still wondering and worrying about their own wayward children (Buchanan & Lappin, 1990; Minkler, Roe, & Price, 1992). This emerging family constellation, "grandparent-headed families," brings with it a number of intergenerational implications (O'Reilly & Morrison, 1993: 147).

Although the majority of grandparents in this situation amazingly cope with tremendous physical and financial strains, it can be the emotional and mental turmoil of surrogate parenting that can prove to too much. O'Reilly and Morrison (1993) note that feelings of anger and helplessness are common for grandparents as their efforts to inspire responsibility in their children fail. Along this same line, grandparents may also struggle with feelings of failure and guilt for their own parenting, as well as a sense of being overwhelmed at the present task of raising children all over again. Sadly, the day-to-day demands of child rearing may prevent many grandparents from finding the time to work on these conflictual feelings.

Clinicians are becoming sensitive to the challenges facing grandparents who are raising grandchildren. Several authors have reported positive outcomes in psychotherapy and support groups and family therapy clinics where grandparent-headed families and their unique struggles are the focus of treatment (Kennedy & Keeney, 1988; O'Reilly & Morrison, 1993; Strom & Strom, 1993). O'Reilly and Morrison (1993) suggest that treatment plans often center around three key issues. First, clinicians must address issues relating to child development to help grandparents reacquaint themselves with the appropriate behavior and growth patterns for younger children. Second, many grandparents are at a loss when dealing with outside agencies such as child protective services, the court system, and financial assistance programs; to survive as surrogate parents, grandparents must have an understanding of how these agencies can work for and against them. And third, clinicians should focus on intergenerational conflict patterns that further induce anxiety and tension as parents and grandparents argue over how to rear the third generation.

Two issues are particularly likely to create conflict and, therefore, require the attention of clinicians. The first issue, *hierarchy*, focuses on the distribution of power in the family system (Minuchin, 1974). In well-functioning families, there is a clear hierarchy, with the parents assuming the leadership role for their children. In most American families, the role for grandparents is to respect the authority of the parents and assume a caring, but noninterfering role (Cherlin & Furstenberg, 1986a). This pattern seems appropriate in nuclear families, but who is "in charge" in grandparent-headed families? Do the grandparents have the final say regarding the raising of the grandchildren, or do the parents maintain primary authority over the children?

Because the circumstances of grandparent-headed families vary widely, it is impossible to formulate a general rule regarding the optimal structure of the hierarchy. Rather, the point is that the hierarchy must be *clarified* in each family so that the role of the grandparents and parents regarding the leadership of the family is not confused. When all of the family members, including the grandchildren, understand the distribution of authority, there will be much less stress and conflict in the system.

The second issue, *boundary ambiguity*, was coined by Pauline Boss to refer to confusion within families about who is and who is not in the system (Boss, 1988). Boss found that families experience additional stress when it is unclear whether or not a person is a part of the family system. In order for a person to be fully in the system, he or she must be both physically and psychologically present. When only one of these criteria is met, the family experiences a high level of boundary ambiguity.

Grandparent-headed families are at risk for a high level of boundary ambiguity. When the grandchildren are living with their grandparents instead of their parents, it is often difficult for the grandchildren to understand their relationship with their parents. This problem is exacerbated when the parents seemingly arbitrarily become heavily involved with their children, only to disappear from their lives again. In these cases, the children often ask, "Is my Mom still my Mom?" It is also frustrating for the grandparents, whose role in the family system changes depending upon the unpredictable and variable involvement of their adult children in the family.

Similar to the concept of hierarchy, the key is to minimize boundary ambiguity by *clarifying* the boundaries in the family. Stress would be reduced if clinicians could help families strive to determine a consistent and predictable pattern of involvement of the parents in the lives of their children.

CLINICAL ISSUES OF DIVORCE

Divorce of the middle generation often has profound effects on the relationship between grandparents and grandchildren (see Chapter 13). Grandparents, when their divorced children retain primary residential custody of the grandchildren, typically experience increased interaction with and closeness toward their grandchildren (Cherlin & Furstenberg, 1986a). This is especially true during the transition period following the divorce, when grandparents are very involved in helping their adult child adjust to the divorce.

Noncustodial grandparents, on the other hand, typically experience a dramatic decrease in interaction with their grandchildren. In many cases, the custodial parent severely limits grandparents' access to their grandchildren by moving away or forbidding contact with their ex-spouses' parents. In cases where grandparents have been cut off from their grandchildren, the loss is profound (Kornhaber & Woodward, 1981). Grandparents struggle with the often abrupt transition from enjoying an ongoing relationship with their grandchildren to losing contact with them.

To date, the primary intervention to help cut-off grandparents regain contact with their grandchildren has been through establishing social policy that gives them visitation rights. The Grandparents Rights Movement has lobbied for legislation across the country to grant grandparents the right to legally seek reasonable visitation with their grandchildren. As a result, grandparents are now legally empowered to seek the right to maintain relationships with their grandchildren (see Chapter 16).

However, like custody battles between former spouses, establishing the right to specified visitation patterns between grandparents and grandchildren does not necessarily reduce the acrimony between the battling parties. Rather than decreasing the hostility and ill-will between the grandparents and the custodial parent, going to court to establish visitation rights usually increases the conflict. The result is that the grandchildren are caught in the middle of a powerful triangle between their custodial parent and noncustodial grandparents. It is likely that children suffer adversely when put in the role of a pawn in the battleground between the two parties.

Unfortunately, very little has been written about clinical strategies to help grandparents become reconnected with grandchildren who have been cut off from them. Erlanger (1997) suggests that therapists should help grandparents grieve and accept the loss of their grandchildren, but that approach does not offer hope or help to grandparents who want to work on reestablishing ties with their grandchildren.

It seems that family systems theory has the theoretical tools to help resolve some of the patterns of hostility, anger, and conflict between grandparents, adult children, and their former spouses that are the root cause of the unwillingness of custodial parents to have their children visit their former spouse's parents. Strategies and techniques of divorce therapy that have been useful in helping former spouses achieve a nondestructive divorce hold promise in helping intergenerational families adjust to divorce in a way that permits grandparents and grandchildren to maintain positive relationships. Therapists need to turn their attention to applying divorce-therapy approaches to intergenerational relationships.

CONCLUSION

Although there has been signf[c]ant progress made toward providing therapeutic theories and strategies to help grandparents and grandchildren enjoy positive relationships, there is still much work to be done. For example, with the exception of life review and reminisence (Burnside, 1996; Butler, 1996), virtually no clinical research has been conducted to test the efficacy of clinical interventions that are used with grandparents. Consequently, there is little empirical evidence supporting the effectiveness of much of the clinical work that is done with grandparens and their grandchildren. In addition, there has been little research examining the *process* of therapy with this population. That is, we have little understanding, based on empirical research, about *why* therapy might work. Although clinical experience suggests that therapy is effective with intergenerational families, clinical research needs to be conducted to provide empirical support. Such research will also provide insights into what aspects of specific approaches are therapeutic, which will enable these theories to be refined and improved.

There has been a promising trend in recent years toward integrating the general theoretical approaches when working with intergenerational families. For example, Hargrave (Hargrave, 1994; Hargrave & Anderson, 1992) and Walsh (1989) include life review in their family therapy approaches, and DeGenova (1991) uses family therapy to help her assist older persons in their process of life review. By integrating useful techniques from different perspectives, therapists can increase their ability to work with a variety of intergenerational family problems. Such integration also enhances communication and cross-fertilization between therapists from different theoretical perspectives.

Finally, therapists who work from a systems perspective need to turn their attention more to grandparenting issues. Although the pioneers of family therapy addressed three-generational issues, most family therapists today focus on the nuclear family. Family therapy has a rich array of conceptual tools that have great promise in helping troubled grandparent-grandchild relationships. The task is for family therapists to become more involved in applying these tools to grandparents and their familial relationships.

Chapter 16

Public Policy and Grandparents: Contrasting Perspectives

Joan Aldous

Grandparents' rights are being abused. What are grandparents to do when they can't afford a lawyer to fight for the right to see their grandchildren or to get custody? (Morrison, 1996: A10)

As a grandparent, I was dismayed at the 2,000 grandparents of the GRINS organization lobbying the Indiana General Assembly for the absolute right to visit their grandchildren against the objections of the parents. (Sightes, 1996: A18)

These two excerpts from letters to a newspaper express some of the strong feelings giving rise to and aroused by public policy concerning grandparents. By policy in this connection, I am referring to measures taken by governmental bodies with specific reference to or effect on grandparents. This chapter will focus on two issues concerning the relations of grandparents and grandchildren that have involved controversy: grandchild visitation and custody. My coverage of each will include the associated legal questions along with social science findings that could provide some perspective on court decisions in these areas. Those are particularly important with respect to the contentious issue of visitation, but grandparents with live-in grandchildren also deal with legal matters. There is a discussion of some of these problems residential grandparents experience. To the extent possible, this section also contains material on how recent changes in welfare policies affect grandparents who are caring for grandchildren. The chapter begins with a consideration of how grandparents are generally seen, since this view influences policies directed toward them.

VIEWS OF GRANDPARENTS AND VISITATION RIGHTS

Governmental policies directed toward individuals in their status as grand-parents arise out of perceptions of them and the kind of relationships they are thought to have with their grandchildren. The picture most people hold is highly favorable and even sentimental. As columnist, Russell Baker (1996: A8) has noted, the majority of people "speak of their grandparents with more affection than they do of their parents." How the middle generation fits into this inter-generational linkage as I will show in later discussions is often overlooked. Although some continue to see grandparents as frail individuals, enfeebled by old age, the *Whistler's Mother* image, others know from personal observations that persons in this family position can still be leading active lives, holding down jobs, and keeping family lineages together. However, many are unaware that today's grandparents are more likely to be healthy, well off, and to have a living spouse than was true as recently as half a century ago. After all, most attain this status while in their 40's and 50's (Aldous, 1995), although increasing longevity and the continuing greater poverty of older women means this favor-able situation does not hold for all grandparents. However, the greater economic well-being along with the physical fitness of many persons likely to be grand-parents has contributed to the popular, and perhaps somewhat idealized, images of the roles grandparents play in child development (Thompson et al., 1989: 1221).

Grandparents can serve as both direct and indirect models for passing on values and behaviors to grandchildren. They can also relieve the middle gen-eration of some of the cares that accompany rearing children through the older generation's financial, task assistance, and emotional support (Apfel & Seitz, 1991; Solomon & Marx, 1995). Legislators, like the general public, are favor-ably impressed by these possibilities and find it agreeable to do things for grandparents. The fact that voters over 60 are more likely to go to the polls (Binstock, 1992) does not lessen this desire. It has been argued that the "dra-matic broadening of grandparent rights in recent years" is due to their greater political power (Thompson et al., 1989: 1218).

One of the first areas in which this regard for grandparents appeared had to do with their visits to grandchildren. As early as 1894, grandparents were seek-ing access to their grandchildren through legal means if necessary. At that time, an appellate court ruled that such visitation was a moral, not a legal, obligation of parents. They were not legally required to permit such visits (Wacker, 1995: 287). Higher divorce rates, the subsequent remarriages of former partners and stepparent adoptions led to situations in which parents of the noncustodial par-ent, usually on the father's side, lost touch with their grandchildren (Cherlin & Furstenberg, 1986a). Parents in the middle generation could be unenthusiastic about such visits and put obstacles in their way. It was apparent that the older generation's love and concern for the children of their offspring did not cease even if the offsprings' marriages had come to an end. Grandparents faced with seemingly insurmountable barriers to seeing their grandchildren turned to legal strategies to gain access. As a consequence, state legislators began passing laws to give grandparents the right to visit their grandchildren.

The push for the right of grandparents to visit their grandchildren started in the 1960's and 1970's, when divorce rates began rising. The early statutes used the standard of the "in the best interest of the child" to be used in courts granting grandparents visitation. Moreover, the circumstances under which grandparents could seek legal remedy were limited to parental death or divorce, the granting of final adoption to the spouse of the child's custodial parent or some comparable event. By 1993, every state in the union had passed a law specifically permitting grandparent visitation or giving such rights to third persons over the objections of the parents (Greene, 1994). Typical of such laws was one initially passed by the Wisconsin Legislature in 1975 and "re-created" in 1977. It granted grandparents the right to petition for visitation privileges under any circumstance. The court was to grant the petition if visits were in the "best interest" of the child (Hintz, 1994: 492–493).

In any discussion of such legally authorized visitation, the concept of boundary maintenance is a useful one (Aldous, 1978, 1996). It refers to the family unit, in this instance composed of parents and children, and the boundaries that exist to mark its identity and preserve its autonomy from outside interference. The Supreme Court as early as 1923 in *Meyer v. Nebraska* held that the fourteenth amendment guaranteed the right of individuals to establish homes and to rear children as they deem proper. The state under the doctrine of outside protector, *patriae parens*, can intervene within family boundaries to influence parent-child relations only when the children are being harmed or there is threat of harm to them. Even protecting the health of the child is not sufficient to justify state action that would go against parental wishes. Errors in parental judgment do not necessarily constitute harm or the level of harm necessary for state intervention (Bean, 1985–1986: 407–408). The sanctity of the parent-child unit boundaries is to be maintained.

More recent visitation statutes continue to be based upon the doctrine of the "best interest" of the child, but they are "open ended." This means that the particular parent-child family situation can be overlooked. In Florida, for example, the courts can grant grandparent visitation rights for children living with both natural parents, who are still married, despite the opposition of one or both parents (Greene, 1994: 54–55). According to such visitation legislation, grandparents have gained legal rights without corresponding duties. Parents are still completely responsible for giving care to their children and can be held liable if they do not. As a result of these laws, parents have experienced a decrease in their autonomy to rear their children as they see proper but have not been relieved of any duties to care for them (Bostock, 1994: 359). Increasingly, therefore, both legal scholars and social scientists are questioning whether these visitation policies contribute to the well-being of the three generations involved.

CONCERNS ABOUT LEGALLY ENFORCED VISITATION

To begin with the arguments of the first group, they are concerned that courts not order grandparent visiting unless harm to the child from parental decisions or lack of them has been demonstrated. Moreover, even if harm has been determined according to these lawyers, courts need to consider what remedy is best for the child without giving undue "sentimental weight" to preserving the child's contacts with the grandparents. Too often in this view, the best interest of the particular child is "overshadowed" by the "court's desire to contribute to the maintenance of a grandparent-grandchild relationship" (Bean, 1985–1986: 394). Instead of requiring grandparents to show that their visits are in the best interests of the child, courts "invariably" demand that the parents demonstrate harm from the contacts (Bean, 1985–1986: 400–401).

It also appears that there has been some gender bias in granting visitation rights. Courts are more likely to grant visitation to paternal grandparents when mothers have custody than in the reverse situation. Judges seem to take more seriously objections to visits from maternal grandparents if fathers are the custodial parents. The same male-oriented tradition influences decisions in grandparent visitation cases where stepparents have adopted the children from a previous marriage. Increasingly, courts are granting grandparents through the biological line contact with their grandchildren in such situations. Again though, such rights are more likely to be granted to grandparents over the objections of a stepmother than a stepfather. The rationale appears to be that women are better prepared to handle conflictual relations and that men should have control over their families (Czapansky, 1994: 1343, 1348–1349). In these cases, whether divorce, remarriage, or adoption is involved, the actual relationship among the three generations is often overlooked. Instead, decisions are based on "stereotypes" concerning "which grandparents are seen as good or bad or which parents deserve respect for autonomy," and which ones can heal hurtful relations (Czapansky, 1994: 1350).

Lawyers point out that there is little research about the importance of grandparent-grandchild relations or about the effects of legal disputes over visitation on the grandchildren (Bostock, 1994: 321). They note that the rationale for the importance of the grandparent-grandchild relation underlying the visitation policy is based on such factors as the older generation's supposed transmission of family values, grandparents' unconditional love unsullied by the irritations of lengthy, daily contacts, and their ability to reduce stress within the parent-child family (Bostock, 1994: 361–364).

Turning to the arguments of social scientists, we find that psychologists, Barbara R. Tinsley and Ross D. Parke (1984) have also described the functions grandparents can provide for the succeeding generations. For the middle generation they can serve as an auxiliary support staff. They can be baby-sitters as well as counselors and advice givers. They can display good parenting practices for new parents to follow. These in extreme cases can lessen the effects of brutal or abusive parents. As good companions, grandparents can also make their grandchildren's lives happier. In addition, the stability that a previously existing, comfortable relation with grandparents can provide ameliorates the disruption in children's lives if their parents divorce. But grandparents' involvement in their children's and grandchildren's lives is not always positive (Hintz, 1994: 510). They may serve as poor parenting models, and even if they are good parental surrogates, they may become too intrusive in their offspring's family lives.

There appears to be a curvilinear relation between grandparents' involvement within the family boundaries of their children and their descendants' well-being. Either too much or too little can be dysfunctional. Grandparents themselves are loathe to cross the boundaries of their children's families for any sustained time. They want to conform to the norm of noninterference in their adult children's families (Cherlin & Furstenberg, 1986a). At the same time, they usually wish to be involved enough to see the development of their grandchildren. Maintaining a comfortable balance between the extremes of disinterest and over-solicitousness can be difficult.

The few, large-scale studies that document the effect of grandparents' contacts on grandchildren indicate that there is great diversity in the extent and type of interaction according to the age, gender, race, and social class of the grandparent and the age of the grandchild (Aldous, 1995). One such study, based on a national sample of 510 grandparents, did cover the issue of how much grandparents were involved in their grandchildren's lives. The findings were that the older generation plays only a minimal role in the socialization of their grandchildren. Regardless of race, only a "tiny fraction" of the grandchildren reported that they turned to their grandparents when problems appeared. The few who did include them when they listed the persons whom they considered within their family boundaries were no more apt than the other grandchildren to see them as guides for forming their social perspectives. Grandparents' influence on the transmission of values was through the parents (Cherlin & Furstenberg, 1986a: 182).

Relationships when grandchildren are in problematic family situations may be different. Again, however, as with so much research in this area, we are dependent upon small-scale studies for our information. One using 391 college students, for example, showed that grandchildren in single-parent families (n = 70) and particularly grandchildren in stepfamilies (n = 55) did report being closer and more involved with their grandparents than were the students from families with two biological parents present (n = 266). The researchers speculated that young adults in stepfamilies turned to grandparents for support when the boundaries of the former single-parent family unit expanded to include the parent's new partner. These adult children were no longer the focus of their single parent's attention. They were having to accept another individual in an intimate relation with their parent. Grandmothers especially provided continuing sources of pleasure and companionship for the young people living in a reconfigured family (Kennedy & Kennedy, 1993). Presumably, as suggested above, grandparents helped ease the disruption in family relations these young adults faced.

In times of stress, as when partners are in conflict or divorcing, maternal grandparents often do step in, taking on more parental roles and assisting the mother, usually the custodial parent, financially and by providing her and her children with emotional support. Thus, 32 of 80 middle-class, Canadian grandmothers with preteen grandchildren were more often in contact with them after a divorce, particularly when they lived close to each other. However, among services to grandchildren, such as as baby-sitting, caring for an ill grandchild, or giving them personal advice, the only one that increased after the parents' marital breakup was taking the grandchildren to some commercial entertainment. Increased interaction was less true of paternal grandmothers whose sons are less likely to have custody of their children. This would account for the greater social distance between the grandmothers and grandchildren (Gladstone, 1988).

The national study of grandparents cited above showed that three of ten parents of daughters who divorced opened their homes to them and their children at the time of the dissolution of the marriage. Four of ten parents of sons who divorced gave financial aid, and one of seven had a grandchild living with them. (Cherlin & Furstenberg, 1986a: 142). A longitudinal study of the effects of parents' divorces and grandchildren's relations with their maternal grandparents also showed a similar greater grandparent involvement following divorce but not remarriage. The children were 9 to 13 years old. As compared with the 73 intact and 49 stepparent families in the middle-class sample, the children in single-mother families reported closer relations to grandparents over the 22 months of the research (Clingempeel et al., 1992). Paternal grandparents whose sons are unlikely to have child custody are more apt to lose access to their children's children (Cherlin & Furstenberg, 1986a).

The relations of grandparents and grandchildren and their mutual involvement, however, depend heavily upon how well the middle and the older generations get along. In the national sample referred to above, grandparents who reported being close to their daughters saw their grandchildren almost twice as often as did grandparents whose relationships were less agreeable (Cherlin & Furstenberg, 1986a). More recent research based on the reports of 398 intact couples and their ninth-grade children living in a rural area produced similar findings. As was true in the national sample, the factor of proximity played the major part in grandparent-grandchild contacts. But parents who reported poor relations between themselves and their parents were more likely to have adolescents who said they saw their grandparents less frequently and did not get along with them as well as did their peers whose parents and grandparents had good relations (Whitbeck, Hoyt, & Huck, 1993). This is likely to be especially true if such contacts are the result of litigation where parents and grandparents are put in adversarial positions in a courtroom setting (Thompson et al., 1989).

In addition to exposing children to the acrimony between parents and the preceding generation, legally imposed visitation results in children's experiencing conflicting loyalties. On the one hand, they are being cared for by one set of adults, but on the other they are being forced against these adults' wishes to be in contact with another. The young parties to these disputes may well feel uncertain as to which adults are in authority and thus their protectors (Goldstein, Freud, & Solnit, 1979). Moreover, unlike the usual close relation between parent and child, grandparents granted visitation through court intervention may not have such a long established affectionate tie. One child psychiatrist, A. F. Derdyn (1985: 284), has concluded that visitation "provides a new legal means for children to be involved in and to be used in the service of conflicts of their elders." The best interest of the child, supposedly the legal basis upon which such rights are granted, can be lost due to the dissension between adults.

The solidarity of the family unit may also be threatened if its boundaries are breached and its privacy destroyed (Nolan, 1993). As lawyer, Kathleen S. Bean (1985–1986: 423–430) has written that in order for courts to override the assumption of parental autonomy to rear their children as they deem proper, judges must find that a child is being harmed in a particular way from being deprived of grandparent visits. If it so determined, the court can then intervene in the best interest of the child to decide that seeing the grandparents is necessary to remedy the harm and benefit the child in question. This intervention, though, is placing the court's judgment above that of the parental caretaker. And if relationships between parents and grandparents are strained, such an order can add to the intergenerational conflict. Under such circumstances, parents are unlikely to see their parents as sources of support and assistance.

Lawyers also note that there is the element of the time parents have to spend with their children. Divorced parents who have custody often find themselves seeking more time to spend with their children. Job responsibilities to support them along with the time children spend in school and with friends, as well as with the noncustodial parent, all cut into the time the custodial parent has with them. Thus, in addition to the attorney costs and mental strain that visitation cases impose upon parents, court-ordered visits with grandparents decrease even more the time children have to spend with the parents in their homes (Galasso, 1994; Morris, 1989).

Children often do find relations with their grandparents helpful, especially as discussed above when they may be having difficulties in their own families. However, "the law is a very blunt instrument for ensuring that they are maintained, especially when the costs to the child of a court battle" and the resulting intergenerational rancor are taken into account (Thompson et al., 1989: 1222). It is just because of such considerations that some grandparents, prevented from seeing their grandchildren, do not seek legal recourse. In a small British study (Lowe & Douglas, 1989), 12 of 46 grandparents who received advice to go to court to gain access to their grandchildren did not choose to do so. Included in their reasons for this decision was their concern to avoid contributing to destructive family relations. Thus, grandparents themselves may recognize that there are risks as well as rewards to be gained in using legal means to keep in contact with their grandchildren.

GRANDPARENTS AND LIVE-IN GRANDCHILDREN

A second issue involving grandparents and their grandchildren that has legal ramifications has to do with grandchildren living with grandparents. Changes in parent-child family units over the last several decades have made this issue like that of visitation salient. The numbers of separations, divorces, teenage pregnancies, single-parent families, parents who are abusive or on drugs and mothers who are holding jobs has led to situations where grandparents have had to take on parenting roles again. They might be dubbed the ''pick-up generation,'' since grandmothers especially are having to pick up the living remainders of adult children's failed partnerships and care for them.

Just as grandparent visitation rights enforced by law may erase family boundaries to the dismay of parents and their children, so too grandparents having to assume custody of their children's children are not always happy to pick up the youngsters from inoperative families for inclusion into their own. It goes against the norm of noninterference in the lives of adult children who are supposedly independent, and grandparents usually have left behind the responsibilities entailed in active parenting for a daily existence in which they can exercise more choice. Custodial grandparents are understandably disappointed that their offspring have failed to fulfill the duties associated with parenthood (Shore & Hayslip, 1994). Thus, Andrew J. Cherlin and Frank F. Furstenberg, Jr. (1986a: 189–190) on the basis of their national study concluded that for today's grandparent being part of her grandchildren's lives is important ''but not at the cost of her autonomy.''

As with so many other aspects of the two generations' relations, there is not much information on families that are characterized by coresidence of grandparents and grandchildren. The U.S. Bureau of the Census data from 1995 show how many children lived with a grandparent as householder at that time, that is the person owning, renting or maintaining the housing unit (Saluter, 1995: B2). Children living in these households constituted 5.6% of all children under 18 years of age (Saluter, 1995: table 4, 26). This is up from the 1.6% of children living in such households in 1980 (U.S. Bureau of the Census, 1981, Table 4, 27- 30).

A recent study based on the 1992–1994 wave of the National Survey of Families and Households provides more detailed information on such families from the perspective of the grandparents (Fuller-Thomson, Minkler, & Driver, 1997). The proportion of grandparents in this representative national sample who said they had the primary responsibility for rearing a grandchild for six months or more, a different question than that of the U.S. Census survey described above, was 10.9%. These caregiving grandparents had distinctive characteristics. Not unexpectedly, they were more likely to be grandmothers than grandfathers.

They had more of their children living with them than did other grandparents. The odds of being in charge of grandchildren also were higher for African Americans and went up with each grandchild an individual had. Older grandparents, however, were less likely to be caregivers. There were differences in income between caregiving grandparents and the other grandparents. About a fourth (23%) of those who were caregivers had incomes below the poverty line as compared with 14% of the noncustodial grandparents. In respect to gender and age, therefore, residential grandparents were somewhat better prepared for their parenting roles than their noncaregiving peers. But grandparents' lower incomes and larger numbers of coresident grandchildren would make fulfilling these responsibilities harder.

Factors similar to those contributing to legal intervention in grandparent visitation are related to the issue of grandparent coresidency or custody of grandchildren. Grandparents as a group are less likely to be needing care from a child than in the past, but as noted above they are more likely now to have to pick up the care of their children's children. Disruption in adult children's partnerships can lead in some cases to an increased emphasis on the boundaries of the parent-child unit leaving grandparents outside, but in some cases to their opening them to include grandparents. And in yet other cases, it may be grandparents' family boundaries that must expand. In one small-scale study, 30 grandparents with legal custody of their grandchildren told why they had sought to incorporate the children into their families. The major reason given by 22 was the mothers' emotional problems. Sixteen also reported they did not want the children to be placed in foster care, and a similar number said the mother of the children was on drugs (Jendrek, 1993).

Grandparents are most likely to gain custody of their grandchildren when such conditions indicate to the courts that the natural parents are unfit. The other standard judges use to assign custody to third parties in regard to the granting of visitation is the best interest of the child. One indication that granting custody to nonparents meets this standard is when the child is already living with these persons (Haralambie, 1991). Thus, grandparents are more apt to win custody resulting from litigation if they have been rearing the children in question for several years under informal arrangements. Similarly, parents who wish to regain custody of their children should be able to show that they have remained in contact with them. That the parents provided some support for their children during the period of the third party's custody is also a factor contributing to parents' probabilities of regaining custody. Provision of supports like visits to the children provides evidence of the parents' continuing concern for their children (Atkinson, 1986: 411–417). Even so, it appears that courts are likely to decide in favor of grandparents when a child has spent a considerable period with them. The rationale is that remaining in the stable environment to which the child has become accustomed is better for the child than being "snatched from the only home he or she has known" (Victor, 1989: 9).

Caretaking grandparents who have some regularized arrangement concerning their live-in grandchildren are in a minority. The older generation is exercising parental responsibilities but often lacks the legal legitimation to do so. Most exist in a "legal limbo" with respect to decisions regarding the child and to needed financial aid (Rudasill, 1995: 217). Without some legally recognized arrangement, the grandmother cannot enroll the child in school, obtain financial services, or take nonemergency health actions regarding the child unless the parent consents. If a parent is ill, disabled, uninterested, or missing and the grandmother has to make decisions that will benefit the child, she will be going against the exclusive rights vested in the parent (Czapansky, 1994: 1318).

Grandparents and other third parties responsible for the day-to-day care of children in this anomalous status suffer other difficulties. Landlords of private housing units can refuse to rent to grandparents when they take grandchildren into their homes. Those living in subsidized housing for the elderly may no longer be eligible for these units if children join them in the living quarters. Younger grandparents may have to move out of their present homes due to the increased family size. To take one example of such a case, officials instituted eviction proceedings from a public housing unit against a 49–year-old grand-mother whose seven grandchildren lived with her. The reasons for the grand-mother's parenting responsibilities indicate some of the dramatic situations that thrust the elder generation into picking up the pieces from failed families. Her daughter-in-law, the mother of five of the grandchildren, had been on drugs at different times and had died of a drug overdose. The son-father was in prison for armed robbery. The mother of the other two children, a daughter, had died of an AIDS-related sickness. Lacking legal custody of the children, this grand-mother faced having to deal with the possible loss of her subsidized housing (Karp, 1993).

Obtaining financial support for grandchild rearing can also be a problem when the living arrangement is not regularized. As previously noted, grandparents who are caretakers of grandchildren cannot always afford it. Since they are more likely to be women, they are more apt to be poor. A number of such grandpar-ents also are retired and living on fixed incomes. In 1992, the U.S. Bureau of the Census reported 23% of them were 65 years of age or older. Over a fourth, 27% of grandparent caretakers in the same year, were living in poverty. An additional 14% were among the near-poor. The median income of these shared households was $18,000 (Rudasill, 1995: 216, footnote 7; U.S. Bureau of the Census, 1992). Consequently, grandparents opening their homes to grandchil-dren may well be looking for outside financial assistance.

Before the transfer of greater responsibility for the financial support of poor families with dependent children from the federal government to the states through the 1996 Personal Responsibility and Work Opportunity Act, 28% of middle-aged and older grandparents were estimated to receive Aid to Families with Dependent Children (AFDC) for coresident children. However, even then "many" grandparents who sought such benefits were turned down. The prob-lems they faced are worth reviewing, since they will continue and be exacerbated now when states with their varying regulations and funding priorities have taken over administration of welfare programs. Some states categorically denied AFDC to nonparents while others only gave it if the grandparents had custody (Rudasill, 1995: 270). This was especially a problem when the mother was under 18 years of age and obtaining certain kinds of education. Federal law required that the grandparents' income be considered available to the grandchildren. As a consequence, they could have been considered ineligible for AFDC, or, in some states, state-provided public assistance. This would be the situation even when the daughter was taking complete care of the child. Legally, the older generation's responsibility for the daughter was seen to extend to the grandchild as long as the daughter was a minor (Czapansky, 1994: 1316–1317). As far as Social Security benefits go for grandchildren, grandparents having a grandchild living with them do not always receive such payments. The grandchild's parent must be dead or disabled, or the grandparent has to have adopted the child to obtain them (Czapansky, 1994: 1318, footnote 13.)

Often, grandparents lack the money and knowledge of how to institute action to adopt or to obtain legal custody. In most states, adoption is not possible unless the parent consents, or has abandoned the child or harmed her or him. Third parties wanting to obtain custody must show that the parents are unfit. Grandparents can have difficulty proving this or may feel disloyal doing it. When the adult child is dying, for example, parents may be unwilling to add to her stress by seeking the partial removal or complete ending of that child's parental rights (Czapansky, 1994: 1319). Others are unsure of how long they will have the children in their care and so are wary of obtaining legal custody (Rudasill, 1995: 218).

Another option besides seeking adoption or custody for the grandmother who is in charge of grandchildren and lacks legal standing for their care is to place them in state foster care. She would then seek to be named foster parent. Although she would then be receiving considerably higher payments than she would from welfare allotments, there are disadvantages. She would have to be licensed, meet state training requirements, and conform to state standards on adequacy of the residence and child care. For less well off grandparents, such standards as number of bedrooms or minimum residential square footage can be hard to fulfill. Moreover, their having higher foster-care payments could discourage parents eligible only for lower welfare payments from reuniting with their families (Karp, 1993: 586).

Another need grandparents who are serving as parental surrogates face is medical care for the children in their charge. Although the elders may be receiving Medicare benefits, Medicare does not cover dependent children. Only some private companies will insure the children, and only then if the grandparents have custody. If the children are on welfare or receive Supplemental Social Security Benefits, however, Medicaid, the federal health program for needy people, is automatically available (Rudasill, 1995: 272).

The 1996 welfare legislation provides for federal block grants to the states to substitute for AFDC and Medicaid payments. These provisions will give states greater freedom in setting eligibility and benefit levels. There will be even greater state variability in these standards than existed before the changes. One of the more potentially harmful features to grandparents of the legislation is the work requirement for child caretakers. Those in charge of children over five will be required to obtain a job within two years of receiving benefits, and the 1996 law sets a limit of five years for assistance from federal block grant funds. Mothers and presumably other caretakers of younger children are exempt from this provision if they can demonstrate a lack of suitable, affordable child care (Kilborn, 1996: A10). As we have seen, custodial grandparents tend to be younger, so they may be required to obtain a job or engage in a job training program after a certain period of obtaining welfare payments. Thus, grandparents of young grandchildren would be having to face the problem of child care. More seriously, their ability to obtain benefit payments on behalf of grandchildren is put in jeopardy by the cut-off dates for giving welfare states face. Some states like Massachusetts and Virginia are exempting the ''elderly'' from the time limits on receiving welfare, but this would not cover younger grandparents (Cohen, 1996).

There are some strategies to deal with the legal limbo in which many grandparents responsible for grandchildren find themselves. New state laws exist that grant caregivers the legal recognition they need which does not ''unduly'' diminish the authority of the child's parents. New York and Illinois among others now have standby guardianship statutes. Under them, a parent who is terminally ill can designate a guardian for his or her children. This individual then is able to exercise parental rights when the parent becomes too sick to care for the child. The caretaker assumes custody of the child when the parent dies (Czapansky, 1994: 1352; Karp, 1996). ''Consent'' legislation also exists that permits the transfer of specific kinds of authority without court action. Parents or legal guardians can simply sign a document allowing another adult to permit health treatment for children in their care. Such a procedure is authorized in Washington, DC. In California, any adult caregiver can also enroll a child in school, and if the caregiver is a relative, the caregiver can allow medical or dental care for the minor. The grandparent or other caregiver must have an affidavit that she or he has informed the child's parent or legal custodian of the planned care and received no objection or been unable to reach this person (Karp, 1996). Pro bono lawyers and service providers can also inform parental surrogates about the ways to obtain legal authority and represent them in custody and guardianship cases (Karp, 1993). However, there have been drastic congressional cuts of over 31% from 1994–1996 in the budget of the federally funded Legal Services Corporation. Their lawyers are devoted to representing the poor in civic legal matters. In 1996, the funding for the agency was $283 million as compared with $415 million in 1994. Thus, the services such lawyers can provide to needy grandparents is considerably curtailed (Cohen, 1996; Coleman, 1989).

Other federal and state actions can affect grandparents by requiring that they open their homes to grandchildren. This is most apparent with welfare reform measures. States have increasingly enacted laws requiring minors who have children to live with their "parents or another responsible adult," as the Indiana welfare description has it (State of Indiana, 1994). It is now a requirement of the 1996 welfare law that unmarried mothers under 18 years of age will usually have to live with an adult and attend school to obtain welfare (Kilborn, 1996: A10). Yearly, the number of unmarried adolescents under 18 giving birth is not large. In 1991, for example, it was 159,139. But a disproportionate number of these young mothers, 42.2%, are black mothers and more likely to be poor (National Center for Health Statistics, 1995: 110, 211, tables 1–56, 1–84). Thus, among all female householders in 1994, 46.2% of blacks and 29% of whites were in poverty (U. S. Bureau of the Census, 1996: XVII, Table F).

The rationale for this welfare requirement that adults, generally parents and adolescent mothers with children, share a home is that parents will supervise the adolescent mother in her schooling, and in her peer and parenting roles, and assist her in fulfilling them. This supervision is supposed to be especially devoted to seeing that the young mothers complete their high-school educations. The ideas that parental monitoring can decrease adolescent childbirths and/or help youths in school are commendable, but evidence to support them is skimpy. For example, research based on National Longitudinal Survey of Youth data found only "limited support" for the hypothesis that lack of supervision in single-parent households accounted for adolescent premarital births. Moreover, the families these young women were living in were very often characterized by instability and poverty. Parents had changed partners through divorce and remarriage or cohabitation shifts. These changes are also related to their lack of the financial resources that would provide opportunities to the adolescent children in the occupational world (Wu, 1996: 404). Thus, requiring teenagers with their children to live with parents may simply keep them in the same deprived settings that contributed to their precocious childbearing.

RELEVANT RESEARCH ON CORESIDENCE OF GRANDPARENTS AND GRANDCHILDREN

As with other aspects of grandparent policy, there is not much research that sheds light on whether grandchildren benefit from sharing a home with grandparents. Studies that are available often do not single out the children of teenage mothers in their findings. Several have been based on a 1966–1967 first-grade cohort from a low-income, black, urban community. There were interview data from 130 families in which grandmothers were living. Mothers were present in 89 of these residences. When grandmothers were playing maternal roles, they performed more caregiving activities than in mothers-present homes. They also did more punishing and exercised more control over the children when mothers were absent. In grandmother-mother-child families, grandmothers gave more support to children than in families where fathers also lived. Fathers may have provided the child care that grandmothers otherwise would have felt it necessary to provide (Pearson et al., 1990).

First- and third-grade teachers also rated these children along with half of all the 1964 first graders as to their abilities to perform certain social tasks. In these early years, children in single-mother families did less well on the ratings. When grandmothers were present, however, they performed almost as well as children in two-parent families. Grandmothers seemed to have "important ameliorative functions" so that they lessened the disadvantages children in father-absent homes experienced (Kellam, Ensminger, & Turner, 1977: 1012). A follow-up study nine years later using the same sample of children now 15 to 16 years old, looked at their school adaptation in relation to their family backgrounds. Children in families of single mothers did more poorly in school. However, where grandmothers and mothers shared a home, children did almost as well as children in two-parent families (Kellam, Ensminger, & Turner, 1977). In these low-income, black families, grandmothers appeared to play a positive role when mothers, but not fathers, were present.

Another study on custodial grandparenting of predominantly white grandparents in an urban area has a comparison group of nonresidential grandparents. Its findings indicated less satisfactory relations between the first and third generations when the middle generation was absent (Shore & Hayslip, 1994). There were 103 in the grandparent caretaker group, with somewhat over half having legal custody, and 100 grandparents in the comparison group without responsibilities for their grandchildren. As might have been expected from the previous discussion, the latter grandparents were better off economically than the residential grandparents. In addition, questionnaire results showed that almost two-thirds (65%) of the grandparents who were serving as surrogate parents reported their charges were demonstrating serious enough behavioral problems that they had sought or were planning to obtain outside help. They also perceived their involvement with their grandchildren to be less agreeable than did the traditional noncaretaking grandparents.

Some of these problems and the attendant dissatisfaction may have been associated with the overrepresentation of grandsons among the grandchildren living with their grandparents. Sons are more exposed to parental conflict than daughters and have more difficulty after parents divorce than do daughters (Hetherington, Cox, & Cox, 1982, 1985). Consequently, sons may be more often given to grandparents to raise in times when parents are experiencing conflict and marital dissolution. The senior generation has to deal with the family disarray their children and their children's children are living through. The above findings, therefore, suggest that conditions associated with grandparents' having to assume parental roles for grandchildren, especially sons, may not encourage positive relationships between the two generations when the middle generation is absent.

Research indicates that grandparents' feelings are not always positive about having live-in grandchildren. In the study of coresidential and traditional grandparents described above, the first group on average were less satisfied with grandparenting and had lower well-being scores than was true of grandparents without parenting responsibilities (Shore & Hayslip, 1994). Having to perform the duties of parental surrogates for often obstreperous grandsons and on less money than the grandparents without such demands seemed to take its toll. Similar findings appeared in a study of 36 custodial grandparents, 24 coresidential grandparents without custody, and 52 grandparents who provided regular daycare. The custodial grandparents reported the "off-time" parenting took them away from friends without such responsibilities. The latter were free to pursue their own concerns, a state the grandparents had looked forward to but failed to enter due to continuing parental duties (Jendrek, 1993).

Grandparents who had the care of grandchildren where a parent was absent but who lacked custody had the worries of possibly losing the child they were parenting to an unprepared or even harmful parent. When a parent was also present in the grandparents' home, the family elders faced the problem of boundary maintenance. How could they play a caregiving role without going against the norm of noninterference in the parent-child unit? They faced the unpleasant situation of giving needed physical care to the child which the parent might resent.

Grandparents did report that there were some compensations. About two-thirds of the custodial and one-half of the living-with grandparents said the caretaking tasks gave them a purpose in life. Daycare grandparents enjoyed more personal freedom since their charges were only present during the day. Some liked the parenting tasks, although others bemoaned their lack of freedom (Jendrek, 1993).

CONCLUSION

This review of the literature on visitation and custodial policy affecting grandparents shows the contrasting perspectives surrounding it. Such policies often rest on the sentimental assumption that grandparents can be a positive influence on their grandchildren's lives. Some of the limited research available with reference to intergenerational contacts indicates the circumstances when this is likely to be true. The older generation can ease the discomforts children in single-parent and stepfamilies may experience. Children who are living through the upheaval usually surrounding the breakup of their parents' partnerships are especially likely to benefit from the attentions of loving grandparents.

Yet, there are situations where lawyers and social scientists question whether contacts between grandparents and grandchildren are necessarily in the best interest of the children. Their concern centers on visitations imposed by legal bodies. It appears that when family boundaries are forced to expand for visiting reasons, the adults in the original units are seldom happy. The middle generation generally views these legal mandates granting grandparents the right to visit their grandchildren as an unwelcome intrusion. Since research shows the relations between elders and parents affect the tone of grandparent-grandchild feelings, the circumstances surrounding enforced visits generally do not foster the favorable outcomes a sentimental perspective sees associated with these interpersonal ties.

It also seems that some grandparents prefer not to be actively involved in rearing their children's children. Grandparents like visiting at their discretion, where they can enter and leave their grandchildren's lives at will. Such a style is consistent with the norm of noninterference that usually governs the relations between adults of different generations. Most grandmothers are anxious to keep in touch with grandchildren but enjoy not having to provide physical care. For elders to have to open their homes to grandchildren suggests to them that they have failed in bringing up their own offspring to be responsible adults. The timing can be inconvenient. Grandparents may lack the energy, money, and residential facilities necessary for off-time parenting.

The evidence suggests, therefore, that whether with reference to living together or visiting, the ability of grandparents, parents, or grandchildren to choose the extent of interaction is important for positive interaction. Legal decisions setting the terms of involvement are often counterproductive. The above discussion shows that lawyers, legislators, and judges are seeking solutions to ease the difficulties grandparents experience in being forced to rear grandchildren when their adult children prove inadequate parents. But the previous analysis also indicates that in setting the terms of grandchildren-grandparent contacts the law should be a last resort.

What can be done to make it more likely that the sentimental perspective on grandparent policy, that is, that children always benefit from being with grandparents, will be a reality in visitation conflicts? Certainly, the doctrine of the best interest of the child should be paramount in such decisions. To see that the child's welfare is central, judges and lawyers must take into account the feelings of her or his caretakers about grandparent-grandchild contacts. When relations between the first and second generations are strained, and they usually are if the law must be called upon to settle visitation disputes, the advantages of grandparent visits are threatened. Calling for some mediating procedure between the disagreeing parties before a final decision is reached is one strategy court officials can use for easing the entrance of grandparents into the previously closed parent-children boundaries. Judges have the power to urge the parties in conflict to seek mediation assistance, and most good-sized communities have such centers staffed with trained mediators (Wood & Kestner, 1989). The contending parties can then negotiate how to divide these costs. When the grandparents and parents have themselves worked out arrangements for the oldest and youngest generations to get together, it is more likely that these meetings will result in the benefits "contemplated by grandparent visitation statutes" (Hartfield, 1996).

Governmental policies affecting grandparents necessarily involve intergenerational ties as well as relationships. Often, when contacts between grandparents and grandchildren are forced, whether in matters of visiting or co-residence, members of at least one generation are in difficulty or unhappy. It is apparent from the above discussion that laws, courts, and lawyers can be helpful in easing possible difficulties involving the generations. They can provide the means for enabling hard-pressed grandparents to take over caring for grandchildren who have inadequate or unavailable parents. They can also encourage the oldest and middle generations to work out their conflicts over contacts between elders and their grandchildren. However, the law and its functionaries, although they can require individuals to be in touch, cannot create the good feelings that make these visits the kind memorialized in the stories, songs and reminiscences of countless grandchildren. For these, judges and lawyers have to turn back to the contending parties and direct them to settings where they can be forced to work out their own arrangements. Family insiders with skilled mediators are better able than outsiders to develop policies that all the generations can at least live with. Therefore, it appears that grandparent policies are best when they are enabling rather than forced. Under those circumstances sentimental, legal and social science perspectives can be accommodated to the benefit of the generations of grandparents, parents, and children alike.

NOTE

I would like to thank Robert M. Birkey for reading over and making comments on this chapter, and Eric Stromberg for doing the necessary library research for it.

Chapter 17

Programs for Grandparents

Maximiliane E. Szinovacz and Angela Roberts

Today's grandparents face numerous challenges. The transition to grandparenthood itself as a countertransition is outside grandparents' control and may or may not fit the new grandparents' role repertory or correspond with their current life goals (Hagestad & Burton, 1986; Sprey & Matthews, 1982). Becoming a "good" grandparent is difficult when norms are vague and mainly proscriptive (Cherlin & Furstenberg, 1986a; Cunningham-Burley, 1985), and grandparents may experience a "double bind" as they are confronted with simultaneous expectations for support and noninterference on the part of their adult children (Thomas, 1990a). Some grandparents are separated from their grandchildren through family conflicts or divorce (see Chapter 13), and some older adults are altogether deprived of grandparenthood due to their own or their children's childlessness. On the other hand, an increasing number of grandparents are overburdened by demands for child care for their grandchildren (especially when adult daughters or daughters-in-law are employed) or the need to assume a coparenting or surrogate parenting role (see Chapter 14).

In response to these challenges numerous programs have emerged to help grandparents. This chapter offers a brief overview of such programs. We start with a classification of program types, followed by brief descriptions of major programs and their evaluation. The chapter concludes with suggestions for program development and research and a brief list of information resources. Clinical interventions and current policies addressed in preceding chapters are not covered.

GRANDPARENT PROGRAMS—AN OVERVIEW

Programs and information for grandparents fall essentially into three main groups: (1) general education and information that targets all grandparents and aims at improving grandparenting skills; (2) information and supports for grandparents with special needs, particularly grandparents raising grandchildren; and (3) intergenerational programs that provide opportunities for interactions between seniors and children or adolescents. The latter programs typically serve both the senior and young participants but may target special needs among either group.

Educating Grandparents

Educational materials for grandparents come in various formats, ranging from book-length treatments on "how to become a successful grandparent" to brief advice columns in magazines (for example, Chassler, 1994) and to curricula presented either as workshops and seminars or as self-help guides for grandparents. Because this chapter is devoted to programmatic efforts, we will concentrate on the latter.

The two major education programs are those by Strom and Strom (1991a, 1991b) and Kornhaber (1985). Strom and Strom (1991a, 1991b) developed a curriculum for grandparents that aims "to help women and men who aspire to becoming a better grandparent" (1992b: 5) and to enhance "grandparent potential" (Strom & Strom, 1992b). The curriculum addresses children's, parents', and grandparents' experiences. It encourages grandparents to "become more influential" or to "keep up with times," provides information on parenting, and addresses issues of child rearing and communication with children and adolescents. Recently, efforts have been made to adapt the program to special issues confronted by black grandparents (Strom et al., 1993). The authors report that their pre- and post-test evaluations of the program showed improvement of grandparenting skills among grandparents as well as the adult children and grandchildren of program participants but no improvements for a control group (Strom, Strom, & Collinsworth, 1990; Strom & Strom, 1992a).

Arthur Kornhaber and his wife established the Foundation for Grandparenting in 1980. Its mission is to "raise people's awareness about the importance of grandparenting for all three generations" (Kornhaber, 1996: 8). The foundation publishes a quarterly newsletter *Vital Connections* and developed programs for grandparents. A practical guide for parents and grandparents *Between Parents and Grandparents* was published a decade ago (Kornhaber, 1985). Kornhaber (1996) does not offer information on program evaluations.

Supports for Grandparents

A second group of programs offers supports to grandparents. Most of these efforts have targeted grandparents who raise their grandchildren, while programs and supports for grandparents with other problems (e.g., those with divorced adult children) are still lacking (Brown, 1982; Strom & Strom, 1993).

The broadest effort to help grandparents as surrogate parents was initiated by the Brookdale Foundation. The project now entails an information center, a newsletter, seed grants for the development of local programs and services for grandparent caregivers, as well as research and advocacy. The Grandparent Information Center, funded by the Brookdale Foundation and administered by AARP, has two main goals: (1) to raise awareness about grandparent caregivers and (2) to accumulate and distribute information about grandparent caregivers to service providers and grandparents themselves (Brookdale Grandparent Newsletter, 1992, 1993; AARP Grandparent Newsletter, 1994). Since its inception in 1993, the Information Center has published "Tips for Grandparents" detailing problems encountered by surrogate grandparents (e.g., on health care for grandchildren, on obtaining access to public benefit programs such as AFDC or Medicaid, or on establishing a support group) and advice on how to deal with these problems (Chalfie, 1994). In addition, the triannual newsletter provides information on the center, addresses selected issues in grandparent caregiving, describes local support groups, reports on policies and their impact on grandparent caregivers, and lists resources for service providers and grandparent caregivers. The center's most recent initiative is the development of a minority grandparent component (Brookdale Newsletter, 1994, 1995, 1996).

The Brookdale Foundation Group also provides small seed grants for grandparent caregiver support groups (five grants were awarded as of 1996). A book designed for grandparent caregivers offers advice on common problems (Takas, 1995). Efforts by the Brookdale Foundation and other agencies, including AARP, the National Council on the Aging, and Generations United resulted in the adoption of a Resolution on Grandparents Raising Grandchildren at the 1995 White House Conference on Aging.

Two other national organizations serve grandparent caregivers. ROCKING (Raising Our Children's Kids: An Intergenerational Network of Grandparenting, Inc.) maintains a directory of support groups for grandparent caregivers, helps individuals locate support groups, and offers support to individuals who care for their grandchildren. It thus serves as a network for caregiving grandparents. The nonprofit organization also aims to initiate policy changes in support of grandparent caregivers. ROCKING is particularly effective because it provides information and programmatic efforts applicable to the broad spectrum of grandparent issues that emerged during the past decades. For example, the platform adopted by ROCKING in 1993 includes issues related to grandparents' visitation rights (Generations United, 1993). Education and advocacy goals are also the focus of the National Coalition on Grandparents, established in 1992. Its membership consists of local chapters representing grandparent caregivers as well as of professionals from a variety of disciplines.

At the heart of aid to grandparent caregivers are, of course, the many local support groups. As of winter 1996, the AARP Grandparent Information Center identified over 400 such support groups nationwide (Brookdale Newsletter, 1996), and, undoubtedly, there are others not yet listed by the center. Organizationally, the groups are quite diverse. Some were initiated by local agencies or professionals, others by individual grandparents; some are funded through grants from foundations or state and local funds, while others rely primarily on their members' own resources; some target specific groups of grandparents (e.g., parents of teenage parents, parents of parents who have drug addictions, or parents of mothers who are incarcerated), while others address a broader audience (Barnhill, 1996; Brookdale Grandparent Newsletter, 1993; Cervera, 1989; Dressel & Barnhill, 1994; Kornhaber, 1996; Minkler & Roe, 1993, 1996; Roe, Minkler, & Saunders, 1995).

Because most support groups are either not funded at all or funded through local agencies, they typically do not have access to trained professionals as facilitators or program developers and rarely include evaluations. Some problems experienced by these groups have been noted by national support group network leaders. They include too much complaining by group members, which tends to foster pessimistic rather than optimistic attitudes, problematic group dynamics such as a few group members monopolizing the conversation, an emphasis on communication with peers which may discourage communication with family and friends, limited educational components, overburdened group leaders, and an overemphasis on self-help (Minkler & Roe, 1993; Strom & Strom, 1993).

Furthermore, many of the support groups cannot provide the kinds of supports that grandparent caregivers need on a higher system level, that is, federal and statewide policies and programs that help grandparent caregivers or at least diminish problems they have in access to benefits (see Chapter 16). The individual support group members who are themselves grandparent caregivers can help one another by listening to or baby-sitting for each other, providing leads to resources, or sharing tips on dealing with schools and agencies, on child rearing, or on stress management, but they often have little time or energy left over to advance their cause. Additionally, members of the grandparent care movement sometimes advocate solutions and ideas that diverge from those of the ''rank and file,'' thus creating a potential split in the ranks and a nonuniform approach to the creation of policy and expanded support services. For example, some advocates focus solely on the responsibility of social services and the government to provide financial resources, but many surrogate parents need other services as well. Such problems can undermine program efficiency and, in some cases, even lead to the disbandment of a group.

Intergenerational Programs

A third group of programs encourages interaction between different generations (usually children or youth and older persons) through joint participation in planned productive activities with shared goals. Typically, program objectives emphasize reciprocity between generations, dispelling of ageist stereotypes, and focus on activities that benefit both the elders and the youth involved in the programs as well as their communities. Established programs usually include training of volunteers and program revisions based on program evaluations (Roberts, 1995; Wilson, 1994).

In the United States, the major impetus for intergenerational programs started in the 1960's with the establishment of the Foster Grandparent program, the Adopt a Grandparent program, RSVP (Retired and Senior Volunteer Program), and the National Student Volunteer program (Kornhaber, 1996). Meanwhile, similar programs have been developed in other countries (for Great Britain see O'Connor, 1993). Today many of these programs are sponsored by or linked through national organizations, including AARP, the Corporation for National Service, the Elvirita Lewis Forum, Generations Together administered by the University of Pittsburgh, Generations United, the National Association for the Education of Young Children, the National Council on Aging, or the Temple University Center for Intergenerational Learning (Kornhaber, 1996; Wilson, 1994). However, individual programs are often grassroots efforts at the local level that may receive funding and other assistance from national organizations and/or state and federal government and rely on available program guides.

There are now numerous types of intergenerational programs. Most programs fit one of the following modules: older adults meeting the needs of the younger generations, young persons meeting the needs of older adults, young and old serving together in community projects or programs, older and younger individuals participating in shared activities designed to enhance intergenerational understanding, and intergenerational advocacy (Roberts, 1995: 3–4). We concentrate on those programs that are well established nationally and have relevance as "substitutes" for older persons without grandchildren or as supports for grandparents with special needs.

The oldest and one of the largest efforts is the Foster Grandparent Program, founded in 1965. This is "a federally supported volunteer program . . . that offers older people living on limited incomes aged 60 and over opportunities to provide person to person assistance in community and home-based settings to children with special or exceptional needs" (Wilson, 1994: 13). Volunteers serve a minimum of 20 hours a week and receive a small stipend. A variety of children with special needs have been included in Foster Grandparent programs, including children with disabilities or AIDS, juvenile delinquents, teenage parents, abused or neglected children, youth with drug addictions, or hospitalized children (J. Wilson, 1994). Today over 32,000 seniors serve in Foster Grandparent programs across the nation.

The Adopt a Grandparent Program, started in 1965 in Gainesville, Florida, aims to enhance interactions among children and seniors through grade schoolers' visits to nursing homes or similar facilities (Haber & Short-DeGraff, 1990; Proller, 1989). Grade-school children "adopt" nursing home residents and write to them, visit them, read stories to them, or engage in other activities with the seniors. The intent is to increase seniors' exposure to social contacts with nonresidents in general and with children in particular, and to enhance schoolchildren's understanding of aging processes.

Several other intergenerational programs involve youth serving older persons. Similar to the Adopt a Grandparent Program, "Community" involves schoolchildren visits to nursing homes and YES (Youth Exchanging with Seniors), developed under the sponsorship of Texas Tech University, is a program where youth help home-bound elderly through assisted-living services (Wilson, 1994). A guide for similar programs is available from the National Council on Aging (NCOA).

The Retired and Senior Volunteer Program (RSVP) "helps people age 55 and over find service opportunities in their communities" (Roberts, 1995: cover). Under the auspices of the federally supported National Senior Service Corps, RSVP programs involve seniors in a variety of volunteer activities, many of them intergenerational. Recent demonstration projects aim to form partnerships among organizations and agencies to enhance intergenerational contacts and exchanges. For example, the RSVP Senior/Youth Alliance of Camden County, New Jersey, involves the Camden City Housing Authority, the Rutgers University Urban Literacy Program, the Genesis Counseling Center, Kennedy Memorial hospital, and the Work Group. This alliance functions under a model where youth and seniors work as teams on community projects, including a drug elimination program, senior and youth tutors for schools, or peer counseling. Another RSVP program, Linking Intergenerational North Coast Kids and Seniors (LINKS) in Cleveland, involves youth and seniors in activities ranging from an oral history project where seniors share their life experiences with youth to a project where RSVP volunteers teach schoolchildren about gardening. Summer Horizons, in Harrisburg, Pennsylvania, involves RSVP seniors and at-risk middle-school students in learning experiences during summers, whereas Atlanta RSVP sponsors a program where RSVP volunteers visit youth in a juvenile detention facility, and the St. Paul RSVP runs a program where RSVP volunteers and teenagers jointly teach cultural, safety, and health awareness to young children after-school hours (Roberts, 1995).

Numerous other intergenerational programs have been developed over the past three decades. They include intergenerational arts programs, students providing respite for caregivers of frail elders, older seniors as mentors for schoolchildren and at-risk youth, intergenerational child-care programs where older persons either serve as child-care workers or child-care centers are placed in nursing homes and other senior residential facilities, after school programs where seniors listen to and help children through telephone help-lines or serve as role models, and many school-based programs and curricula (Crites, 1989; Haber & Short-DeGraff, 1990; Kuehne, 1992; Tice, 1991; Wilson, 1994).

Although there is now a plentitude of intergenerational programs, systematic and well-designed evaluations of these programs are much less common. Many evaluations are based on very small samples, some rely on retrospective accounts rather than pre- and post-tests, and many fail to include control groups. Furthermore, existing evaluations have provided mixed results. In some cases, improvements may occur for the youth but not the elders involved in the program;

in other cases the elders may profit more than the children or adolescents. However, initial problems are often solved through program modifications (Haber & Short-DeGraff, 1990; Kuehne, 1992; Newman & Riess, 1992; Proller, 1989; Saltz, 1989). Overall, intergenerational programs do seem to be successful. As Haber and Short-DeGraff (1990: 46–47) note, "Despite the general lack of experimental research regarding intergenerational programming, the positive observations and attitudes reported by staff and participants in the programs suggest that the programs are worthwhile and beneficial to the elderly as well as the young."

The Convergence of Grandparent and Intergenerational Networks

In 1991, Generations United, a national coalition on intergenerational issues and programs, incorporated a grandparenting track into its national conference. This formative step led to a closer alliance between grandparent and intergenerational networks and helped move them from mostly grassroots-level local efforts to national movements. The affiliation of the intergenerational and grandparent constituencies gained momentum throughout the 1990's and led to joint efforts in the drafting and eventual passage of a grandparenting resolution at the 1995 White House Conference on Aging as well as to cooperation among advocates of both networks. For example, in the background paper for its sixth national conference, Generations United highlighted the support needs of grandparents raising grandchildren. The paper called for consideration of grandparent-headed households in national and state policies and suggested that intergenerational programs could be used as vehicles to deliver services in a cost-effective manner (Generations United, 1995, 1996).

NEEDED: EVALUATION, EXPANSION, AND ALTERNATIVES

The programs described in the preceding sections offer grandparents and seniors a variety of opportunities to improve their grandparenting skills and to engage in intergenerational activities. That many grandparents and seniors participate in these programs demonstrates their willingness to expand time and effort to enhance their skills, to be the "family watchdogs," and to help their grandchildren or other youths. Nevertheless, many needs of grandparents remain unmet, selected programs may prove beneficial for some grandparents but not for others, and some grandparents or grandchildren may require other solutions to their problems than those offered and propagated by existing programs and policies. What then needs to be done to improve programmatic efforts that benefit grandparents and grandchildren?

First, there is a need for systematic and independent evaluations of existing programs. As noted above, even such widespread programs as Foster Grandparents or support groups for grandparents raising grandchildren continue to lack systematic periodic evaluations. Given the heterogeneity of today's grandparent population it would be especially important to assess whether specific subgroups of grandparents have limited access to programs, encounter difficulties with specific program goals or their underlying values, or drop out of programs they feel do not serve their needs. Perhaps more importantly, the success of programs for grandparents is not only contingent on whether they meet the grandparents' own needs but also on whether they benefit the grandparents' adult children and especially the grandchildren. One urgent research need is, therefore, to evaluate existing programs among diverse population subgroups and from the perspectives of the grandparents, the parents, and the grandchildren. If young grandchildren are involved, this may require elaborate observations in experimental or quasi-experimental settings.

There also is a need to expand programmatic efforts in several areas. For example, current programs target grandparents who are surrogate parents and those who are involved in formal child-care settings. However, few programs exist for the much larger number of grandparents who coparent their grandchildren or are the major child-care providers for employed adult children. Research showing tensions in coparenting situations (Thomas, 1990a) and demonstrating that a noteworthy minority of parents would prefer other child-care arrangements because of quality concerns (Brayfield, Deich, & Hofferth, 1993) suggest that more programs may be needed to enhance grandparents' child-care skills and to ease tensions between grandparents and the grandchildren's parents.

Many (though certainly not all) intergenerational programs bring together seniors and children or youths where one or both groups have special needs or problems. For example, eligibility in the Foster Grandparent Program is limited to the low-income elderly. Furthermore, programs for grandchildren may be needed under some circumstances. For instance, both research and programs have focused on the needs of caregivers (including caregivers with dependent children), but we know very little about the impact of caregiving on caregivers' children (Creasey & Jarvis, 1989; Pruchno, Peters, & Burant, 1995) and few programs address these children's needs. Similarly, not only grandparents raising grandchildren but youth raised by grandparents may profit from support groups and other opportunities to interact with peers in comparable situations. Alternatively, programs that include both youths and their parents or grandparents may benefit both. Such an approach would be consistent with a family systems perspective (see Chapter 16) and is likely to omit scapegoating of children and adolescents that may occur if individual counseling is used (i.e., the child becomes the defined "problem").

Lastly, careful consideration must be given to the question whether selected programs divert attention from better or at least equally beneficial alternatives. For example, enrollment in a support group may alleviate some stresses and provide an outlet for communication with peers, but under some circumstances it may also reinforce feelings of obligation and beliefs that other solutions are either not available, inappropriate, or unethical (e.g., only "bad" grandparents allow adoption of their grandchildren by strangers or placement of grandchildren in foster care, and only "bad" children put their ailing parents in nursing homes). Stressful situations that involve several generations require weighing of benefits and costs for *all* family members. Of course, lack of resources and of available alternatives often constrain families' options. From this perspective it seems particularly important to enhance and broaden policies and programs that enable families to chose among alternatives rather than to streamline them into solutions that are deemed appropriate by policy makers or program developers but may cause harm to some families or individual family members.

RESOURCES

Information on grandparent and intergenerational programs and research is available from the following organizations:

American Association of Retired Persons
Grandparent Information Center
601 E Street, NW
Washington, DC 20049
(202) 434–2296

American Society on Aging
833 Market Street, Suite 511
San Francisco, CA 94103
(415) 974–9600

Association for Gerontology in Higher Education
1001 Connecticut Ave., NW, Suite 410
Washington, DC 20036
(202) 429–9277

Brookdale Foundation
Center on Aging
140 Warren Hall
University of California
Berkeley, CA 94720
(510) 643–6427

Generations Together
University Center for Social and Urban Research
University of Pittsburgh
12 University Place, Suite 300
Pittsburgh, PA 15260
(412) 648–7150

Generations United
c/o CWLA, 440 First Street, NW, Suite 310
Washington, DC 20001
(202) 638–2952

Gerontological Society of America
1275 K Street NW, Suite 350
Washington, DC 20005
(202) 842–1275

National Council on Aging
409 Third Street, SW, Suite 200
Washington, DC 20024
(202) 479–1200

Temple University Center for Intergenerational Learning
1601 North Broad Street, Rm. 206
Philadelphia, PA 19122
(215) 204–6836

NOTE

The description of programs and educational materials for grandparents in this chapter does not imply an endorsement of them by the authors nor were our descriptions endorsed by the authors or agencies that develop, publicize, distribute, or implement these programs or materials.

Chapter 18

Research on Grandparenting: Needed Refinements in Concepts, Theories, and Methods

Maximiliane E. Szinovacz

Grandparent research expanded rapidly during the past two decades. However, many studies were problem oriented and descriptive rather than grounded in theory. Advancement in the field requires conceptual/theoretical frameworks that can serve as guidelines for research as well as methodologies that are informed by such conceptual/theoretical frameworks. Grandparent research can build upon general theories in pertinent fields such as psychology or sociology, as well as on theoretical and methodological contributions from specific research areas such as human development, family studies, or intergenerational relationships. However, such applications must be modified or expanded to adequately address the very special characteristics and circumstances of grandparenthood and of grandparent-grandchild relationships.

Because current theorizing on grandparenthood is rudimentary at best, this chapter is meant to direct future efforts rather than to provide final or even preliminary solutions. I begin with a discussion of conceptual issues. A brief overview of current theories and theoretical frameworks is presented next, followed by suggestions for further theory development. The chapter concludes with a discussion of methodological issues and recommendations for future research.

CONCEPTUAL ISSUES

Studying grandparenthood poses several conceptual challenges. Perhaps the most important among these issues are the conceptualization of the multiple relationships within extended families; the distinction among family, dyadic, and individual characteristics; and the multidimensionality of the grandparent role and of grandparent-grandchild and extended-family relationships.

Multiple Relationships among Extended Family Members

Analyses based on the National Survey of Families and Households (NSFH) conducted during 1992–94 indicate that, on average, grandparents have 5 to 6 grandchildren, and some have considerably more—up to 30 (Szinovacz, 1998). Similarly, most grandchildren today have more than one surviving grandparent at least into early adolescence and often well into adulthood (see Chapters 2 and 12; Szinovacz, 1998). However, grandparent research typically focuses either on relationships between *specific* grandparents and *specific* grandchildren or on grandparents' *overall* relationship to grandchildren. Although both approaches have some merit, they clearly fall short of capturing the complexity of multiple interrelationships among grandparents, grandchildren, and other members of the extended family (Giarrusso, Silverstein, & Bengtson, 1996). The presence of stepgrandparents or stepgrandchildren and fictional grandparent-grandchild relationships (see Chapters 3 and 5) further complicates this picture. In addition, both approaches have theoretical as well as methodological flaws: they imply that grandparents maintain similar relationships with all grandchildren, and that either the grandparent-grandchild dyad or the grandparent-parent-grandchild triad constitute isolated units.

Structural Complexity

Neglecting the multiple linkages among grandparents, grandchildren, and the middle generation (the grandchildren's parents) constitutes a serious limitation of current research and theorizing. The importance of such linkages becomes evident when one considers the complexity and diversity of extended-family systems. Figure 18.1 illustrates linkages among extended and nuclear family units. There are four couples—the parent generation (identified by lowercase a, b, c, d), each spouse's parents (the grandparents, identified by lineage), and each couple's children (the grandchildren, identified by gender). The grandchildren are further identified by the same lowercase letters as their parents. Because grandparents who have several children with children are members of several generational units, they are identified by their children's lowercase letter. For example, PGFa/MGFb is the father of a son (Fa) and the grandfather of his child (GSa) as well as the father of a daughter (Mb) and the grandfather of her children (GSb, GDb). As long as all grandparents are alive, each grandchild has four biological grandparents—though under very different conditions. In contrast, the number of grandchildren for each grandparent ranges from one (MGFa, MGMa) to seven (PGFb,c,d and PGMb,c,d). In addition, the lineage structure and sex composition of the grandchildren varies for each grandparent couple. Some grandparents are exclusively paternal grandparents (PGFb,c,d and PGMb,c,d), others are exclusively maternal grandparents (MGFa, MGMa, MGFc, MGMc, MGFd, MGMd), and others are both (PGFa, MGFb, PGMa, MGMb). Similarly, some grandparents have grandchildren of both sexes (PGFa, MGFa, PGMa, MGMb), some have only grandsons (MGFa, MGMa), and some

Figure 18.1
Configuration of Three-Generation Family Systems

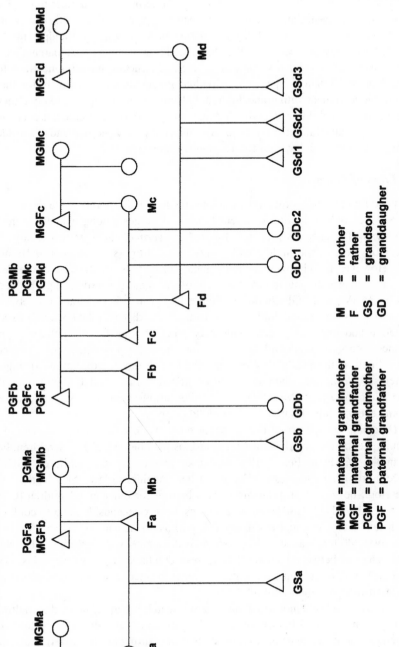

MGM = maternal grandmother
MGF = maternal grandfather
PGM = paternal grandmother
PGF = paternal grandfather

M = mother
F = father
GS = grandson
GD = granddaugher

Lowercase letters a, b, c, and d identify extended nuclear family units. Grandparents who have several children with children are members of several extended nuclear family units.

have only granddaughters (MGFc, MGMc). Furthermore, the number of possible ties and of nuclear family units (grandparent—parent—grandchild) in which each grandparent is involved differs, contingent on how many grandparents are alive, how many grandchildren they have, and how many of grandparents' children have children. Such variations in size and structure have implications for grandparents' relationships with individual grandchildren as well as for their overall involvement with grandchildren. Selective relationships are likely if there are many grandchildren (Cherlin & Furstenberg, 1986a), and grandparents with numerous grandchildren may be overburdened by multiple demands (consider Christmas and birthday gifts for 15 grandchildren!).

Types of Linkages

In addition to such structural variations, the figure also points to the theoretical importance of considering different types of linkages among extended family members. To date, research has focused on *vertical* linkages, especially the mediating role of the middle or "bridge" generation (see Chapters 4, 10, and 12). However, both horizontal and diagonal linkages also deserve attention. *Horizontal* linkages among family members of the *same* generation (e.g., between MGFa/MGMa and PGFa/PGMa in Figure 18.1) can affect interactions between grandparents and grandchildren. For example, a distant relationship between paternal and maternal grandparents may preclude joint family gatherings and render access to grandchildren more competitive. Such competition is particularly likely if the availability of grandchildren differs for the involved grandparents, for example, when one grandparent couple has grandchildren from only one adult child (e.g., MGMc/MGFc) while the other couple has grandchildren from several adult children (e.g., PGFc/PGMc).

Diagonal linkages (i.e., linkages that cross nuclear family boundaries) also can impact on the grandparents' relationships with individual grandchildren. For example, PGMc in Figure 18.1 may take care of the grandchildren (GDc1, GDc2) from her oldest son (Fc) while her daughter-in-law (Mc) works and, therefore, be somewhat reluctant to also babysit for other grandchildren (GSb, GDb, GSd1, GDd2, GSd3) during evenings or on weekends, leading to conflicts with her youngest daughter-in-law (Md) whose own parents (MGFd/MGMd) live over 300 miles away. Also, sibling rivalries among the grandparents' adult children (e.g., between Fa and Mb) may restrict interactions among cousins (GSa and GSb, GDb) and thus, force grandparents to interact separately with grandchildren from different adult children.

These examples demonstrate that future research has to acknowledge multiple linkages in extended-family systems. The structural and dynamic features of extended-family systems need to be studied in their own right, and theoretically relevant characteristics of extended-family systems should be included as independent or control variables in explanatory models.

Conceptual Levels

Once grandparent research moves beyond its current emphasis on individual grandparents and grandparent-grandchild dyads, distinctions among diverse levels of conceptualization and analysis become essential. Grandparent research can be conceptualized at one of four levels: the individual, the dyad, the family unit, and the macro or societal level (Copeland & White, 1991; Kahana & Kahana, 1971).

At the *individual level,* research is concerned with the characteristics, attitudes, and behaviors of individuals (e.g., a grandparent or a grandchild). For example, studies dealing with the importance a person attaches to becoming a grandparent (Cunningham-Burley, 1984a, 1985), how grandparents interpret their role (Hurme, 1991; Kivett, 1996; Miller & Cavanaugh, 1990), or how much effort a grandparent invests in activities with grandchildren (Bass & Caro, 1996) would fall into this category.

Dyadic concepts refer to the relationship between two individuals as well as similarities and differences between them. Research addressing frequency of interactions between a grandparent and a grandchild (Hodgson, 1992; Lawton, Silverstein, & Bengtson, 1994b), their consensus on values (Lawton, Silverstein, & Bengtson, 1994), their feelings for each other (King & Elder, 1995a; Lawton, Silverstein, & Bengtson, 1994b), or grandparents' influence on grandchildren (Cherlin & Furstenberg, 1986a; Chapter 11) operates at this level. While most studies focus on relationships between grandparent and grandchild, other dyads have theoretical relevance in grandparent research. The division of labor between a grandparent couple or conflicts between two grandchildren or two adult children with children may also deserve investigation.

The *family level* encompasses studies that deal with relationships among three or more family members. Most prominent within grandparent research are generational studies (Mangen, Bengtson, & Landry, 1988) as well as investigations of the mediating role parents have in grandparent-grandchild relationships (Robertson, 1976; Chapters 10 and 12). Studies concerning the impact of coresidence with a grandparent on grandchildren's development (Pearson et al., 1994; Chapter 11) or the effects of an adult child's divorce on grandparent-grandchild interactions (Cooney & Smith, 1996; Chapter 13) can be conceptualized at this level, but other family subgroups may be theoretically relevant as well (e.g., extended families residing in one household).

At the *societal* or *macro level,* researchers are primarily concerned with societal norms about and images of grandparenthood, grandparents' societal functions, and/or structural features pertaining to grandparenthood (e.g., laws and policies affecting grandparents, grandparents' role in the supply of child care, or kinship structures derived from residence or lineage rules) and with cultural/ subcultural as well as historical variations in these characteristics. For example, lineage and residence rules may determine grandparents' access to grandchildren (see Chapter 3), societal norms may impact on the prevalence and perceived appropriateness of extended family coresidence (see Chapters 3, 7, and 14), and trends in mortality and fertility may impact on the supply of grandparents and grandchildren (see Chapter 2).

Levels of Variable Construction and Assessment

The theoretical unit of interest or conceptual level must be differentiated from the level of variable construction as well as from the unit or level of assessment (Copeland & White, 1991; Huston & Robins, 1982; Larsen & Olson, 1990; Ransom et al., 1990; Thompson & Walker, 1982). The *unit of assessment* refers to *who* is studied, that is, whether the study relies on individuals, dyads, or a group of three of more family members, whereas the *level of variable construction* "refers to the level at which measures are used in coding or statistical analyses" (Copeland & White, 1991: 24). Combinations of different conceptual, variable construction, and assessment levels in one study are quite common and theoretically, as well as methodologically, acceptable. However, it is essential that the measures and assessment units are appropriate and that their limitations are taken into account when interpreting the data. For example, parental mediation (a family-level concept) of grandparent-grandchild relationships is often inferred from the effect grandparent-parent relationship characteristics such as closeness (a dyadic concept) have on the grandparent-grandchild relationship. This approach may overestimate the extent of parental mediation. Statistical associations between parent-grandparent and grandchild-grandparent closeness can reflect earlier attachments among family members that develop into parallel (but no longer *mediated*) close relationships between parents-grandparents and between grandparents-grandchildren (King & Elder, 1995a; Rossi & Rossi, 1990). In this case, the unit of variable construction may indeed be inappropriate given the conceptual focus of the research.

Dimensions of the Grandparent Role and Grandparent Relationships

A third important conceptual issue in grandparent research is the identification and categorization of relevant dimensions of grandparenthood or grandparent/ grandchild and extended-family relationships. Past research has dealt with a wide variety of dimensions, but concepts vary across studies, are often defined in different ways, and refer to divergent conceptual levels. For example, there are several classifications of the "meaning" of grandparenthood (Kivnick, 1983; Wood & Robertson, 1976). Neugarten and Weinstein (1964) describe meanings of grandparenthood but refer to them as "significance," whereas Kivett (1996) infers "importance" of grandparenthood from the frequency of grandparents' activities and contacts with grandchildren. Others proposed multidimensional schemes. For instance, Kahana and Kahana (1971) view grandparenthood as a social role, an emotional state, a transaction, a group process, and a symbol, and Hurme (1991) differentiates among different "aspects" of grandparenthood (attitudinal, behavioral, emotional, and symbolic). Some researchers derive grandparenting "styles" from multiple dimensions (Cherlin & Furstenberg, 1985; 1986a; Silverstein, Lawton, & Bengtson, 1994b; Chapter 10), while others define grandparenting styles exclusively in terms of grandparents' activities with grandchildren (Neugarten & Weinstein, 1964). Most dimensions of grandparenthood are conceptualized at the individual level, whereas the intergenerational solidarity model operates essentially at the dyadic level (normative and structural solidarity are an exception) and is multidimensional (Roberts, Richard, & Bengtson, 1991; see Chapter 10). Existing classifications tend to ignore structural relationship features such as boundaries and hierarchies as well as extended-family relationship structures and characteristics such as density, multiplexity, or affect balance. Furthermore, indicators or scales used to measure various dimensions differ across studies and often have not been tested for validity or reliability (Miller & Cavanaugh, 1990).

In view of this conceptual confusion, a systematic categorization of grandparenthood dimensions is needed. Classification of grandparenthood dimensions is essential for several reasons: It can pinpoint both emphases and gaps in the literature on grandparenthood, it can constitute a basis for the development of conceptual and theoretical frameworks that guide measurement construction and data analyses, and it can facilitate integration of research findings which is essential for theory development (see also Chapter 10).

The conceptual scheme discussed in this section is primarily grounded in role theory and its applications (Burr et al., 1979; LaRossa & Reitzes, 1993; Peplau, 1983; J. Turner, 1982) but also includes concepts from other theories such as exchange (Ekeh, 1974; Sabatelli & Shehan, 1993; J. Turner, 1982) or family systems theory (Whitchurch & Constantine, 1993). It further draws on earlier conceptualizations of family and intergenerational relations and social networks in general (Antonucci, 1990; Bengtson & Roberts, 1991; House, Umberson, & Landis, 1988; Peplau, 1983; Surra, 1988) and of grandparenthood in particular (Hurme, 1991; Kahana & Kahana, 1971; Neugarten & Weinstein, 1964). In contrast to earlier categorizations, dimensions at the individual, dyadic, family, and societal level are presented separately.

The Grandparent Role

Dimensions of the grandparent role are conceptualized at the individual level. Six major dimensions are distinguished: role assignment, role-defining characteristics, role expectations, role identity, role enactment, and role satisfaction (see Table 18.1). Definitions for each dimension and major subdimension are given in the table.

Table 18.1

Dimensions of Grandparent Role (Individual Level)

DIMENSIONS	DEFINITIONS
Role assignment	Definitional processes and criteria used by self and others in accepting/allocating the status/role of grandparent
Role-defining characteristics	Sex, lineage, and age of grandparent
Role expectations	Perceived rights (including authority), duties, and rules pertaining to the status of grandparent
Role identity	Meaning of the grandparent role to the status incumbent
essence	Substance or meaning content of the grandparent role
salience	Importance attached to the grandparent role
emotional investment	Extent (weak - strong) and quality (positive - negative) of feelings about the grandparent role
Role enactment	Execution or implementation of the grandparent role by the status incumbent
behavioral	Activities performed by status incumbents in their role as grandparent (socializing, support, education and information, symbolic)
affective	Emotional experiences of the grandparent associated with the enactment of the grandparent role
cognitive	Motivations for and interpretations of role enactment by the grandparent or others
quality	Evaluation of the grandparent's role performance by self or others
Role satisfaction	Evaluation of the grandparent role by the status incumbent

Role Assignment

Grandparenthood constitutes a status, that is, a social position defined by a collection of rights and duties (Turner, 1982: 319). Persons who occupy this status (the status incumbents) "play" the role of grandparent and, in doing so, may redefine and renegotiate rights, duties, and rules, a process commonly described as role making (LaRossa & Reitzes, 1993; Turner, 1982). In the case of grandparenthood role making may start at the very elementary level of whether or not a person defines him- or herself as a grandparent. Adoption, new fertility techniques, remarriage, and fictional kinship render the definition and assignment of grandparenthood ambiguous. Schmid (1995) reports, for example, that some grandparents consider adoptive children of their adult children "like their own biological grandchildren," whereas others perceive them as "not really" a grandchild. Differential treatment of biological and stepgrandchildren (Coleman, Ganong, & Cable, 1997) also implies some ambiguity about the role of stepgrandparent.

Role-Defining Characteristics

Grandparents' age, sex, and lineage are considered role-defining characteristics. These characteristics are ascribed statuses that modify the grandparent role.

Because families are organized by age, sex, and lineage (Rossi & Rossi, 1990), the grandparent role may be further differentiated into the roles of young maternal grandmother, old paternal grandfather, and so forth. Studies indicating sex, age, and lineage differences in grandparenting support this distinction (Burton & Bengtson, 1985; Rossi & Rossi, 1990; Chapters 3, 8, 10, and 12).

Role Expectations

Role expectations refer to the rights, duties, and rules associated with a role as perceived by self (e.g., the grandparent) and others, especially those in counterpositions (i.e., the grandchild). As noted by several contributors to this volume, expectations about the grandparent (or grandchild) role tend to be ambiguous and "emergent," that is, derived from negotiations among family members and changing situational circumstances rather than determined by social norms (Finch & Mason, 1993; Wood, 1982; see also Chapters 6 and 10). The content of role expectations can be proscriptive or prescriptive. One of the proscriptive rules that apparently receives widespread support is that grandparents should *not* interfere in their adult children's parenting, whereas grandparents *are* expected to be available in family crises (Cherlin & Furstenberg, 1986a, 1986b; Cunningham-Burley, 1985; Hagestad, 1985; Roberto, 1990; Sprey, 1991; Troll, 1983, 1986; Wilson, 1987; see also Chapters 10, 13, 14, and 16).

Role Identity

Role identity reflects the meaning a role has for the status incumbent (LaRossa & Reitzes, 1993: 145). Three subdimensions are distinguished: essence, salience, and emotional investment. Explorations of the *essence* of grandparenthood have predominated in early studies but continue to this date (see Chapter 1). Grandparents differ widely in the substantive meaning they attach to the role of grandparent, ranging from buddy and confidant to valued elder and biological renewal (Creasey & Koblewski, 1991; Franks et al., 1993; Hurme, 1991; Kennedy, 1990; Kivnick, 1982, 1985; Roberto & Stroes, 1992; Thomas, 1989). The essence of the grandparent role may differ among subcultural groups (see Chapters 5, 6, and 7) and can change over time. For example, biological renewal might be of primary importance when the first grandchild is born but lose its significance for additional grandchildren.

Salience indicates the relative importance a role has in a person's role repertory. While some argue that being a grandparent constitutes the "master" or most salient role for many older people (Kahana & Kahana, 1970, 1971), others claim that today's grandparents are most interested in the pursuit of hedonistic goals and thus are rather detached from their grandchildren (Gutmann, 1985; Kornhaber, 1996). Empirical evidence suggests that grandparenthood is important to most grandparents (Cherlin & Furstenberg, 1986a). However, the relative importance of the grandparent role compared to other roles remains to be tested.

Whereas salience is a cognitive concept, *emotional investment* refers to the feelings grandparents have about being a grandparent. Note that emotional investment in the role and feelings of closeness to grandchildren, though probably interrelated, are nevertheless distinct concepts. For example, a grandmother may have strong negative feelings about being a grandparent "too early" (Hagestad & Burton, 1986) but still feel close to the "too-early" grandchild.

Role Enactment

Role enactment pertains to the dynamic aspects of a role, how actors "play" a role. *Behavioral components* of role enactment encompass the *quantity* and *types of activities* involved in executing the grandparent role. Grandparents' role enactment involves *all* activities pertaining to the role (e.g., how often a grandfather has contacts with *any* grandchild or whether a grandmother baby-sits for *any* grandchild) and should thus be distinguished from interactions with specific grandchildren. Also, not all grandparenting activities involve interactions with the grandchildren. For example, a grandmother who establishes a trust fund for her grandchild's college education engages in grandparenting but does not interact with the grandchild. Thus, the *quantity* of grandparenting activities should be assessed in terms of grandparents' total investment (time, money) or involvement (frequency of contacts with any grandchild) rather than on the basis of interactions with specific grandchildren.

Earlier research suggests that grandparents engage in four major *types of activities*: (1) socializing (visits, contacts by phone or letter, play), (2) support (emotional, instrumental, or economic), (3) information and education, and (4) symbolic activities. *Socializing* essentially serves to maintain contact, to keep in touch, and may involve either face-to-face contacts or other means of communication. Depictions of grandparents as "funseekers," "buddies," or "companionates" refer primarily to socializing activities such as playing games with grandchildren or doing things and having fun together (Cherlin & Furstenberg, 1986a; Franks et al., 1993; Kennedy, 1990; Neugarten & Weinstein, 1964;).

Supports are activities whose purpose is to help the grandchild or, as in the case of baby-sitting, the grandchild's parents. *Emotional supports* may be particularly important during family crises, for example when the grandchild's parents are divorcing (Kennedy & Kennedy, 1993), but are certainly not restricted to such situations. Grandparents' functions as confidants and attachment figures (Hurme, 1991; Kennedy, 1992a, 1992b; Tinsley & Parke, 1984) constitute examples of emotional supports. *Instrumental supports* consist of services and tasks grandparents provide to grandchildren or their parents such as physical care of the grandchild, transportation, or help with school work. *Economic supports* may either involve direct financial transactions (e.g., gifts of money, no-interest loans, trust funds, inheritance) or consist of activities that have economic value (for instance, care for grandchildren during mothers' work hours, purchases of needed items for the grandchild). Research suggests that most economic transfers are to or from adjacent generations, and that the flow of supports favors the younger generation at least until grandparents reach "old-old" age (Bass & Caro, 1996; Kronebusch & Schlesinger, 1994).

Numerous studies emphasize the importance of grandparents as transmitters of values, socialization agents, or family historians (Barusch & Steen, 1996; Chapter 3). Such *educational* and *informational* activities may be particularly important among ethnic groups when parents lack knowledge of cultural traditions (see Chapters 6 and 7) or when "immature" parents are unable to serve as adequate role models (see Chapter 14).

Symbolic activities are influenced by an individual's role as grandparent but not targeted at the grandchildren. Telling friends about one's grandchildren (Cunningham-Burley, 1984a) or including grandchildren in one's prayer signify symbolic enactment of the grandparent role.

The strength and type of emotions grandparents experience when playing the grandparent role constitute the *affective* component of role enactment. For example, a grandparent may feel happy when playing with a grandchild or sad that his or her grandchildren will not visit over a holiday. This dimension is to be dinstinguished from emotional closeness to grandchildren, a concept at the dyadic level.

Cognitive processes involve the motivations guiding grandparents' behaviors and the interpretations of their actions by the grandparents themselves and by other family members. Two theoretical traditions are particularly relevant. Reactance theory suggests "that individuals experience negative feelings when freedom of choice and autonomy are eliminated" (Uphold & Morgan, 1988: 7). For example, perceptions that supports are obligatory may result in negative feelings about the relationship and the demanding family member (Uphold & Morgan, 1988). Attribution theory holds that relationship satisfaction derives not only from the interactions and supports between family members but also from the intent attributed to family members' actions (Uphold & Morgan, 1988). Thus, the same "objective" features of role enactment (e.g., baby-sitting) may have different outcomes, contingent on their interpretation (does the grandmother believe she is asked to baby-sit because this is the least expensive option for her adult daughter or because the daughter trusts that she will provide the best care).

Quality of role enactment refers to the status incumbents' role performance, that is, how well a grandparent plays his or her role. Generally, role performance will be judged according to some standards about what a "good" grandparent is and does. Normative ambiguity (see Chapter 10) may render such evaluations difficult and highly idiosyncratic. This also means that there might be considerable disparity in the evaluation of a grandparent's performance by different family members.

Role Satisfaction

The evaluation of outcomes associated with *being* a grandparent is called role satisfaction. It is important to differentiate between role satisfaction that reflects an overall assessment of the grandparent role from satisfaction with specific grandparent-grandchild relationships. For example, a grandfather may be quite dissatisfied with the relationship he has with his youngest granddaughter but still satisfied with his role as grandfather, derived from his relationships with other grandchildren and/or from occupying the status of grandfather. Exchange theorists argue that satisfaction with a role evolves from actors' evaluation of the outcomes (the reward/cost ratio) obtained in the role against the so-called comparison level, that is, a standard of what can be reasonably expected from a role. If the outcomes are perceived to exceed the comparison level, the role will be considered satisfactory, whereas outcomes below the comparison level will be judged as unsatisfactory (Sabatelli & Shehan, 1993). This implies, of course, that grandparents with very similar experiences may differ considerably in their role satisfaction.

Grandparent-Grandchild and Extended-Family Relationships

Whereas dimensions of the grandparent role reflect processes associated with being a grandparent and are conceptualized at the individual level, grandparent-grandchild and extended-family relationships concern interactions among family members at the dyadic or family level. Major dimensions at these conceptual levels are shown in Table 18.2. The conceptual scheme presented in the table builds on Bengtson's intergenerational solidarity model, but it has been adapted to fit special features of grandparent-grandchild and extended-family relationships. Consequently, there are several deviations from the intergenerational solidarity model (see Chapter 10), and some definitions differ from those given by Bengtson and his colleagues (Bengtson & Roberts, 1991; Roberts, Richards, & Bengtson, 1991). Specifically, normative solidarity is not covered because it is essentially an individual-level concept and synonymous with role expectations. Also not included is structural solidarity. This concept pertains primarily to factors that impinge upon intergenerational relations but not to relationship features (see Chapter 10). Several other concepts were added to the model, namely, structural relationship characteristics as well as symbolic and gratificational solidarity. Because the intergenerational solidarity model was described in detail in Chapter 10, the following discussion highlights new and altered concepts of the model, including concepts at the family level.

Structural Features

Three structural characteristics are particularly important in grandparent research: composition, hierarchy, and boundaries.[1] As noted in the section on multiple relationships, the *composition* of grandparent-grandchild dyads or extended family groups impinges on relationships and their consequences. For example, cross-sex grandparent-grandchild dyads may engage in different activities than same-sex dyads (see Chapter 8), or extended families with four surviving grandparents entail different dynamics than those in which only one or two grandparents are still alive.

Family systems theorists stress the importance of hierarchy and boundaries

Table 18.2

Dimensions of Grandparent-Grandchild and Extended-Family Relationships and Solidarity

	GRANDPARENT-GRANDCHILD RELATIONSHIP (DYADIC LEVEL)	EXTENDED FAMILY OF FAMILY SUBGROUPS (FAMILY LEVEL)
Structural features		
composition	Age, sex, and lineage composition of the grandparent-grandchild dyad	Age, sex, lineage, and generational composition of family group
hierarchy	Extent to which grandparent and grandchild have power and exert influence and control over each other	Hierarchy - power, control, and influence structure within extended family groups Mediation - extent to which the grandparent-grandchild relationship is influenced or controlled by other family members
boundaries	permeability of the grandparent-grandchild system	permeability of the extended family system or of family subsystems within the extended family
Consensual solidarity	Extent of agreement or similarity between grandparent and grandchild regarding role expectations, role interpretations, role performance, and other attitudes, beliefs, and values	Extent of family or group consensus - derived from agreements and similarities within dyads - proportion of family members agreeing on a specific issue - distribution of consenting and conflicting family members (e.g., along generational lines)
Affectual solidarity	Extent and quality of feelings between grandparent and grandchild Extent of mutuality of feelings for each other	Emotional enmeshment - extent to which extended family members are emotionally involved with each other Affect balance - positive and negative affect patterns within family groups
Associational solidarity	Frequency and types of interactions between grandparent and grandchild	Frequency and types of interactions that involve the entire extended family or family subgroups Interaction patterns among extended family members (density, clustering, centrality, overlap, selectivity)
Functional solidarity	Frequency and types of supports, services, and other contributions exchanged between grandparent and grandchild Reciprocity of exchanges between grandparent and grandchild	Frequency and types of supports, services, and contributions exchanged among extended family members Patterns of exchanges among extended family members (reciprocity, complementarity, specialization, multiplexity)
Symbolic solidarity	Manifest and latent influences of having a grandchild on the grandparent's behaviors, feelings, and attitudes	Manifest and latent influences of the presence of specific extended family members (e.g., of grandparents) on other extended family members' behaviors, feelings, and attitudes
Gratificational solidarity	Satisfaction with the grandparent-grandchild relationship Equity of the grandparent-grandchild relationship	Satisfaction with extended family relationships Distribution of rewards and costs derived from extended family relationships among family members

(Whitchurch & Constantine, 1993; see also Chapter 15). *Hierarchy* is determined by family members' relative power and manifests itself in influence and control processes and structures (see Huston, 1983; Szinovacz, 1987, for definitions of these concepts). Current societal norms discourage control by grandparents (norm of noninterference). Thus, control attempts by grandparents are often seen in a negative light and can cause intergenerational tensions (Thomas, 1990a). In other cultural or subcultural contexts, however, control by grandparents may be accepted and considered legitimate (Gratton & Haber, 1996; Chapters 3, 5, and 7). Parental mediation of grandparent-grandchild relationships (Robertson, 1975; Chapters 4, 10, and 12) constitutes a special case of control within the extended-family unit. It may thus be more appropriate to assess parental mediation through parental control and influence behaviors rather than on the basis of associations between grandparent-parent and grandparent-grandchild interactions and closeness.[2]

Boundaries delineate the extent to which family systems or subsystems are open to outside influences by other family members, nonrelated persons, or institutions (for a more detailed discussion of boundaries, see Chapter 15). Of particular interest in grandparent research is the permeability of the grandparent-grandchild dyad as well as of generational units that include grandparents from one lineage. For example, surrogate grandparents may shield the grandchildren from the grandchildren's parents (see Chapter 14), and matrifocal generational units that are closed to paternal kin may form after divorce (see Chapter 13).

Consensual Solidarity

Consensual solidarity reflects agreement (or conflict) and similarities in family members' attitudes, values, and beliefs. Particularly important for relationships between grandparents and grandchildren will be consensus on diverse aspects of the grandparent or grandchild roles. For example, coresidence of teenage parents with their parents often gives rise to conflicts because of the grandparents' and teenage parents' divergent role expectations (Thomas, 1990a). On the other hand, agreement on political or religious values may be of less importance, especially when family members are not very political or religious. In such cases, establishment of "demilitarized zones" (Hagestad, 1985) is likely. At the extended-family level, assessments of consensual solidarity may either capture the overall prevalence of consensus within the family or the configuration of extended-family subgroups who agree or disagree on a specific issue. For example, grandparents and grandchildren may side together against the parents.

Affectual Solidarity

Affectual solidarity concerns both the *extent* of affection between grandparents and grandchildren as well as the *quality* (positive versus negative affect) of their feelings for each other. While most studies assess emotional closeness as perceived either by the grandparent or grandchild (King & Elder, 1995a; Lawton, Silverstein, & Bengtson, 1994b), the *mutuality* of their feelings may be particularly important for the development of the relationship over time.

Two affect dimensions have special significance at the family level: emotional enmeshment and affective balance. *Emotional enmeshment* signifies the extent of affective involvement within the extended family or family subgroups, either based on perceptions of "family closeness" or derived from the prevalence of close and distant dyadic relationships within the extended-family system. *Affect balance* (Heider, 1958) reflects symmetry or asymmetry of positive and negative affect relationships within family systems. Heider stresses that systems characterized by asymmetrical affect balance (e.g., one negative and two positive affect relations within a triad) are unstable. Thus, conflicts between a parent and a grandparent or rivalries among grandparents may be resolved through the formation of relationship clusters or the exclusion of a family member from family interactions to reestablish affective balance. However, the somewhat obligatory character of kin relationships may lead to enduring unbalanced relationships and ongoing tensions among extended kin.

Associational Solidarity

Associational solidarity refers to the *quantity* and *type* of interactions between grandparents and grandchildren or among extended-family members. Research has focused on the frequency of contacts between grandparents and grandchildren. Perhaps equally important for understanding grandparent-grandchild relationships would be to assess who initiates interactions and whether grandparents and grandchildren engage in similar or distinct activities during interactions. For example, Nussbaum & Bettini (1994) show that grandparents engaged in storytelling while grandchildren talked about their values and life goals.

Assessment of associational solidarity at the family level may either refer to the *frequency* and *type of activities* that involve grandparents, grandchildren, and other family members such as family gatherings, joint trips, or the Sunday dinner with members of the nuclear family and one set of grandparents, or to *interaction patterns* among extended kin. Concepts derived from analyses of social or family networks such as density, clustering, centrality, overlap, or selectivity (see Antonucci, 1990; Surra, 1988 for definitions of these terms) can be used to describe interaction patterns among extended-family members. Particularly important for grandparent research would be how central a grandparent is in the extended-family system, to what extent extended-family clusters are divided along lineage lines, and whether grandparents interact selectively with specific grandchildren or with grandchildren from specific adult children. For example, the maternal grandmother often assumes a central role in the extended-kin network (Chapter 8), whereas paternal grandparents play a more peripheral role. Matrifocal networks among African American grandparents and among grandparents of divorced daughters suggest clustering (see Chapters 5 and 13). Among grandparents with numerous grandchildren selectivity often characterizes relationships with grandchildren, that is, some grandchildren receive preferential treatment (Cherlin & Furstenberg, 1986a; Young & Willmott, 1957).

Functional Solidarity

Grandparents' contributions to individual grandchildren (dyadic level) or to nuclear and extended family systems (family level) and grandchildren's or other family members' contributions to the grandparents represent functional solidarity. Such contributions may involve various types of supports and services (see Chapter 10 and also the description of role enactment behaviors above).

Of interest in grandparent research is not only whether or not grandparents and grandchildren provide supports to each other but whether such exchanges are reciprocated (see Chapter 10). *Reciprocity* can characterize dyadic relationships as well as family systems. However, the typical quid-pro-quo type of reciprocity (what Ekeh, 1974, calls "restricted exchange") assessed in most research may be inadequate for family relationships. In families, reciprocation often occurs over relatively long time spans (for example, when children "repay" their parents through supporting them in old age), or it may involve several family members through generalized exchange chains (Ekeh, 1974; Szinovacz, 1997b). Generalized exchange implies indirect exchanges among three or more parties. For example, grandparents may expect their children to reciprocate for their upbringing not through supports to the grandparents but through supports to the children's children, the grandchildren, following the motto: "I expect you to do for your children what I did for you."

Exchange patterns among extended kin reflect how specific supports are distributed by and among family members. Exchanges may be *reciprocal* in content, involving exchanges of the same supports (e.g., mutual gift giving), they may *complement* each other (e.g., the employed maternal grandmother offers economic supports while the nonemployed paternal grandmother baby-sits), or be characterized by a division of activities and supports where family members *specialize* in specific support activities (e.g., it is always the paternal grandfather who takes the grandchildren to the zoo while the maternal grandfather is the storyteller). *Multiplexity* refers to the number of different supports exchanged within specific dyads or larger family groups (Antonucci, 1990). Relationships with remote grandparents may involve but a few types of supports (e.g., gift giving), whereas more involved grandparents may offer and receive numerous types of supports.

Symbolic Solidarity

In their preceding discussion of the intergenerational solidarity model (Chapter 10), Silverstein and his colleagues subsume symbolic solidarity under functional solidarity. Though clearly a "function," I prefer to treat symbolic solidarity as a separate dimension for two reasons. First, in contrast to functional solidarity, it does not involve overt actions on the part of the grandparent (or grandchild), that is, latent and manifest consequences of having a grandparent (or a grandchild) derive from the mere presence of the grandparent and/or his/her characteristics but do not involve specific contributions in the form of supports and services. Second, the symbolic functions of grandparents have special significance (Bengtson, 1985) and thus warrant separate treatment.

Symbolic solidarity refers to latent or manifest consequences of having (or having had) a grandparent on the grandchild's and other family members behaviors, attitudes, and feelings. The knowledge that "grandparents are (or were) there" (Bengtson, 1985) may in itself prompt specific behaviors in the grandchildren, for example, when a grandchild visits a grandparent's grave or when parents use grandparents' existence to enforce discipline ("just imagine if

Table 18.3
Dimensions of Grandparent Status (Societal Level)

DIMENSIONS	DEFINITIONS
Status	Institutionalized definition of the status of grandparent (e.g., in laws or policies)
Supply and distribution	Proportion of population or of population subgroups who are grandparents; demographic characteristics of grandparents
Norms	Institutionalized rights (including authority), duties, and rules pertaining to the status of grandparent within societies or societal subgroups
Functions	Contributions by grandparents to societal institutions and groups
Esteem	Worth and significance attached to the status of grandparent, as reflected in representations and treatments of grandparenthood in language, media, and other societal or cultural events and artifacts

grandma saw you do this''). The mere knowledge that grandparents are there as backup in case of family crises also may prompt parents and grandchildren to act differently than if grandparents were not available.

Gratificational Solidarity

While role satisfaction derives from gratifications of *being* a grandparent, gratificational solidarity evolves from satisfaction with grandparent-grandchild or extended-family relationships. The extent of gratification derived from a relationship can either be conceived in terms of the fit between expectations and reality (i.e., whether a grandchild visits as often as the grandfather would like) or in terms of the relative profits (equity) the grandparent and the grandchild (or other family members) derive from the relationship. Equity theorists (Adams, 1965) claim that highly inequitable relationships (e.g., grandparent's and grandchild's outcomes are highly dissimilar benefitting either the grandparent or the grandchild) will, at least over time, be unsatisfactory to both involved parties and either dissolved or renegotiated to achieve equity. Because kin relationships are rarely entirely voluntary, inequitable relationships may be maintained especially if family authority figures (e.g., the parents) mandate their continuation. However, the underbenefitted party may try to ''escape'' interactions as much as possible and the overbenefitted party may feel ''guilty'' enough to initiate renegotiations of the relationship to render it more equitable.

Grandparent Status (Societal Level)

Whereas dimensions pertaining to the grandparent role and to grandparent-grandchild relationships refer to microlevel phenomena, dimensions concerning grandparent's status and related social structures and social facts are concepts at the macrolevel. Major dimensions at this level are shown in Table 18.3.

Because research on grandparenthood at the macrolevel is particularly scarce, the following discussion is restricted to the few dimensions where some infomation is available.

Status

Grandparents' status derives from biological or legalized (marriage, adoption) ties to their children and their children's children. Thus, biological grandparents and grandparents with adopted children with children or adopted grandchildren would be assigned the status of grandparent, whereas fictional grandparents would not.

Norms

Until recently norms guiding grandparents' rights and obligations were either grounded in common law that aimed at preserving parents' autonomy in child rearing except under special circumstances (Hartfield, 1996; Thompson et al., 1989; see also Chapter 16) or in filial responsibility statutes that typically favor family members of adjacent or the same generation in support requirements and are rarely enforced (Bulcroft, Van Leynseele, & Borgatta, 1989). Both norms (parental autonomy and primary support obligations of adjacent generations) conform with widespread attitudes (at least among ethnic majority groups) that grandparents should not interfere in their adult children's lives in general and their parenting in particular (Cunningham-Burley, 1985; Kivett, 1991b). They also are consistent with observed support hierarchies among kin (Rossi & Rossi, 1990). Grandparent visitation statutes enacted during the past decades have broadened grandparents' rights to some extent (see Chapter 16 for a detailed discussion). They also shifted, at least in intent though not necessarily in their application, the rationale underlying norms about grandparents' access to grandchildren from an emphasis on parental autonomy to a focus on children's "best interest" (Thompson et al., 1989). Thus, grandparents' rights are increasingly linked to their grandchildren's rather than their adult children's rights and interests. Because most research has centered on support obligations rather than access rules (Rossi & Rossi, 1990; Coleman, Ganong, & Cable, 1997), it is not known whether the new grandparent visitation statutes reflect prevailing opinions about grandparents' rights. On the other hand, responsibility for children continues to rest on parents, a norm that often blocks grandparents who are raising grandchildren from access to needed services and benefits (Chalfie, 1994; see also Chapter 16).

Supply and Distribution

Supply and distribution of grandparents and grandchildren in the population at large or among population subgroups may influence grandparent-grandchild relationships, grandparents' position in society, or the prevalence of specific family and household structures. For example, grandchildren's relationships with grandparents may be contingent on how many of their peers have surviving grandparents. Scarcity of grandparents, especially when they function as important sources of tradition and wisdom, may enhance grandparents' status (Chapter 3). However, a large number of grandparents in the population can raise their political power as indicated by the grandparent movement (Chapters 16 and 17). Also, the relatively low supply of grandparents in preindustrial societies typically precluded widespread formation of extended households or the experience of great-grandparenthood (Farkas & Hogan, 1994; Hareven, 1994).

Functions

At the societal level, grandparents' functions represent their contributions to societal institutions and groups. Within the context of debates on generational equity (Kingson, Hirshorn, & Cornman, 1986), grandparents' economic function has special significance. Because many of grandparents' contributions are in the form of services (e.g., child care) rather than in the form of financial transactions (e.g., financial gifts, loans, or inheritance), their economic value is difficult to estimate. Recent analyses do suggest, however, that grandparents' contributions to their families are substantial (Bass & Caro, 1996; Kronebusch & Schlesinger, 1994; Wilson, 1987) and that grandparents play an important role in the nation's supply of child-care providers (Brayfield, Deich, & Hofferth, 1993; Hofferth, et al., 1991; Presser, 1989; Willer et al., 1991). In addition, grandparents' contributions to cultural heritage and historical continuity have gained increased recognition (Barush & Steen, 1996). To further capture grandparents' significance in this realm, it would be particularly helpful to assess from which sources (school, parents, grandparents) children derive knowledge about cultural heritage and history.

Esteem

Grandparents' esteem reflects the worth, significance, respect, and authority associated with the status of grandparent. Research on this topic is scarce. The few available studies, based on depictions of grandparents in children's literature (Balkwell, Ritblatt, & Deutsch, 1995; Janelli, 1988) and in Grandparent's Day cards (Greene & Polivka, 1985), indicate a stereotyped image of grandparents as benign, passive, powerless, and old, although magazines have started to portray grandparents as younger and more active (Hagestad, 1985). National events such as the celebration of Grandparent's Day, the proclamation of 1995 as the Year of the Grandparent, the inclusion of sessions on grandparents in the 1995 White House Conference on Aging, or a special request for proposals on grandparenthood by the National Institute on Aging (Brookdale Newsletter, Summer, 1995; Kornhaber, 1996; National Institute on Aging, 1995) also speak to enhanced recognition of grandparents' societal significance. The apparent contrast between these latter events and continued stereotyped representations of grandparents in books and other media underline the need for more research on grandparents' esteem and image. Particularly important would be further analyses of grandparents' depiction in a wide variety of media and artifacts as well as surveys addressing public opinion about grandparents' image and worth. In conducting such studies, it will be essential to investigate whether and to what extent images of grandparents blend with or are distinct from images of the elderly.

THEORETICAL ISSUES

Current Theoretical Approaches

Conceptual clarification and classification constitutes a first step in theory building. However, systematic theory construction also requires the development of interconnected propositions and hypotheses. Grandparent research to date largely lacks such systematic theory development. Instead, most research has tested isolated hypotheses or, at best, relatively simple theoretical models. The most commonly used approach is to test whether specific demographic and structural variables such as gender, age, proximity, race, or marital status impinge upon selected dimensions of grandparenthood or grandparent-grandchild relationships (Kivett, 1991b). Frequently such studies are not linked to specific theoretical perspectives and, therefore, have only limited use for further theory development. Thus, it is often not clear why a specific variable correlates with selected grandparenthood dimensions. A case in point is the effect of gender. As noted in Chapter 8, observed gender differences are consistent with several quite divergent theoretical explanations (e.g., evolutionary, socialization, or exchange theories), and available studies provide few insights as to which theoretical explanation is the most valid. In other cases, a variable may explain a significant proportion of the variance in grandparenting but have little theoretical relevance. For example, proximity is highly predictive of the frequency of grandparent-grandchild interactions and of instrumental supports provided by grandparents. While it is certainly important to control for geographic distance and other constraining conditions such as illness in empirical models, the influence of these factors is not necessarily of major theoretical importance.

Another common approach is to derive specific hypotheses from broader theoretical perspectives. As Kivett (1991b) notes, a variety of theoretical perspectives have been suggested for and used in grandparent research, ranging from more individual-oriented psychodynamic perspectives to more group- or macro-oriented family and sociological/anthropological theories. Psychodynamic models stress the "fit" between grandparents' and grandchildren's developmental needs and the demands placed on them in their roles as grandparent or grandchild (Kivnick, 1988), the influence of grandchildren's cognitive development on their perceptions of grandparents (Tyszkowa, 1991, 1993), or the timing of grandparenthood in terms of the individual's life context (Troll, 1985). The life-course perspective is currently perhaps the most prominent among these perspectives (Bengtson & Allen, 1993). Family systems and family developmental perspectives have informed grandparent research by focusing on the interconnections among extended-family members (Matthews, 1992; Sprey & Matthews,

1982; Whitchurch & Constantine, 1993), the importance of past relationship histories (King & Elder, 1995a; Whitbeck, Hoyt, & Huck, 1993), or the intersection of family members' lives and roles over time (Troll, 1985). Sociological and anthropological theories serve as the basis for the explanation of gender differences (Rossi & Rossi, 1990; M. S. Smith, 1991; Chapter 8). In addition, they stress the social and historical context of grandparenthood experiences and grandparent-grandchild relationships. For example, using the ecological perspective, King and colleagues (Chapter 4) explore the impact of rural/urban residence. Others have focused on subcultural (especially racial or ethnic) norms (see Chapters 5–7) or on societal and cultural change (see Chapters 3 and 7). Though certainly more promising than the first approach, the insights gained from the reliance on broader theoretical perspectives remain limited for several reasons. First, broad perspectives such as the ecological model presented in Chapter 4 serve well as guidelines for theory development (as is the intent of that chapter) but do not necessarily provide specific propositions or hypotheses. In addition, they are often too complex to be tested empirically. Consequently, empirical research relying on such broad perspectives has been typically restricted to test one or two concrete hypotheses derived from such perspectives. For example, the life-course perspective motivated a series of studies that demonstrate that "off-time" grandparenthood is associated with decreased satisfaction and increased stress, but we still know very little about the "intersecting life courses" of grandparents and grandchildren, which are at the core of the life-course perspective. Similarly, the stress on "family systems" in early writings on grandparenthood (Young & Willmott, 1957; Sprey & Matthews, 1982) has produced very few studies that systematically explore how specific grandparent-grandchild relationships are affected by the grandparent's relationships to other grandchildren or the grandchild's relationships to other grandparents.

A third and much rarer approach consists of causal models that include several interrelated dimensions of grandparenthood or grandparent-grandchild relationships as well as contextual factors (exogenous variables). The intergenerational solidarity model (see Chapter 10) is one example, although its applicability to grandparenthood requires further theoretical refinement and empirical tests. Shore and Hayslip (1994) present a causal model for the well-being of custodial grandparents, and Uphold and Morgan (1988) offer an expanded model to explain affectual solidarity. Some fairly complex models used in the general family literature such as Burr's (Burr et al., 1979) theory of the ease of role transitions or the ABC-X model of family stress (Boss, 1987) may, with some modifications, also be useful in grandparent research.

Needed Theoretical Refinements

What then needs to be done to advance theory development on grandparenting? The major challenge to researchers in this field is that, on the one hand they will have to pay tribute to the complexity of multiple relationships, dimensions, and contextual factors, and, on the other hand, achieve parsimonious and testable theoretical models. To achieve both goals most likely requires a stepwise approach to theory development and stronger integration of research findings. The following discussion provides a few suggestions for theory development on grandparenting (for additional suggestions, see Chapter 1). These suggestions are grounded in prevailing theoretical traditions. As alternative paradigms (e.g., feminist and critical theories) gain more widespread acceptance, they may guide grandparent research in different directions.

Identification of Relevant Contextual Variables

As noted in previous chapters (see especially Chapter 4), numerous contextual factors may impinge on grandparenthood and grandparent-grandchild relationships. *Individual context* variables include major demographic characteristics of the status incumbents (e.g., sex, age, marital status), constraints on role enactment (e.g., geographical distance, illness, or access barriers through parental intervention), resources (e.g., skills, income, time, knowledge), personality characteristics, developmental stage and needs, attitudes and values, role repertory, role as well as relationship history, and relevant life events. It is important that analyses of grandparent-grandchild relationships include contextual factors for both parties and/or their consensus or similarity on selected factors such as values and attitudes.

Family context variables consist of family structural features (e.g., household composition, lineage compression or extension, openness of boundaries, authority hierarchies), the history of relationships among extended-family members, and some of the network and exchange patterns described in Table 18.2.

The *societal context* impacts on grandparenting through cultural and subcultural norms, laws and policies, available support structures, and historical or natural events. Each of these contexts must be assumed to change over time (Chapter 4), although the societal context will typically be more stable than individual and family contexts. While it is theoretically important to identify those contextual factors that *may* impinge on grandparenthood, it is quite impossible to test the effect of these factors simultaneously. It will, therefore, be necessary to gradually identify those contextual factors that have the strongest impact on selected dimensions of grandparenting and that are of particular relevance within specified theoretical models.

Categorizing Grandparents and Grandchildren

While it is important to capture the multidimensional nature of grandparenting, it is equally impossible to include numerous dimensions in empirical models. Typologies derived from multiple dimensions are more amenable to empirical testing than are models that include many individual grandparent dimensions (see also Chapter 10). Data reduction techniques (e.g., factor analysis, multidimensional scaling, or cluster analysis) can identify which dimensions of grandparenting cluster together (i.e., can be treated as *one* factor or construct).

The so-identified constructs can then be used to cross-classify grandparents or grandchildren. We must recognize, however, that such techniques always involve a loss of detail and that constructs that "fit" one population group may be inappropriate for another group. For example, the similarity of factor structures for intergenerational solidarity achieved for parent-adult child and grandparent-grandchild dyads (Lawton, Silverstein, & Bengtson, 1994; see also Chapter 10) may very well be due to the fact that this particular study relied exclusively on relationships with adult grandchildren. Different factor structures may occur for younger grandchildren, for grandfathers versus grandmothers, or for families of different racial or ethnic background. Statistical programs (LISREL, EQS) for analyses of covariance structures permit tests for such subgroup variations (Acock & Schumm, 1993).

Linkages among Dimensions/Constructs of Grandparenting

Another possible shortcoming of typologies and empirically derived constructs is that they obscure potential causal linkages among constructs. Whether this is a problem depends on the theoretical objective of the study. If the researcher is primarily interested in assessing which contextual factors predict specific grandparent types or if the study focuses on the outcomes (e.g., grandparent's or grandchild's well-being) associated with specific grandparent-grandchild relationships, then the causal structure among dimensions or constructs of grandparent-grandchild relationships are of little import. On the other hand, if the research addresses the development and change of grandparent-grandchild relationships over time or specific transitions (including the transition to grandparenthood itself), then the causal structure of the model is essential. Especially important is to identify types of linkages among constructs (e.g., are they direct or indirect, one-directional or reciprocal; see Menaghan & Godwin, 1993) and to assess changes in covariance structures over time (Acock & Schumm, 1993).

Contexts as Mediating Forces

As noted throughout this volume, grandparent experiences vary considerably among diverse populations. Such contexts (e.g., culture, race/ethnicity, rural/urban residence) not only exert direct influences on grandparenting but also mediate how specific dimensions of grandparenthood relate to each other and how they impinge on selected outcomes. Of particular importance are cultural factors that alter the meaning context of specific grandparenting experiences. For example, perceptions and consequences of surrogate parenting by grandparents and of early grandparenthood differ depending on cultural context (see Chapter 14). Because contexts may overlap and interact (e.g., mediating effects of urban/rural residence may be different for Caucasians and African Americans and among them for grandmothers and grandfathers), it may be necessary to develop separate theoretical models for selected population subgroups. Such model building typically requires statistical techniques that allow subgroup comparisons (e.g., tests for interaction effects, structural equation models) and samples that include diverse subpopulations (Acock & Schumm, 1993; Menaghan & Godwin, 1993). Small samples based on selected population subgroups that have abounded in grandparent research are particularly inadequate for this type of theory development.

Emphasis on Transitions

Even though there is general consensus among researchers that grandparent-grandchild relationships change over time and that such changes are theoretically important, most studies use cross-sectional designs. Because long-term panel studies that follow relationships from the birth of the grandchild to his or her adulthood (or the grandparent's death) are often not feasible, it would be advantageous to direct research efforts toward studying specific transitions in grandparents' or grandchildren's lives (see also Chapter 9). Especially important is, of course, the transition to grandparenthood itself as well as changes in existing grandparent-grandchild relationships following the births of additional grandchildren.

A focus on transitions in the lives of the grandparents, the grandchildren, or the middle generation is consistent with life-course and family systems perspectives which conceive of grandparenthood as a "career" contingent on family members' life situations and on synchronous life events (Troll, 1985; Chapters 4 and 9). An emphasis on transitions also is consistent with theoretical perspectives such as symbolic interactionism which stress the temporal embeddedness of individuals' role expectations and role enactment (Berger & Kellner, 1964). For example, Knipscheer (1988), relying on George Herbert Mead's work, identified four dimensions of the past that impinge on perceptions of grandparenting and the enactment of the grandparent role. The "implied objective past" refers to necessary conditions for grandparents' current situation. In most cases, grandparenthood requires parenthood on the part of both the grandparent and one of his or her adult children, or specific instrumental supports to grandchildren require that grandparents and grandchildren have remained in or moved within close geographic proximity. Thus, selected demographic and other situational conditions set the stage for future grandparenting. Transitions often encompass a redefinition of past relationships and interactions, a process termed "symbolic reconstructed past" in Knipscheer's framework. Research indicates, for example, that the transition to grandparenthood often leads to the renegotiation of relationships with the adult child who became a parent, but it may also involve altered perceptions of the relationship to the grandparents' own parents or even new understanding of past relationships with their grandparents. The "social-structural past" is thought to condition current and future activities by defining paths for behaviors. For example, close relationships with one's own grandparents may predispose individuals toward adopting a positive grandparent role identity, and close relationships with grandparents during childhood may serve as a basis for close relationships with grandparents when the grandchildren have become adults (Lawton, Silverstein & Bengtson, 1994b; Whitbeck et al., 1993; Chapter 12). Lastly, the "mythical past" consists of symbolically created collective beliefs among family members that guide future actions. Thus, new parents' expectations about their parents' grandparent role may derive from an image of grandparenthood that emerges from (but does not necessarily accurately reflect) both spouses' own experiences as grandchildren.

Focusing on transitions in grandparents' or grandchildren's lives also has the advantage of theoretical relevance beyond grandparenting. For example, research on the effects of adult children's divorce, grandparents' retirement, or grandchildren's marriage is not only important to understand grandparenthood but also contributes to our understanding of divorce, retirement, or marriage.

Beyond Individuals and Dyads

As noted throughout this chapter, grandparent research has to go beyond investigations of individual grandparents or selected grandparent-grandchild relationships. Such research requires not only different concepts (see Table 18.2) but also different theoretical approaches and models than those used for individual or dyadic studies. Because the theoretical focus in such studies is on the group of grandchildren or grandparents, many variables used in individual and dyadic models are only of limited importance. Instead, the researcher needs to identify structural features of the extended family (including network characteristics) as well as other factors that may explain differences in the treatment of diverse grandchildren, competition among grandparents, or singling out a grandparent for specific supports and activities. For example, "normative solidarity" or role expectations about "what a grandparent should do" may be useful for individual and dyadic analyses, whereas distributive justice norms (Deutsch, 1975) may have greater theoretical relevance in a model designed to assess the differential treatment of grandchildren by a grandparent. Similarly, whether grandchildren (or their parents) turn to a specific grandparent for help in family crises may not only depend on the grandchild's or the parent's closeness to the selected grandparent but also on the symbolically constructed "helper reputation" of a grandparent within the extended family *or* on calculations of past commitments and debts (Finch & Mason, 1993) to specific grandparents (e.g., because the maternal grandmother already helped in the past, the family now turns to the paternal grandmother to whom they "owe" less).

METHODOLOGICAL ISSUES

Many of these theoretical refinements will not be possible without increased attention to methodological issues. This section addresses some of the more common methodological problems in grandparent research and offers some recommendations for improvement.

Design of Grandparenting Studies

Perhaps most important for theory development is that grandparent research is designed to capture the heterogenity and complexity of grandparenting. Many existing studies fail this test. Specific flaws in design include restricted samples, cross-sectional studies, reliance on individuals rather than dyads or families, and prevalence of surveys and interviews.

One frequently mentioned limitation of grandparent studies is their reliance on *small* or *non-representative* samples. Whether and how such sample selection constitutes a serious problem depends on the goal of the investigation. If the study's purpose is mainly exploratory, the sample need not be representative or large. However, the heterogeneity of grandparent experiences among diverse population subgroups or under different situational conditions renders it essential that even exploratory research covers a sufficiently divergent population. Many existing studies have failed to do so. For example, Johnson's leading research on the effects of adult children's divorce on grandparenting (see Chapter 13) is based exclusively on white, middle-class respondents even though divorce among the middle generation and stepgrandparenthood prevail among African Americans (Szinovacz, 1998). Similarly, many studies of grandparents raising grandchildren rely on African Americans and refer to specific causal conditions (e.g., adult children with drug addictions), and investigations of the meaning of grandparents' roles are often based on samples of college students (Kennedy, 1990; Roberto & Skoglund, 1996) or grandparents from selected socioeconomic status groups (Neugarten & Weinstein, 1964; Burton, 1992). Findings derived from such restricted samples will reflect only a subset of possible responses to crises or only a limited range of grandparent roles. Consequently, it will be necessary to either conduct comparable studies in other cultural or social contexts or to replicate existing investigations with larger and more representative samples.

Research designed to describe demographic trends in grandparenthood or the prevalence of specific grandparenting experiences, on the other hand, does require fairly large and representative samples. Uhlenberg and Kirby's work (Chapter 2) on historical and demographic trends, based on U.S. census data, fulfills this requirement, as does Szinovacz's (1998) demographic profile of grandparents using the National Survey of Families and Households, but most studies assessing grandparents' or grandchildren's experiences do not. Among the most frequently cited large-scale studies are those by Cherlin and Furstenberg (1986a), Bengtson and Harootyan (1994), and King and Elder (1995a). None of these studies is truly representative. Cherlin and Furstenberg's (1986a) as well as King and Elder's (1995a) research relies exclusively on grandparents with teenage grandchildren, whereas Bengtson and Harootyan (1994) include only grandparents with adult grandchildren. Thus, especially grandparents with small grandchildren are seriously underrepresented in current research efforts. One reason for the age restriction in previous studies is that these investigations included interviews with the grandchildren. Representative surveys of grandparents with grandchildren of all ages must rely on the grandparents' or the adult children's perspective since young children cannot be interviewed. Although it is possible to obtain information on the interactions between grandparents and very young grandchildren through observations and other techniques (Tomlin & Passman, 1991), the high cost of such methods renders large-scale representative research difficult.

A second design problem is the use of *cross-sectional data* and *retrospective accounts*. Cross-sectional research is inadequate to capture the dynamics of grandparenting over time and retrospective accounts may be biased (Cunningham-Burley, 1986b; Leik et al., 1990). Instead of long-term longitudinal designs, which are usually too costly, researchers can use panel studies that focus on transitions or carefully designed retrospective studies that involve recall-enhancing techniques such as temporal mapping (Leik et al., 1990). Regardless of which approach is used, it will be essential to control for synchronous events in grandparents', grandchildren's, or parents' lives. Unless such controls are included, causal attributions may remain questionable even if the data are longitudinal.

The third research design issue concerns choice of the *unit of assessment*. To date most research relied on information obtained from one respondent, either the grandparent or the grandchild (Bengtson & Harootyan, 1994; Kennedy, 1992a, 1992b; Kivett, 1996; Thomas, 1989). A few studies include two generations, often parent-child dyads (King & Elder, 1995a), and some investigations rely on generational lineages (Mangen, Bengtson, & Landry, 1988; Rossi & Rossi, 1990; Taylor, Chatters, & Jackson, 1993). As noted earlier, information from one respondent can be used to derive dyad- and group-level variables, but researchers need to keep in mind that responses from one family member always reflect this individual's perspective, which may differ considerably from the perspectives of other family members (Copeland & White, 1991). Indeed, comparative models based on separate information from grandparents and grandchildren may provide important insights into the dynamics of grandparent-grandchild relationships. Furthermore, interactions among two or more family members are influenced by characteristics of each family member. However, grandparents may not be aware of some aspects of their grandchildren's lives, and grandchildren may not have detailed information on some characteristics of their grandparents. Consequently, information gathered from one respondent may lead to theoretically incomplete modeling. For example, most studies using grandparents as respondents include only rudimentary information on the grandchildren such as their age or gender, but fail to include other characteristics (e.g., grandchildren's involvement in other activities, their contacts with other grandparents, or their feelings toward the grandparent) that may impact on frequency of interactions or activities performed with specific grandchildren. In addition, distinctions between respondents' own perceptions and the perceptions of other family members may be theoretically important. For example, in assessing parental mediation of grandparent-grandchild relations it may be essential to determine whether grandparents' perceptions of their adult children's mediation efforts (i.e., what the grandparent *thinks* the adult child wants) or parents' actions (i.e., what parents actually *do* to influence grandparent-grandchild interactions) have a stronger impact on grandparents' behaviors. Similarly, studies on such issues as competition among grandparents will typically require input from all concerned parties to obtain a valid overall picture of group dynamics.

Fourth, the nearly exclusive *reliance on interviews and surveys* in grandparent research also needs reconsideration. Observational studies can provide important insights about interaction processes among family members, and such information may be crucial to assess grandparents' influence especially on younger grandchildren as well as to determine the impact of gender and situational contexts (e.g., parents' or siblings' presence) on grandparent-grandchild interactions (see Chapter 11). Various coding and statistical techniques to analyze family interactions are now available in the family literature (Copeland & White, 1991; Draper & Marcos, 1990). In addition, quasi-experimental or experimental designs are needed to assess the impact of grandparent policies, programs, and clinical interventions. As noted in the preceding chapters (15, 16, and 17), current interventions frequently proceed without clear evidence whether intended effects are achieved or which unintended consequences are caused by the intervention.

Measurement and Analysis Issues

Attention to design issues constitutes but one step toward improved methodologies in grandparent research. Equally important are the measures and analyses used in grandparent studies. To date, grandparent research has suffered from lack of valid instruments and insufficient attention to the special problems of dyadic or family-based measures. Researchers have tended to develop their own instruments, usually without adequate tests for validity, and even operationalizations of well-developed concepts such as intergenerational solidarity have not been consistent (Bengtson & Harootyan, 1994; Mangen, Bengtson, & Landry, 1988; Roberts & Bengtson, 1990). The few available scales such as Kivnick's (1982) scale of grandparenthood meaning and Robertson's (1977) scale of grandparents' role conception (adapted by Hartshorne & Manaster, 1982) are now somewhat dated and also may lack validity. For example, researchers found few relationships between meaning types and expected behaviors (McGreal, 1986) or similar predictors of divergent grandparent styles (Miller & Cavanaugh, 1990). Development of valid scales for the divergent concepts of grandparenting is essential not only to ensure valid results but also to achieve some comparability among studies.

In constructing such scales it will be important to consider the heterogeneity and complexity of grandparenthood meanings and roles. If the instruments are to yield valid results across divergent population subgroups, the items included in these scales and the dimensions derived from them must have equivalent meanings for diverse populations. Some research indicates, however, that grandmothers and grandfathers respond differently to interviewers' questions (Cunningham-Burley, 1984b), and similar differences by gender or race/ethnicity may occur in responses to scale items in questionnaires. Also, some aspects of grandparents' roles may be restricted to specific population subgroups. For example, the transmission of cultural heritage may be particularly important among Native American or Asian grandparents (see Chapters 3 and 7) but have little relevance among Caucasians.

Many studies target specific grandparent-grandchild relationships, that is, respondents are asked to report about their relationship with one specific grandchild or one specific grandparent. *Which* grandparent or grandchild is the target of the investigation may have a major impact on findings. Often, questions refer to the grandparent/child to whom the respondent has "the closest" relationship (Kivett, 1996). This procedure is likely to yield results that overestimate contacts and shared activities among grandparents and grandchildren because it excludes, by definition, those grandparent-grandchild dyads who have distant or conflictual relationships. The resulting reduction in variance will also affect statistical tests and thus may produce misleading findings about predictors of grandparent-grandchild interactions. A better alternative is to chose a grandparent or grandchild randomly from the available pool of grandparents or grandchildren and to include a few general questions about respondents' relationships with other grandchildren.

Other studies rely on overall assessments of grandparent-grandchild relationships (e.g., questions on grandparenting in the National Survey of Families and Households, NSFH). While it is appropriate to examine grandparents' or grandchildren's total involvement in grandparent-grandchild interactions (e.g., how often *any* grandchild is seen or how much time is spent in *all* grandparent-grandchild activities), some dimensions are relationship-specific (e.g., closeness) and cannot be aggregated across different relationships. Indeed, when asked to rate how close they felt to their grandchildren some NSFH respondents refused to provide a general answer, indicating that their feelings for different grandchildren varied (NSFH codebook). If the investigation does not target specific grandparent-grandchild relationships, then it may be best to assess whether the grandparents have any grandchild to whom they feel extremely close or distant, or to ask with how many of their grandchildren they entertain emotionally close or remote relationships.

If information is obtained from or about two or more family members, it is possible to construct dyadic or group-level variables (see Ransom et al., 1990, for detailed discussions about the construction of such variables). The construction of such variables must be theoretically founded, and consideration must be given to their statistical properties. If one individual provides information on several family members (e.g., a grandmother describes her relationships with all of her grandchildren), dyadic or family-level variables derived from this information will reflect differences or similarities among the grandchildren from the perspective of the grandmother. This perspective may differ considerably from the perceptions of other family members. Furthermore, variables or constructs obtained from responses by one individual are likely to involve different types of measurement error than those obtained from several family members. For example, both norms stressing equal treatment of grandchildren and a consistent response pattern across answers about all grandchildren (i.e., some grandparents will tend toward checking extreme scores while others show a preference for moderate scores) may artificially enhance similarity of responses. On the other hand, data from different family members (e.g., grandparents and grandchildren) may be biased because of divergent response patterns, so that it is not clear how much of the difference between responses reflects ''true'' discrepancies between grandparents and grandchildren and how much is due to measurement error. If multiple-item indicators are used, then these problems may be alleviated to some extent through determination of correlated measurement error.

Another problem facing researchers using data from several family members is nonindependence of observations and subjects. Nonindependence of observations (Mangen, 1988) occurs when scores from one family member are used in two different constructs. For example, to assess value consensus across generations a researcher may calculate consensus between a grandmother and her adult daughter (the mother) from answers given by both, and consensus between the mother and her daughter, again from answers given by both. In this case, scores from the mother are included in both constructs, and the inclusion of both variables in one analysis may lead to considerable measurement error as well as multicollinearity problems. In addition, most statistical tests presume that individuals included in a study were independently sampled. Obviously, this assumption is violated when two or more members of one family are part of the research and in some way compared to each other. In this situation statistical techniques designed for correlated samples can be used (Copeland & White, 1991).

Even if independence criteria are met, scores for different relationships (e.g., grandmother-mother, grandmother-granddaughter) or for different relationship dimensions (e.g., frequency of face-to-face visits and instrumental help) may be highly correlated. For example, Thompson and Walker (1987) found it impossible to distinguish between grandmothers' closeness to their daughters and their grandchildren. Because highly correlated variables cannot be included in the same statistical model, constructs derived from both variables will have to be used in the analyses. Such constructs may be based on simple typologies or can be obtained through data reduction techniques such as confirmatory factor analyses or multidimensional scaling (Larzelere & Klein, 1987).

Though certainly not exhaustive, the above examples demonstrate the difficulties in designing and executing grandparent research. Dealing with these difficulties may require more complex and diverse designs and measures and use of more sophisticated statistical techniques than has been typical for grandparent research in the past. However, increased attention to methodological issues is necessary to promote theory development and to inform and evaluate policies, programs, and clinical interventions.

CONCLUSION

A grandmother, employed part time, cares for her 3-year-old granddaughter while her daughter is at work.

A 45-year-old grandfather rushes to the hospital to see his newborn first grandson.

A Native American grandmother tells her teenage grandchildren about tribal rituals and customs.

A recently retired couple plans an extended trip to visit grandchildren who are enrolled in different colleges.

An Asian grandmother, living with her oldest son and his family, supervises her daughter-in-law's child rearing.

A 72-year-old grandmother who was recently diagnosed with Alzheimer's dementia is taken in by her middle-aged daughter who lives with her husband and two teenage children.

An African American grandmother coaches her teenage daughter in caring for her newborn son.

A remarried grandmother buys Christmas presents for her grandchildren as well as her stepgrandchildren.

A 55-year-old farmer shows his 10-year-old grandson how to care for farm animals.

An 80-year-old grandmother who lives in a retirement home looks forward all week to the visit of her 40-year-old granddaughter and her 12-year-old great-grandson on Sunday.

These examples illustrate the heterogeneity, complexity, and dynamics of grandparenthood. Grandparent experiences vary over time; they involve divergent care scenarios, have different meanings in distinct cultural and subcultural settings, and occur within the context of multiple relationships among extended-family members. The multifaceted nature of grandparenthood documented throughout this handbook and also emphasized in Bengtson and Robertson's (1985) earlier edited volume poses a special challenge for researchers, policy makers, and practitioners. To meet this challenge, we need to refine our concepts, theories, methods, and interventions so that they adequately address the contextual, dynamic, and systemic features of grandparenting experiences. Achieving this goal requires that we integrate, evaluate, build upon, and, where necessary, redirect our past efforts. The chapters contained in this handbook were designed for this purpose—to assess past grandparent research and to initiate and provide guidelines for new research endeavors on this topic. Future research efforts spanning into the next century will show whether our efforts were successful.

NOTES

1. Proximity may constitute an additional structural relationship characteristic.

2. The term "mediation" has been used in a variety of ways in grandparent research. Some authors refer to intervening variables in a statistical sense (see Chapter 10), others imply influence of parent-grandparent on grandparent-grandchild relationships (King & Elder, 1995a), and others mean active intervention of parents in grandparent-grandchild relationships (see Chapter 12). I use the latter definition.

Bibliography

AARP Grandparent Information Newsletter. (1994). Washington, DC: AARP.

Achenbaum, W. A. (1978). *Old age in the new land.* Baltimore: Johns Hopkins University Press.

Achenbaum, W. A. (1996). Historical perspectives on aging. In Robert H. Binstock & Linda K. George (Eds.), *Handbook of aging and the social sciences* (4th ed.) (pp. 137–152). San Diego: Academic Press.

Acock, A. C., & Schumm, W. R. (1993). Analysis of covariance structures applied to family research and theory. In P. G. Boss, W. J. Doherty, R. LaRossa, W. R. Schumm, & S. K. Steinmetz (Eds.), *Sourcebook of family theories and methods* (pp. 451–468). New York: Plenum.

Adams, J. S. (1965). Inequity in social exchange. In L. Berkowitz (Ed.), *Advances in experimental social psychology,* Vol. 2 (pp. 267–299). New York: Academic Press.

Ahrons, C. R., & Bowman, M. E. (1982). Changes in family relationships following divorce of adult child: Grandmothers' perceptions. *Journal of Divorce, 5,* 49–68.

Ahrons, C., & Rodgers, R. H. (1987). *Divorced families: A multidisciplinary, developmental view.* New York: Norton.

Ainsworth, M. D. S., Blehar, M. C., Waters, E., & Wall, S. (1978). *Patterns of attachment: A psychological study of the strange situation.* Hillsdale, NJ: Erlbaum.

Ainsworth, M. D. S., & Eichberg, C. (1981). Effects on infant-mother attachment of mothers: Unresolved loss of an attachment figure, or other traumatic experience. In C. M. Parkes, J. Stevenson-Hinde, & P. Marris (Eds.), *Attachment across the life cycle* (pp. 160–183). London: Routledge.

Al Awad, A. M., & Sonuga-Barke, E. J. (1992). Childhood problems in a Sudanese city: A comparison of extended and nuclear families. *Child Development, 63,* 906–914.

Albrecht, R. (1954). The parental responsibilities of grandparents. *Marriage and Family Living, 16,* 201–204.

Aldous, J. (1978). *Family careers: Developmental change in families*. New York: Wiley.

Aldous, J. (1985). Parent-adult child relations as affected by the grandparent status. In V. L. Bengtson & J. F. Robertson (Eds.), *Grandparenthood* (pp. 117–132). Beverly Hills, CA: Sage.

Aldous, J. (1990). Family development and the life course: Two perspectives on family change. *Journal of Marriage and the Family, 52*, 571–583.

Aldous, J. (1995). New views of grandparents in intergenerational context. *Journal of Family Issues, 16*, 104–122.

Aldous, J. (1996). *Family careers: Rethinking the developmental perspective*. Thousand Oaks, CA: Sage.

Aldous, J., & Klein, D. (1991). Sentiment and services: Models of intergenerational relationships in mid-life. *Journal of Marriage and the Family, 53*, 595–608.

Aldrich, R., & Austin, G. (1991). *Grandparenting for the 90's*. Escondido, CA: Erdmann.

Allen, K., & Pickett, R. (1987). Forgotten streams in the family life course: Utilization of qualitative retrospective interviews in the analysis of lifelong single women's family careers. *Journal of Marriage and the Family, 49*, 514–526.

Allen, W. R. (1978). The search for applicable theories of black family life. *Journal of Marriage and the Family, 40*, 117–129.

Amato, P. R. (1993). Urban-rural differences in helping friends and family members. *Social Psychology Quarterly, 56*, 249–262.

Amoss, P. (1981). Coast Salish elders. In P. T. Amoss & S. Harrell (Eds.), *Other ways of growing old: Anthropological perspectives* (pp. 227–247). Stanford: Stanford University Press.

Anderson, K. L., & Allen, W. R. (1984). Correlates of extended household structure. *Phylon Review of Race and Culture, 45*, 144–157.

Anderson, M. (1977). The impact on the family relationships of the elderly of changes since Victorian times in governmental income-maintenance provision. In E. Shanas & M. B. Sussman (Eds.), *Family, bureaucracy, and the elderly* (pp. 36–59). Durham, NC: Duke University Press.

Angel, J. L., Angel, R. J., McClellan, J. L., & Markides, K. S. (1996). Nativity, declining health, and preferences in living arrangements among elderly Mexican Americans: Implications for long-term care. *The Gerontologist, 36*, 464–473.

Angel, J. L., & Hogan, D. P. (1992). The demography of minority aging populations. *Journal of Family History, 17*, 95–115.

Angelou, M. (1969). *I know why the caged bird sings*. New York: Random House.

Anspach, D. (1976). Kinship and divorce. *Journal of Marriage and the Family, 38*, 343–350.

Antonucci, T. (1990). Social supports and social relationships. In R. H. Binstock & L. K. George (Eds.), *Handbook of aging and the social sciences* (3rd ed.) (pp. 205–226). New York: Academic Press.

Antonucci, T. C., & Akiyama, H. (1991). Convoys of social support: Generational issues. *Marriage and Family Review, 16*, 103–123.

Apfel, N. H., & Seitz, V. (1991). Four models of adolescent mother-grandmother relationships in black inner-city families. *Families Relations, 40*, 421–429.

Aponte, R. (1991). Urban Hispanic poverty: Disaggregations and explanations. *Social Problems, 39*, 516–528.

Apple, D. (1956). The social structure of grandparenthood. *American Anthropologist, 58*, 656–663.

Aquilino, William. (1996). The life course of children born to unmarried mothers: Childhood living arrangements and young adult outcomes. *Journal of Marriage and the Family, 58*, 293–310.

Arber, S., & Ginn J. (1991). *Gender and later life: A sociological analysis of resources and constraints.* London: Sage.

Aschenbrenner, J. (1973). Extended families among black Americans. *Journal of Comparative Family Studies, 4*, 257–268.

Aschenbrenner, J. (1975). *Lifeline: Black families in Chicago.* Chicago: Holt & Winston.

Astone, N. M., & Washington, M. L. (1994). The association between grandparental coresidence and adolescent childbearing. *Journal of Family Issues, 15*, 574–589.

Atkinson, J. (1986). *Modern child custody practice.* New York: Kluwer Law Book Publishers.

Atkinson, M. P., Kivett, V. R., & Campbell, R. T. (1986). Intergenerational solidarity: An examination of a theoretical model. *Journal of Gerontology, 41*, 408–416.

Bach, G. R., & Deutsch, R. (1970). *Pairing.* New York: Peter H. Wyden.

Bahr, K. S. (1994). The strengths of Apache grandmothers: Observations on commitment, culture, and caretaking. *Journal of Comparative Family Studies, 25*, 233–248.

Bahr, K. S., & Bahr, H. M. (1993). Autonomy, community, & the mediation of value: Comments on Apachean grandmothering, cultural change, & the media. *Family Perspective, 27*, 347–374.

Baker, R. (1996, March 26). Who likes old age? Not the old. *South Bend Tribune*, p. A8.

Balkwell, C., Ritblatt, S., & Deutsch, F. (1995). Images of grandparents presented in children's literature: Multicultural comparisons of intergenerational family relations. San Diego: San Diego State University.

Bane, M. J. (1976). *Here to stay: American families in the twentieth century.* New York: Basic Books.

Bane, M. J., & Jargowsky, P. A. (1988). The links between government policy and family structure. In A. Cherlin (Ed.), *The changing american family and public policy* (pp. 219–255). Washington, DC: Urban Institute.

Bankoff, E. A. (1983). Aged parents and their widowed daughters: A support relationship. *Journal of Gerontology, 38*, 226–230.

Baranowski, M. D. (1982). Grandparent-adolescent relations: Beyond the nuclear family. *Adolescence, 17*, 575–584.

Baranowski, M. D. (1985). Men as grandfathers. In S. M. Hanson & F. W. Bozett (Eds.), *Dimensions of fatherhood* (pp. 217–242). Beverly Hills, CA: Sage.

Baranowski, M. D. (1987). *The grandfather-grandchild relationship: Patterns and meaning.* Paper presented at the 40th Annual Scientific Meeting of the Gerontological Society of America, Washington, DC.

Baranowski, M. D. (1990). The grandfather-grandchild relationships: Meaning and exchange. *Family Perspective, 24*, 201–215.

Barnhill, S. (1996). Three generations at risk: Imprisoned women, their children, and grandmother caregivers. *Generations, 1*, 39–40.

Barranti, C. C. R. (1985). The grandparent/grandchild relationship: Family resource in an era of voluntary bonds. *Family Relations, 34*, 343–352.

Barusch, A. S., & Steen, P. (1996). Keepers of community in a changing world. *Generations, 20*, 49–52.

Bass, S. A., & Caro, F. G. (1996). The economic value of grandparent assistance. *Generations, 20*, 29–33.

Bastida, E. (1988). Reexamining assumptions about extended familism: Older Puerto Ricans in a comparative perspective. In M. Sotomayor & H. Curiel (Eds.), *A cultural signature* (pp. 163–183). Edinburg, TX: Pan American University Press.

Bastida, E., & Gonzalez, G. (1993). Ethnic variations in measurement of physical health status: Implications for long-term care. In C. Barresi & D. Stull (Eds.), *Ethnic elderly in long-term care* (pp. 22–35). New York: Springer.

Battistelli, P., & Farnetti, A. (1991). Grandchildren's images of their grandparents: A psychodynamic perspective. In P. K. Smith (Ed.), *The psychology of grandparenthood: An international perspective* (pp. 143–156). New York: Routledge.

Bean, K. S. (1985–1986). Grandparent visitation: Can the parent refuse? *Journal of Family Law, 24,* 393–450.

Beck, R. W., & Beck, S. H. (1989). The incidence of extended households among middle aged black and white women: Estimates for a five year panel study. *Journal of Marriage and the Family, 10,* 147–168.

Beck, S. H., & Beck, R. W. (1984). The formation of extended households during middle age. *Journal of Marriage and the Family, 46,* 277–287.

Bellah, R., Madsen, R., Sullivan, W., Swidler, A., & Tipton, S. (1985). *Habits of the heart.* Berkeley: University of California Press.

Belsky, J., & Rovine, M. (1984). Social-network contact, family support, and the transition to parenthood. *Journal of Marriage and the Family, 46,* 455–462.

Bengtson, V. L. (1985). Diversity and symbolism in grandparent roles. In V. L. Bengtson & J. F. Robertson (Eds.), *Grandparenthood* (pp. 11–25). Beverly Hills, CA: Sage.

Bengtson, V. L. (1989). The problem of generations: Age group contrasts, continuities, and social change. In V. L. Bengtson & K. W. Schaie (Eds.), *The course of later life: Research and reflections* (pp. 25–54). New York: Springer.

Bengtson, V. L., & Allen, K. R. (1993). The life course perspective applied to families over time. In P. G. Boss, W. J. Doherty, R. LaRossa, W. R. Schumm, & S. K. Steinmetz (Eds.), *Sourcebook of family theories: A contextual approach* (pp. 469–504). New York: Plenum.

Bengtson, V. L., & Black, K. D. (1973). Intergenerational relations and continuities in socialization. In P. B. Baltes & K. W. Schaie (Eds.), *Life-span developmental psychology: Personality and socialization* (pp. 207–234). New York: Academic Press.

Bengtson, V. L., & Harootyan, R. (Eds.). (1994). *Hidden connections: A study of intergenerational linkages in American society.* New York: Springer.

Bengtson, V. L., & Roberts, R. E. L. (1991). Intergenerational solidarity in aging families: An example of formal theory construction. *Journal of Marriage and the Family, 53,* 856–870.

Bengtson, V. L., & Robertson, J. F. (1985). *Grandparenthood.* Beverly Hills, CA: Sage.

Bengtson, V. L., Rosenthal, C., & Burton, L. (1990). Families and aging: Diversity and heterogeneity. In R. H. Binstock and L. K. George (Eds.), *Handbook of aging and the social sciences* (3rd ed.). New York: Academic Press.

Bengtson, V., Rosenthal C., & Burton L. (1996). Paradoxes of families and aging. In R. H. Binstock & L. K. George (Eds.), *Handbook of aging and the social sciences* (4th ed.). San Diego: Academic Press.

Bengtson, V. L., & Schrader, S. (1982). Parent-child relations. In D. Mangen & W. A. Peterson (Eds.), *Research instruments in social gerontology,* Vol. 2 (pp. 115–186). Minneapolis: University of Minnesota Press.

Benn, R., & Saltz, E. (1989, April). *The effect of grandmother support on teen parent and infant attachment patterns within the family.* Paper presented at the Society for Research in Child Development, Kansas City, KS.

Berardo, F. (1990). Trends and directions in family research. *Journal of Marriage and the Family, 52*, 809–817.

Berger, P. L., & Kellner, H. (1964). Marriage and the construction of reality. *Diogenes, 46*, 1–23.

Billingsley, A. (1968). *Black families in white America.* Englewood Cliffs, NJ: Prentice-Hall.

Binstock, R. H. (1992). Older voters and the 1992 presidential election. *The Gerontologist, 32*, 601–606.

Blackwelder, D. E., & Passman, R. P. (1986). Grandmothers' and mothers' disciplining in three-generational families: The role of social responsibility in rewarding and punishing grandchildren. *Journal of Personality and Social Psychology, 50*, 80–86.

Blassingame, J. W. (1972). *The slave community: Plantation life in the antebellum South.* New York: Oxford University Press.

Blau, T. H. (1984). An evaluative study of the role of the grandparent in the best interests of the child. *The American Journal of Family Therapy, 12*, 45–50.

Bledsoe, E., & Isiugo-Abanihe, U. (1989). Strategies of child fosterage among Mende grannies. In R. J. Lesthaeghe (Ed.), *Reproduction and social organization in Sub-Saharan Africa* (pp. 442–474). Berkeley: University of California Press.

Blust, E. P. N., & Scheidt, R. J. (1988). Perceptions of filial responsibility by elderly Filipino widows and their primary caregivers. *International Journal of Aging and Human Development, 26*, 91–106.

Bogolub, E. (1989). Families of divorce: A three-generational prospective. *Social Work, 34*, 375–376.

Bohannon, P. (1971). *Divorce and after: An analysis of the emotional and social problems of divorce.* New York: Anchor Books.

Borden, B. (1946). The role of grandparents in children's behavior problems. *Smith College Studies in Social Work, 17*, 115–116.

Boss, P. (1987). Family stress. In M. B. Sussman & S. K. Steinmetz (Eds.), *Handbook on marriage and the family* (pp. 695–723). New York: Plenum.

Boss, P. (1988). *Family stress management.* Newbury Park, CA: Sage.

Bostock, C. (1994). Does the expansion of grandparent visitation rights promote the best interests of the child? A survey of grandparent visitation laws in the fifty states. *Columbia Journal of Law and Social Problems, 27*, 319–373.

Boswell T. D., & Curtis, J. R. (1984). *The Cuban-American experience.* Totowa, NJ: Rowman and Allanheld.

Boszormenyi-Nagy, I. (1974). Ethical and practical implications of intergenerational family therapy. *Psychosomatic, 24*, 261–268.

Boszormenyi-Nagy, I., & Spark, G. M. (1973). *Invisible loyalties: Reciprocity in intergenerational family therapy.* New York: Harper & Row.

Bowen, M. (1978). *Family therapy in clinical practice.* New York: Jason Aronson.

Bray, J. H., & Berger, S. H. (1990). Noncustodial father and paternal grandparent relationships in stepfamilies. *Family Relations, 39*, 414–419.

Brayfield, A. A., Deich, S. G., & Hofferth, S. L. (1993). *Caring for children in low-income families: A substudy of the national child care survey 1990.* Washington, DC: Urban Institute Press.

Bretherton, I. (1993). Theoretical contributions from developmental psychology. In P. G. Boss, W. J. Doherty, R. LaRossa, W. R. Schumm, & S. K. Steinmetz (Eds.), *Sourcebook of family theories and methods* (pp. 275–297). New York: Plenum.

Brewer, M., Dull, V., & Lui, L. (1981). Perceptions of the elderly: Stereotypes as prototypes. *Journal of Personality and Social Psychology, 41*, 656–670.

Brim, O. G., & Kagan, J. (Eds.). (1980). *Constancy and change in human development.* Cambridge, MA: Harvard University Press.

Brim, O. G., & Riff, C. D. (1980). On the properties of life events. In P. B. Baltes & O. G. Brim (Eds.), *Lifespan development and behavior*, Vol. 3. New York: Academic Press.

Brody, E. M. (1983). Women in the middle and family help to older people. *The Gerontologist, 21*, 471–480.

Bronfenbrenner, U. (1986). Ecology of the family as a context for human development: Research perspectives. *Developmental Psychology, 22*(6), 723–742.

Bronfenbrenner, U., & Crouter, A. C. (1983). The evolution of environmental models in developmental research. In P. H. Mussen (Vol. Ed.) & W. Kessen (Series Ed.), *Handbook of child psychology: Vol. 1. History, theory, and methods* (4th ed.) (pp. 357–414). New York: Wiley.

Brookdale Grandparent Caregiver Information Project Newsletter (1992–1993). Center on Aging. Berkeley: University of California.

Brookdale Newsletter from the AARP Grandparent Information Center (1994–1996). Parenting grandchildren: A voice for grandparents. Washington, DC: AARP.

Brown, D. R., (1995). *Midlife and older African Americans as intergenerational caregivers of school-aged children.* Final report to the AARP–Andrus Foundation. Detroit: Wayne State University.

Brown, E. M. (1982). Divorce and the extended family. A consideration of services. *Journal of Divorce, 5*, 169.

Brubaker, T. (1990). Families in later life: A burgeoning research area. *Journal of Marriage and the Family, 52*, 959–981.

Bubolz, M. M., & Sontag, M. S. (1993). Human ecology theory. In P. G. Boss, W. J. Doherty, R. LaRossa, W. R. Schumm, & S. K. Steinmetz (Eds.), *Sourcebook of family theories and methods: A contextual approach* (pp. 419–448). New York: Plenum.

Buchanan, B., & Lappin, J. (1990). Restoring the soul of the family. *The Family Therapy Networker, 10*, 46–52.

Bulcroft, K. A., & Bulcroft, R. A. (1991). The timing of divorce: Effects on parent-child relationships in later life. *Research on Aging, 13*, 226–243.

Bulcroft, K. A., Van Leynseele, J., & Borgatta, E. F. (1989). Filial responsibility laws. Issues and state statutes. *Research on Aging, 11*, 374–393.

Bumpass, L. L. (1990). What's happening to the family? Interactions between demographic and institutional change. *Demography, 27*, 483–498.

Burgess, E. W., & Locke, H. J. (1960). *The family: From institution to companionship* (2nd ed.). New York: American Book Company.

Burke, P. J. (1991). Identity process and social stress. *American Journal of Sociology, 56*, 836–849.

Burnette, D. (1997). Grandparents raising grandchildren in the inner city. *Families in Society: The Journal of Contemporary Human Services, 78*, 489–499.

Burns, E. M. (1991). Grandparent visitation rights: Is it time for the pendulum to fall? *Family Law Quarterly, 25*, 59–81.

Burnside, I. M. (1996). Reminiscence. In *Encyclopedia of Gerontology*, Vol. 2. (pp. 399–406). San Diego, CA: Academic Press.

Burr, W. R., Leigh, G. K., Day, R. D., & Constantine, J. (1979). Symbolic interaction and the family. In W. R. Burr, R. Hill, F. I. Nye, & I. L. Reiss (Eds.), *Contemporary theories about the family*, Vol. 2 (pp. 42–111). New York: Free Press.

Burton, L. M. (1987). Young grandmothers: Are they ready? *Social Science, 72*, 191–194.

Burton, L. M. (1990). Teenage childbearing as an alternating life-course strategy in multigeneration black families. *Human Nature, 1*, 123–143.

Burton, L. M. (1992). Black grandparents rearing children of drug-addicted parents: Stressors, outcomes, and social service needs. *The Gerontologist, 32*, 744–751.

Burton, L. M. (1994, August). *Age norms, the timing of family role transitions, and intergenerational caregiving among aging African American women.* Paper presented at the annual meeting of the American Sociological Association, Los Angeles, CA.

Burton, L. M. (1995). Intergenerational patterns of providing care in African-American families with teenage childbearers: Emergent patterns in ethnographic study. In V. L. Bengtson, K. W. Schaie, & L. M. Burton (Eds.), *Adult intergenerational relations: Effects of social change* (pp. 79–118). New York: Springer.

Burton, L. M. (1996). Age norms, the timing of family role transitions, and intergenerational caregiving among aging African American women. *The Gerontologist, 36*, 199–208.

Burton, L. M., & Bengtson, V. L. (1985). Black grandmothers: Issues of timing and continuity of roles. In V. L. Bengtson & J. Robertson (Eds.), *Grandparenthood* (pp. 61–77). Beverly Hills, CA: Sage.

Burton, L. M., & deVries, C. (1992). Challenges and rewards: African American grandparents as surrogate parents. *Generations, 16*, 51–54.

Burton, L. M., & Dilworth-Anderson, P. (1991). The intergenerational family roles of aged black Americans. *Marriage and Family Review, 16*, 311–330.

Burton, L. M., Dilworth-Anderson, P., & Merriwether-deVries, C. (1995). Context and surrogate parenting among contemporary grandparents. *Marriage and Family Review, 20*, 349–366.

Burton, L. M., & Stack, C. (1993). Kinscripts. *Journal of Comparative Family Studies, 24*, 157–170.

Butler, R. N. (1963). The life review: An interpretation of reminiscence in the aged. *Psychiatry, 26*, 65–76.

Butler, R. N. (1996). Life review. In *Encyclopedia of Gerontology*, Vol. 2 (pp. 53–58). San Diego, CA: Academic Press.

Butler, R. N., & Lewis, M. L. (1982). *Aging and mental health* (3rd ed.). St. Louis: Mosby.

Campbell, R. (1995). Weaving a new tapestry of research: A bibliography of selected readings on feminist research methods. *Women's Studies International Forum, 18*, 215–222.

Carlson, G. E. (1993). When grandmothers take care of grandchildren. *The American Journal of Maternal/Child Nursing, 18,* 206–207.

Caroll, V. (1971). *Adoption in Eastern Oceania.* Honolulu: University of Hawaii Press.

Cath, S. H. (1986). Clinical vignettes: A range of grandparental experiences. *Journal of Geriatric Psychiatry, 19,* 57–68.

Cattell, M. (1989). Knowledge and social change in Samia, Western Kenya. *Journal of Cross-Cultural Gerontology, 4*(3), 225–244.

Cattell, M. (1994). "Nowadays it isn't easy to advise the young": Grandmothers and granddaughters among Abaluyia of Kenya. *Journal of Cross-Cultural Gerontology, 9*(2), 157–178.

Cervera, N. (1989). Groupwork with parents of unwed pregnant teens: Transition to unexpected grandparenthood. Special issue: Social work with multi-family groups. *Social Work with Groups, 12,* 71–93.

Chalfant, H. P., & Heller, P. L. (1991). Rural/urban versus regional differences in religiosity. *Review of Religious Research, 33,* 76–86.

Chalfie, D. (1994). *Going it alone: A closer look at grandparents parenting grandchildren.* Washington, DC: AARP.

Chan, A., Madsen, R., & Unger, J. (1992). *Chen village under Mao and Deng* (2nd ed.). Berkeley: University of California Press.

Chan, C. G., & Elder, G. H., Jr. (1996, November). *Opportunity and the structure of grandparent-grandchild relations.* Paper presented at the annual meeting of the Gerontological Society of America, Washington, DC.

Chase-Lansdale, P. L., Brooks-Gunn, J., & Zampsky, E. L. (1994). Young African-American multigenerational families in poverty: Quality of mothering and grandmothering. *Child Development, 65,* 373–393.

Chassler, S. (1994). New rules for grandparenting in the '90's. *New Choices for Retirement Living, 34,* 28–31.

Chatters, L. M., & Jayakody, R. (1995). Commentary: Intergenerational support within African-American families: Concepts and methods. In V. L. Bengtson, K. W. Schaie, & L. M. Burton (Eds.), *Adult intergenerational relations* (pp. 97–118). New York: Springer.

Chatters, L. M. & Taylor, R. J. (1993). Intergenerational support: The provision of assistance to parents by adult children. In J. S. Jackson, L. M. Chatters, & R. J. Taylor (Eds.), *Aging in black America* (pp. 69–83). Newbury Park, CA: Sage.

Chatters, L. M., Taylor, R. J., & Jackson, J. S. (1985). Size and composition of the informal helper networks of elderly blacks. *Journal of Gerontology, 40,* 605–614.

Chatters, L. M., Taylor, R. J., & Jayakody, R. (1994). Fictive kinship relations in black extended families. *Journal of Comparative Family Studies, 25,* 297–312.

Chatters, L. M., Taylor, R. J., & Neighbors, H. W. (1989). Size of the informal health network mobilized in response to serious personal problems. *Journal of Marriage and the Family, 51*(3), 667–676.

Chen, R., & Morgan, S. P. (1991). Recent trends in the timing of first births in the United States. *Demography, 28,* 513–553.

Cherlin, A. (1978). Remarriage as an incomplete institution. *American Journal of Sociology, 84,* 634–650.

Cherlin, A. J., & Furstenberg, F. F. (1985). Styles and strategies of grandparenting. In V. L. Bengtson & J. F. Robertson (Eds), *Grandparenthood* (pp. 97–116). Beverly Hills, CA: Sage.

Cherlin, A. J., & Furstenberg, F. F. (1986a). *The new American grandparent*. New York: Basic Books.

Cherlin, A. J., & Furstenberg, F. F. (1986b). Grandparents and family crisis. *Generations, 10*, 26–28.

Cherlin, A. J., & Furstenberg, F. F. (1994). Stepfamilies in the United States: A reconsideration. *Annual Review of Sociology, 20*, 359–381.

Chescheir, M. W. (1980). The use of elderly as surrogate parents—A clinical perspective. *Journal of Gerontological Social Work, 3*, 3.

Chevan, A., & Sutton, G. H. (1985). Race and sex differentials in the life course. In G. H. Elder (Ed.), *Life course dynamics* (pp. 282–301). Ithaca, NY: Cornell University Press.

Chodorow, N. (1978). *The reproduction of mothering*. Berkeley: University of California Press.

Cicirelli, V. (1983). A comparison of helping behavior to elderly parents of adult children with intact and disrupted marriages. *The Gerontologist, 23*, 619–625.

Clingempeel, W. G., Colyar, J. J., Brand, E. M., & Hetherington, M. (1992). Children's relationships with maternal grandparents: A longitudinal study of family structure and pubertal status effects. *Child Development, 63*, 1404–1422.

Cogswell, J. F. (1983). Reflections of a grandfather. *Counseling Psychologist, 11*, 61.

Cohen, H. (1996). Congressional Research Services, Personal Communication, December 30.

Cohen, M. (1976). *House united, house divided: The Chinese family in Taiwan*. New York: Columbia University Press.

Cohler, B. J., & Altergott, K. (1995). Family of the second half of life: Connecting theories and findings. In R. Blieszner & V. H. Bedford (Eds.), *Handbook of aging and the family* (pp. 59–64). Westport, CT: Greenwood.

Cohler, B. J., & Grunebaum, H. U. (1981). *Mothers, grandmothers, and daughters: Personality and childcare in three-generation families*. New York: Wiley.

Cole, T. R. (1992). *The journey of life: A cultural history of aging in America*. Cambridge, UK: Cambridge University Press.

Coleman, J. S. (1988). Social capital in the creation of human capital. *American Journal of Sociology, 94*, S95–S120.

Coleman, J. S., & Hoffer, T. (1987). *Public and private high schools: The impact of communities*. New York: Basic Books.

Coleman, M., & Ganong, L. H. (1990). Remarriage and stepfamily research in the 1980s: Increased interest in an old family form. *Journal of Marriage and the Family, 52*, 925–940.

Coleman, M., Ganong, L., & Cable, S. M. (1997). Beliefs about women's intergenerational family obligations to provide support before and after divorce and remarriage. *Journal of Marriage and the Family, 59*, 165–176.

Coleman, N. (1989). The delivery of legal assistance to the elderly in the United States. In J. M. Eekelaar & D. Pearl (Eds.), *An aging world: Dilemmas and challenges for law and social policy* (pp. 463–477). Oxford, UK: Clarendon.

Colletta, N. D., & Lee, D. (1983). The impact of support for black adolescent mothers and their mothers: An analysis of supportive and problematic interactions. *Journal of Community Psychology, 22*, 12–20.

Collins, P. H. (1990). *Black feminist thought: Knowledge, consciousness, and the politics of empowerment*. New York: Routledge.

Colman, G., & Elbert, S. (1984). Farming families: The farm needs everyone. *Research in Rural Sociology and Development, 1,* 61–78.

Cookson, M. A. (1988). Successful grandparenting. *Focus on the Family, 12,* 10–12.

Cool, L. (1980). Ethnicity and aging: Continuity through change for elderly Corsicans. In C. L. Fry & contributors, *Aging in culture and society: Comparative viewpoints and strategies* (pp. 149–169). New York: Bergin.

Cooney, T. M., & Smith, L. A. (1996). Young adults' relations with grandparents following recent parental divorce. *Journal of Gerontology: Social Sciences, 51B,* S91–S95.

Cooney, T. M., & Uhlenberg, P. (1992). Support from parents over the life course: The adult child's perspective. *Social Forces, 71,* 63–84.

Copeland, A. P., & White, K. M. (1991). *Studying families.* Newbury Park, CA: Sage.

Cottrell, J. L. (1986). Work and community influences on the quality of child rearing. *Child Development, 57,* 362–374.

Coward, R. T., & Cutler, S. J. (1991). The composition of multigenerational households that include elders. *Research on Aging, 13,* 55–73.

Coward, R. T., & Dwyer, J. W. (1990). The association of gender, sibling network composition, and patterns of parent care by adult children. *Research on Aging, 12,* 158–181.

Coward, R. T., & Smith, W. M., Jr. (1981). Introduction. In R. T. Coward & W. M. Smith, Jr. (Eds.), *The family in rural society* (pp. 1–6). Boulder, CO: Westview.

Cowgill, D. O. (1974). Aging and modernization: A revision of the theory. In J. F. Gubrium (Ed.), *Late life: Communities and environmental policy* (pp. 123–146). Springfield, IL.: Charles C. Thomas.

Cowgill, D. O., & Holmes, L. (1972). *Aging and modernization.* New York: Appleton-Century-Crofts.

Crawford, M. (1981). Not disengaged: Grandparents in literature and reality, an empirical study in role satisfaction. *Sociological Review, 29,* 499–519.

Creasey, G. L. (1993). The association between divorce and late adolescent grandchildren's relations with grandparents. *Journal of Youth and Adolescence, 22*(5), 513–529.

Creasey, G. L., & Jarvis, P. (1989). Grandparents with Alzheimer's disease: Effect of parental burden on grandchildren. *Family Therapy, 16,* 79–85.

Creasey, G. L., & Koblewski, P. J. (1991). Adolescent grandchildren's relationships with maternal and paternal grandmothers and grandfathers. *Journal of Adolescence, 14,* 373–387.

Crimmins, E. M., Hayward, M. D., & Saito, Y. (1994). Changing mortality and morbidity rates and the health status and life expectancy of the older population. *Demography, 31,* 159–175.

Crispell, D. (1993). Grandparents galore. *American Demographics, 15,* 63.

Crites, M. S. (1989). Child development & intergenerational programming. *Journal of Children in Contemporary Society, 20,* 33–43.

Crittenden, P. M. (1985). Social networks, quality of childrearing, and child development. *Child Development, 56,* 1299–1313.

Crosby-Barnett, M., & Lewis, E. A. (1993). Functioning to address the challenges of European-American postdivorce families. *Family Relations, 42,* 243–248.

Cunningham-Burley, S. (1984a). On telling the news: Grandparenthood as an announceable event. *International Journal of Sociology and Social Policy, 4,* 52–69.

Cunningham-Burley, S. (1984b). We don't talk about it: Issues of gender and methods in portrayals of grandfatherhood. *Sociology, 18*, 325–328.

Cunningham-Burley, S. (1985). Constructing grandparenthood: Anticipating appropriate action. *Sociology, 19*, 421–436.

Cunningham-Burley, S. (1986a). Becoming a grandparent. *Ageing and Society, 6*, 453–470.

Cunningham-Burley, S. (1986b). Becoming a grandparent. *New Society, 75*, 229–230.

Czapansky, K. (1994). Grandparents, parents and grandchildren: Actualizing interdependency in law. *Connecticut Law Review, 26*, 1315–1395.

Davis, D. (1993). Urban households: Supplicants to a socialist state. In D. Davis & S. Harrell (Eds.), *Chinese families in the post-Mao era* (pp. 50–76). Berkeley: University of California Press.

Davis, O. (1940). The sociology of parent-child conflict. *American Sociological Review, 5*, 523–535.

DeFrain, J. D., Jakub, D. K., & Mendoza, B. L. (1991–92). The psychological effects of sudden infant death on grandmothers and grandfathers. *Omega: Journal of Death and Dying, 24*, 165–182.

DeFrain, J. D., LeMasters, E. E., & Schroff, J. A. (1991). Environment and fatherhood: Rural and urban influences. In F. W. Bozett & S. M. H. Hanson (Eds.), *Fatherhood and families in cultural context* (pp. 162–186). New York: Springer.

DeGenova, M. K. (1991). Elderly life review therapy: A Bowen approach. *The American Journal of Family Therapy, 19*(2), 160–166.

Dellman-Jenkins, M., Papalia, D., & Lopez, M. (1987). Teenagers' reported interaction with grandparents: Exploring the extent of alienation. *Lifestyles: A Journal of Changing Patterns, 8*, 35–46.

Demkovich, L. (1988). Staying in touch: Grandparent groups push for greater access to grandchildren. *Fathers' Journal, August*, 4.

Denham, T. E., & Smith, C. W. (1989). The influence of grandparents on grandchildren: A review of the literature and resources. *Family Relations, 38*, 345–350.

Derdyn, A. F. (1985). Grandparent visitation rights: Rendering family dissension more pronounced? *American Journal of Orthopsychiatry, 55*, 277–287.

Detzner, D. F. (1996). No place without a home: Southeast Asian grandparents in refugee families. *Generations, 20*, 45–48.

Deutsch, M. (1975). Equity, equality, and need: What determines which value will be used as the basis of distributive justice? *Journal of Social Issues, 31*, 137–149.

De Vos, S., & Lee, Y. (1993). Changes in extended family living among elderly people in South Korea, 1970–1980. *Economic Development and Cultural Change, 41*, 377–393.

Dilworth-Anderson, P. (1992). Extended kin networks in black families. *Generations, 16*, 29–32.

Dilworth-Anderson, P. (1994). The importance of grandparents in extended kin caregiving to black children with sickle cell disease. *Journal of Health and Social Policy, 5*, 185–202.

Doka, K. J., & Mertz, M. E. (1988). The meaning and significance of great-grandparenthood. *The Gerontologist, 28*, 192–197.

Donner, W. (1987). Compassion, kinship and fosterage: Contexts for the care of the childless elderly in a Polynesian community. *Journal of Cross-Cultural Gerontology, 2*(1), 43–59.

Dornbusch, S. M., Carlsmith, J. M., Bushwall, S. J., Ritter, A. I., Leiderman, H., Hastorf, A. H., & Gross, R. T. (1985). Single parents, extended households, and the control of adolescents. *Child Development, 56,* 326–341.

Dowd, J. J., & Bengtson, V. L. (1978). Aging in minority populations: An examination of the double jeopardy hypothesis. *Journal of Gerontology, 33,* 427–36.

Dowdell, E. B. (1995). Caregiver burden: Grandparents raising their high risk children. *Journal of Psychosocial Nursing, 33,* 27–30.

Draper, T. W., & Marcos, A. C. (Eds.). (1990). *Family variables: Conceptualization, measurement and use.* Newbury Park, CA: Sage.

Dressel, P. (1996). Grandparenting at century's end: An introduction to the issue. *Generations, 20,* 5–6.

Dressel, P. L., & Barnhill, S. K. (1994). Reframing gerontological thought and practice: The case of grandmothers with daughters in prison. *The Gerontologist, 34,* 685–691.

Drucker-Brown, S. (1982). Joking at death: The Mamprusi grandparent-grandchild joking relationship. *Man* (N.S.) 17, 714–727.

Du Bois, W. E. B. (1899). *The Philadelphia negro: A social study.* Philadelphia: University of Pennsylvania Press.

Du Bois, W. E. B. (1908). *The Negro American family.* Atlanta: Atlanta University Press.

Duffy, M. (1981). Divorce and the dynamics of the family kinship system. *Journal of Divorce, 5,* 3.

Duffy, M. (1986). The techniques & contexts of multi-generational therapy. *Clinical Gerontologist, 5,* 347–362.

Duncan, G. J., & Smith, K. R. (1989). The rising affluence of the elderly: How far, how fair, and how frail? *Annual Review of Sociology, 15,* 261–289.

Duran-Aydintug, C. (1991). Relationships with former in-laws: Normative guidelines and actual behavior. *Journal of Divorce and Remarriage, 19,* 69–82.

Durkheim, E. (1993). *The division of labor in society.* New York: Free Press.

Eggebeen, D. J. (1992a). Family structure and intergenerational exchanges. *Research on Aging, 14,* 427–447.

Eggebeen, D. J. (1992b). From generation unto generation: Parent-child support in aging American families. *Generations, 16,* 45–49.

Ehrle, G. M., & Day, H. D. (1994). Adjustment and family functioning of grandmothers rearing their grandchildren. *Contemporary Family Therapy, 16*(1) 67–82.

Eisenberg, A. R. (1988). Grandchildren's perspectives on relationships with grandparents: The influence of gender across generations. *Sex Roles, 19,* 205–217.

Ekeh, P. P. (1974). *Social exchange theory: The two traditions.* Cambridge, MA: Harvard University Press.

Elder, G. H. (1974). *Children of the Great Depression: Social change in life experience.* Chicago: University of Chicago Press.

Elder, G. H. (1975). Age differentiation and the life course. *Annual Review of Sociology, 1,* 165–190.

Elder, G. H. (1978a). Approaches to social change and the family. *American Journal of Sociology, 84,* 1–37.

Elder, G. H. (1978b). Family history and the life course. In T. Hareven (Ed.), *Transitions* (pp. 17–64). New York: Academic Press.

Elder, G. H. (1984). Families, kin, and the life course: A sociological perspective. In R.

Parke (Ed.), *Advances in child development research: The family* (pp. 80–136). Chicago: University of Chicago Press.

Elder, G. H. (1985). Household, kinship and the life course: Perspectives on black families and children. In M. Spencer, G. Brookins, & W. Allen (Eds.), *Beginnings: The social and affective development of black children* (pp. 29–43). Hillsdale, NJ: Erlbaum.

Elder, G. H. (1986). Military times and turning points in men's lives. *Developmental Psychology, 22*, 233–245.

Elder, G. H. (1991). Family transitions, cycles, and social change. In P. A. Cowan & E. M. Hetherington (Eds.), *Family Transitions* (pp. 31–57). Hillsdale, NJ: Erlbaum.

Elder, G. H. (1994). Time, human aging, and social change: Perspectives on the life course. *Social Psychology Quarterly, 57*, 4–15.

Elder, G. H. (1995). The life course paradigm: Social change and individual development. In P. Moen, G. H. Elder, Jr., & K. Luscher (Eds.), *Examining lives in context: Perspectives on the ecology of human development* (pp. 101–139). Washington, DC: American Psychological Association.

Elder, G. H. (forthcoming). The life course and human development. In R. M. Lerner (Ed.), *Handbook of child psychology, Vol. 1: Theory.* New York: Wiley.

Elder, G. H., Caspi, A., & Downey, G. (1986). Problem behavior and family relationships: Life course and intergenerational themes. In A. B. Sorenson, F. E. Weinert, and L. R. Sherrod (Eds.), *Human development and the life course: Multidisciplinary perspectives* (pp. 293–342). Hillsdale, NJ: Erlbaum.

Elder, G. H., & Conger, R. D. (forthcoming). *Leaving the land: Rural youth at century's end.* Chicago: University of Chicago Press.

Elder, G. H. & King, V. (forthcoming). Wisdom of the ages. Chapter 6 in G. H. Elder, Jr., & R. D. Conger (Eds.), *Leaving the land: Rural youth at century's end.* Chicago: University of Chicago Press.

Elder, G. H., King, V., & Conger, R. D. (1996). Intergenerational continuity and change in rural lives: Historical and developmental insights. *International Journal of Behavioral Development, 19*(2), 433–455.

Elder, G. H., Rudkin, L., & Conger, R. D. (1994). Intergenerational continuity and change in rural America. In K. W. Schaie, V. Bengtson, & L. Burton (Eds.), *Societal impact on aging: Intergenerational perspectives.* New York: Springer.

Emerson, R. (1962). Power and dependency. *American Sociological Review, 27*, 31–40.

Emick, M., & Hayslip, B. (1996). Custodial grandparenting: New roles for middle aged and older adults. *International Journal of Aging and Human Development, 43*, 135–154.

Erikson, E. H. (1950). *Childhood and society.* New York: Norton.

Erikson, E. H. (1963). *Childhood and society* (2nd ed.). New York: Norton.

Erikson, E. H., Erikson, J. M., & Kivnick, H. Q. (1986). *Vital involvement on old age.* New York: Norton.

Erlanger, M. A. (1997). Changing roles and life-cycle transitions. In T. D. Hargrave & S. M. Hanna (Eds.), *The aging family* (pp. 163–177). New York: Brunner/Mazel.

Everett, C. A., Russell, C. S., & Keller, J. (1992). *Family therapy glossary* (pp. 1–40). Washington, DC: The American Association for Marriage and Family Therapy.

Facio, E. (1996). *Understanding older Chicanas.* Thousand Oaks, CA: Sage.

Falbo, T. (1991). The impact of grandparents on children's outcomes in China. *Marriage & Family Review, 16*, 369–376.

Farkas, J., & Hogan, D. (1994). The demography of changing intergenerational relationships. In V. L. Bengtson, K. W. Schaie, & L. M. Burton (Eds.), *Adult intergenerational relations: Effects of social change* (pp. 1–29). New York: Springer.

Farley, R., & Allen, W. (1987). *The color line and the quality of life in America.* New York: Russell Sage Foundation.

Feng, H-Y. (1967). *The Chinese kinship system.* Cambridge, MA: Harvard University Press.

Fernandez, P. S. (1988). Grandparent access: A model statute. *Yale Law & Policy Review, 6*, 109–136.

Field, D., & M. Minkler. (1988). Continuity and change in social support between young-old and old-old or very-old age. *Journal of Gerontology: Psychological Sciences, 43*, P100–P106.

Finch, J., & Mason, J. (1993). *Negotiating family responsibilities.* New York: Routledge, Chapman & Hall.

Fischer, C. S. (1982). *To dwell among friends: Personal networks in town and city.* Chicago: University of Chicago.

Fischer, C. S. (1984). *The urban experience* (2nd ed.). New York: Harcourt, Brace, Jovanovich.

Fischer, L. R. (1981). Transitions in the mother-daughter relationship. *Journal of Marriage and the Family, 43*, 613–622.

Fischer, L. R. (1983). Transition to grandmotherhood. *International Journal of Aging and Human Development, 16*, 67–78.

Fischer, L. R. (1988). The influence of kin on the transition to parenthood. *Marriage and Family Review, 12*, 201–219.

Fischer, L. R., & Silverman, J. (1982). *Grandmothering as a tenuous role relationship.* Paper presented at the annual meetings of the National Council on Family Relations, Portland, OR.

Flaherty, M. J. (1988). Seven caring functions of black grandmothers in adolescent mothering. *Maternal-Child Nursing Journal, 17*, 191–207.

Flaherty, M. J., Facteau, L., & Garver, P. (1987). Grandmother functions in multigenerational families: An exploratory study of black adolescent mothers and their infants. *Maternal-Child Nursing Journal, 16*, 61–73.

Folk, K. F. & Beller, A. H. (1993). Part-time work and child care choices for mothers of preschool children. *Journal of Marriage and the Family, 55*, 146–157.

Ford, T. R. (1978). Contemporary rural America: Persistence and change. In T. R. Ford (Ed.), *Rural U.S.A.: Persistence and change* (pp. 3–18). Ames: Iowa State University Press.

Foster, H. H., & Freed, D. J. (1984). The child's right to visit grandparents: An emerging question to visitation rights. *Trial, 20*, 39.

Framo, J. L. (1976) Family of origin as a therapeutic resource for adults in marital and family therapy: You can and should go home again. *Family Process, 15*, 193–210.

Framo, J. L. (1992). *Family-of-origin therapy: An intergenerational approach.* New York: Brunner/Mazel.

Franklin, J. H. (1948). *From slavery to freedom: A history of American negroes.* New York: Knopf.

Franks, L. J., Hughes, J. P., Phelps, L. H., & Williams, D. G. (1993). Intergenerational influences on Midwest college students by their grandparents and significant elders. *Educational Gerontology, 19*, 265–271.

Frazier, E. F. (1939). *The Negro family in the United States*. Chicago: University of Chicago Press.

Freedman, M. (1966). *Chinese lineage and society: Fukien and Kwangtung*. London: Athlone.

Freedman, R., Chang, M., & Sun, T. (1982). Household composition, extended kinship, and reproduction in Taiwan. *Population Studies, 36*, 395–411.

Fried, E. G., & Stern, K. (1948). The situation of the aged within the family. *American Journal of Orthopsychiatry, 18*, 31–54.

Fry, C. (1995). Kinship and individuation: Cross-cultural perspectives on intergenerational relations. In V. L. Bengtson & L. Burton (Eds.), *Adult intergenerational relations: Effects of social change* (pp. 126–156). New York: Springer.

Fry, C. L. (1986). Cognitive anthropology and age differentiation. In C. L. Fry & J. Keith (Eds.), *New methods for old age research*. South Hadley, MA: Bergin and Garvey.

Fu, V. R., Hinkle, D. E., & Hanna, M. K. (1986). A three-generational study of the development of individual dependency and family interdependence. *Genetic, Social and General Psychology Monographs, 112*, 155–172.

Fuller, A. M. (1984). Part-time farming: The enigmas and the realities. *Research in Rural Sociology and Development, 1*, 187–219.

Fuller-Thomson, E., Minkler, M., & Driver, D. (1997). A profile of grandparents raising grandchildren in the United States. *The Gerontologist, 37*, 406–411.

Furstenberg, F. F. (1976). Unplanned parenthood: The social consequences of teenage childbearing. New York: Free Press.

Furstenberg, F. F. (1980). Burdens and benefits: The impact of early childbearing on the family. *Journal of Social Issues, 36*, 64–87.

Furstenberg, F. F. (1981). Remarriage and intergenerational relations. In R. Fogel et al. (Eds.), *Aging: Stability and change in the family* (pp. 115–142). New York: Academic Press.

Furstenberg, F. F., Brooks-Gunn, J., & Chase-Lansdale, L. (1989). Teenage pregnancy and childbearing. *American Psychologist, 44*, 313–320.

Furstenberg, F. F., Brooks-Gunn, J., & Morgan, P. (1987). *Adolescent mothers in later life*. Cambridge, UK: Cambridge University Press.

Furstenberg, F. F., & Hughes, M. E. (1995). Social capital and successful development among at-risk youth. *Journal of Marriage and the Family, 57*, 580–592.

Furstenberg, F. F., Nord, C. W., Peterson, J. L., & Zill, N. (1983). The life course of children of divorce: Marital disruption and parental contact. *American Sociological Review, 48*, 656–668.

Furstenberg, F. F., & Spanier, G. (1984). *Recycling the family: Remarriage after divorce*. Beverly Hills, CA: Sage.

Galasso, P. J. (1994, April 29). Whose children are they anyway? *New York Law Journal, 211*, 1, 4.

Ganong, L. H., & Coleman, M. (1984). The effects of remarriage on children: A review of the empirical literature. *Family Relations, 33*, 389–406.

Garcia, J. M. (1993). *The Hispanic population in the United States: March 1992*. U.S. Bureau of the Census, Current Population Reports P20–465PV. Washington, DC: U.S. Government Printing Office.

Garcia, M. C. (1996). *Havana USA*. Berkeley: University of California Press.

Gelfand, D. E. (1994). *Aging and Ethnicity*. New York: Springer.

Generations United. (1993). *Generations United public policy agenda*. Washington, DC: Author.

Generations United. (1995). *Setting an agenda for an aging society*. Final Program, 6th National Conference. Washington, DC: Author.

Generations United. (1996). *Connecting communities*: Final Program, 7th National Conference. Washington, DC: Author.

George, J. (1987). Children and grandparents: The right to visit. *Legal Rights Journal, 8*, 2–8.

George, L. K. (1980). *Role transitions in later life*. Monterey, CA: Brooks/Cole.

George, L. K. (1993). Sociological perspectives on life transitions. *Annual Review of Sociology, 19*, 353–373.

George, L. K., & Gold, D. T. (1991). Life course perspectives on intergenerational and generational connections. *Marriage and Family Review, 16*, 67–88.

Giarrusso, R., Feng, D., Wang, Q., & Silverstein, M. (1996). Parenting and co-parenting of grandchildren: Effects on grandparents' well-being and family solidarity. *International Journal of Sociology and Social Policy, 16*, 124–154.

Giarrusso, R., Silverstein, M., & Bengtson, V. L. (1996). Family complexity and the grandparent role. *Generations, 21*, 17–23.

Giarrusso, R., Stallings, M., & Bengtson, V. L. (1995). The "intergenerational stake" hypothesis revisited: Parent-child differences in perceptions of relationships 20 years later. In V. L. Bengtson, K. W. Schaie, & L. M. Burton (Eds.), *Adult Intergenerational relations: Effects of societal change* (pp. 227–263). New York: Springer.

Gilligan, C. (1982). *In a different voice*. Cambridge, MA: Harvard University Press.

Gladstone, J. W. (1988). Perceived changes in grandmother-grandchild relations following a child's separation or divorce. *The Gerontologist, 28*, 66–72.

Gladstone, J. W. (1989). Grandmother-grandchild contact: The mediating influence of the middle generation following marriage breakdown and remarriage. *Canadian Journal on Aging, 8*, 355–365.

Gladstone, J. W. (1991). An analysis of changes in grandparent-grandchild visitation following an adult child's remarriage. *Canadian Journal on Aging, 10*(2), 113–126.

Glascock, A., & Feinman, S. (1981). Social asset or social burden: Treatment of the aged in non-industrial societies. In C. Fry (Ed.), *Dimensions: Aging, culture, and health* (pp. 13–31). New York: J. F. Bergin.

Glenn, N. D., & Hill, L., Jr. (1977). Rural-urban differences in attitudes and behavior in the United States. *Annals of the American Academy of Political and Social Science, 429*, 36–50.

Glick, P. C. (1989). Remarried families, stepfamilies, and stepchildren: A demographic profile. *Family Relations, 38*, 24–27.

Gold, S. J. (1993). Migration and family adjustment: Continuity and change among Vietnamese in the United States. In H. P. McAdoo (Ed.), *Family ethnicity: Strength in diversity* (pp. 300–314). Newbury Park, CA: Sage.

Goldberg, C. (1997). Hispanic households struggle as poorest of the poor in U.S. *New York Times* (January 20), A1, A12.

Goldscheider, F. K., & Goldscheider, C. (1989). Ethnicity and the new family economy.

In F. K. Goldscheider & C. Goldscheider (Eds.), *Ethnicity and the new family economy: Living arrangements and intergenerational financial flows* (pp. 185–197). Boulder, CO: Westview.

Goldstein, J., Freud, A., & Solnit, A. (1979). *Beyond the best interests of the child.* New York: Free Press.

Goldstein, S. E. (1982). Grandparents and their children. *Journal of the American Geriatrics Society, 30,* 150.

Goode, W. (1956). *Women in divorce.* New York: Free Press.

Goode, W. J. (1963). *World revolution and family patterns.* London: Free Press.

Gould, R. (1978). *Transformations.* New York: Simon & Schuster.

Gratton, B. (1987). Familism among black and Mexican-American elderly: Myth or reality? *Journal of Aging Studies, 1,* 19–32.

Gratton, B., & Haber, C. (1996). Three phases in the history of American grandparents: Authority, burden, companion. *Generations, 20,* 7–12.

Gravenish, B. A., & Thomson, E. (1995). Marital disruptions and grandparent relationships. *NSFH Working Paper No. 74.* Madison: University of Wisconsin.

Grebler, L., Moore, J., & Guzman, R., (1970). *The Mexican American people: The nation's second largest minority.* New York Free Press.

Greenberg, S. J., Becker, M., & Dessonville-Hill, C. (1988). Aging parents as family resources. *The Gerontologist, 28,* 786–791.

Greene, C. L. (1994). Grandparents' visitation rights: Is the tide turning? *Journal of the Academy of Matrimonial Lawyers, 12,* 51–74.

Greene, R. R., & Polivka, J. S. (1985). The meaning of grandparents' day cards: An analysis of the intergenerational network. *Family Relations, 34,* 221–228.

Greenfield, L. A., & Minor-Harper, S. (1991). *Women in prison* (BJS Publication No. 91–405). Rockville, MD: U.S. Department of Justice.

Gutman, H. G. (1976). *The black family in slavery and freedom: 1750–1925.* New York: Vintage Press, Random House.

Gutmann, D. L. (1975). Parenthood: A key to the comparative study of the life circle. In N. Datan & L. H. Ginsberg (Eds.), *Life-span developmental psychology: Normative life crises* (pp. 167–184) New York: Academic Press.

Gutmann, D. L. (1977). The cross-cultural perspective: Notes toward a comparative psychology of aging. In J. E. Birren & K. W. Schaie (Eds.), *Handbook of the psychology of aging* (pp. 302–327). New York: Van Nostrand Reinhold.

Guttman, D. L. (1985). Deculturation and the American grandparent. In V. L. Bengtson & J. F. Robertson (Eds.), *Grandparenthood* (pp. 173–181). Beverly Hills, CA: Sage.

Gwaltney, J. L. (1980). *Drylongso: A self-portrait of black America.* New York: Random House.

Haber, C. (1983). *Beyond sixty-five: The dilemma of old age in America's past.* Cambridge, MA: Cambridge University Press.

Haber, C., & Gratton, B. (1994). *Old age and the search for security: An American social history.* Bloomington, IN: Indiana University Press.

Haber, E. A., & Short-DeGraff, M. A. (1990). Intergenerational programming for an increasingly age-segregated society. *Activities, Adaptation & Aging, 14,* 35–49.

Hader, M. (1965). The importance of grandparents in family life. *Family Process, 4,* 228–240.

Hagestad, G. O. (1978). *Patterns of communication and influence between grandparents and grandchildren in a changing society.* Paper presented at the World Congress of Sociology, Sweden.

Hagestad, G. O. (1981). Problems and promises in the social psychology of intergenerational relations. In R. W. Fogel, E. Hatfield, S. Kiesler, & E. Shanas (Eds.), *Aging, stability and change in the family.* New York: Academic Press.

Hagestad, G. O. (1982). Parent and child: Generations in the family. In T. M. Field, A. Huston, H. C. Quay, L. Troll, & G. E. Finley (Eds.), *Review of human development* (pp. 485–498). New York: Wiley.

Hagestad, G. O. (1985). Continuity and connectedness. In V. L. Bengtson & J. F. Robertson (Eds.), *Grandparenthood* (pp. 31–48). Beverly Hills, CA: Sage.

Hagestad, G. O. (1986). The family: Women and grandparents as "kinkeepers." In A. Pifer & L. Bronte (Eds.), *Our aging society: Paradox and promise.* New York: Norton.

Hagestad, G. O. (1987). Able elderly in the family context: changes, chances, and challenges. *The Gerontologist, 27,* 417–422.

Hagestad, G. O. (1988). Demographic change and the life course: Some emerging trends in the family realm. *Family Relations, 37,* 405–410.

Hagestad, G. O. (1990). Social perspectives on the life course. In R. Binstock & L. George (Eds.), *Handbook of aging and the social sciences* (pp. 151–168). New York: Academic Press.

Hagestad, G. O., & Burton, L. M. (1986). Grandparenthood, life context, and family development. Special issue: Developmental tasks in later life. *American Behavioral Scientist, 29,* 471–484.

Hagestad, G. O., & Lang, M. (1986). The transition to grandparenthood: Unexplored issues. *Journal of Family Issues, 7,* 115–130.

Hagestad, G., & Neugarten, B. (1985). Age and life course. In R. Binkston & E. Shanas (Eds.), *Handbook of aging and the social sciences* (pp. 35–61). New York: Van Nostrand Reinhold.

Hagestad, G. O., & Smyer, M. A. (1982). Dissolving long-term relationships: Patterns of divorcing in middle age. In S. Duck (Ed.), *Personal relationships, Vol. 4: Dissolving personal relationships* (pp. 155–196). New York: Academic Press.

Hagestad, G. O., Smyer, M. A., & Stierman, K. (1984). The impact of divorce in middle age. In R. S. Cohen and S. H. Weissman (Eds.), *Parenthood: A psychodynamic perspective* (pp. 247–262). New York: Guilford Press.

Haley, J. (1976). *Problem-solving therapy.* San Francisco: Jossey-Bass.

Hall, E. J., & Cummings, E. M. (1997). The effects of marital and parent-child conflicts on other family members: Grandmothers and grown children. *Family Relations, 46,* 135–143.

Halle, E., Schmidt, C. W., & Meyer, J. K. (1980). The role of grandmothers in transsexualism. *The American Journal of Psychiatry, 137,* 497.

Halperin, S. M. (1989). A neglected triangle: Grandmother, mother, and daughter. *Contemporary Family Therapy, 11,* 151–168.

Hansen, L. B., & Jacob, E. (1992). Intergenerational support during the transition to parenthood: Issues for new parents and grandparents. *Families in Society: The Journal of Contemporary Human Services, 73,* 471–479.

Hansson, R. O., & Carpenter, B. N. (1994). *Relationships in old age: Coping with the challenge of transitions.* New York: Guilford Press.

Haralambie, A. M. (1991). Grandparents have rights, too: Custody leaps across new legal borders. *The Compleat Lawyer, 8*(30), 46–48.

Hareven, T. K. (1977). Family time and historical time. *Daedalus, 107*, 57–70.

Hareven, T. K. (1994). Family change and historical change. In M. W. Riley, R. L. Kahn, & A. Foner (Eds.), *Age and structural lag* (pp. 130–150). New York: Wiley.

Hargrave, T. (1994). Using video life reviews with older adults. *Journal of Family Therapy, 16*, 259–268.

Hargrave, T., & Anderson, W. T. (1992). *Finishing well: Aging and reparation in the intergenerational family.* New York, NY: Brunner/Mazel.

Harrell, S. (1982). *Ploughshare village: culture and context in Taiwan.* Seattle: University of Washington Press.

Harrigan, M. P. (1992). Advantages and disadvantages of multigenerational family households: Views of three generations. *The Journal of Applied Gerontology, 11*, 457–474.

Hartfield, B. W. (1996). Legal recognition of the value of intergenerational nurturance: Grandparent visitation statutes in the nineties. *Generations, 20*, 53–56.

Hartshorne, T. S., & Manaster, G. J. (1982). The relationship with grandparents: Contact, importance, role conception. *International Journal of Aging and Human Development, 15*, 233–245.

Hays, J. G., Fillenbaum, G. C., Gold, D. T., Shanley, M. C., & Blazer, D. G. (1995). Black-white and urban-rural differences in stability of household composition among elderly persons. *Journal of Gerontology, 50B*, S301–S312.

Hayslip, B. et al. (forthcoming). Custodial grandparenting and grandchildren with problems: Their impact on role satisfaction and role meaning. *Journal of Gerontology: Social Sciences.*

Heider, F. (1958). *The psychology of interpersonal relations.* New York: Wiley.

Hendricks, Jon. (1995). *The Meaning of Reminiscence and Live Review.* Amityville, NY: Baywood.

Henry, C. S., Ceglian, C. P., & Matthews, D. W. (1992). The role behaviors, role meanings, and grandmothering styles of grandmothers and stepgrandmothers: Perceptions of the middle generation. *Journal of Divorce and Remarriage, 17*, 1–22.

Henry, C. S., Ceglian, C. P., & Ostrander, D. L. (1993). The transition to stepgrandparenthood. *Journal of Divorce and Remarriage, 19*, 25–44.

Hepworth, M. (1995). Where do grannies come from? *Generations Review 5*, 2–4.

Hernandez, D. J., & Myer, D. E. (1993). *America's children: Resources from family, government, and the economy.* New York: Russell Sage Foundation.

Hernandez, G. G. (1992). The family and its aged members: The Cuban experience. *Clinical Gerontologist, 11*, 45–57.

Hess, B. B., & Waring, J. M. (1978). Parent and child in later life: Rethinking the relationship. In R. Lerner & G. B. Spanier (Eds.), *Child influences on marital and family interaction: A life-span perspective* (pp. 241–273). New York: Academic Press.

Hetherington, E. M. (1989). Coping with family transitions: Winners, losers, and survivors. *Child Development, 60*, 1–14.

Hetherington, E. M., Cox, M., & Cox, R. (1982). Effects of divorce on parents and children. In M. Lamb (Ed.), *Nontraditional Families: Parenting and child development* (pp. 233–288). Hillsdale, NJ: Erlbaum.

Hetherington, E. M., Cox, M., & Cox, R. (1985). Long-term effects of divorce and remarriage on the adjustment of children. *Journal of American Academy of Psychiatry, 24*, 518–530.

Hill, R., Foote, N., Aldous, J., Carlson, R., & MacDonald, R. (1970). *Family development in three generations.* Cambridge, MA: Schenkman.

Hill, R., & Klein, D. (1973). Toward a research agenda and theoretical synthesis. In E. B. Sheldon (Ed.), *Family economic behavior* (pp. 371–404). Philadelphia: Lippincott.

Hill-Lubin, M. (1991). The African-American grandmother in autobiographical works by Frederick Douglass, Langston Hughes, & Maya Angelou. *International Journal of Aging & Human Development, 33*, 173–185.

Hintz, P. A. (1994). Grandparents' visitation rights following adoption: Expanding traditional boundaries in Wisconsin. *Wisconsin Law Review, 30*, 483–510.

Hirshorn, B. A., & Van Meter, M. J. (1996). *Final report to the W. K. Kellog Foundation, year I. Strengthening parenting across generations: A self management learning program for grandparents raising grandchildren.* Detroit: Wayne State University.

Hochschild, A. R. (1976). Disengagement theory: A logical, empirical, and phenomenological critique. In J. F. Gubrium (Ed.), *Time, roles, and self in old age* (pp. 53–87). New York: Human Sciences Press.

Hodgson, L. G. (1987). The graying grandchild: Some personal observations. *Perspective on Aging, 16* 20–23.

Hodgson, L. G. (1991). *Adult grandchildren and their grandparents: Dimensions of intergenerational support.* Paper presented at the Population Association of America annual meeting in Washington, DC.

Hodgson, L. G. (1992). Adult grandchildren and their grandparents: The enduring bond. *International Journal of Aging and Human Development, 34*, 209–225.

Hodgson, L. G. (1995). Grandchildren and their grandparents: The enduring bond. In J. Hendricks (Ed.), *The ties of later life* (2nd ed.) (pp. 155–170). Amityville, NY: Baywood.

Hodgson, L. G., Falcigno, P. A., Ke, H., & Huang, J. (1994). Grandparent/adult grandchild relationships: A comparison between the U.S. and China. Paper presented at the annual meeting of the Gerontological Society of America, Atlanta, GA.

Hofferth, I. L. (1984). Kin networks, race, and family structure. *Journal of Marriage and the Family, 46*, 791–806.

Hofferth, S. (1985). Children's life course: Family structure and living arrangements in cohort perspective. In G. H. Elder (Ed.), *Life course dynamics: Trajectories and transitions* (pp. 57–112). Ithaca, NY: Cornell University Press.

Hofferth, S. L., Brayfield A., Deich, S., & Holcomb, P. (1991). *National Child Care Survey 1990.* Urban Institute Report, 91–95. Washington, DC: Urban Institute Press.

Hoffman, E. (1979). Young adults' relations with their grandparents: An exploratory study. *International Journal of Aging and Human Development, 10*, 299–310.

Hogan, D. P., Eggebeen, D. J., & Clogg, C. C. (1993). The structure of intergenerational exchanges in American families. *American Journal of Sociology, 98*, 1428–1458.

Hogan, D. P., Hao, L.-X., & Parish, W. L. (1990). Race, kin networks, and assistance to mother-headed families. *Social Forces, 68*, 797–812.

Holman, T. B., & Burr, W. R. (1980). Beyond the beyond: The growth of family theories in the 1970's. *Journal of Marriage and the Family, 42*, 729–741.

Holmes, E. R., & Holmes, L. D. (1995). *Other cultures, elder years* (2nd ed.). Thousand Oaks, CA: Sage.

Holz-Eakin, D., & Smeeding, T. M. (1994). Income wealth and intergenerational economic relations of the aged. In L. G. Martin & S. H. Preston (Eds.), *Demography of aging* (pp. 102–145). Washington DC: National Academy Press.

Hooyman, R. (1995). Feminist perspectives on family care: Policies for gender justice. Thousand Oaks, CA: Sage.

House, J. S., Umberson, D., & Landis, K. R. (1988). Structures and processes of social support. *Annual Review of Sociology, 14*, 293–318.

Huling, W. E. (1978). Evolving family roles for black elderly. *Aging, 287*, 21–27.

Hummert, M. 1991. Physiognomic associations with stereotypes of the elderly. Paper presented at meetings of Gerontological Society of America, San Francisco.

Hunter, A. G. (1993). Making a way: Economic strategies of southern urban African-American families, 1900 and 1936. *Journal of Family History, 18*, 231–248.

Hunter, A. G. (1997). Counting on grandmothers: Black mothers' and fathers' reliance on grandmothers for parenting support. *Journal of Family Issues, 18*(3), 251–269.

Hunter, A. G., & Ensminger, M. E. (1992). Diversity and fluidity in children's living arrangements: Family transitions in an urban Afro-American community. *Journal of Marriage and the Family, 54*, 418–426.

Hurd, M. (1990). Research on the aged: Economic status, retirement and consumption and savings. *Journal of Economic Literature, 28*, 565–637.

Hurme, H. (1991). Dimensions of the grandparent role in Finland. In P. K. Smith (Ed.), *The psychology of grandparenthood: An international perspective* (pp. 19–31). New York: Routledge.

Huston, T. L. (1983). Power. In H. H. Kelley, E. Berscheid, A. Christensen, J. H. Harvey, T. L. Huston, G. Levinger, E. McClintock, L. A. Peplau, & D. R. Peterson (Eds.), *Close relationships* (pp. 169–219). New York: W. H. Freeman.

Huston, T. L., & Robins, E. (1982). Conceptual and methodological issues in studying close relationships. *Journal of Marriage and the Family, 44*, 901–926.

Ikels, C. (1996). *The return of the god of wealth: The transition to a market economy in urban China.* Stanford: Stanford University Press.

Ingersoll, D. B., & Neal, M. B. (1991). Grandparents in family therapy: A clinical research study. *Family Relations, 40*, 264–271.

Ingersoll-Dayton, B., Arndt, B., & Stevens, D. (1988). Involving grandparents in family therapy. *Social Casework. The Journal of Contemporary Social Work, 69*, 280–289.

Ishii-Kuntz, M. (Forthcoming). Japanese American families. In M. K. DeGenova (Ed.), *Families in cultural perspective.* Palo Alto, CA: Mayfield.

Jackson, J. J. (1971). Aged blacks: A potpourri in the direction of the reduction of inequities. *Phylon, 23*, 260–280.

Jackson, J. S. (1986). Black grandparents: Who needs them? In R. Staples (Ed.), *The black family: Essays and stories* (pp. 186–194). Belmont, CA: Wadsworth.

Jackson, J. S., Chatters, L. M., & Taylor, R. J. (Ed.). (1993). *Aging in black America.* Newbury Park, CA: Sage.

Jackson, J. S., & Hatchett, S. J. (1986). Intergenerational research: Methodological considerations. In N. Datan, A. L. Greene & H. W. Reese (Eds.), *Intergenerational relations* (pp. 51–75). Hillsdale, NJ: Erlbaum.

Jackson, J. S. Jayakody, R., & Antonucci, T. (1996). Exchanges within black American three-generation families: The family environment context model. In T. Hareven (Ed.), *Aging and generational relations over the life course* (pp. 351–381). New York: Walter de Gruyter.

James, J. (1984). Grandparents and the family script parade. *Transactional Analysis Journal, 14*, 18.

Janelli, L. M. (1988). Depictions of grandparents in children's literature. *Educational Gerontology, 14*, 193–202.

Jarrett, R. (1994). Living poor: Family life among single parent, African-American women. *Social Problems, 41*, 30–45.

Jaskowski, S. K., & Dellasega, C. (1993). Effects of divorce on the grandparent-grandchild relationship. *Issues in Comprehensive Pediatric Nursing, 16*, 125–133.

Jayakody, R., Chatters, L. M., & Taylor, R. J. (1993). Family support to single and married African American mothers: The provision of financial, emotional, and child care assistance. *Journal of Marriage and the Family, 55*, 261–276.

Jendrek, M. P. (1993). Grandparents who parent their grandchildren: Effects on lifestyle. *Journal of Marriage and the Family, 55*, 609–621.

Jendrek, M. P. (1994). Grandparents who parent their grandchildren: Circumstances and decisions. *The Gerontologist, 34*, 206–216.

John, R. (1988). The Native American family. In C. H. Mindel, R. W. Haberstein, & R. Wright, Jr. (Eds.), *Ethnic families in America: Patterns and variations* (pp. 325–366). New York: Elsevier.

Johnson, C. L. (1983a). A cultural analysis of the grandmother. *Research on Aging, 5*, 547–568.

Johnson, C. L. (1983b). Dyadic family relations and social support. *The Gerontologist, 23*, 377–383.

Johnson, C. L. (1985). Grandparenting options in divorcing families: An anthropological perspective. In V. L. Bengtson & J. F. Robertson (Eds.), *Grandparenthood* (pp. 81–96). Beverly Hills, CA: Sage.

Johnson, C. L. (1988a). Postdivorce reorganization between divorcing children and their parents. *Journal of Marriage and the Family, 50*, 221–231.

Johnson, C. L. (1988b). Socially-controlled civility: The functioning of rituals in the divorce process. *American Behavioral Scientist, 31*(6), 685–701.

Johnson, C. L. (1988c). Active and latent functions of grandparenting during the divorce process. *The Gerontologist, 28*, 185–191.

Johnson, C. L. (1988d). *Ex familia: Grandparents, parents, and children adjust to divorce*. New Brunswick, NJ: Rutgers University Press.

Johnson, C. L. (1989a). Definitions of family and kinship with divorce and remarriage. In I. Rauch & G. Carr (Eds.), *The Semiotic Bridge* (pp. 241–259). Berlin: Mouton de Guyter.

Johnson, C. L. (1989b). In-law relationships in the American kinship system: The impact of divorce and remarriage. *American Ethnologist, 16*, 87–99.

Johnson, C. L. (1992). Divorced and reconstituted families: Effects on the older generation. *Generations, 16*, 17–20.

Johnson, C. L. (1994). Differential expectations and realities: Race, socioeconomic status and health of the oldest-old. *Journal of Aging and Human Development, 38*(1), 13–27.

Johnson, C. L., & Barer, B. M. (1987). Marital instability and the changing kinship networks of grandparents. *The Gerontologist, 27*, 330–335.

Johnson, C. L., Klee, L., & Schmidt, C. (1988). Conceptions of parentage and kinship among children of divorce. *American Anthropologist, 90*, 136–144.

Johnson, E. S. (1981). Older mothers' perceptions of their child's divorce. *The Gerontologist, 21*, 395–401.

Johnson, E. S., & Vinick, B. H. (1982). Support of the parent when an adult son or daughter divorces. *Journal of Divorce, 5*, 69–77.

Johnson, W. (1995a). *Socially contextualized paternal identity: The construction of possible selves among urban poor African American adolescent males.* Paper presented at the Manpower Demonstration Research Corp., New York, NY.

Johnson, W. (1995b). *Perceptions and patterns of parental role functioning among urban, lower socio-economic status adolescent African American males.* Unpublished manuscript, University of Michigan.

Jones, F. C. (1973). The lofty role of the black grandmother. *Crisis, 80*, 19–21.

Joslin, D., & Brouard, A. (1995). The prevalence of grandmothers as primary caregivers in a poor pediatric population. *Journal of Community Health, (20)5*, 383–401.

Kahana, B., & Kahana, E. (1970). Grandparenthhood from the perspective of the developing grandchild. *Developmental Psychology, 3*, 98–105.

Kahana, E., & Kahana, B. (1971). Theoretical and research perspectives on grandparenthood. *Aging and Human Development, 2*, 261–268.

Kalish, R. A., & Visher, E. (1982). Grandparents of divorce and remarriage. *Journal of Divorce, 5*, 127–140.

Kalter, J. (1993). It's gran and poppa—instead of mommy and daddy. *New Choices for Retirement Living, 33*, 26–28.

Kamo, Y. (1990). Husbands & wives living in nuclear & stem family households in Japan. *Sociological Perspectives, 33*, 397–417.

Kamo, Y. (1995a). Grandparenthood. In D. Levinson (Ed.), *Encyclopedia of marriage and the family* (pp. 432–436). New York: Macmillan.

Kamo, Y. (1995b). *Racial differences in extended family households: A comprehensive approach.* Paper presented at the 90th Annual Meeting of the American Sociological Association. Washington, DC, August 1995.

Kamo, Y., & Zhou, M. (1994). Living arrangements of elderly Chinese and Japanese in the United States. *Journal of Marriage and the Family, 56*, 544–558.

Kantor, D., & Lehr, W. (1975) *Inside the family.* San Francisco: Jossey-Bass.

Kardiner, A., & Oversey, L. (1951). *The mark of oppression: A psychosocial study of the American Negro.* New York: Norton.

Karp, N. (1993). Kinship care: The legal problems of grandparents and other relative care takers. *Clearing House Review, 27*, 585–587.

Karp, N. (1996). Legal problems of grandparents and other kinship caregivers. *Generations, 20*, 57–63.

Kaslow, F. W., & Hyatt, R. (1981). Divorce: A potential growth experience for the extended family. *Journal of Divorce, 5*, 1159.

Kearl, M. C., & Hermes, M. P. (1984). Grandparents, grandchildren, and the Kondratieff: Thoughts on ''period effects'' in intergenerational analyses. *International Journal of Aging and Human Development, 19*, 257–265.

Keith, J., Fry, C., Glascock, A., Ikels, C., Dickerson-Putman, J., Harpending, H., & Draper, P. (1994). *The aging experience: Diversity and commonality across cultures.* Thousand Oaks, CA: Sage.

Kellam, S. G., Ensminger, M. E., & Turner, R. J. (1977). Family structure and the mental health of children: Concurrent and longitudinal community-wide studies. *Archives of General Psychiatry, 34,* 1012–1022.

Kennedy, G. E. (1990). College students' expectations of grandparent and grandchild behaviors. *The Gerontologist, 30,* 43–48.

Kennedy, G. E. (1992a). Quality in grandparent/grandchild relationships. *International Journal of Aging and Human Development, 35,* 83–98.

Kennedy, G. E. (1992b). Shared activities of grandparents and grandchildren. *Psychological Reports, 70,* 211–227.

Kennedy, G. E, & Kennedy, C. E. (1993). Grandparents: A special resource for children in stepfamilies. *Journal of Divorce and Remarriage, 19,* 45–68.

Kennedy, J. F., & Keeney, V. T. (1988). The extended family revisited: Grandparents rearing grandchildren. *Child Psychiatry and Human Development, 19,* 26–35.

Kilborn, P. T. (1996, August 23). With welfare overhaul now law, states grapple with the consequences. *New York Times,* p. A10.

Kim, K. C., Kim, S., & Hurh, W. M. (1991). Filial piety and intergenerational relationship in Korean immigrant families. *International Journal of Aging and Human Development, 33,* 233–245.

King, V., & Elder, G. H. (1995a). American children view their grandparents: Linked lives across three rural generations. *Journal of Marriage and the Family, 57,* 165–178.

King, V., & Elder, G. H. (1995b). *Grandparenthood as a social construction: Multiple perspectives.* Paper presented at the annual meeting of the Gerontological Society of America, Los Angeles, CA.

King, V., & Elder, G. H. (1997). The legacy of grandparenting: Childhood experiences with grandparents and current involvement with grandchildren. *Journal of Marriage and the Family, 59,* 848–859.

Kingson, E. R., Hirshorn, B. A., & Cornman, J. M. (1986). *Ties that bind: The independence of generations.* Washington, D.C.: Seven Locks.

Kitano, H. H. L., & Daniels, R. (1995). *Asian Americans: Emerging minorities* (2nd ed.). Englewood Cliffs, NJ: Prentice-Hall.

Kivett, V. R. (1985a). Consanguinity and kin level: Their relative importance to the helping network of older adults. *Journal of Gerontology, 40,* 228–234.

Kivett, V. R. (1985b). Grandfathers and grandchildren: Patterns of association, helping, and psychological closeness. *Family Relations, 34,* 565–571.

Kivett, V. R. (1991a). Centrality of the grandfather role among older rural black and white men. *Journal of Gerontology: Social Sciences, 46,* S250–S258.

Kivett, V. R. (1991b). The grandparent-grandchild connection. *Marriage and Family Review, 16,* 267–290.

Kivett, V. R. (1993). Racial comparisons of the grandmother role: Implications for strengthening the family support system of older black women. *Family Relations, 42,* 165–172.

Kivett, V. R. (1996). The saliency of the grandmother-granddaughter relationship: Predictors of association. *Journal of Women & Aging, 8,* 25–39.

Kivett, V. R., Dugan, E., & Moxley, S. C. (1994). Family supports and relationships of older urban and rural migrants in North Carolina. Final Report to the AARP–Andrus Foundation. Greensboro, NC: University of North Carolina at Greensboro.

Kivnick, H. Q. (1981). Grandparenthood and the mental health of grandparents. *Ageing and Society, 1,* 365–391.

Kivnick, H. Q. (1982). Grandparenthood: An overview of meaning and mental health. *The Gerontologist, 22,* 59–66.

Kivnick, H. Q. (1982/1980). *The meaning of grandparenthood.* Ann Arbor: University of Michigan.

Kivnick, H. Q. (1983). Dimensions of grandparenthood meaning: Deductive conceptualization and empirical derivation. *Journal of Personality and Social Psychology, 44,* 1056–1068.

Kivnick, H. Q. (1984). Grandparents and family relations. In W. H. Quinn & G. A. Hughston (Eds.), *Independent aging: Family and social systems perspectives* (pp. 35–57). Rockville, MD: Aspen Systems.

Kivnick, H. Q. (1985). Grandparenthood and mental health. In V. L. Bengtson & J. F. Robertson (Eds.), *Grandparenthood* (pp. 151–158). Beverly Hills, CA: Sage.

Kivnick, H. Q. (1986). Grandparenthood and a life cycle. *Journal of Geriatric Psychiatry, 19,* 39–55.

Kivnick, H. Q. (1988). Grandparenthood, life review, and psychosocial development. Special issue: Twenty-five years of the life review: Theoretical and practical considerations. *Journal of Gerontological Social Work, 12,* 63–81.

Knipscheer, C. P. M. (1988). Temporal embeddedness and aging within the multigenerational family: The case of grandparenting. In J. E. Birren & V. L. Bengtson (Eds.), *Emergent theories of aging* (pp. 426–446). New York: Springer.

Kobrin, F. E. (1981). Family extension and the elderly: Economic, demographic, and family cycle factors. *Journal of Gerontology, 36,* 370–377.

Kojima, H. (1989). Intergenerational household extension in Japan. In F. K. Goldscheider & C. Goldscheider (Eds.), *Ethnicity and the new family economy: Living arrangements and intergenerational financial flows* (pp. 163–184). Boulder, CO: Westview.

Koller, M. R. (1954). Studies of three-generation household. *Marriage and Family Living, 16,* 205–206.

Kornhaber, A. (1985). Grandparenthood and the "new social contract." In V. L. Bengtson & J. F. Robertson (Eds.), *Grandparenthood* (pp. 159–171). Beverly Hills, CA: Sage.

Kornhaber, A. (1986). Grandparenting: Normal and pathological—A preliminary communication from the grandparent study. *Journal of Geriatric Psychiatry, 19,* 19–37.

Kornhaber, A. (1996). *Contemporary grandparenting.* Thousand Oaks, CA: Sage.

Kornhaber, A., & Woodward, K. L. (1981). *Grandparents/grandchildren.* Garden City, NY: Anchor.

Kornhaber, A., & Woodward, K. (1985). *Grandparents/grandchildren: The vital connection.* New Brunswick, NJ: Transaction.

Krause, N., & Borawski-Clark, E. (1994). Clarifying the functions of social support in later life. *Research on Aging, 16,* 251–279.

Kronebusch, K., & Schlesinger, M. (1994). Intergenerational transfers. In V. L. Bengtson & R. A. Harootyan (Eds.), *Intergenerational linkages: Hidden connections in American society* (pp. 112–151). New York: Springer.

Kuehne, V. S. (1992). Older adults in intergenerational programs: What are their experiences really like? *Activities, Adaptation & Aging, 16,* 49–67.

La Gaipa, J. (1981). A systems approach to personal relationships. In S. Duck & R.

Gilmour (Eds.), *Personal Relationships*, Vol. 1 (pp. 67–90). New York: Academic Press.

Langer, N. (1990). Grandparents & adult grandchildren: What do they do for one another? *International Journal of Aging and Human Development, 31*, 101–110.

LaRossa, R., & Reitzes, D. C. (1993). Symbolic interactionism and family studies. In P. G. Boss, W. J. Doherty, R. LaRossa, W. R. Schumm, & S. K. Steinmetz (Eds.), *Sourcebook of family theories and methods: A contextual approach* (pp. 135–162). New York: Plenum.

Larsen, A., & Olson, D. H. (1990). Capturing the complexity of family systems: Integrating family theory, family scores, and family analysis. In T. W. Draper & A. C. Marcos (Eds.), *Family variables: Conceptualization, measurement, and use* (pp. 19–47). Newbury Park, CA: Sage.

Larson, O. F. (1978). Values and beliefs of rural people. In T. R. Ford (Ed.), *Rural USA: Persistence and change* (pp. 91–112). Ames: Iowa State University Press.

Larzelere, R. E., & Klein, D. M. (1987). Methodology. In M. B. Sussman and S. K. Steinmetz (Eds.), *Handbook of marriage and the family* (pp. 125–155). New York: Plenum.

Lasch, C. (1978). *The culture of narcissism*. New York: Norton.

Lasslett, B. (1978). Family members, past and present. *Social Problems, 25*, 476–490.

Latimer, D. J. (1994). Involving grandparents & other older adults in the preschool classroom. *Dimensions of Early Childhood, 22*, 26–30.

Lawton, L., Silverstein, M., & Bengtson, V. (1994a). Affection, social contact, and geographic distance between adult children and their parents. *Journal of Marriage and the Family, 56*, 57–68.

Lawton, L., Silverstein, M., & Bengtson, V. L. (1994b). Solidarity between generations in families. In V. L. Bengtson & R. A. Harootyan (Eds.), *Intergenerational linkages: Hidden connections in American society* (pp. 19–42). New York: Springer.

Lee, G. R. (1992). Gender differences in family caregiving: A fact in search of a theory. In J. W. Dwyer & R. T. Coward (Eds.), *Gender, families, and elder care*. Newbury Park, CA: Sage.

Lee, G. R., & Cassidy, M. L. (1981). Kinship systems and extended family ties. In R. T. Coward & W. M. Smith, Jr. (Eds.), *The family in rural society* (pp. 57–71). Boulder, CO: Westview.

Lee, G. R., Coward, R. T., & Netzer, J. K. (1994). Residential differences in filial responsibility expectation among older persons. *Rural Sociology, 59*(1), 100–109.

Lee, G. R., Dwyer, J. M., & Coward, R. T. (1990). Residential location and proximity to children among impaired elderly parents. *Rural Sociology, 55*, 579–589.

Lee, G. R., & Lassey, M. L. (1982). The elderly. In D. A. Dillman & D. J. Hobbs (Eds.), *Rural society in the U.S.: Issues for the 1980s* (pp. 85–93). Boulder, CO: Westview.

Lee, G. R., Netzer, J. K., & Coward, R. T. (1994). Filial responsibility expectations and patterns of intergenerational assistance. *Journal of Marriage and the Family, 56*, 559–565.

Lee, G. R., & Whitbeck, L. B. (1987). Residential location and social relations among older persons. *Rural Sociology, 52*(1), 89–97.

Leek, M., & Smith, P. K. (1991). Cooperation and conflict in three-generation families. In P. K. Smith (Ed.), *The psychology of grandparenthood: An international perspective*. New York: Routledge.

Leik, R. K., Roberts, C. L., Caron, W. A., Mangen, D. J., & Leik, S. A (1990). Temporal mapping: A method for analyzing process. In T. W. Draper & A. C. Marcos (Eds.), *Family variables: Conceptualization, measurement, and use* (pp. 197–218). Newbury Park, CA: Sage.

Levin, J. S., Markides, K. S., & Ray, L. A. (1996). Religious attendance and psychological well-being in Mexican Americans: A panel analysis of three-generations data. *The Gerontologist, 36*, 454–463.

Levinson, D. J., Darrow, C. N., Klein, E. B., Levinson, M. H., & McKee, B. (1978). *The seasons of a man's life*. New York: Knopf.

Levitt, M. J., Guacci, N., & Weber, R. A. (1992). Intergenerational support, relationship quality, and well-being: A bicultural analysis. *Journal of Family Issues, 13*, 465–481.

Levitt, M. J., Weber, R. A., & Clark, M. C. (1986). Social network relationships as sources of maternal support and well-being. *Developmental Psychology, 22*, 310–316.

Lewis, O. (1958). *Village life in northern India: Studies in a Delhi village*. Urbana: University of Illinois Press.

Lichter, D. T., Johnston, G. M., & McLaughlin, D. K. (1994). Changing linkages between work and poverty in rural America. *Rural Sociology, 59*(3), 395–415.

Loevinger, J. (1976). *Conceptions and theories*. San Francisco: Jossey-Bass.

Logan, J., & Spitze, G. (1996). *Family ties: Enduring relations between parents and their grown children*. Philadelphia: Temple University Press.

Long, L. (1988). *Migration and residential mobility in the United States*. New York: Russell Sage Foundation.

Longino, C. F., & Earle, T. R. (1996). Who are the grandparents at the century's end? *Generations, 20*, 13–16.

Lopata, H. Z. (1973). *Widowhood in an American city*. Cambridge, MA: Schenckman.

Lowe, N., & Douglas, G. (1989). The grandparent-grandchild relationship in English law. In J. Eekelaar & D. Pearl (Eds.), *An aging world: Dilemmas and challenges for laws and social policy* (pp. 755–774). Oxford, UK: Clarendon.

Lowenthal, M. F., Thurnher, M., & Chiriboga, D. (1975). *Four stages of life: A comparative study of men and women facing transitions*. San Francisco: Jossey-Bass.

Lubben, J. E., & Becerra, R. M. (1987). Social support among black, Mexican, and Chinese elderly. In D. E. Gelfand & C. M. Barresi (Eds.), *Ethnic dimensions of aging* (pp. 130–144). New York: Springer.

Madan, T. (1989). *Family and kinship: A study of the Pandits of rural Kashmir* (2nd ed.). Delhi: Oxford University Press.

Madsen, W. (1964). *The Mexican-Americans of south Texas*. New York: Holt, Rinehart, & Winston.

Main, M., Kaplan, N., & Cassidy, J. (1985). Security in infancy, childhood, and adulthood: A move to the level of representation. In I. Bretherton & E. Waters (Eds.), *Growing points of attachment theory and research* (pp. 66–104). Chicago: University of Chicago Press.

Maldonado, D. (1978). On Chicano aged. *Social Work, 20*, 213–216.

Mancini, J. A., & Benson, M. J. (1989). Aging parents and adult children: New views on old relationships. In J. A. Mancini (Ed.), *Aging parents and adult children* (pp. 285–295). Lexington, MA: Lexington Books.

Mancini, J. A., & Blieszner, R. (1989). Aging parents and adult children: Research themes in intergenerational relations. *Journal of Marriage and the Family, 51*, 275–290.

Mangen, D. J. (1988). Measuring intergenerational family relations. In D. J. Mangen, V. L. Bengtson, and P. H. Landry, Jr. (Eds.), *Measurement of intergenerational relations* (pp. 31–53). Newbury Park, CA: Sage.

Mangen, D. J. (1995). Methods and analysis of family data In R. Blieszner & V. H. Bedford (Eds.), *Handbook of aging and the family* (pp. 148–177). Westport, CT: Greenwood.

Mangen, D. J., Bengtson, V. L., & Landry, P. H. (1988). *Measurement of intergenerational relations*. Beverly Hills: Sage.

Manthorpe, J., & Atherton, C. (1989). *Grandparent's rights*. Mitchom, England: Age Concern.

Manton, K. G., Corder, L. S., & Stallard, E. (1993). Estimates of change in chronic disability and institutional incidence and prevalence rates in the U.S. elderly population from the 1982, 1984, and 1989 National Long Term Care Survey. *Journal of Gerontology: Social Sciences, 48*, S153–S166.

Marin, B. V. (1989). Hispanic culture: Implications for AIDS prevention. In J. Boswell, R. Hexter, & J. Reinisch (Eds.), *Sexuality and disease: Metaphors, perceptions, and behavior in AIDS era*. New York: Elsevier.

Marin, B. V., & Triandis, H. C. (1985). Allocentrism as a cultural characteristic of Hispanics and Latin Americans. In R. Diaz-Guerrero (Ed.), *Cross-cultural and national studies on social psychology*. New York: Elsevier.

Markides, K. S., Boldt, J. S., & Ray, L. A. (1986). Sources of helping and intergenerational solidarity: A three-generations study of Mexican Americans. *Journal of Gerontology, 41*, 506–511.

Markides, K. S., & Krause, N. (1985). Intergenerational solidarity and psychological well-being among older Mexican Americans: A three-generation study. *Journal of Gerontology, 40*, 506–511.

Markides, K. S., Liang, J., & Jackson, J. S. (1990). Race, ethnicity, and aging: Conceptual and methodological issues. In R. H. Binstock & L. K. George (Eds.), *Handbook of aging and the social sciences* (3rd ed.) (pp. 112–129). San Diego: Academic Press.

Markides, K. S., & Martin, H. W. (1990). *Older Mexican Americans*. San Antonio: Tomas Rivera Center.

Markides, K. S., Martin, H. W., & Gomez, E. (1983). *Older Mexican Americans: A study in an urban barrio*. Austin: Center for Mexican American Studies, University of Texas at Austin.

Markides, K. S., & Mindel, C. H. (1987). *Aging & Ethnicity*. Newbury Park, CA: Sage.

Marsiglio, W. (1995). Fathers' diverse life course patterns and roles: Theory and social interventions. In W. Marsiglio (Ed.), *Fatherhood: Contemporary theory, research, and social policy*. Thousand Oaks, CA: Sage.

Martin, E., & Martin, J. M. (1978). *The black extended family*. Chicago: University of Chicago Press.

Martin, L. G. (1989). Living arrangement of the elderly in Fiji, Korea, Malaysia, and the Philippines. *Demography, 26*, 627–643.

Matthews, S. H. (1992). Placing filial behavior in the context of the family. In B. Bauer (Ed.), *Conceptual and methodological issues in family caregiving research. Pro-*

ceedings of the invitational conference on family caregiving research (pp. 55–62). Toronto: University of Toronto Press.

Matthews, S. H., & Rosner, T. T. (1988). Shared filial responsibility: The family as the primary caregiver. *Journal of Marriage and the Family, 50*, 185–195.

Matthews, S. H., & Sprey, J. (1984). The impact of divorce on grandparenthood: An exploratory study. *The Gerontologist, 24*, 41–47.

Matthews, S. H., & Sprey, J. (1985). Adolescents' relationships with grandparents: An empirical contribution to conceptual clarification. *Journal of Gerontology, 40*, 621–626.

Maxwell, R., & Silverman, P. (1970). Information and esteem: Cultural considerations in the treatment of the aged. *International Journal of Aging and Human Development, 1*, 361–392.

McBride, A. B. (1983). Differences in parents and their grown children's perceptions of parenting. *Developmental Psychology, 19*, 686.

McCready, W. (1985). Styles of grandparenting among white ethnics. In V. Bengtson & J. Robertson (Eds.), *Grandparenthood* (pp. 49–60). Beverly Hills, CA: Sage.

McCulloch, B. J. (1995). Aging and kinship in rural context. In R. Blieszner & V. H. Bedford (Eds.), *Handbook of aging and the family* (pp. 332–354). Westport, CT: Greenwood.

McDaniel, A. (1990). The power of culture: A review of the idea of Africa's influence on family structure in antebellum American. *Journal of Family History, 15*, 225–238.

McGreal, C. E. (1986). Grandparental role-meaning types: A critical evaluation. *Infant Mental Health Journal, 7*, 235–241.

McKeever, P. (1980). When Jason's grandpa died: The response of a toddler to the events surrounding the death of a grandparent. *Essence, 4*, 19–25.

McLanahan, S., & Bumpass, L. (1988). Intergenerational consequences of family disruption. *American Journal of Sociology, 94*, 130–152.

McPherson, B. D. (1983). *Aging as a social process.* Toronto: Butterworths.

Mead, G. H. (1934). *Mind, self, and society.* Chicago: University of Chicago Press.

Mead, M. (1974). Grandparents as educators. In H. J. Leichter (Ed.), *The family as educator* (pp. 66–75). New York: Teachers College Press.

Menaghan, E. G., & Godwin, D. D. (1993). Longitudinal research methods and family theories. In P. G. Boss, W. J. Doherty, R. LaRossa, W. R. Schumm, & S. K. Steinmetz (Eds.), *Sourcebook of family theories and methods* (pp. 259–274). New York: Plenum.

Miller, D. (1994). Influences on paternal involvement of African-American adolescent fathers. *Child and Adolescent Social Work, 11*, 363–378.

Miller, R. B. (1989). *Role transitions and grandparent-grandchild solidarity: A longitudinal analysis.* Unpublished doctoral dissertation, University of Southern California.

Miller, R., & Glass, J. (1989). Parent-child attitude similarity across the life course. *Journal of Marriage and the Family, 51*(4), 991–997.

Miller, S. S., & Cavanaugh, J. C. (1990). The meaning of grandparenthood and its relationship to demographic, relationship, and social participation variables. *Journal of Gerontology: Social Sciences, 45*, 244–247.

Min, P. G. (1988). The Korean American family. In C. H. Mindel, R. W. Habenstein, &

R. Wright, Jr. (Ed.), *Ethnic families in America: Patterns and variations* (3rd ed.) (pp. 199–229). New York: Elsevier.

Min, P. G. (1993). Korean immigrants' marital patterns and marital adjustments. In H. P. McAdoo (Ed.), *Family ethnicity: Strength in diversity* (pp. 287–299). Newbury Park, CA: Sage.

Minkler, M., Driver, D., Roe, K. M., & Bedeian, K. (1993). Community interventions to support grandparent caregivers. *The Gerontologist, 33*, 807–811.

Minkler, M., & Roe, K. M. (1993). *Grandmothers as caregivers.* Newbury Park, CA: Sage.

Minkler, M., & Roe, K. M. (1996). Grandparents as surrogate parents. *Generations, 20*, 34–38.

Minkler, M., Fuller-Thomson, E., Miller, D., & Driver, D. (1997). Depression in grandparents raising grandchildren. *Archives of Family Medicine, 6*, 445–452.

Minkler, M., Roe, K. M., & Price, M. (1992). The physical and emotional health of grandmothers raising grandchildren in the crack cocaine epidemic. *The Gerontologist, 32*, 752–761.

Minkler, M., Roe, K. M., & Robertson-Beckley, R. J. (1994). Raising grandchildren from crack-cocaine households: Effects on family and friendship ties of African-American women. *American Journal of Orthopsychiatry, 64*, 20–29.

Minuchin, S. (1974). *Families & family therapy.* Cambridge, MA: Harvard University Press.

Minuchin, S., Montalvo, B., Guerney, B. C., Rosman, B. L., & Schumer, F. (1967). *Families of the slums: An exploration of their structure and treatment.* New York: Basic Books.

Moen, P. (1995). Introduction. In P. Moen, G. H. Elder, Jr., & K. Luscher (Eds.), *Examining lives in context: Perspectives on the ecology of human development* (pp. 1–11). Washington, DC: American Psychological Association.

Moen, P. (1996). Gender, age, and the life course. In R. H. Binstock & L. K. George (Eds.), *Handbook of aging and the social sciences* (pp. 171–187). San Diego: Academic Press.

Mogey, J. (1991). Families: Intergenerational and generational connections—Conceptual approaches to kinship and culture. *Marriage & Family Review, 16*, 47–66.

Møller, V., & Sotshongaye. (1996). "My family eat this money too": Pension sharing and self-respect among Zulu grandmothers. *Southern Africa Journal of Gerontology, 5*(2), 9–19.

Montejano, D. (1987). *Anglos and Mexicans in the making of Texas, 1836–1986.* Austin: University of Texas Press.

Montepare, J. M., Steinberg, J., & Rosenberg, B. (1992). Characteristics of vocal communication between young adults and their parents and grandparents. *Communication Research, 19*, 479–492.

Moore, J. (1971). Mexican Americans. *The Gerontologist, 11*, 30–35.

Moore, J., & Pachon, H. (1985). *Hispanics in the United States.* Englewood Cliffs, NJ: Prentice-Hall.

Moore, J., & Pinderhughes, R. (1993). Introduction. In J. Moore & R. Pinderhughes (Eds.), *In the barrios: Latinos and the underclass debate* (pp. xi–xxxix). New York: Russell Sage Foundation,

Morris, S. J. (1989). Grandparents, uncles, aunts, cousins, friends: How is the court to decide which relationships will continue? *Family Advocate, 12*, 11–14.

Morrison, D. R., & Cherlin, A. J. (1995). The divorce process and young children's wellbeing: A prospective account. *Journal of Marriage and the Family, 57,* 800–812.

Morrison, J. (1996, March 7). Voice of the people. *South Bend Tribune* (IN), p. A10.

Moynihan, D. (1965). The negro family: The case for national action. Washington, DC: U.S. Department of Labor, Office of Planning and Research.

Mulhern, R. K., & Passman, R. H. (1977). The child's behavioral pattern as a determinant of maternal punitiveness. *Child Development, 50,* 815–820.

Mulhern, R. K., & Passman, R. H. (1981). Parental discipline as affected by the sex of the parent, the sex of the child, and the child's apparent responsiveness to discipline. *Developmental Psychology, 17,* 604–613.

Mullen, F. (1996). Public benefits: Grandparents, grandchildren, and welfare reform. *Generations, 20,* 61–64.

Musick, J. S. (1994). Grandmothers and grandmothers-to-be: Effects on adolescent mothers and adolescent mothering. *Infants and Young Children, 6,* 1–9.

Mutchler, J. E., & Burr, J. A. (1991). A longitudinal analysis of household and non-household living arrangements in later life. *Demography, 28,* 375–390.

Mutran, E. (1985). Intergenerational family support among blacks and whites: Response to culture or to socioeconomic differences. *Journal of Gerontology, 40,* 382–389.

Myers, B. J., Jarvis, P. A., & Creasey, G. L. (1987). Infants' behavior with the mothers and grandmothers. *Infant Behavior and Development, 10,* 245–259.

Myers, J. E., & Perrin, N. (1993). Grandparents affected by parental divorce: A population at risk? *Journal of Counseling and Development, 72,* 62–66.

Nadel, S. (1951). *The foundations of social anthropology.* Glencoe, IL: Free Press.

Nahemow, N. (1983). Grandparenthood among the Baganda: Role option in old age? In J. Sokolovsky (Ed.), *Growing old in different societies: Cross-cultural perspectives* (pp. 104–115). Belmont, CA: Wadsworth.

Nahemow, N. (1985). The changing nature of grandparenthood. *Medical Aspects of Human Sexuality, 19,* 81–92.

National Center for Health Statistics. (1994). *Vital statistics of the United States, 1990. Vol. 1, Natality.* Washington, DC: Public Health Service.

National Center for Health Statistics. (1995). *Vital Statistics of the United States, 1991. Vol. I, Natality.* Washington, DC: Public Health Service.

National Institute on Aging (1995). *Grandparenting: Issues for aging research.* Program Announcement Number PA-95-086. Bethesda, MD: Author.

Neugarten, B. L. (1979). Time, age, and the life cycle. *American Journal of Psychiatry, 136,* 887–894.

Neugarten, B. L., & Weinstein, K. K. (1964). The changing American grandparent. *Journal of Marriage and the Family, 26,* 199–204.

Newman, S., & Riess, J. (1992). Older workers in intergenerational child care. *Journal of Gerontological Social Work, 19,* 45–66.

Nock, S. L. (1988). The family and hierarchy. *Journal of Marriage and the Family, 50,* 957–966.

Nolan, L. C. (1993). Honor thy father and thy mother: But court ordered grandparent visitation in the intact family? *Brigham Young Journal of Public Law, 8,* 51–73.

Nussbaum, J. F., & Bettini, L. M. (1994). Shared stories of grandparent-grandchild relationship. *International Journal of Aging and Human Development, 39,* 67–80.

Nydegger, C. N. (1983). Family ties of the aged in cross-cultural perspective. *The Gerontologist, 23*, 26–32.

Nye, F. I. (1979). Choice, exchange, and the family. In W. R. Burr, R. Hill, F. I. Nye, & I. L. Reiss (Eds.), *Contemporary theories about the family*, Vol. 2 (pp. 1–41). New York: Free Press.

O'Connor, M. (1993). *Generation to generation: Older people as an educational resource.* London: Cassell.

Olson, P. (1990). The elderly in the People's Republic of China. In J. Sokolovsky (Ed.), *The cultural context of aging: Worldwide perspectives* (pp. 143–161). New York: Bergin & Garvey.

O'Reilly, E., & Morrison, M. L. (1993). Grandparent-headed families: New therapeutic challenges. *Child Psychiatry and Human Development, 23*, 147–159.

Ou, Y., & McAdoo, H. P. (1993). Socialization of Chinese American Children. In H. P. McAdoo (Ed.), *Family ethnicity: Strength and diversity* (pp. 245–270). Newbury Park, CA: Sage.

Oyserman, D., Radin, N., & Benn, R. (1993). Dynamics in a three-generational family: Teens, grandparents, and babies. *Developmental Psychology, 29*, 564–572.

Oyserman, D., Radin, N., & Saltz, E. (1994). Predictors of nurturant parenting in teen mothers living in three-generational families. *Child Psychiatry and Human Development, 24*, 215–230.

Paine, R. (1974). Anthropological approaches to friendship. In E. Leyton (Ed.), *The compact: Selected dimensions of friendship* (pp. 1–14). Newfoundland: Memorial University of Newfoundland.

Palmore, E. (1975). *The honorable elders: A cross-cultural analysis of aging in Japan.* Durham, NC: Duke University Press.

Palmore, E., & Maeda, D. (1985). *The honorable elders revisited: A revised cross-cultural analysis of aging in Japan.* Durham, NC: Duke University Press.

Palmore, E., & Manton, K. (1974). Modernization and status of the aged: International correlations. *Journal of Gerontology, 29*, 205–210.

Parish, W. L., Hao, L., & Hogan, D. P. (1991). Family support networks, welfare, & work among young mothers. *Journal of Marriage and the Family, 53*, 203–215.

Parsons, T. (1954/1943). The kinship system of the contemporary United States. In T. Parsons (Ed.), *Essays in sociological theory* (pp. 177–196). New York: Macmillan.

Parsons, T. (1971). Reply to his critics. In M. Anderson (Ed.), *Sociology of the family* (pp. 120–121). Hammondsworth, England: Penguin.

Parsons, T., & Bales, R. F. (1955). *Family, socialization and interaction process.* Glencoe, IL: Free Press.

Pasley, K., & Ihinger-Tallman, M. (1987). Remarriage and stepparenting. New York: Guilford Press.

Passman, R. H., & Blackwelder, D. E. (1981). Rewarding and punishing mothers: The influence of progressive changes in the quality of their sons' apparent behavior. *Developmental Psychology, 17*, 614–619.

Pearlin, L. I. (1980). Life-strains and psychological distress among adults. In N. J. Smelser & E. H. Erikson (Eds.), *Themes of work and love in adulthood* (pp. 319–336). Cambridge, MA: Harvard University Press.

Pearson, J. L. (1993). Parents' reactions to their children's separation & divorce at two

& four years: Parent gender & grandparent status. *Journal of Divorce and Remarriage, 20,* 25–43.

Pearson, J. L., Hunter, A. G., Cook, J. M., Ialongo, N. S., & Kellam, S. G. (1997). Grandmother involvement in child caregiving in an urban community. *The Gerontologist, 37,* 650–657.

Pearson, J. L., Hunter, A. G., Ensminger, M. E., & Kellam, S. G. (1990). Black grandmothers in multigenerational households: Diversity in family structure and parenting involvement in the Woodlawn community. *Child Development, 61,* 434–442.

Pearson, J. L., Ialongo, N. S., Hunter, A. G., & Kellam, S. G. (1994). Family structure and aggressive behavior in a population of urban elementary school children. *Journal of the American Academy of Child & Adolescent Psychiatry, 33,* 540–548.

Peplau, L. A. (1983). Roles and gender. In H. H. Kelley, E. Berscheid, A. Christensen, J. H. Harvey, T. L. Huston, G. Levinger, E. McClintock, L. A. Peplau, & D. R. Peterson (Eds.), *Close relationships* (pp. 220–264). New York: W. H. Freeman.

Peres, L. (1986). Immigrant economic adjustment and family organization: The Cuban success story reexamined. *International Migration Review, 22,* 4–20.

Peterson, E. T. (1989). Grandparenting. In S. J. Bahr & E. T. Peterson (Eds.), *Aging and the family* (pp. 159–174). Lexington, MA: Lexington Books.

Pettigrew, T. F. (1964). *A profile of the Negro American.* Princeton, NJ: Van Nostrand.

Phinney, J. (1990). Ethnic identity in adolescents and adults: Review of research. *Psychological Bulletin, 108,* 499–514.

Plath, D. (1983). "Ecstasy years"—old age in Japan. In J. Sokolovsky (Ed.), *Growing old in different societies: Cross-cultural perspectives* (pp. 147–153). Belmont, CA: Wadsworth.

Poe, L. M. (1992). *Black grandparents as parents.* Author.

Ponzetti, J. J. (1992). Bereaved families: A comparison of parents' and grandparents' reactions to the death of a child. *Omega: Journal of Death and Dying, 25,* 63–71.

Ponzetti, J. J., Jr., & Folkrod, A. W. (1989). Grandchildren's perceptions of their relationships with their grandparents. *Child Study Journal, 19,* 41–50.

Popenoe, D. (1993). American family decline, 1960–1990: A review and appraisal. *Journal of Marriage and the Family, 55,* 527–541.

Powers, E. A., Keith, P. M., & Goudy, W. J. (1981). Family networks of the rural aged. In R. T. Coward & W. M. Smith, Jr. (Eds.), *The family in rural society* (pp. 199–217). Boulder, CO: Westview.

Powers, E. A., & Kivett, V. R. (1992). Kin expectations and kin support among rural older adults. *Rural Sociology, 57,* 194–215.

Press, L., & McKool, M. (1972). Social structure and status of the aged: Toward some valid cross-cultural generalizations. *International Journal of Aging and Human Development, 3,* 297–306.

Presser, H. B. (1980). Sally's Corner. *Journal of Social Issues, 36,* 107–129.

Presser, H. B. (1989). Some economic complexities of child care provided by grandmothers. *Journal of Marriage and the Family, 51,* 581–591.

Proller, N. L. (1989). The effects of an adoptive grandparent program on youth & elderly participants. *Journal of Children in Contemporary Society, 20,* 195–203.

Pruchno, R. (1995). *Grandparents in American society: Review of recent literature.* Paper prepared for the National Institute on Aging. Bethesda, MD: NIA.

Pruchno, R. A., & Johnson, K. W. (1996). Research on grandparenting: Review of current studies and future needs. *Generations, 20*, 65–70.

Pruchno, R. A., Peters, N. D., & Burant, C. J. (1995). Mental health of coresident family caregivers: Examination of a two-factor model. *Journal of Gerontology: Psychological Sciences, 50B*, P247–P256.

Purcell, M. (1979). Foster grandparents in a residential treatment center. *Child Welfare, 58*, 409–411.

Purnell, M., & Bagby, B. H. (1993). Grandparents' rights. Implications for family specialists. *Family Relations, 42*, 173–178.

Radcliffe-Brown, A. (1940). On joking relationships. *Africa, 13*, 195–210.

Radin, N., Oyserman, D., & Benn, R. (1991). Grandfathers, teen mothers and children under two. In P. K. Smith (Ed.), *The psychology of grandparenthood: An international perspective.* New York: Routledge.

Raley, R. K. (1995). Black-white differences in kin contact and exchange among never married adults. *Journal of Family Issues, 16*, 77–103.

Ram, M., & Wong, R. (1994). Covariates of household extension in rural India: Change over time. *Journal of Marriage and the Family, 56*, 853–864.

Ransom, D. C., Fisher, L., Phillips, S. Kokes, R. F., & Weiss, R. (1990). The logic of measurement in family research. In T. W. Draper & A. C. Marcos (Eds.), *Family variables: Conceptualization, measurement, and use* (pp. 48–63). Newbury Park, CA: Sage.

Raphael, E. I. (1989). Grandparents: A study of their role in Hispanic families. *Physical and Occupational Therapy in Geriatrics, 6*, 31–62.

Rappaport, E. A. (1957). The grandparent syndrome. *Psychoanalytic Quarterly, 27*, 518–537.

Rempusheski, V. F. (1990). Role of the extended family in parenting: A focus on grandparents of preterm infants. *Journal of Perinatal & Neonatal Nursing, 4*, 43–55.

Richards, T., White, M. J., & Tsui, A. O. (1987). Changing living arrangements: A hazard model of transitions among family types. *Demography, 24*, 77–97.

Richardson, R. A., Barbour, N. B., & Bubenzer, E. G. (1991). Bittersweet connections: Informal social networks as sources of support and interference for adolescent mothers. *Family Relations, 40*, 430–434.

Riesman, D., Denney, R., & Glazer, N. (1950). *The lonely crowd.* New Haven, CT: Yale University Press.

Riley, J. C. (1990). The risk of being sick: Morbidity trends in four countries. *Population and Development Review, 16*, 403–432.

Roberto, K. A. (1990). Grandparent and grandchild relationships. In T. H. Brubaker (Ed.), *Family relationships in later life* (pp. 100–112). Newbury Park, CA: Sage.

Roberto, K. A., & Skoglund, R. R. (1996). Interactions with grandparents and great-grandparents: A comparison of activities, influences, and relationships. *International Journal of Aging and Human Development, 43*, 107–117.

Roberto, K. A., & Stroes, J. (1992). Grandchildren and grandparents: Roles, influences, and relationships. *International Journal of Aging and Human Development, 34*, 227–239.

Roberts, A. (1995). *The retired and senior volunteer program: A catalyst for intergenerational partnerships*. Washington, DC: Generations United.

Roberts, R. E. L., & Bengtson, V. L. (1990). Is intergenerational solidarity a unidimensional construct? A second test of a formal model. *Journal of Gerontology: Social Sciences, 45,* S12–S20.

Roberts, R. E. L., Richards, L. N., & Bengtson, V. L. (1991). Intergenerational solidarity in families: Untangling the ties that bind. *Marriage & Family Review, 16,* 11–46.

Robertson, E. B., Elder, G. H., Skinner, M. L., & Conger, R. D. (1991). The costs and benefits of social support in families. *Journal of Marriage and the Family, 53,* 403–416.

Robertson, J. F. (1975). Interaction in three generation families, parents as mediators: Toward a theoretical perspective. *International Journal of Aging and Human Development, 6,* 103–110.

Robertson, J. F. (1976). Significance of grandparents. *The Gerontologist, 16*(2), 137–140.

Robertson, J. F. (1977). Grandparenthood: A study of role conceptions. *Journal of Marriage and the Family, 39,* 165–174.

Robertson, J. F. (1995). Grandparenting in an era of rapid change. In R. Blieszner & V. H. Bedford (Eds.), *Handbook on aging and the family* (pp. 243–260). Westport, CT: Greenwood.

Robinson, L. H. (1989). Grandparenting: Intergenerational love and hate. *Journal of the American Academy of Psychoanalysis, 17,* 483–491.

Rodgers, R. H., & White, J. M. (1993). Family development theory. In P. G. Boss, W. J. Doherty, R. LaRossa, W. R. Schumm, & S. K. Steinmetz (Eds.), *Sourcebook of family theories: A contextual approach* (pp. 225–254). New York: Plenum.

Rodriguez, C. E. (1997). A summary of Puerto Rican migration to the United States. In M. Romero, P. Hondagneu-Sotelo, & V. Ortiz (Eds.), *Challenging fronteras: Structuring Latina and Latino lives in the U.S.* (pp. 101–113). New York: Routledge.

Roe, K. M., Minkler, M., & Barnwell, R. (1994). The assumption of caregiving: Grandmothers raising the children of the crack cocaine epidemic. *Qualitative Health Research, 4,* 281–303.

Roe, K. M., Minkler, M., & Saunders, F. F. (1995). Combining research, advocacy and education: The methods of the grandparent caregiver study. *Health Education Quarterly, 22,* 458–475.

Rogers, A., Rogers, R. G., & Belanger, A. (1990). Longer life but worse health? Measurement and dynamics. *The Gerontologist, 30,* 640–649.

Rogler, L. H., & Cooney, R. S. (1991). Puerto Rican families in New York City: Intergenerational processes. *Marriage and Family Review 16,* 331–349.

Romis, J. C. (1981). The role of grandparents in adjustment to epilepsy. *Social Work Health Care, 6,* 37–43.

Rosenmayr, L. (1972). The elderly in Austrian society. In D. Cowgill & L. Holmes (Eds.), *Aging and modernization* (pp. 183–196). New York: Appleton-Century-Crofts.

Rosenthal, C. J. (1985). Kinkeeping in the familial division of labor. *Journal of Marriage and the Family, 47,* 965–974.

Rosenthal, C. J. (1987). Aging and intergenerational relations in Canada. In V. W. Marshall (Ed.), *Aging in Canada: Social perspectives* (2nd ed.) (pp. 311–342). Toronto: Fitzhenry & Whiteside.

Rossi, A. S. (1984). Gender and parenthood. *American Sociological Review, 49*, 1–19.

Rossi, A. S., & Rossi, P. H. (1990). *Of human bondings: Parent-child relations across the life course.* New York: Aldine de Gruyter.

Rubel, A. (1966). *Across the tracks: Mexican-Americans in a Texas city.* Austin: University of Texas Press.

Rubin, L. B. (1976). *Worlds of pain: Life in the working-class family.* New York: Basic Books.

Rudasill, M. C. (1995). Grandparents raising grandchildren: Problems and policy from an Illinois perspective. *Elder Law Journal, 3*, 215–274.

Ruggles, S. (1994). The origins of African-American family structure. *American Sociological Review, 59*, 136–151.

Ruoppila, I. (1991). The significance of grandparents for the formation of family relations. In P. K. Smith (Ed.), *The psychology of grandparenthood: An international perspective* (pp. 123–139). New York: Routledge.

Russell, G. (1986). Grandfathers: Making up for lost opportunities. In R. A. Lewis & R. E. Salt (Eds.), *Men in families* (pp. 233–259). Beverly Hills, CA: Sage.

Sabatelli, R. M., & Shehan, C. L. (1993). Exchange and resource theories. In P. G. Boss, W. J. Doherty, R. LaRossa, W. R. Schumm, & S. K. Steinmetz (Eds.), *Sourcebook of family theories and methods* (pp. 385–411). New York: Plenum.

Sabogal, F., Martin, G., & Otero-Sabogal, R. (1987). Hispanic familism and acculturation: What changes and what doesn't. *Hispanic Journal of Behavioral Sciences, 9*, 397–412.

Sadavoy, J., & Fogel, B. (1988). Personality disorders in old age. In J. E. Birren, R. B. Sloane, & G. D. Cohen (Eds.), *Handbook of mental health and aging* (pp. 433–462). San Diego, CA: Academic Press.

Safier, E. J. (1992). Daughter becomes mother, mother becomes grandmother: Life cycle transitions for mothers and daughters. *Journal of Feminist Family Therapy, 4*, 53–68.

Salamon, S. (1992). *Prairie patrimony: Family, farming, and community in the Midwest.* Chapel Hill: University of North Carolina Press.

Salamon, S., & Lockhart, V. (1980). Land ownership and the position of elderly in farm families. *Human Organization, 39*(4), 324–331.

Saltz, R. (1989). Research evaluation of a foster grandparent program. *Journal of Children in Contemporary Society, 20*, 205–216.

Saluter, A. F. (1991). *Marital status and living arrangements: March 1990.* U.S. Bureau of the Census, Current population reports, Series P-20, no. 450. Washington, DC: U.S. Government Printing Office.

Saluter, A. F. (1992). *Marital status and living arrangements: March 1992.* U.S. Bureau of the Census, Current Population Reports, Series P-20, no. 468. Washington, DC: U.S. Government Printing Office.

Saluter, A. (1994a). *Marital status and living arrangements: March 1993.* Current Population Reports, Series P-20, no. 478. Washington, DC: U.S. Government Printing Office.

Saluter, A. (1994b). *Marital status and living arrangements: March 1994.* Current Population Reports, Series P-20, no. 484. Washington, DC: U.S. Government Printing Office.

Saluter, A. F. (1995). *Marital status and living arrangements: March 1995*. Current Population Reports, Series P-20, no. 491. Washington, DC: U.S. Government Printing Office.

Sanchez-Ayendez, M. (1988). Elderly Puerto Ricans in the United States. In S. R. Applewhite (Ed.), *Hispanic elderly in transition: Theory, research, policy and practice* (pp. 17–31). Westport, CT: Greenwood.

Sanders, G. F. (1993). Strengths in the grandparent-grandchild relationship. *Activities, Adaptation & Aging, 17*, 43–53.

Sanders, G. F., & Trygstad, D. W. (1989). Stepgrandparents and grandparents: The view from young adults. *Family Relations, 38*, 71–75.

Sandler, A. G., Warren, S. H., & Raver, S. A. (1995). Grandparents as a source of support for parents of children with disabilities. *Mental Retardation, 33*, 248–250.

Sangree, W. H. (1992). Grandparenthood and modernization: The changing status of male and female elders in Tiriki, Kenya, and Irigwe, Nigeria. *Journal of Cross-Cultural Gerontology, 7*(4), 331–361.

Schlosberg, J. (1990). Grandparents: Before you can market to grandparents, you must find them, describe them, and measure their spending. *American Demographics, 12*, 32–35, 51.

Schlossberg, N. K. (1984). *Counseling adults in transition*. New York: Springer.

Schmidt, A. M., & Padilla, A. (1983). Grandparent-grandchild interaction in a Mexican American group. *Hispanic Journal of Behavioral Sciences, 5*, 181–198.

Schmid, K. (1995). *Grandparent-grandchild relationships in adoptive families*. Paper presented at the meeting of the Gerontological Society of America, Los Angeles, CA.

Schneider, B., & Coleman, J. T. (1993). *Parents, their children, and school*. Boulder, CO: Westview.

Schneider, D. (1968). *American kinship: A cultural account*. Englewood Cliffs, NJ: Prentice-Hall.

Schorr, A. (1980). . . . Thy father & thy mother . . . : A second look at filial responsibility and family policy. Washington, DC: U.S. Government Printing Office.

Schultz, N. W. (1980). A cognitive-developmental study of the grandchild-grandparent bond. *Child Study Journal, 10*, 7–26.

Schvaneveldt, J. D., Pickett, R. S., & Young, M. H. (1993). Historical methods in family research. In P. G. Boss, W. J. Doherty, R. LaRossa, W. R. Schumm, & S. K. Steinmetz (Eds.), *Sourcebook of family theories and methods: A contextual approach* (pp. 99–116). New York: Plenum.

Schwartz, J., & Waldrop, J. (1992). The growing importance of grandparents. *American Demographics, 14*, 10–11.

Schweitzer, M. M. (1987). The elders: Cultural dimension of aging in two American Indian communities. In J. Sokolovsky (Ed.), *Growing old in different societies*. Acton, MA: Copley.

Scott, J. W., & Black, A. (1994). Deep structures of African American family life: Female and male kin networks. In R. Staples (Ed.), *The black family: essays and studies* (pp. 204–213). Belmont, CA: Wadsworth.

Seligman, M. (1991). Grandparents of disabled grandchildren: Hopes, fears, and adaptation. *Families in Society: The Journal of Contemporary Human Services, 72*, 147–152.

Seltzer, J. A., & Bianchi, S. M. (1988). Children's contact with absent parents. *Journal of Marriage and the Family, 50*, 663–675.

Seltzer, M. M. (1976). Suggestions for the examination of time-disordered relationships. In F. J. Gubrium (Ed.), *Time, roles, and self in old age* (pp 111–125). New York: Human Sciences Press.

Serovich, J. M. (1991). Former in-laws as a source of support. *Journal of Divorce and Remarriage, 17*, 17–25.

Severino, S. K., Teusink, J. P., Pender, V. B., & Bernstein, A. E. (1986). Overview: The psychology of grandparenthood. *Journal of Geriatric Psychiatry, 19*, 3–17.

Shandling, J. L. (1986). The constitutional constraints on grandparents' visitation rights. *Columbia Law Review, 86*, 118–138.

Shimkin, D. B., Shimkin, E. M., & Frate, D. A. (Eds.). (1978). *The extended family in black societies*. Paris: Mouton.

Shomaker, D. (1989). Transfer of children and the importance of grandmothers among the Navajo Indians. *Journal of Cross-Cultural Gerontology, 4*(1), 1–18.

Shomaker, D. (1990). Health care, cultural expectations and frail Navajo grandmothers. *Journal of Cross-Cultural Gerontology, 5*(1), 21–34.

Shore, R. J., & Hayslip, B. (1994). Custodial grandparenting: Implications for children's development. In A. E. Gottfried & A. W. Gottfried (Eds.), *Redefining families: Implications for children's development* (pp. 171–218). New York: Plenum.

Sightes, B. P. (1996, March 17). Voice of the People. *South Bend Tribune* (IN), p. A18.

Silverman, P., & Maxwell, R. (1983). The significance of information and power in the comparative study of the aged. In J. Sokolovsky (Ed.), *Growing old in different societies: Cross-cultural perspectives* (pp. 43–55). Belmont, CA: Wadsworth.

Silverstein, M., Lawton, L., & Bengtson, V. L. (1994). Types of intergenerational relations. In R. Harootyan, V. L. Bengtson, & M. Schlesinger (Eds.), *Hidden connections: Intergenerational linkages in American society* (pp. 43–76). New York: Springer.

Silverstein, M., & Parrott, T. M. (1997). Attitudes toward public support of the elderly: Does early involvement with grandparents moderate generational tensions? *Research on Aging, 19*, 108–132.

Simmons, L. (1945). *The role of the aged in primitive society*. New Haven: Yale University Press.

Simon-Rusinowitz, L., Krach, C. A., Marks, L. N., Piktialis, D., & Wilson, L. B. (1996). Grandparents in the workplace: The effects of economic and labor trends. *Generations, 20*, 41–44.

Smith, L. (1983). A conceptual model of families incorporating adolescent mother and child. *Advances in Nursing Science, 6*(1) 45–60.

Smith, M. S. (1991). An evolutionary perspective on grandparent-grandchild relationships. In P. K. Smith (Ed.), *The psychology of grandparenthood: An international perspective* (pp. 157–176). New York: Routledge.

Smith, P. K. (1991). Introduction: The study of grandparenthood. In P. K. Smith (Ed), *The psychology of grandparenthood: An international perspective* (pp. 1–16). New York: Routledge.

Smith, P. K. (1995). Grandparenthood. In M. H. Bornstein (Ed.), *Handbook of parenting* (pp. 89–111). Mahwah, NJ: Erlbaum.

SmithBattle, L. (1996). Intergenerational ethics of caring for teenage mothers and their children. *Family Relations, 45*, 56–64.

Sokolovsky, J. (1990). *The cultural context of aging*. New York: Bergin & Garvey.

Solomon, J. C., & Marx, J. (1995). "To grandmother's house we go": Health and school adjustment of children raised solely by grandparents. *The Gerontologist, 35*, 386–394.

Sotomayor, M. (1973). *A study of Chicano grandparents in an urban barrio.* Unpublished doctoral dissertation, Graduate School of Social Work, University of Denver.

Sotomayor, M. (1989). The Hispanic elderly and the intergenerational family. *Journal of Children in Contemporary Society, 20*, 55–65.

Spanier, G. B., & Hanson, S. (1982). The role of extended kin in the adjustment to marital separation. *Journal of Divorce, 5*, 33–48.

Spanier, G. B., & Thompson, L. (1984). *Parting.* Beverly Hills, CA: Sage.

Spark, G. M. (1974). Grandparents and intergenerational family therapy. *Family Process, 13*(2), 225–237.

Spicer, J., & Hampe, G. (1975). Kinship interaction after divorce. *Journal of Marriage and the Family, 37*, 113–118.

Spierer, H. (1977). *Major transitions in the human life cycle.* New York: Academy for Educational Development.

Spitze, G., & Logan, J. (1990). Sons, daughters, and intergenerational support. *Journal of Marriage and the Family, 52*, 420–430.

Spitze, G., & Logan, J. (1991). Sibling structure and intergenerational relations. *Journal of Marriage and the Family, 53*, 871–884.

Spitze, G., Logan, J., Deane, G., & Zerger, S. (1994). Adult children's divorce and intergenerational relationships. *Journal of Marriage and the Family, 56*, 279–293.

Sprey, J. (1991). Studying adult children and parents. *Marriage and Family Review, 16*, 221–235.

Sprey, J., & Matthews, S. H. (1982). Contemporary grandparenthood: A systemic transition. *The Annals of the American Academy of Political and Social Science, 464*, 91–103.

Stack, C. B. (1974). *All our kin: Strategies for survival in a black urban community.* New York: Harper & Row.

Stack, C. B., & Burton, L. M. (1993). Kinscripts. *Journal of Comparative Family Studies, 24*, 157–170.

Stacy, J. (1993). Good riddance to the family: A response to Dr. Popenoe. *Journal of Marriage and the Family, 55*, 545–547.

Staples, R. (1971). *The black family: Essays and studies.* Belmont, CA: Wadsworth.

Staples, R., & Smith, J. W. (1954). Attitudes of grandmothers and mothers toward child rearing practices. *Child Development, 25*, 91–97.

Starrels, M., Ingersoll-Dayton, B., Neal, M. B., & Yamada, H. (1995). Intergenerational solidarity and the workplace: Employees' caregiving for their parents. *Journal of Marriage and the Family, 57*, 751–762.

State of Indiana. (1994, December). *Impacting families through work: Partnership for personal responsibility.* Indianapolis, IN: Author.

Stein, J. A., Newcomb, M. D., & Bentler, P. M. (1993). Differential effects of parents and grandparent drug abuse on behavior problems of male and female children. *Developmental Psychology, 29*, 31–43.

Stevens, J. H. (1984). Black grandmothers and black adolescent mothers' knowledge about parenting. *Developmental Psychology, 20*, 1017.

Sticker, E. J. (1991). The importance of grandparenthood during the life cycle in Germany. In P. K. Smith (Ed.), *The psychology of grandparenthood: An international perspective* (pp. 68–82). London: Routledge.

Sticker, E. J., & Flecken, M. (1986). Die Beziehung zwischen Grosseltern und ihren Enkeln im Vorschulalter. *Zeitschrift für Gerontologie, 19,* 336–341.

Stokes, J., & Greenstone, J. (1981). Helping black grandparents and older parents cope with child rearing: A group method. *Child Welfare, 60,* 691.

Stolba, A., & Amato, P. R. (1993). Extended single-parent households and children's behavior. *The Sociological Quarterly, 34,* 543–549.

Strauss, C. A. (1943). Grandma made Johnny delinquent. *American Journal of Orthopsychiatry, 13,* 343–347.

Strawbridge, W. J., Wallhagen, M. I., Shema, S. J., & Kaplan, G. A. (1997). New burdens or more of the same? Comparing grandparent, spouse, and adult-child caregivers. *The Gerontologist, 37,* 505–510.

Streib, G. F. (1958). Family pattern in retirement. *Journal of Social Issues, 14,* 46–60.

Strom, R. (1988). Intergenerational learning & curriculum development. *Educational Gerontology, 14,* 165–181.

Strom, R. (1989). Grandparents & learning. *International Journal of Aging & Human Development, 29,* 163–169.

Strom, R. (1992a). Grandparent education for black families. *The Journal of Negro Education, 61,* 554–569.

Strom, R. (1992b). *Achieving grandparent potential: A guidebook for building intergenerational relationships.* Newbury Park, CA: Sage.

Strom, R. (1993). Grandparent development and influence. *Journal of Gerontological Social Work, 20,* 3–16.

Strom, R., Collinsworth, P., Strom, S., & Griswold, D. (1993). Strengths and needs of black grandparents. *International Journal of Aging and Human Development, 36,* 255–268.

Strom, R., & Strom, S. (1987). Preparing grandparents for a new role. *The Journal of Applied Gerontology, 6,* 476–486.

Strom, R., & Strom, S. K. (1991a) *Becoming a better grandparent: Viewpoints on strengthening the family.* Newbury Park, CA: Sage.

Strom, R., & Strom, S. K. (1991b). *Grandparent education: A guide for leaders.* Newbury Park, CA: Sage.

Strom, R., & Strom, S. (1992a). Grandparents and intergenerational relationships. *Educational Gerontology, 18,* 607–624.

Strom, R., & Strom, S. K. (1992b). *Achieving grandparent potential: Viewpoints on building intergenerational relationships.* Newbury Park, CA: Sage.

Strom, R., & Strom, S. K. (1993). Grandparents raising grandchildren: Goals and support groups. *Educational gerontology, 19,* 705–715.

Strom, R., Strom, S., & Collinsworth, P. (1990a). Improving grandparent success. *Journal of Applied Gerontology, 9,* 480–491.

Strom, R., Strom, S., & Collinsworth, P. (1990b). Raising expectations for grandparents: A three generational study. *International Journal of Aging & Human Development, 31,* 161–167.

Strom, R., Strom, S., Collinsworth, P., & Strom, P. (1996). Black grandparents: Curriculum development. *International Journal of Aging and Human Development, 43,* 119–133.

Stryker, S. (1959). Symbolic interaction as an approach to family research. *Journal of Marriage and the Family, 21,* 111–119.

Stryker, S. (1972). Symbolic interaction theory: A review and some suggestions for comparative family research. *Journal of Comparative Family Studies, 3,* 17–32.

Stryker, S. (1987). Identity theory: Developments and extensions. In K. Yardley & T. Honess (Eds.), *Self and identity: Psychological perspectives* (pp. 83–103). New York: Wiley.

Suchindran, C. M., & Koo, H. P. (1992). Age at last birth and its components. *Demography, 29,* 227–245.

Surra, C. A. (1988). The influence of the interactive network on developing relationships. In R. M. Milardo (Ed.), *Families and social networks* (pp. 48–82). Newbury Park, CA: Sage.

Sussman, M. B. (1953). The help pattern of the middle class family. *American Sociological Review, 18,* 22–28.

Szinovacz, M. E. (1987). Family power. In M. B. Sussman & S. K. Steinmetz (Eds.), *Handbook of marriage and the family* (pp. 651–694). New York: Plenum.

Szinovacz, M. E. (1996). Living with grandparents: Variations by cohort, race, and family structure. *International Journal of Sociology and Social Policy, 16,* 89–123.

Szinovacz, M. E. (1997a). *Grandparenthood: Profiles, supports, and transitions.* Final report submitted to the AARP–Andrus Foundation. Norfolk, VA: Old Dominion University.

Szinovacz, M. E. (1997b). Adult children taking parents into their homes: Effects of childhood living arrangements. *Journal of Marriage and the Family, 59,* 700–717.

Szinovacz, M. E. (1998). Grandparents today: A demographic profile. *The Gerontologist, 38,* 37–52.

Takas, M. (1995). *Grandparents raising grandchildren: A guide to finding help and hope.* N.P.: Brookdale Foundation Group/Author.

Tam, V. C., & Detzner, D. F. (1995). Grandparents as a family resource in Chinese-American families. In H. I. McCubbin, E. A. Thomson, A. I. Thompson, and J. E. Fromer (Eds.), *Resiliency in ethnic minority families, Vol. 1: Native and immigrant American families* (pp. 243–263). Madison: University of Wisconsin Press.

Taylor, R. J. (1985). The extended family as a source of support for elderly blacks. *The Gerontologist, 25,* 488–495.

Taylor, R. J. (1993). A profile of familial relations among three-generation black families. *Family Relations, 42,* 332–341.

Taylor, R. J., & Chatters, L. M. (1986a). Church-based informal support among elderly blacks. *The Gerontologist, 26*(6), 637–642.

Taylor, R. J. & Chatters, L. M. (1986b). Patterns of informal support to elderly black adults: Family, friends, and church members. *Social Work, 31*(6), 432–438.

Taylor, R. J., & Chatters, L. M. (1991). Extended family networks of older black adults. *Journal of Gerontology: Social Sciences, 46,* S210–S217.

Taylor, R. J., Chatters, L. M., & Jackson, J. S. (1993, July). A profile of familial relations among three generation black American families. *Family Relations, 42,* 332–341.

Taylor, R. J., Tucker, M. B., Chatters, L. M., & Jayakody, R. (1997). Recent demographic trends in African American family structure. In R. J. Taylor, J. S. Jackson, & L. M. Chatters (Eds.), *Family life in black America.* Newbury Park, CA: Sage.

Thoits, P. A. (1991). On merging identity theory and stress research. *Social Psychology Quarterly, 54*(2), 101–112.

Thomas, J. L. (1986a). Age and sex differences in perceptions of grandparenting. *Journal of Gerontology, 41,* 417–423.

Thomas, J. L. (1986b). Gender differences in satisfaction with grandparenting. *Psychology and Aging, 1,* 215–219.

Thomas, J. L. (1989). Gender and perceptions of grandparenthood. *International Journal of Aging and Human Development, 29,* 269–282.

Thomas, J. L. (1990a). Grandparent role: A double bind. *International Journal of Aging and Human Development, 31,* 169–177.

Thomas, J. L. (1990b). Grandparenthood and mental health: Implications for the practitioner. Special issue: Retirement migration: Boon or burden? *Journal of Applied Gerontology, 9,* 464–479.

Thomas, J. L. (1994). Older men as fathers and grandfathers. In E. H. Thompson, Jr. (Ed.), *Older men's lives* (pp. 197–217). Thousand Oaks, CA: Sage.

Thomas, J. L. (1995). Gender and perceptions of grandparenthood. In J. Hendricks (Ed.), *The ties of later life* (pp. 181–193). Amityville, NY: Baywood.

Thomas, W. I., & Znaniecki, F. (1958). The Polish peasant in Europe and America. New York: Dover.

Thompson, L., & Walker, A. J. (1982). The dyad as the unit of analysis: Conceptual and methodological issues. *Journal of Marriage and the Family, 44,* 889–900.

Thompson, L., & Walker, A. J. (1987). Mothers as mediators of intimacy between grandmothers and their young adult granddaughters. *Family Relations, 36,* 72–77.

Thompson, L., & Walker, A. J. (1995). The place of feminism in family studies. *Journal of Marriage and the Family, 57,* 847–865.

Thompson, R. A., Tinsley, B. R., Scalora, M. J., & Parke, R. D. (1989). Grandparents' visitation rights: Legalizing the ties that bind. *American Psychologist, 44,* 1217–1222.

Tice, C. H. (1991). Developing informal networks of caring through intergenerational connections in school settings. *Marriage & Family Review, 16,* 377–389.

Tienda, M. (1995). Latinos and the American pie: Can Latinos achieve economic parity? *Hispanic Journal of Behavioral Sciences, 17,* 403–429.

Tienda, M., & Angel, R. (1982). Headship and household composition among blacks, Hispanics, and other whites. *Social Forces, 61,* 508–531.

Timberlake, E. M. (1980). The value of grandchildren to grandmothers. *Journal of Gerontological Social Work, 3,* 63–76.

Timberlake, E. M., & Chipungu, S. S. (1992). Grandmotherhood: Contemporary meaning among African American middle-class grandmothers. *Social Work, 37,* 216–222.

Tinsley, B. J., & Parke, R. D. (1984). Grandparents as support and socialization agents. In M. Lewis (Ed.), *Beyond the dyad* (pp. 161–194). New York: Plenum.

Tinsley, B. J., & Parke, R. D. (1987). Grandparents as interactive and social support agents for families with young infants. *International Journal of Aging and Human Development, 25,* 259–277.

Tomlin, A. M., & Passman, R. P. (1989). Grandmothers' responsibility in raising two-year-olds facilitates their grandchildren's adaptive behavior: A preliminary intrafamilial investigation of mothers' and maternal grandmothers' effects. *Psychology and Aging, 4,* 119–121.

Tomlin, A. M., & Passman, R. P. (1991). Grandmothers' advice about disciplining grandchildren: Is it accepted by mothers, and does its rejection influence grandmothers' subsequent guidance? *Psychology and Aging, 6,* 182–189.

Tran, T. V., & Dhooper, S. D. (1996). Ethnic and gender differences in perceived needs for social services among three elderly Hispanic groups. *Journal of Gerontological Social Work, 25,* 121–147.

Trent, K. (1994). Teenage mothers in nuclear & extended households: Differences by marital status & race/ethnicity. *Journal of Family Issues, 15,* 309–337.

Trent, K., & Harlan, S. L. (1994). Teenage mothers in nuclear and extended households: Differences by marital status and race/ethnicity. *Journal of Family Issues, 15,* 309–337.

Troll, L. E. (1971). The family of later life: A decade review. In Carlfred B. Broderick (Ed.), *A decade of family research and action* (pp. 187–214). Minneapolis: National Council on Family Relations.

Troll, L. E. (1980). Grandparenting. In L. Poon (Ed.), *Aging in the 1980s* (pp. 475–481). Washington, DC: American Psychological Association.

Troll, L. (1983). Grandparents: The family watchdogs. In T. H. Brubaker (Ed.), *Family relationships in later life* (pp 63–74). Beverly Hills, CA: Sage.

Troll, L. E. (1985). The contingencies of grandparenting. In V. L. Bengtson & J. F. Robertson (Eds.), *Grandparenthood* (pp. 135–149). Beverly Hills, CA: Sage.

Troll, L. E. (1986). Parents and children in later life. *Generations, 10,* 23–25.

Troll, L. E., & Bengtson, V. L. (1979). Generations in the family. In W. Burr, R. Hill, I. Reiss, & F. I. Nye (Eds.), *Theories about the family* (pp. 127–161). New York: Free Press.

Troll, L., Miller, S., & Atchley, R. (1979). *Families in later life.* Belmont, CA: Wadsworth.

Trupin, S. (1993). Moral support for "grandparents who care." *American Journal of Nursing, 93,* 52–56.

Trygstad, D. W., & Sanders, G. F. (1989). The significance of stepgrandparents. *International Journal of Aging and Human Development, 29,* 119–134.

Tsuya, N. O., & Martin, L. G. (1992). Living arrangements of Japanese elderly and attitudes toward inheritance. *Journal of Gerontology: Social Sciences, 47,* S45–S54.

Tu, E. J, Liang, J., & Li, S. (1989). Mortality decline and Chinese family structure: Implications for old age support. *Journal of Gerontology: Social Sciences, 44,* 157–168.

Turner, B., & Turner, C. (1994). Social cognition and gender stereotypes for women varying in age and race. In B. Turner & L. Troll (Eds.), *Women growing older: Psychological perspectives* (pp. 94–139). Thousand Oaks, CA: Sage.

Turner, J. H. (1982). *The structure of sociological theory* (3rd ed). Homewood, IL: Dorsey.

Turner, R. (1976). The real self: From institution to impulse. *American Journal of Sociology 81,* 989–1016.

Tyrer, P., & Seivewright, H. (1988). Studies of outcome. In P. Tyrer (Ed.), *Personality disorders: Diagnosis, management and course* (pp. 119–136). London: Wright.

Tyszkowa, M. (1991). The role of grandparents in the development of grandchildren as perceived by adolescents and young adults in Poland. In P. K. Smith (Ed.), *The psychology of grandparenthood: An international perspective* (pp. 50–67). New York: Routledge.

Tyszkowa, M. (1993). Adolescents' relationships with grandparents: Characteristics and developmental transformations. In S. Jackson & H. Rodriguez-Tome (Eds.), *Adolescence and its social world* (pp. 121–143). Hillsdale, NJ: Erlbaum.

Uba, L. (1994). *Asian Americans: Personality patterns, identity, and mental health.* New York: Guilford Press.

Uhlenberg, P. (1980). Death and the family. *Journal of Family History, 5,* 313–320.

Uhlenberg, P. (1993). Demographic change and kin relationships in later life. *Annual Review of Gerontology and Geriatrics, 13,* 219–238.

Uhlenberg, P. (1996). Mortality decline in the twentieth century and supply of kin over the life course. *The Gerontologist, 36,* 681–685.

Umberson, D. (1992). Relationships between adult children and their parents: Psychological consequences of both generations. *Journal of Marriage and the Family, 54,* 664–674.

Unger, D. G., & Cooley, M. (1992). Partner and grandmother contact in black and white teen parent families. *Journal of Adolescent Health, 13*(7), 546–552.

Uphold, C. R., & Morgan, L. A. (1988). Understanding intergenerational relationships: A theoretical review and synthesis. *Gerontology Review, 1,* 3–15.

U.S. Bureau of the Census. (1945). *Differential fertility, 1940 and 1910: Women by number of children under 5 years old.* Washington, DC: U.S. Government Printing Office.

U.S. Bureau of the Census. (1953). *Census of population: 1950, Vol 2, Characteristics of the populations: Part 1, United States summary.* Washington, DC: U.S. Government Printing Office.

U.S. Bureau of the Census. (1964). Persons by family characteristics. *Census of population: 1960, subject reports. PC(2)-4B.* Washington, DC: U.S. Government Printing Office.

U.S. Bureau of the Census. (1965). *Census of population: 1960. PC(2)-1A.* Washington, DC: U.S. Government Printing Office.

U.S. Bureau of the Census. (1973a). *Census of population: 1970. PC(2)-1A.* Washington, DC: U.S. Government Printing Office.

U.S. Bureau of the Census. (1973b). Persons by family characteristics. *Census of population: 1970, subject reports. PC(2)-4B.* Washington, DC: U.S. Government Printing Office.

U.S. Bureau of the Census. (1975a). *Historical statistics of the United States: Colonial times to 1970.* Washington, DC: U.S. Government Printing Office.

U.S. Bureau of the Census. (1975b). *Census of population: 1970. PC(2)-3B.* Washington, DC: U.S. Government Printing Office.

U.S. Bureau of the Census. (1981). Marital status and living arrangements, March, 1980. *Current Population Reports, Series P-20, No. 365.* Washington, DC: U.S. Government Printing Office.

U.S. Bureau of the Census. (1985). Living arrangements of children and adults. *Census of population: 1980, subject reports PC80–2-4B.* Washington, DC: U.S. Government Printing Office.

U.S. Bureau of the Census. (1990). *Statistical abstract of the United States: 1990* (110th ed.). Washington, DC: U.S. Government Printing Office.

U.S. Bureau of the Census. (1991). Marital status and living arrangements. *Current population reports. Series P-20*, no. 450. Washington, DC: U.S. Government Printing Office.

U.S. Bureau of the Census. (1992a). *1990 Census of population and housing: Public use microdata samples, United States*. Technical Documentation. Washington, DC: U.S. Government Printing Office.

U.S. Bureau of the Census. (1992b). Marital status and living arrangements: March 1991. *Current population reports. Series P-20, no. 461*. Washington, DC: U.S. Government Printing Office.

U.S. Bureau of the Census. (1992c). Marital status and living arrangements, March 1992. *Current population reports. Series P-20, no. 468*. Washington, DC: U.S. Government Printing Office.

U.S. Bureau of the Census. (1994a). *Current population reports. Series P-20, no. 478*. Washington, DC: U.S. Government Printing Office.

U.S. Bureau of the Census. (1994b). *Current population reports. Series P-70, no. 38*. Washington, DC: U.S. Government Printing Office.

U.S. Bureau of the Census. (1994c). Age of Population by Ethnicity. *Current population reports. Series P-60, no. 189*. Washington, DC: U.S. Government Printing Office.

U.S. Bureau of the Census. (1995a). *Current population reports. Series P-20, no. 485*. Washington, DC: U.S. Government Printing Office.

U.S. Bureau of the Census. (1995b). *Statistical abstract of the United States: 1995*. Washington, DC: U.S. Government Printing Office.

U.S. Bureau of the Census. (1996). Income, poverty, and valuation of noncash benefits, 1994. *Current Population Reports. Series P-60, no. 189*. Washington, DC: U.S. Government Printing Office.

Vaden-Kiernan, N., Ialongo, N. S., Pearson, J., & Kellam, S. G. (1995). Household family structure and children's aggressive behavior: A longitudinal study of urban elementary school children. *Journal of Abnormal Child Psychology, 23*, 553–568.

Vaillant, G. E. (1977). *Adaptation to life*. Boston: Little, Brown.

Van Nostrand, J. F. (Ed.). (1993). *Common beliefs about the rural elderly: What do national data tell us?* Hyattsville, MD: National Center for Health Statistics, Vital Health Statistics 3(28).

Van Ranst, N., Verschueren, K., & Marcoen, A. (1995). The meaning of grandparents as viewed by adolescent grandchildren: An empirical study in Belgium. *International Journal of Aging and Human Development, 41*, 311–324.

Van Tran, T. (1988). The Vietnamese American family. In C. H. Mindel, R. W. Habenstein, & R. Wright, Jr. (Eds.), *Ethnic families in America: Patterns and variations* (pp. 276–299). New York: Elsevier.

Vega, W. A. (1991). Hispanic families in the 1980s: A decade of research. In A. Booth (Ed.), *Contemporary families: Looking forward, looking backward* (pp. 297–306). Minneapolis: National Council on Family Relations.

Verbrugge, L. M. (1984). Longer life but worsening health? Trends in health and mortality of middle-aged and older persons. *Milbank Memorial Fund Quarterly, 62*, 474–519.

Vermulst, A. A., de Brock, A. J. L. L., & van Zutphen, R. A. H. (1991). Transmission of parenting across generation. In P. K. Smith (Ed.), *The psychology of grandparenthood: An international perspective* (pp. 100–132). New York: Routledge.

Victor, R. S. (1989). When third parties come first: Asserting the custodial rights of nonparents. *Family Advocate, 12,* 8–9, 45.

Von Hentig, H. (1946). The sociological function of the grandmother. *Social Forces, 24,* 389–392.

Voran, M., & Phillips, D. (1993). Correlates of grandmother childcare support to adolescent mothers: Implications for development in two generations of women. *Children and Youth Services Review, 15,* 321–334.

Wacker, R. R. (1995). Legal issues and family involvement in later-life families. In R. Blieszner & V. H. Bedford (Eds.), *Handbook of aging and the family* (pp. 284–306). Westport, CT: Greenwood.

Waley, A. (1971). *The analects of Confucius.* London: Allen & Unwin.

Walker, M. M., & Macklin, M. C. (1992). The use of role modeling in targeting advertising to grandparents. *Journal of Advertising Research, 32,* 37–44.

Wallerstein, J., & Kelly, J. (1979). Children of divorce: A review. *Social Work, 24,* 468–475.

Walsh, F. (1989). The family in later life. In B. Carter & M. McGoldrick (Eds.), *The changing family life cycle* (pp. 311–332). Boston: Allyn & Bacon.

Walsh, W. M., & McGraw, J. A. (1996). *Essentials of family therapy: A therapist's guide to eight approaches.* Denver: Love.

Ward, R. A., Logan, J., & Spitze, G. (1992). The influence of parent and child needs on coresidence in middle and later life. *Journal of Marriage and the Family, 54,* 209–221.

Watkins, J. A., & Koblinsky, S. A. (1997). Strengths and needs of working-class African-American and Anglo-American grandparents. *International Journal of Aging and Human Development, 44,* 149–165.

Watkins, S. C., Menken, J. A., & Bongaarts, J. (1987). Demographic foundations of family change. *American Sociological Review, 52,* 346–358.

Weibel-Orlando, J. (1988). Indians, ethnicity as a resource and aging: You can go home again. *Journal of Cross-Cultural Gerontology, 3*(4), 323–348.

Weibel-Orlando, J. (1990). Grandparenting styles: Native American perspectives. In J. Sokolovsky (Ed.), *The cultural context of aging: worldwide perspectives* (pp. 109–125). New York: Bergin & Garvey.

Weitzman, L. (1985). *The divorce revolution: The unexpected social and economic consequences for women and children in America.* New York: Free Press.

Wentowski, G. J. (1985). Older women's perceptions of great-grandmotherhood: A research note. *The Gerontologist, 25,* 593–596.

Werner, E. E. (April 1989). Children of the Garden Island. *Scientific American, 260,* 106–111.

Werner, E. E. (1991). Grandparent-grandchild relationships amongst US ethnic groups. In P. K. Smith (Ed.), *The psychology of grandparenthood: An international perspective* (pp. 68–82). New York: Routledge.

Werner, E. E., and Smith, R. S. (1977). *Kauai's children come of age,* Honolulu: University of Hawaii Press.

Werner, E. E., & Smith, R. S. (1982). *Vulnerable but invincible: A longitudinal study of resilient children and youth.* New York: McGraw-Hill.

Whitbeck, L. B., Hoyt, D. R., & Huck, S. M. (1993). Family relationship history, contemporary parent-grandparent relationship quality, and the grandparent-grandchild relationship. *Journal of Marriage and the Family, 55,* 1025–1035.

Whitbeck, L. B., Simons, R. L., & Conger, R. D. (1991). Effects of early family relationships on contemporary relationships and assistance patterns between adult children and their parents. *Journal of Gerontology: Social Sciences, 46,* S330–S337.

Whitchurch, G. G., & Constantine, L. L. (1993). Systems theory. In P. G. Boss, W. J. Doherty, R. LaRossa, W. R. Schumm, & S. K. Steinmetz (Eds.), *Sourcebook of family theories and methods* (pp. 325–352). New York: Plenum.

White, D. G. (1985). *Ain't I a woman? Family slaves in the plantation south.* New York: Norton.

White, L. K. (1992). The effect of parental divorce and remarriage on parental support for adult children. *Journal of Family Issues, 13,* 234–250.

White, L. K., & Riedmann, A. (1992). When the Brady bunch grows up: Step/half- and full-sibling relationships in adulthood. *Journal of Marriage and the Family, 54,* 197–208.

Wilcoxon, S. A. (1987). Grandparents and grandchildren: An often neglected relationship between significant others. *Journal of Counseling and Development, 65,* 289–290.

Wilk, L. (1993). Grosseltern und Enkelkinder. In K. Lüscher and F. Schulther (Eds.), *Generationenbeziehungen in "postmodernen" Gesellschaften* (pp. 203–214). Konstanz: Universitätsverlag.

Wilkening, E. A., Guerrero, S., & Ginsberg, S. (1972). Distance and intergenerational ties of farm families. *Sociological Quarterly, 13,* 383–396.

Willer, B., Hofferth, S. L., Kisker, E. E., Divine-Hawkins P., Farquhar, E., & Glantz, F. B. (1991). *The demand and supply of child care in 1990.* Washington, DC: Urban Institute Press.

Williams, L., & Domingo, L. J. (1993). The social status of elderly women and men within the Filipino family. *Journal of Marriage and the Family, 55,* 415–426.

Williams, N. (1990). *The Mexican American family: Tradition and change.* Dix Hills, NY: General Hall.

Williams, N. (1993). Elderly Mexican American men: Work and family patterns. In J. C. Hood (Ed.), *Men, work, and family* (pp. 68–85). Newbury Park, CA: Sage.

Williams, N. (1994). Health and social services, formal organizations, and the Mexican American elderly. *Clinical Sociology Review, 12,* 222–234.

Williams, N., Himmel, K. F., Sjoberg, A. F., & Torrez, D. J. (1995). The assimilation model, family life, and race and ethnicity in the United States: The case of minority welfare mothers. *Journal of Family Issues, 16,* 380–405.

Willits, F. K., Bealer, R. C., & Crider, D. M. (1982). Persistence of rural/urban differences. In D. A. Dillman & D. J. Hobbs (Eds.), *Rural society in the U.S.: Issues for the 1980s* (pp. 69–76). Boulder, CO: Westview.

Wilson, F. W., & Clarke, S. C. (1992). Remarriage: A demographic profile. *Journal of Family Issues, 13,* 123–141.

Wilson, G. (1987). Women's work: The role of grandparents in intergenerational transfers. *The Sociological Review, 35,* 703–720.

Wilson, J. B. (1994). *Connecting the generations: A guide to intergenerational resources.* Washington, DC: Generations Together/AARP.

Wilson, K. B., & LeShane, M. R. (1982). The legal rights of grandparents: A preliminary discussion. *The Gerontologist, 22,* 67–71.

Wilson, M. N. (1984). Mothers and grandmothers: Perceptions of parental behaviors in three-generational black families. *Child Development, 55,* 1333–1339.

Wilson, M. N. (1989). Child development in the context of the black extended family. *American Psychologist, 44,* 380–385.

Wilson, M. N., Tolson, T., Hinton, I. D. & Kiernan, M. (1990). Flexibility and sharing of child care duties in black families. *Sex Roles, 22,* 409–425.

Winton, C. A. (1995). *Frameworks for studying families.* Guilford, CT: Dushkin.

Wirth, L. (1938). Urbanism as a way of Life. *American Journal of Sociology, 44,* 3–24.

Wood, E. F., & Kestner, P. B. (1989). *Mediation: The coming of age—a mediator's guide in serving the elderly.* Washington, DC: American Bar Association.

Wood, V. (1982). Grandparenthood: An ambiguous role. *Generations, 7,* 22–23.

Wood, V., & Robertson, J. F. (1976). The significance of grandparenthood. In J. F. Gubrium (Ed.), *Time, roles, and self in old age* (pp. 278–304). New York: Human Sciences Press.

Wu, L. L. (1996). Effects of family instability, income, and income instability on the risk of a premarital birth. *American Sociological Review, 61,* 386–406.

Yan, Y. (1996). *The flow of gifts: Reciprocity and social networks in a Chinese village.* Stanford: Stanford University Press.

Yang, H., & Chandler, D. (1992). Intergenerational relations: Grievances of the elderly in rural China. *Journal of Comparative Family Studies, 23,* 431–453.

Yanigasako, S. (1977). Women-centered kin networks in urban bilateral kinship systems. *American Ethnologist, 4,* 207–226.

Yee, B. W. K. (1992). Elders in Southeast Asian refugee families: A cultural transformation. *Generations, 16,* 24–28.

Young, M., & Willmott, P. (1957). *Family and kinship in East London.* Harmondsworth, England: Penguin.

Author Index

Subject Index

About the Contributors

JOAN ALDOUS is the William R. Kenan, Jr., Professor of Sociology at the University of Notre Dame. Her latest book is *Family Careers: Rethinking the Developmental Perspective* (1996). Her articles on grandparents include "New Views of Grandparents in Intergenerational Context," *Journal of Family Issues* (1995).

VERN L. BENGTSON is AARP/University Professor of Gerontology and Professor of Sociology at the University of Southern California, and is past president of the Gerontological Society of America. For 25 years he has been Principal Investigator of the Longitudinal Study of Four Generation Families at USC. Among his most recent co-authored publications are *The Changing Contract between Generations* (1993), *Hidden Connections: Intergenerational Linkages in American Society* (1994), and *Intergenerational Issues in Aging* (1995).

GLEN H. ELDER, JR. is Howard W. Odum Professor of Sociology and Research Professor of Psychology at the University of North Carolina, Chapel Hill, where he directs a research program on the life course and social change. His theoretical work on the life course and related longitudinal studies began in the early 1960's at the University of California, Berkeley (Institute of Human Development), and he has continued this research program to the present through faculty appointments at Cornell University and the University of North Carolina, where he is co-director of the Carolina Consortium of Human Development. Professor Elder's books (authored, co-authored, or co-edited) include *Children of the Great Depression* (1974), *Life Course Dynamics* (1985), *Children in Time and Place* (1993), and *Families in Troubled Times* (1994).

ROSEANN GIARRUSSO is Research Assistant Professor of Gerontology and Sociology at the University of Southern California and the Project Director of the Longitudinal Study of Four-Generation Families. Her research interests include intergenerational family relations, social psychology, and sociology of aging and the life course. Her most recent publications include an examination of grandparents who raise their grandchildren; the tendency of older generations to perceive family relations in a more favorable light than younger generations; and the extent to which self-esteem exhibits stability or change over the life course.

BARBARA A. HIRSHORN is Director of the Division of Intergenerational Studies at the Institute for Families in Society at the University of South Carolina. Dr. Hirshorn has worked in university, public policy, and community settings. She co-authored the first report on intergenerational transfers at the Gerontological Society of America and has worked on intergenerational programming in the continuing care retirement community setting and with grandparents raising grandchildren when the middle generation is substance-abusing.

LYNNE GERSHENSON HODGSON is Chair of the Department of Sociology and Gerontology at Quinnipiac College in Hamden, Connecticut. Her most recent publications and continuing research interests focus on two areas: grandparent/adult grandchild relationships and concerns about developing Alzheimer's disease ("anticipatory dementia").

ANDREA G. HUNTER is an Assistant Professor in the Department of Psychology and Women's Studies Program and a Faculty Associate at the Institute for Social Research at the University of Michigan. She received her Ph.D. in Human Development and Family Studies from Cornell University and continued post-doctoral work as a National Institute of Mental Health Fellow in Family Process and Psychopathology. Her research areas include African American families; grandparenting and intergenerational family relationships; African American men and gender constructions; feminist ideology among African Americans; race, gender, and the life course; and families and social change.

CHARLOTTE IKELS is the Armington Professor in the Department of Anthropology at Case Western Reserve University. She has been conducting research on Chinese elderly and their family relationships for over 20 years. Her works (authored and co-authored) include *Aging and Adaptation: Chinese in Hong Kong and the United States* (1983), "The Resolution of Intergenerational Conflict: Perspectives of Elders and their Family Members," in *Modern China* (1990), "Settling Accounts: The Intergenerational Contract in an Age of Reform," in *Chinese Families in the Post-Mao Era* (1993), *The Aging Experience: Diversity and Commonality across Cultures* (1994), and *The Return of the God of Wealth: The Transition to a Market Economy in Urban China* (1996).

COLLEEN L. JOHNSON is a professor of Medical Anthropology at the University of California, San Francisco. In addition to her research on grandparenting and divorce, she has studied ethnicity and the family, and family-support processes. She currently has a MERIT Award from the National Institute on Aging to study adaptation of the oldest old. In addition to numerous articles, her books include *Ex-Familia: Grandparents, Parents, and Children Adjust to Divorce* (1988) and *Life Beyond 85 Years: The Aura of Survivorship*.

YOSHINORI KAMO is currently an Associate Professor of Sociology at Louisiana State University. He specializes in family and aging. His recent work deals with elderly living arrangements in the United States, including those of Chinese and Japanese Americans, elderly in Japan, grandparents (*Handbook on Marriage and the Family*), division of household labor, marital stability, and methodological issues.

VALARIE KING is currently Assistant Professor of Sociology and Research Associate with the Population Research Institute at Penn State University. Her research focuses on intergenerational relationships and processes across the life course. Recent work examines the functionality of grandparents in rural America, sources of variation in grandparenting, grandparent self-efficacy, effects of grandparent involvement for grandchild well-being, and the importance of childhood experiences with grandparents for the current involvement of elderly men and women with their own grandchildren.

JAMES B. KIRBY is a graduate student in the Department of Sociology at the University of North Carolina, Chapel Hill. His research includes the social causes and consequences of mortality, morbidity, and aging.

VIRA R. KIVETT is Elizabeth Rosenthal Excellence Professor in the Department of Human Development and Family Studies at The University of North Carolina at Greensboro, Greensboro, North Carolina. She has worked at the Duke Center for the Study of Aging and Human Development, and has published widely in the areas of intergenerational roles, relationships, and solidarity, especially among rural groups. Her current grants relate to longitudinal studies of older rural adults and to structure and outcomes of caregiving to the black elderly.

RICHARD B. MILLER is Associate Professor and Program Director of Marriage and Family Therapy in the School of Family Studies and Human Services at Kansas State University. He received his Ph.D. in sociology with specializations in social gerontology and marriage and family therapy from the University of Southern California. His current research interests include marital interaction over the life course, relationships in aging families, and Marriage and Family Therapy outcome research.

ANGELA ROBERTS is currently a Program Officer for the National Senior Service Corps, Corporation for National Service, in Washington, DC. She is the co-author of *Young and Old Serving Together: Meeting Community Needs Through Intergenerational Partnership*, and the author of *The Retired and Senior Volunteer Program: A Catalyst for Intergenerational Partnerships* and a *Resource Development Handbook* for Senior Corps project directors.

STEPHEN T. RUSSELL completed his Ph.D. in Sociology at Duke University in 1994. He has worked as a research associate in the Life Course Studies Program at the Carolina Population Center at the University of North Carolina in Chapel Hill. He is now Assistant Professor in the Department of Family and Consumer Sciences at the University of Nebraska–Lincoln. His research focuses on the family contexts of adolescent and mid-life development, and intergenerational family relationships.

JONATHAN G. SANDBERG is currently a doctoral candidate in marriage and family therapy at Kansas State University. He has also earned a graduate certificate in gerontology. His research interests include depression and marital process in older couples, clinical issues of aging, and Marriage and Family Therapy outcome research.

MERRIL SILVERSTEIN is the Hanson Family Trust Assistant Professor of Gerontology and Sociology at the Andrus Gerontology Center of the University of Southern California. His research is concerned with understanding how individuals age within the context of the family, including such issues as intergenerational social support and migration in later life. Dr. Silverstein is currently a national Fellow of the Brookdale Foundation and has recently received a FIRST Investigator Award from the National Institute of Aging to study processes and psychological consequences of grandparenting over the life course.

GLENNA SPITZE is Professor of Sociology at the State University of New York at Albany. Her areas of interest are gender, families, and aging. She is co-author of *Family Ties: Enduring Relations between Parents and their Grown Children* (1997), based on an NIA-funded survey of an Albany-area sample. Her current research interests include household labor, marital quality, and adult children's coresidence with parents.

MAXIMILIANE E. SZINOVACZ is Visiting Research Professor at Old Dominion University and Dozent at the University of Vienna, Austria. She edited two volumes on retirement and family issues in later life: *Women's Retirement*, and *Families and Retirement* (with David Ekerdt and Barbara Vinick). She has also published on these topics in various journals. Her most recent projects include analyses of grandparenting, based on the National Survey of Families and Households, a qualitative study on the impact of caregiving on caregivers' adolescent children; and NIH-funded longitudinal research on marriage, families, and retirement.

ROBERT J. TAYLOR is Associate Professor of Social Work and a faculty associate at the Institute for Social Research at the University of Michigan. His NIH funded research focuses on family and friend social support networks across the life span, with a particular emphasis on the networks of older adults. Another major area is the investigation of the correlates of religious participation and church support among African Americans. He has published articles on these topics in *Journal of Gerontology: Social Sciences, Journal of Marriage and the Family; Family Relations; Review of Religious Research, Journal for the Scientific Study of Religion, Journal of Black Psychology,* and *Social Work.*

ANGELA M. TOMLIN earned her degree in clinical psychology from the University of Wisconsin-Milwaukee in 1989. She has published and presented on three-generational families, including issues of attachment to grandmothers and grandmothers' influence on mothers' disciplining of grandchildren. Currently she is the Coordinator of Psychology and the Continuing Education Director for the Riley Child Development Center, and LEND Program (Leadership Education in Neurodevelopmental Disabilities) funded by Maternal and Child Health.

DIANA J. TORREZ is an Associate Professor in the Sociology Department at the University of North Texas. Her research is in the area of aging and health, with a focus on Mexican Americans. She has published in the *Journal of Family Issues, Race, Class and Gender, Clinical Sociological Review,* and *Latino Studies Journal.* Dr. Torrez is currently conducting research in Mexico City, which examines the treatment of chronic illnesses among Mexican older adults.

PETER UHLENBERG is Professor of Sociology and Fellow, Carolina Population Center at the University of North Carolina, Chapel Hill. His research interests include the demography of aging and intergenerational relationships. Recent publications include "Mortality Decline in the Twentieth Century and Supply of Kin Over the Life Course," *The Gerontologist* (1996) and "The Burden of Aging: A Theoretical Framework for Understanding the Shifting Balance of Care Giving and Care Receiving as Cohorts Age," *The Gerontologist* (1996).

RUSSELL A. WARD is Professor of Sociology at the State University of New York at Albany. His interests in the sociology of aging have included age identity, patterns of informal support, and health-related behavior. Recent work has addressed such dimensions of family relations as the antecedents and implications of coresidence by parents and adult children, and the implications of household labor for marital satisfaction among older couples.

NORMA WILLIAMS is Professor of Sociology at the University of Texas at Arlington. She has been president of the Southwestern Sociological Association. She is the author of *The Mexican American Family: Tradition and Change*, (1990) as well as numerous articles and chapters in books on the family, race and ethnic relations, aging, social psychology, and organizations.

ISBN 0-313-29886-6

9 780313 298868

HARDCOVER BAR CODE